Introduction to Global Studies

Politics and Economics

Richard P. Appelbaum

University of California, Santa Barbara

KENDALL/HUNT PUBLISHING COMPANY
4050 Westmark Drive   Dubuque, Iowa 52002

Cover images © 2004 by Digital Stock

Copyright © 2004 by Richard P. Appelbaum

ISBN 0-7575-0792-1

Printed in the United States of America
10 9 8 7 6 5 4 3 2

Contents

Preface

Global 2 *(Introduction to Global Studies: Politics and Economics)* is one of two gateway courses to the Global Studies major at the University of California at Santa Barbara. (The other gateway course introduces students to global issues in culture and ideology). The UCSB Global Studies major, one of the first of its kind in the United States, was created in 1998. Within a few years it had grown to approximately 800 students. The major seeks to prepare students to become knowledgeable citizens in a world where global social forces and processes are radically transforming the lives of everyone on the planet.

Global processes are transnational: they impact people across national boundaries. From global warming to global commodity production, from currency devaluations to the political instability created by transnational ethnic and religious movements, it is important to understand the new forms of political and socioeconomic interactions that are changing our world today.

Numerous examples could be cited. The Cold War that defined world politics between the end of World War II and the collapse of the Soviet Union has been replaced by countless local conflicts, often driven by ethnic or religious nationalism. Since September 11, 2001, "fear of terrorism" has replaced "fear of communism" in the American consciousness. Two wars—in Afghanistan and Iraq—have been waged in the name of a global "war on terror;" both—although offically "over," remain on-going as of this writing. With the collapse of the Soviet Union and the transformation of the China to a market-driven economy, global capitalism has triumphed over state socialist alternatives. The "Washington consensus" on the global economy—the neo-liberal notion that free markets and unrestricted competition provide the key to economic growth—is being spread to all parts of the world. Yet in the world economic system, America's global dominance is increasingly challenged in parts of Asia and Europe, even as U.S. military dominance remains undisputed. At the same time, Africa and much of Latin America sink deeper into poverty.

Global social movements have emerged to challenge globalization itself. From Seattle to Cancún to the populist economic forums in Porto Alegre, Brazil, hundreds of thousands of individuals and organizations have come together to protest unbridled capitalist globalization and seek to invent an alternative. And various forms of religious nationalism, most notably today in the Islamic world, have equated globalization with western dominance and called for turning back the clock entirely, requiring to strict adherence to thousand year-old religious scripture.

Even the nation-state is being challenged. The World Trade Organization requires countries to yield economic sovereignty to global free trade rules, even when it seems disadvantageous to a country's businesses and citizens. Unlike other global organizations (such as the United Nations), the WTO has developed mechanisms for enforcing such rules. In Europe, a growing number of countries have given up their borders and currencies to form the European Union, a behemoth whose economic size now rivals that of the United States. Elsewhere, as in the former Yugoslavia, countries have fractured into warring regions based on ethnic identity. It would seem that the modern nation-state, which has been the principle form of political governance for some 350 years, may be both too large and too small to respond effectively to the enormous power of transnational corporations. In fact, the world's 50 largest "economies" include 15 transnational corporations; Wal-Mart's current annual revenues ($246.7 billion) place it at number 19, somewhere between Switzerland (whose gross domestic product is $247.4 billion) and Belgium ($227.6 billion).

To cover these topics, I have divided this book is divided into five sections. The readings in this book are not meant to be exhaustive; they should be supplemented with additional readings as appropriate. Given the rapidity of changes in the world today (and the inevitable lags in academic publishing), it is important to stay on top of events, both through reading newspapers, academic journals (many of which are on-line), and more popular sources. The Internet is an invaluable tool in this regard.

We begin this book with several articles that explore the meaning of globalization from different perspectives, hopefully exploding some myths about globalization along the way. We then look at two global regions whose futures are inextricably tied in with our own—East Asia and Latin America. We then examine several global issues of importance today: the "global factory" (and its impact of workers), women in poverty (with a special focus on China, which is rapidly becoming the world's workhouse), and global water shortages (which may prove to be the greatest environmental challenge in the next quarter century). This leads to a section that focuses on some of the principal challenges of globalization: the limits of free trade, the inability of national governments to cope with global forces, and the global rise of often-violent religious nationalism. The book concludes with a look to the future, offering three perspectives: one (now-classic) analysis of the global "clash of civilizations," a second that looks at global resistance movements, and a third that looks at the emergence of a new, multiethnic, and highly feminized global working class.

I hope you find this book useful, and would welcome any suggestions for changes (new materials to include, items to exclude in future editions).

Richard P. Appelbaum
Santa Barbara, California (September 25, 2003)
appelbaum@soc.ucsb.edu

Acknowledgments

This book reflects the continuing evolution of Global 2 at UCSB (Introduction to Global Studies: Politics and Economics). Global 2, in turn, has been successful largely because of the support of a small group of graduate students who have worked with me over the years formally as teaching assistants for the course, but more importantly as colleagues in giving the course shape and coherence. Special mention goes to Joe Conti, Francesca deGiuli, and Joy Hylton, who have been TAs in the course in recent years; and, in previous years, Jim Dalton and Chris Kollmeyer. I also want to acknowledge the editorial assistance of Kendall/Hunt who provided me with invaluable assistance in preparing this book. I also wish to thank the students in Global 2, including those in its honors section, who have challenged me and kept me on top of the issues raised in this book.

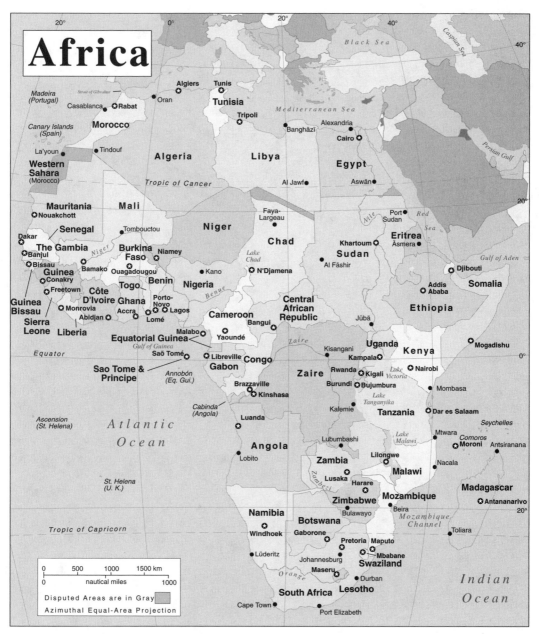

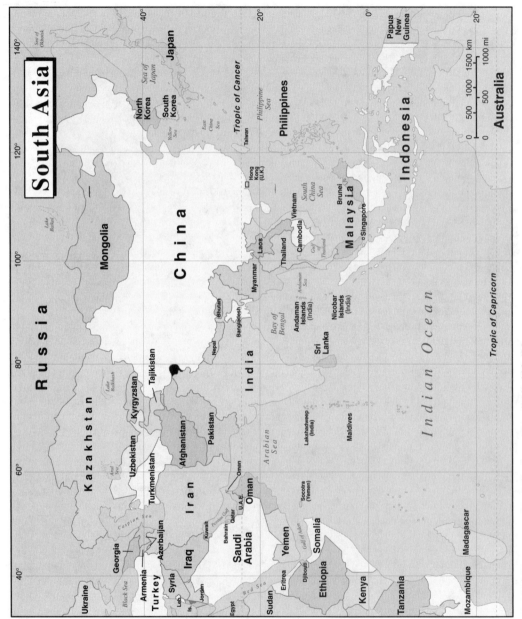

South Asia

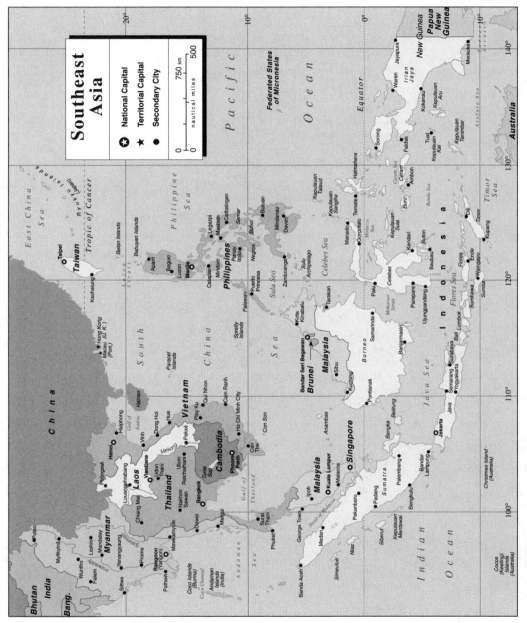

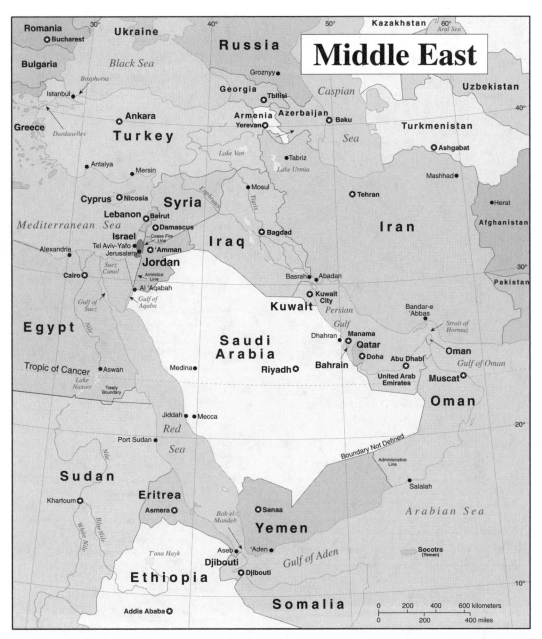

Middle East

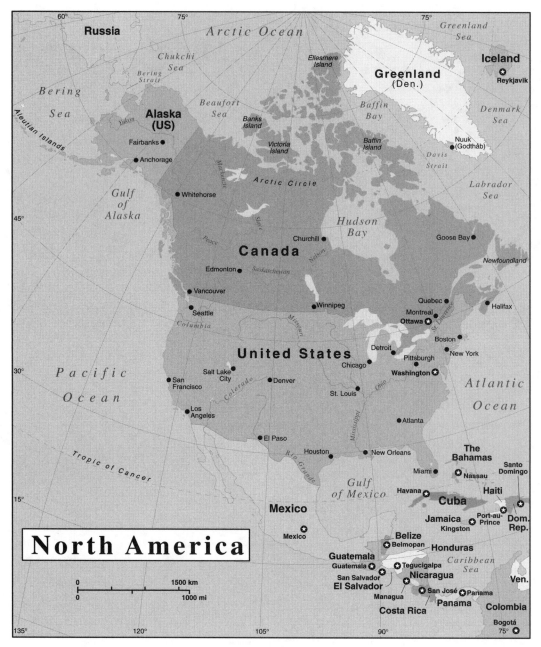

North America

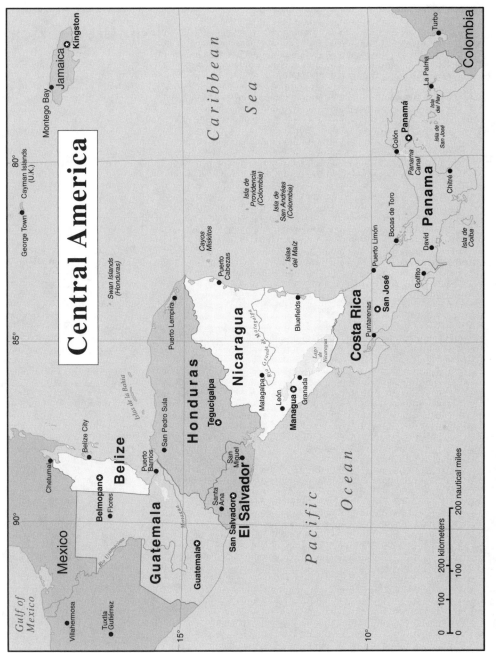

Central America

Gulf of Mexico

Mexico

Villahermosa

Tuxtla Gutiérrez

Chetumal

Belize City

Belmopan✪ **Belize**

Flores

Santa Ana

San Salvador✪ **El Salvador**

San Miguel

Guatemala✪ **Guatemala**

Río Usumacinta

Motagua

Islas de la Bahía

San Pedro Sula

Honduras

Tegucigalpa✪

Puerto Lempira

Puerto Barrios

Jamaica●

Montego Bay

Kingston✪

George Town●

Cayman Islands (U.K.)

80°

85°

90°

15°

10°

Swan Islands (Honduras)

C a r i b b e a n   S e a

Cayos Miskitos

Puerto Cabezas

Nicaragua

Matagalpa

León

Managua✪

Granada

Río Grande de Matagalpa

Lago de Nicaragua

Bluefields

Isla de Providencia (Colombia)

Isla de San Andréas (Colombia)

Islas del Maíz

Costa Rica

Puntarenas

San José✪

Puerto Limón

Golfito

Bocas de Toro

David

Isla de Coiba

Colón

Panamá✪

Panama Canal

Chitré

Panama

La Palma

Isla del Rey

Isla de San José

Turbo●

Colombia

P a c i f i c   O c e a n

0   100   200 kilometers

0   100   200 nautical miles

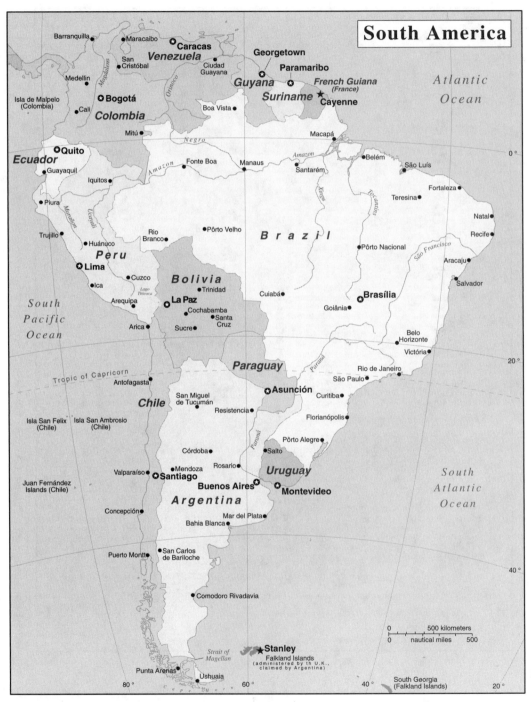

Introduction

Thinking Globally

Jihad vs. McWorld

Benjamin Barber

History is not over. Nor are we arrived in the wondrous land of techné promised by the futurologists. The collapse of state communism has not delivered people to a safe democratic haven, and the past, fratricide and civil discord perduring, still clouds the horizon just behind us. Those who look back see all of the horrors of the ancient slaughterbench reenacted in disintegral nations like Bosnia, Sri Lanka, Ossetia, and Rwanda and they declare that nothing has changed. Those who look forward prophesize commercial and technological interdependence—a virtual paradise made possible by spreading markets and global technology—and they proclaim that everything is or soon will be different. The rival observers seem to consult different almanacs drawn from the libraries of contrarian planets.

Yet anyone who reads the daily papers carefully, taking in the front page accounts of civil carnage as well as the business page stories on the mechanics of the information superhighway and the economics of communication mergers, anyone who turns deliberately to take in the whole 360-degree horizon, knows that our world and our lives are caught between what William Butler Yeats called the two eternities of race and soul: that of race reflecting the tribal past, that of soul anticipating the cosmopolitan future. Our secular eternities are corrupted, however, race reduced to an insignia of resentment, and soul sized down to fit the demanding body by which it now measures its needs. Neither race nor soul offers us a future that is other than bleak, neither promises a polity that is remotely democratic.

The first scenario rooted in race holds out the grim prospect of a retribalization of large swaths of humankind by war and bloodshed; a threatened balkanization of nation-states in which culture is pitted against culture, people against

---

Published originally by Times Books, 1995. Benjamin R. Barber is Kekst Professor of Civil Society at the University of Maryland, Director, New York office, The Democracy Collaborative and the author of many books including *Strong Democracy* (1984), *Jihad vs. McWorld* (Times Books, 1995), *A Place for Us* (Farrar, Strauss & Giroux, 1998), *A Passion For Democracy: American Essays* (Princeton University Press, 1998), *The Truth of Power: Intellectual Affairs in the Clinton White House* (W. W. Norton & Company).

people, tribe against tribe, a Jihad in the name of a hundred narrowly conceived faiths against every kind of interdependence, every kind of artificial social cooperation and mutuality: against technology, against pop culture, and against integrated markets; against modernity itself as well as the future in which modernity issues. The second paints that future in shimmering pastels, a busy portrait of onrushing economic, technological, and ecological forces that demand integration and uniformity and that mesmerize peoples everywhere with fast music, fast computers, and fast food—MTV, Macintosh, and McDonald's—pressing nations into one homogenous global theme park, one McWorld tied together by communications, information, entertainment, and commerce. Caught between Babel and Disneyland, the planet is falling precipitously apart and coming reluctantly together at the very same moment.

Some stunned observers notice only Babel, complaining about the thousand newly sundered "peoples" who prefer to address their neighbors with sniper rifles and mortars; others—zealots in Disneyland—seize on futurological platitudes and the promise of virtuality, exclaiming "It's a small world after all!" Both are right, how can that be?

We are compelled to choose between what passes as "the twilight of sovereignty" and an entropic end of all history; or a return to the past's most fractious and demoralizing discord; to "the menace of global anarchy," to Milton's capital of hell, Pandaemonium; to a world totally "our of control."

The apparent truth, which speaks to the paradox at the core of this book, is that the tendencies of both Jihad *and* McWorld are at work, both visible sometimes in the same country at the very same instant. Iranian zealots keep one ear tuned to the mullahs urging holy war and the other cocked to Rupert Murdoch's Star television beaming in *Dynasty, Donahue,* and *The Simpsons* from hovering satellites. Chinese entrepreneurs vie for the attention of party cadres in Beijing and simultaneously pursue KFC franchises in cities like Nanjing, Hangzhou, and Xian where twenty-eight outlets serve over 100,000 customers a day. The Russian Orthodox church, even as it struggles to renew the ancient faith, has entered a joint venture with California businessmen to bottle and sell natural waters under the rubric Saint Springs Water Company. Serbian assassins wear Adidas sneakers and listen to Madonna on Walkman headphones as they take aim through their gunscopes at scurrying Sarajevo civilians looking to fill family watercans. Orthodox Hasids and brooding neo-Nazis have both turned to rock music to get their traditional messages out to the new generation, while fundamentalists plot virtual conspiracies on the Internet.

Now neither Jihad nor McWorld is in itself novel. History ending in the triumph of science and reason or some monstrous perversion thereof (Mary Shelley's Doctor Frankenstein) has been the leitmotiv of every philosopher and poet who has regretted the Age of Reason since the Enlightenment. Yeats lamented "the center will not hold, mere anarchy is loosed upon the world," and observers of Jihad today have little but historical detail to add. The Christian parable of the Fall and of the possibilities of redemption that it makes possible captures the eighteenth-century ambivalence—and out own—about past and future. I want, however, to do more than dress up the central paradox of human history in modern clothes. It is not Jihad and McWorld but the relationship between them that most interests me. For, squeezed between their opposing forces, the world has been sent spinning out of control. Can it be that what Jihad and McWorld have in common is anarchy: the absence of common will and that conscious and collective human control under the guidance of law we call democracy?

Progress moves in steps that sometimes lurch backwards; in history's twisting maze, Jihad not only revolts against but abets McWorld, while McWorld not only imperils but re-creates and reinforces Jihad. They produce their contraries and need one another. My object here then is not simply to offer sequential portraits of McWorld and Jihad, but while examining McWorld, to keep Jihad in my field of vision, and while dissecting Jihad, never to forget the context of McWorld. Call it a dialectic of McWorld: a study in the cunning of reason that does honor to the radical differences that distinguish Jihad and McWorld yet that acknowledges their powerful and paradoxical interdependence.

There is a crucial difference, however, between my modest attempt at dialectic and that of the masters of the nineteenth century. Still seduced by the Enlightenment's faith in progress, both Hegel and Marx believed reason's cunning was on the side of progress. But it is harder to believe that the clash of Jihad and McWorld will issue in some overriding good. The outcome seems more likely to pervert than to nurture human liberty. The two may, in opposing each other, work to the same ends, work in apparent tension yet in covert harmony, but democracy is not their beneficiary. In East Berlin, tribal communism has yielded to capitalism. In MarxEngelsplatz, the stolid, overbearing statues of Marx and Engels race east, as if seeking distant solace from Moscow: but now, circling them along the streets that surround the park that is their prison are chain eateries like TGI Friday's, international hotels like the Radisson, and a circle of neon billboards mocking them with brand names like Panasonic, Coke, and GoldStar. New gods, yes, but more liberty?

What then does it mean in concrete terms to view Jihad and McWorld dialectically when the tendencies of the two sets of forces initially appear so intractably antithetical? After all, Jihad and McWorld operate with equal strength in opposite directions, the one driven by parochial hatreds, the other by universalizing markers, the one re-creating ancient subnational and ethnic borders from within, the other making national borders porous from without. Yet Jihad and McWorld have this in common: they both make war on the sovereign nation-state and thus undermine the nation-state's democratic institutions. Each eschews civil society and belittles democratic citizenship, neither seeks alternative democratic institutions. Their common thread is indifference to civil liberty. Jihad forges communities of blood rooted in exclusion and hatred, communities that slight democracy in favor of tyrannical paternalism or consensual tribalism. McWorld forges global markets rooted in consumption and profit, leaving to an untrustworthy, if not altogether fictitious, invisible hand issues of public interest and common good that once might have been nurtured by democratic citizenries and their watchful governments. Such governments, intimidated by market ideology, are actually pulling hack at the very moment they ought to he aggressively intervening. What was once understood as protecting the public interest is now excoriated as heavy-handed regulatory browbeating. Justice yields to markets, even though, as Felix Rohatyn has bluntly confessed, "there is a brutal Darwinian logic to these markets. They are nervous and greedy. They look for stability and transparency, but what they reward is not always our preferred form of democracy." If the traditional conservators of freedom were democratic constitutions and Bills of Rights, "the new temples to liberty," George Steiner suggests, "will be McDonald's and Kentucky Fried Chicken."

In being reduced to a choice between the market's universal church and a retribalizing politics of particularist identities, peoples around the globe are threatened with an atavistic return to medieval politics where local tribes and ambitious emperors together ruled the world entire, women and men united by the universal abstraction of Christianity even as they lived out isolated lives in warring fiefdoms defined by involuntary (ascriptive) forms of identity. This was a world in which princes and kings had little real power until they conceived the ideology of nationalism. Nationalism established government on a scale greater than the tribe yet less cosmopolitan than the universal church and in time gave birth to those intermediate, gradually more democratic institutions that would come to constitute the nation-state. Today, at the far end of this history, we seem intent on re-creating a world in which our only choices are the secular universalism of the cosmopolitan market and the everyday particularism of the fractious tribe.

In the tumult of the confrontation between global commerce and parochial ethnicity, the virtues of the democratic nation are lost and the instrumentalities by which it permitted peoples to transform themselves into nations and seize sovereign power in the name of liberty and the commonweal are put at risk. Neither

Jihad nor McWorld aspires to resecure the civic virtues undermined by its denationalizing practices; neither global markets nor blood communities service public goods or pursue equality and justice. Impartial judiciaries and deliberative assemblies play no role in the roving killer hands that speak on behalf of newly liberated "peoples," and such democratic institutions have at best only marginal influence on the roving multinational corporations that speak on behalf of newly liberated markets. Jihad pursues a bloody politics of identity, McWorld a bloodless economies of profit. Belonging by default to McWorld, everyone is a consumer; seeking a repository for identity, everyone belongs to some tribe. But no one is a citizen. Without citizens, how can there be democracy? [. . .]

Jihad is, I recognize, a strong term. In its mildest form, it betokens religions struggle on behalf of faith, a kind of Islamic zeal. In its strongest political manifestation, it means bloody holy war on behalf of partisan identity that is metaphysically defined and fanatically defended. Thus, while for many Muslims it may signify only ardor in the name of a religion that can properly be regarded as universalizing (if not quite ecumenical), I borrow its meaning from those militants who make the slaughter of the "other" a higher duty. I use the term in its militant construction to suggest dogmatic and violent particularism of a kind known to Christians no less than Muslims, to Germans and Hindis as well as to Arabs. The phenomena to which I apply the phrase have innocent enough beginnings: identity polities and multicultural diversity can represent strategies of a free society trying to give expression to its diversity. What ends as Jihad may begin as a simple search for a local identity, some set of common personal attributes to hold out against the numbing and neutering uniformities of industrial modernization and the colonizing culture of McWorld.

America is often taken as the model for this kind of benign multiculturalism, although we too have our critics like Arthur Schlesinger, Jr., for whom multiculturalism is never benign and for whom it signals the inaugural logic of a long-term disintegration. Indeed, I will have occasion below to write about an "American Jihad" being waged by the radical Right. The startling fact is that less than 10 percent (about twenty) of the modern world's states are truly homogenous and thus, like Denmark or the Netherlands, can't get smaller unless they fracture into tribes or clans. In only half is there a single ethnic group that comprises even 75 percent of the population. As in the United Stares, multiculturalism is the rule, homogeneity the exception. Nations like Japan or Spain that appear to the outside world as integral turn our to be remarkably multicultural. And even if language alone, the nation's essential attribute, is made the condition for self-determination, a count of the number of languages spoken around the world suggests the community of nations could grow to over six thousand members.

The modern nation-state has actually acted as a cultural integrator and has adapted well to pluralist ideals: civic ideologies and constitutional faiths around which their many clans and tribes can rally. It has not been too difficult to contrive a civil religion for Americans or French or Swiss, since these "peoples" actually contain multitudes of subnational factions and ethnic tribes earnestly seeking common ground. But for Basques and Normans? What need have they for anything but blood and memory? And what of Alsatians, Bavarians, and East Prussians? Kurds, Ossetians, East Timorese, Quebecois, Abkhazians, Catalonians, Tamils, Inkatha Zulus, Kurile Islander Japanese—peoples without countries inhabiting nations they cannot call their own? Peoples trying to seal themselves off not just from others but from modernity? These are frightened tribes running not to but from civic faith in search of something more palpable and electrifying. How will peoples who define themselves by the slaughter of tribal neighbors be persuaded to peoples to some flimsy artificial faith organized around abstract civic ideals or commercial markets? Can advertising divert warriors of blood from the genocide required by their ancient grievances? [. . .]

McWorld is a product of popular culture driven by expansionist commerce. Its template is American, its form style. Its goods are as much images as matériel, an aesthetic as well as a product line. It is about culture as commodity, apparel as ideology. Its symbols are Harley-Davidson motorcycles and Cadillac motorcars hoisted from the roadways, where they once represented a mode of transportation, to the marquees of global market cafés like Harley-Davidson's and the Hard Rock where they become icons of lifestyle. You don't drive them, you feel their vibes and rock to the images they conjure tip from old movies and new celebrities, whose personal appearances are the key to the wildly popular international café chain Planet Hollywood. Music, video, theater, books, and theme parks—the new churches of a commercial civilization in which malls are the public squares and suburbs the neighborless neighborhoods—are all constructed as image exports creating a common world taste around common logos, advertising slogans, stars, songs, brand names, jingles, and trademarks. Hard power yields to soft, while ideology is transmuted into a kind of videology that works through sound bites and film clips. Videology is fuzzier and less dogmatic than traditional political ideology: it may as a consequence be far more successful in instilling the novel values required for global markets to succeed.

McWorld's videology remains Jihad's most formidable rival, and in the long run it may attenuate the force of Jihad's recidivist tribalisms. Yet the information revolution's instrumentalities are also Jihad's favored weapons. Hutu or Bosnian Serb identity was less a matter of real historical memory than of media propaganda by a leadership set on liquidating rival clans. In both Rwanda and Bosnia, radio broadcasts whipped listeners into a killing frenzy. As *New York Times* rock critic Jon Pareles has noticed, "regionalism in pop music has become as trendy as microbrewery beer and narrowcasting cable channels, and for the same reasons." The global culture is what gives the local culture its medium, its audience, and its aspirations. Fascist pop and Hasid rock are not oxymorons; rather they manifest the dialectics of McWorld in particularly dramatic ways. Belgrade's radio includes stations that broadcast Western pop music as a rebuke to hard-liner Milosevic's super-nationalist government and stations that broadcast native folk tunes laced with antiforeign and anti-Semitic sentiments. Even the Internet has its neo-Nazi bulletin boards and Turk-trashing Armenian "flamers" (who assail every rise of the word *turkey*, fair and fowl alike, so to speak), so that the abstractions of cyberspace too are infected with a peculiar and rabid cultural territoriality all their own.

The dynamics of the Jihad-McWorld linkage are deeply dialectical. Japan has, for example, become more culturally insistent on its own traditions in recent years even as its people seek an ever greater purchase on McWorld. In 1992, the number-one restaurant in Japan measured by volume of customers was McDonald's, followed in the number-two spot by the Colonel's Kentucky Fried Chicken. In France, where cultural purists complain bitterly of a looming Sixième Republique ("la République Américaine"), the government attacks "franglais" even as it funds EuroDisney park just outside of Paris. In the same spirit, the cinema industry makes war on American film imports while it bestows upon Sylvester Stallone one of France's highest honors, the Chevalier des arts et lettres. Ambivalence also stalks India. Just outside of Bombay, cheek by jowl with villages still immersed in poverty and notorious for the informal execution of unwanted female babies or, even, wives, can he found a new town known as SCEEPZ—the Santa Cruz Electronic Export Processing Zone—where Hindi-, Tamil-, and Mahratti-speaking computer programmers write software for Swissair, AT&T, and other labor-cost-conscious multinationals. India is thus at once a major exemplar of ancient ethnic and religious tensions and "an emerging power in the international software industry." To go to work at SCEEPZ, says an employee, is "like crossing an international border." Not into another Country, but into the virtual nowhere-land of McWorld.

More dramatic even than in India, is the strange interplay of Jihad and McWorld in the remnants of Yugoslavia. In an affecting *New Republic* report, Slavenka Drakulic told the brief tragic love story of Admira and Bosko, two young starcrossed lovers from Sarajevo: "They were born in the late 1960s," she writes. "They watched Spielberg movies; they listened to Iggy Pop; they read John le Carré; they went to a disco every Saturday night and fantasized about traveling to Paris or London." Longing for safety, it seems they finally negotiated with all sides for safe passage, and readied their departure from Sarajevo. Before they could cross the magical border that separates their impoverished lane from the seeming sanctuary of McWorld, Jihad caught up to them. Their bodies lay along the riverbank, riddled with bullets from anonymous snipers for whom safe passage signaled an invitation to target practice. The murdered young lovers, as befits émigrés to McWorld, were clothed in jeans and sneakers. So too, one imagines, were their murderers.

Further east, tourists seeking a piece of old Russia that does not take them too far from MTV can find traditional Matryoshka nesting dolls (that fit one inside the other) featuring the nontraditional visages of (from largest to smallest) Bruce Springsteen, Madonna, Boy George, Dave Stewart, and Annie Lennox.

In Russia, in India, in Bosnia, in Japan, and in France too, modern history then leans both ways: toward the meretricious inevitability of McWorld, but also into Jihad's stiff winds, heaving to and fro and giving heart both to the Panglossians and the Pandoras, sometimes for the very same reasons. The Panglossians bank on EuroDisney and Microsoft, while the Pandoras await nihilism and a world in Pandaemonium. Yet McWorld and Jihad do not really force a choice between such polarized scenarios. Together, they are likely to produce some stifling amalgam of the two suspended in chaos. Antithetical in every detail, Jihad and McWorld nonetheless conspire to undermine our hard-won (if only half-won) civil liberties and the possibility of a global democratic future. In the short run the forces of Jihad, noisier and more obviously nihilistic than those of McWorld, are likely to dominate the near future, etching small stories of local tragedy and regional genocide on the face of our times and creating a climate of instability marked by multimicrowars inimical to global integration. But in the long run, the forces of McWorld are the forces underlying the slow certain thrust of Western civilization arid as such may be unstoppable. Jihad's microwars will hold the headlines well into the next century, making predictions of the end of history look terminally dumb. But McWorld's homogenization is likely to establish a macropeace that favors the triumph of commerce and its markers and to give to those who control information, communication, and entertainment ultimate (if inadvertent) control over human destiny. Unless we can offer an alternative to the struggle between Jihad and McWorld, the epoch on whose threshold we stand—postcommunist, postindustrial, postnational, yet sectarian, fearful, and bigoted—is likely also to be terminally postdemocratic.

The Hinge of History: Turbulence and Transformation in the World Economy

Richard P. Appelbaum and
Jeffrey Henderson

This journal grew out of a premise: that the world economy is in time of acute and probably unprecedented flux and transformation. Not only does our present age pose new problems (or old ones in new forms) and throw-up new possibilities, but it is one that calls into question existing frameworks of social scientific, and particularly economic, understanding.

Change, of course, is central to modernity, as is the on-going project of reflexivity that lies at the core of its intellectual traditions (Giddens 1990). Perhaps every age sees itself as a turning point of history—a bifurcation in historical trajectory, a disjuncture between the known past and a new and uncharted future. In a century marked by world wars that were numbered, cold wars that were not, the near-collapse of global capitalism, the rise and fall of state socialism, and even the seeming end of the third world, there would seem to be innumerable candidates for major historical transformations.

Yet we argue that as the twentieth century approaches its close, we are indeed at a hinge of history—a critical point around which history is turning. Hinges by their nature open-up new vistas while closing-down others. But the

From *Competition and Change: The Journal of Global Business and Political Economy, Vol. 1 (1)*
by Richard Appelbaum & Jeffrey Henderson. Reprinted by permission of Taylor and Francis,
www.tandf.co.uk.

opening and closing may be only temporary, always bearing the possibility of partial reversal. Until the new vistas, the new possibilities, are rendered relatively permanent, they are inherently unstable: they reflect periods of simultaneous opportunity and danger.

Theorizing such a change is no easy task, since our present frameworks are inevitably bound up with past understandings. Some frameworks, however, are more intellectually problematic from this perspective than others. Neoclassical economic theory (or at least dominant versions of it), for instance, seems particularly rooted in a reality that has long since past (Hodgson 1988, Lazonick 1991). Other traditions of thought, such as those influenced by dialectics and incorporating such diverse twentieth century contributions as those of the Frankfurt School (Jay 1973), evolutionary economists such as Veblen and Schumpeter (Bottomore 1992, Hodgson 1993) and Bhaskar's 'critical realism' (eg. Bhaskar 1989, 1993; Sayer 1984) are arguably better equipped, conceptually and methodologically, to deal with a world in flux. While current theories inevitably provide the starting point, it is clear we must go beyond them if we are to chart a theoretical pathway to the future.

As a first step, we believe it is necessary to engender discussion across a broad range of intellectual specialisms that are concerned with global economic change: business economics, political economy, organizational sociology, economic geography, international relations and development studies. These are sub-disciplines and multidisciplinary projects that often operate as it in hermetically sealed universes, in virtual ignorance of one another. They frequently embrace mutually incompatible premises, draw on their own specialized literatures, frame their arguments within particularized discourses, and draw widely discrepant conclusions about present circumstances and future possibilities. It is our hope in this journal to foster exchange and debate among scholars in these diverse fields, by focusing their attention on a common set of issues and problems deriving from heightened competition and change in the world economy. We briefly review some of these issues below.

New Faces of Capitalism

The globalization of capital has drawn the world into its vortex, with far-reaching impacts on what only a few years ago were believed to be three nonmiscible 'worlds'.

For market-based industrial nations, economic globalization has meant a transition from nation-based monopoly capital to a new era of global competition. The rebuilding of Europe after World War II, the emergence of Japan as a global economic power, and the newly-industrialized nations of East Asia sounded an early obituary for the short-lived 'American Century' announced by Henry Luce in 1941. Today, transnational corporations—their production and distribution systems extending around the globe—rival nations in wealth and economic power, creating a polycentric world economy whose lattice-like web of economic centres inevitably calls into question the very notion of a geographical core to capitalism. Corporate giants, once sovereign at least in their own back yards, now find themselves competing on a global scale. They are challenged seemingly wherever they turn—by other companies, social movements and governments—and sometimes from unexpected quarters.

The hierarchically-structured, state-centred industrial economies of the socialist world have for the most part ceased to exist. What once appeared to be viable alternative paths for industrial development have crumbled, in part under their own weight. While the reasons for this are many and debated, some credence must be given to the argument that non-market economies are simply unable to respond effectively to the requirements for participation in a global economy. Whatever the limitations of purely market-based allocation systems, the failure of total reliance on state-bureaucratic mechanisms appears even more pronounced in an age where information is near-instantaneous and flexibility the watchword (Castells 1993). Today, with capitalist-roaders firmly in the driving seat of the world's single remaining socialist giant, the only possible barrier to a complete triumph of global capitalism would seem to be religious nationalism—and even the most traditional forms of Islam (or, for that matter, Christianity or Judaism) are less opposed in capitalism than they are to the social institutions and values that accompany it.

For the residual category once labelled the 'third world', the end has been in sight for some time (Harris 1987). This is not to argue that global economic polarization has been overcome; far from it. Nor is it to argue that all regions of the world are somehow becoming economic or political equals. But the 'third world' has ceased to be a homogeneous economic space, and with the end of the Cold War, has ceased—for the moment—to be a prize courted by the other two worlds; a battle ground for their surrogate wars. Rather, to varying degrees, and with decidedly asymmetrical consequences, the 'third world' has been incorporated into the global economic matrix. While its nations still stand in relationships of dependency to the world's principal capitalist countries, concepts such as 'core' and 'periphery' appear less and less useful as attributes of entire countries or indeed of regions within them. Development may be partially dependent on one's location in the global capitalist system, but, as the later industrializers of Pacific

Asia and elsewhere have demonstrated, the notion of purely dependent client states is challenged in an economically polycentric world. Stated somewhat differently, as the global economy becomes more complex, a wider range of roles and relationships are possible: the world-system today engenders core-periphery relations within core and peripheral economies alike.

The world economy is an amalgam of different forms of capitalism. Although these forms have a common core, it is one that appears more circumscribed than previously thought. Indeed if we accept Runciman's recent definition, it consists of no more than 'a mode of production in which formally free labour is recruited for regular employment by ongoing enterprises competing in the market for profit' (Runciman 1995: 33). Outside of this, national (and in some cases subnational) economies exhibit substantial variation in the significance of market allocations based on price signals; industrial policy and state-business relations; the nature of firm ownership and corporate governance; the principal sources of corporate finance; time horizons for profitability; the nature of welfare regimes and their relation to competitiveness; the gearing of capitalist economic arrangements to radically different modes of persuasion and coercion; etc. (among a now substantial literature see, for instance, Lazonick 1991, Porter 1992, Whitley 1992a, 1992b, Albert 1993, Stark 1993, Sheridan 1993, Henderson 1993, Henderson *et al.*, 1995, Hutton 1995, Runciman 1995). We live in a world in which competition is not only a feature of inter-firm relations, but of the relations between different capitalist economic systems. The economic, social and political ramifications of this it something this journal will explore, as is the questionable proposition that increasing globalisation coupled with deepening recession in the principal economies, will result in a systemic convergence around the Anglo-American form.

Space and the Dialectics of Globalism

Recent technological advances—the so-called 'information revolution'—have made possible a degree of organizational flexibility that is without precedent. From facsimile to e-mail, from electronic point-of-sales retailing to programmable robot manufacturing, businesses are increasingly able to effectively coordinate their production and management activities over a global space and hence provide the building blocks for what Castells (1989) terms an 'informational mode of development'. This, in turn, has made it possible to partially dismantle the vertically-integrated firm that dominated industrial capitalism during the immediate post-war period. From Japanese automobile production to the apparel industry's 'manufacturers without factories', firms are increasingly able to choose what to keep 'in house' and what to contract elsewhere (Pfeffer arid Baron 1988). This has had repercussions for the spatial organization of production.

The classic globalization argument, which other than in business schools has often been associated with the 'New International Division of Labour' perspective (Frobel *et al.*, 1980; for critical commentary and refinement see, for instance, Massey 1984, Ernst 1987, Schoenberger 1988, Henderson 1989, Dicken 1992), holds that recent advances in transportation and communications technologies allow multinational corporations to move manufacturing facilities to any site on the globe where productivity is acceptable and profits can be maximized. Labour intensive production in particular is thus dispersed to low-wage countries while capital and skill intensive activities remain in the core. As Henderson (1989) has shown, however, in the global production systems of some industries, intermediate locations which themselves become regionally significant centres for technology, skill and managerial expertise tend to emerge. These become the fulcrums of regionally specific divisions of labour (such as in East and Southeast Asia), establishing their own relative autonomy and development possibilities but constraining their peripheries by further sets of dependent and unequal relations. This perspective on globalization has recently been re-cast by Gereffi and his colleagues within a more encompassing notion of 'global commodity chains' (Gereffi 1992, Gereffi and Korzeniewicz 1994). While bearing some similarity to value chain analysis (Porter 1985, 1990), the work of Gereffi and others builds more on a notion originally advanced by Hopkins and Wallerstein (1986). Here the global commodity chain is offered as a means or understanding production as a dynamic set of processes among firms, rather than as a static property of nations, more typical of world-systems and similar forms of development theory. Commodity chains are conceptualized as global export networks that result in geographical specialization and tightly linked international global sourcing. They favour organizational flexibility, achieved through the externalized contracting and subcontracting of functions that were once internal to large business organizations.

By way of contrast, the 'flexible accumulation' and 'transaction-costs' perspectives note that as organizations become more 'flexible' through vertical and horizontal disintegration, the friction of distance increases in importance, providing a strong incentive for geographical clustering. Geographic proximity to subcontracted labour, suppliers, producer services, and final markets is especially important for smaller, vertically-disintegrated firms when transactions are small-scale, irregular, and involve production for quickly changing markets (Williamson 1975, 1985; Scott 1988a, Storper and Scott 1990). A related set of arguments is advanced by Porter (1990) who—echoing Schumpeter—argues that geographical concentration is advantageous for businesses both because of the transactional advantages it confers, as well as because local competition hones them for global competition.

The global economy today thus fosters both integration and fragmentation. It connects firms by means of global export and labour networks, while pitting them against one another through global competition. While the existence of a globally-accessible labour market (containing enormous wage differentials) encourages geographical dispersion, the advantages of spatial concentration become ever more important in flexible production. In a global economy, space matters; industries continue to produce economic regions, even as regions help to shape industrial competitiveness (see Storper and Walker 1989: chapter 3).

Nation and Development: Rethinking Core and Periphery

We have already noted that in today's world economy, the spatial meaning of core and periphery needs to be rethought. While uneven development remains a char- acteristic of the world-system, stratification also appears to be increasing within once-core industrial nations. While this trend is most pronounced within the United States (Shapiro and Greenstein 1991; Sarbanes 1992; Barancik and Shapiro 1992), it is true in Europe as well. While there are many reasons for this, we believe that increasingly global wage competition plays an important role.

Much of this inequality is found in the prime cities of the world. 'World cities' linked to one another as much as to their own national hinterlands, have come to play a commanding role in the world economy. They are centres of global finance and specialized services, save as the most innovative production sites, and lie at the centre of the leading regional markets (Sassen 1991, 1994, Friedmann and Wolff 1982; Friedmann 1986, King 1990, Smith and Timberlake 1993). Yet world cities are also characterized by economic polarization, fuelled by the expansion of low-wage casual employment, economic informalization, and the presence of large immigrant populations (Sassen 1991, 1994). While such polarization has been statistically noted (Soja 1991, Logan *et al.*, 1992), the mechanisms by which this occurs have not been fully specified—although some have sought to link it specifically with the commanding roles such places play in the world economy (Sassen 1991, Mollenkopf and Castells 1991, Fainstein *et al.*, 1992). One of our hopes in the journal is to better identify the links between social stratification and the respatialization of capital in metropolitan regions.

States and Economic Governance

The turbulence of our present age throws into high relief the economic role of states—national and sub-national—and of international regulatory agencies. National states, of course, have always been central to economic development. This has been so partly because of their historic commitment to war preparation and in this century at least, the regular pursuit of war (Deane 1975, Harris 1992, Harris and Lockwood 1995), and partly because of their structural imperative to take responsibility for both the reproduction of the general conditions necessary for capital accumulation and for legitimating the social and political arrangements associated with the pursuit of wealth and power in any economic system (Habermas 1974, Offe 1975, Carnoy 1984). A multiplicity of policy instruments, on occasion supplemented by informal pressures, have been devised by governments in furtherance of these imperatives. These range from market protection (used from time to time in various forms in practically all industrial economies since the latter part of the nineteen century) to industrial policy to infrastructural projects to welfare provision.

Since the second world war the state-economy relation has been brought into particularly sharp focus by the spectacular rise of the 'late industrializing' societies of Pacific Asia (from a substantial literature see, for instance, the recent contributions by Amsden 1989, Wade 1990, Castells *et at.*, 1990, Woo 1991, Appelbaum and Henderson 1992, Sheridan 1993, Hsiao 1995), the emergence of regional economic and proto-political block—the European Union in particular—and the debates over the sources and appropriate responses to the relative economic decline of the United States (for instance, Reich 1991, Thurrow 1992, Tyson 1992, Krugman 1994). Additionally, the damaging experience of Eastern Europe's flirtation with free market capitalism—the so called 'shock therapy'—seems likely to return industrial policy to the agenda of transformation and development there (Amsden *et al.*, 1994, Henderson *et al.*, 1995).

While governments will continue to generate a variety of initiatives with respect to their economies—ranging from the neo-liberal to the *dirigiste*—it is clear that their room for manoeuvre is now more circumscribed than was previously the case. While pro-active states will remain central to economic growth and prosperity (Carnoy 1993, Hint and Thompson 1995), a world economy that seems to teeter on the verge of chaos arguably demands a far greater role for supra-national regulation. Without it—as has been seen in recent years from the fall-out of the casino capitalism of financial markets—even major firms and economies are under continuous threat. These and the other issues signalled here are amongst those that we seek to explore in the pages of this journal.

Against this backdrop of national state and inter-state economic action emerges the significance of recent initiatives by local states in various parts of the world. Framed intellectually within the debates on post-fordism, 'new industrial spaces' and regulation theory (Scott 1988a, 1988b, Jessop 1990, Amin 1994), the role of subnational state agencies as partners with firms and trade associations in energizing networks of locally-rooted economic action, seems to have become a path to prosperity in societies as disparate as some of those of Pacific Asia, Latin America and Europe (see respectively, Glasmeier ad Sugiura 1991, Schmitz 1994, Cooke and Morgan 1991 among others). Whether the success of such industrial districts can be sustained in changing economic circumstances (see Braczyk *et al.*, 1995 on the problems of BadenWurrtemberg), whether they can be induced from scratch (see Schmitz 1994 for arguments against this possibility), or whether they can ever become more than an adjunct at the level of major national economies to reformed versions of fordism, are among the issues we hope to see debated in this journal.

Labour

Work, working conditions wage rates, trade unions, welfare policy, worker participation in economic and corporate governance, the nature of consumption and leisure, remain central issues for the future of the global economy. For labour, seven world historic processes, some separate in origin, some less so, have combined to radically alter the circumstances under which work is pursued and livelihoods—and with them family lives—are forged. These are (a) the seeming demise or fordism and with it the growth of more flexible but more insecure forms of employment and remuneration affecting workers across the class spectrum; (b) with this, the feminization of large sections of the labour force, albeit within the context of persistently gender-segmented labour markets; (c) the decline of manufacturing industry as a provider of skilled jobs in the advanced economies and a concomitant rise in service sector employment (Sassen 1991); (d) the emergence of a culture of consumerism with its attendant globalization of western (largely US) values resulting in the growing homogenization of indigenous cultures (Sklair 1991); (e) the re-emergence since the early 1950s of migrant labour—legal or illegal—as a principal motor force of the world's industrial economies, with major exception of Japan (Cohen 1981, Sassen 1988); (f) the emergence of neo-liberal policy regimes which irrespective of the idelology of the government in question have constrained trade union activity, reduced welfare provision, compounded job insecurity, and in the developing world—via the structural adjustment policies of the IMF and World Bank—wreaked social havoc; (g) the emergence of new industrial and industrializing economies in the developing worlds of Asia, Latin America and Eastern Europe with huge reservoirs of cheap, but sometimes skilled labour, and subject in some cases to working conditions that would not have been out of place in Engels' Manchester (Elson and Pearson 1981, Leung 1988, Deyo 1989, Bello and Rosenfeld 1992).

These processes, transforming as they are the daily lives of the majority of the populations of the industrial world, are likely to have major consequences for the future of work and leisure, income distribution and social polarization, issues of equality and human rights. In addition, the link between low wages and poor working conditions and standards coupled with high levels of productivity in some of the newly industrialized countries raises the problem of the bases on which international competition ensues, and thus whether meeting internationally acceptable social conditions should be a *sine qua non* of market access. This as well as the other hotly debated issues on the position of labour and its relation to economic performance in various parts of the world is something we expect to see aired regularly in the pages of this journal.

Companies

Changes in the international organization or companies as part of their strategies for responding to economic turbulence have been discussed in various contexts earlier in this article. Consequently there is no need to dwell on this in great detail here. However, it is important to mark that the determinants of corporate strategy, the nature of governance structures, the extent to which companies are capable—in some cases even interested—in institutionalizing innovation as a major objective of their operation, are centrally important not only to national economic performance but to the extent to which prosperous, egalitarian societies can be constructed. We take the view that there is no magical, necessary relation between successful companies, and economies with generalized prosperity and thus low levels of income inequality. That relation has to be deliberately constructed and then institutionally sustained and regulated for the benefit of all. We believe that the present epoch is one in which companies will come under increasing pressure, nationally and internationally, to formulate strategies compatible with these objectives. In this sense and others, the analysis of corporate strategy is an important moment in the intellectual explorations that this journal seeks to encourage.

The Way Forward

Outlined above are the bare bones of the sorts of investigations that *Competition and Change* was set-up to encourage and publish. This is no time for premature theoretical closure and consequently we encourage submissions which may begin from a variety of different premises and which may employ a variety of conceptual apparatuses and methodologies. In each issue we will publish substantive articles as well as shorter pieces which debate the various issues, engage with their policy implications, or mark out research agendas. Additionally we will occasionally publish commentaries which bear directly on articles published in the journal (as in this first issue), and carry review articles of books which make major contributions to our thinking. The contents of this lint issue range across a number of the concerns we have raised here. As such they engage with the some oldie central problems of our time.

References

Albert, M. (1993) *Capitalism Against Capitalism.* London: Whurr.

Amin, A. (ed) (1994) *Post-Fordism.* Oxford: Blackwell.

Amsden, A.H. (1989) *Asia's Next Giant: South Korea and Late Industrialisation.* New York: Oxford University Press.

Amsden, A.H., Kochanowicz, J. and Taylor, L. (1994) *The Market Meets its Match: Restructuring the Economies of Eastern Europe.* Cambridge, MA: Harvard University Press.

Appelbaum, R.P. and Henderson. J. (eds) (1992) *States and Development in the Asian Pacific Rim.* Newbury Park: Sage Publications.

Barancik, S. and Shapiro, I. (1992) *Where Have All the Dollars Gone? A State-By-State Analysis of Income Disparities Over the 1980s.* Washington, D.C.: Center on Budget and Policy Priorities.

Bello, W. and Rosenfeld, S. (1992) *Dragons in Distress: Asia's Miracle Economics in Crisis.* London: Penguin.

Bhaskar, R. (1989) *The Possibility of Naturalism.* London: Harvester Wheatsheaf.

Bhaskar, R. (1993) *Dialectic: The Pulse of Freedom.* London: Verso.

Bottomore, T. (1992) *Between Marginalism and Marxism: The Economic Sociology of J.A. Schumpeter.* London: Harvester Wheatsheaf.

Braczyk, H.J., Schienstock, G. and Stefensen, B. (1995) 'The region of Baden-Wurrtemberg: a "post fordist" success story'? In Eckhart Dittrich, (Gert Schmidt and Richard Whitley (eds) *Industrial Transformation in Europe.* London: Sage Publications, 203–233.

Carnoy, M. (1984) *The State and Political Theory.* Princeton: Princeton University Press.

Carnoy, M. (1993) 'Multinationals in a changing world economy: whither the nation state'? In Martin Carnoy, Manuel Castells, Stephen S. Cohen and Fernando Henrique Cardoso. *The New Global Economy in the Information Age.* University Park: Pennsylvania State University Press, 45–96.

Castells, M. (1989) *The Informational City.* Oxford: Blackwell.

Castells, M. (1993) 'The informational economy and the new international division of labor'. In Martin Carnoy, Manuel Castells, Stephen S. Cohen and Fernando Henrique Cardoso. *The New Global Economy in the Informational Age.* University Park: Pennsylvania State University Press, 15–43.

Castells, M., Goh, L. and Kwok, R.Y. (1990) *The Shek Kip Mei Syndrome: Economic Development and Public Housing in Hong Kong and Singapore.* London: Pion.

Cohen, R. (1987) *The New Helots: Migrants in the International Division of Labour.* Aldershot: Avebury.

Cooke, P. and Morgan, K. (1991) "The Intelligent Region: Industrial and Institutional Innovation in Emilia-Romagna'. *Regional Industrial Research Report No. 7.* University of Wales at Cardiff.

Deane, P. (1975) 'War and industrialisation'. In J.M. Winter (ed) *War and Economic Development: Essays in Memory of David Joslin.* Cambridge: Cambridge University Press, 91–102.

Deyo, F.C. (1989) *Beneath the Miracle: Labor Subordination in the New Asian Industrialism.* Berkeley: University of California Press.

Dicken, P. (1992) *Global Shift: The Internationalization of Economic Activity.* New York: Guilford Publications.

Elson, D. and Pearson, R. (1981) 'Nimble fingers make cheap workers: an analysis of women's employment in Third World export manufacturing'. *Feminist Review, 7,* 87–107.

Ernst, D. (1987) *Innovation, Industrial Structure and Global Competition: the Changing Economics of Internationalization.* New York: Campus Verlag.

Fainstein, S., Gordon, J. and Harloe, M. (eds) (1992) *Divided Cities: New York and London In the Contemporary World.* Cambridge, MA: Blackwell.

Friedmann, J. and Wolff, G. (1982) 'World city formation: an agenda for research and action'. *International Journal of Urban and Regional Research,* 6, 309–344.

Friedmann, J. (1986) 'The world city hypothesis'. *Development and Change, 17:1,* 69–83.

Frobel, F., Heinrichs, J. and Kreye, O. (1980) *The New International Division of Labor Structural Unemployment in Industrialized Countries and Industrialization in Developing Countries.* Cambridge: Cambridge University Press.

Gereffi, G. (1992) 'New realities of industrial development in East Asia and Latin America: global, regional and national trends'. In Richard P. Appelbaum and Jeffrey Henderson (eds) *States and Development in the Asian Pacific Rim.* Newbury Park Sage Publications, 85–112.

Gereffi, G. and Korzeniewicz, M. (eds) (1994) *Commodity Chains and Global Capitalism*. Westport, CT: Greenwood Press.

Giddens, A. (1990) *The Consequences of Modernity*. Cambridge: Polity Press.

Glasmeier, A. and Sugiura, N. (1991) 'Japan's manufacturing system: small business, sub-contracting and regional complex formation'. *International Journal of Urban and Regional Research*, 15(3), 395–414.

Habermas, J. (1974) *Legitimation Crisis*. Boston: Beacon Press.

Harris, N. (1987) *The End of the Third World: Newly Industrialising Countries and the decline of an Ideology*. London: Penguin.

Harris, N. (1992) States, economic development and the Asian Pacific Rim'. In Richard P. Appelbaum and Jeffrey Henderson (eds) *States and Development in the Asian Pacific Rim*. Newbury Park: Sage Publications, 71–84.

Hauls, N. and Lockwood, D. (1995) 'War and privatisation', paper to the *European Science Foundation-European Management and Organisations in Transition Programme Workshop*. Budapest, May.

Henderson, J. (1989) *The Globalisation of High Technology Production: Society, Space and Semiconductors in the Restructuring of the Modern World*. London: Routledge.

Henderson, J. (1993) 'The role of the state in the economic transformation of East Asia'. In Chris Dixon and David Drakakis-Smith (eds) *Economic and Social Development in Pacific Asia*. London: Routledge, 85–114.

Henderson, J., Whitley, R., Lengyel, G. and Czaban, L. (1995) 'Contention and confusion in industrial transformation: dilemmas of state economic management'. In Eckhard Dittrich, Gert Schmidt and Richard Whitley (eds) *Industrial Transformation in Europe*. London: Sage Publications, 79–108.

Hirst, P. and Thompson, G. (1995) 'Globalisation and the future nation state'. *Economy and Society*, 24(3), 408–442.

Hodgson, G.M. (1988) *Economics and Institutions: A Manifesto for a Modern Institutional Economics*. Cambridge: Polity Press.

Hodgson, G.M. (1993) *Economics and Evolution: Bringing Life Back Into Economics*. Cambridge: Polity Press.

Hopkins, T.K. and Wallerstein, I. (1986) 'Commodity chains in the world-economy prior to 1800'. *Review*, 10(1), 157–170.

Hsiao, H.H.M. (1995) 'The state and business relations in Taiwan'. *Journal of Far Eastern Business*, 1(3),76–97.

Hutton, W. (1995) *The State We're In*. London: Jonathan Cape.

Jay, M. (1973) *The Dialectical Imagination*. Boston: Beacon Press.

Jessop. B. (1990) 'Regulation theories in retrospect and prospect'. *Economy and Society*. 19(2), 153–216.

King, A. (1990) *Global Cities: Post-Imperialism and the Internationali-zation of London*. London: Routledge.

Krugman, P. (1994) 'Competitiveness; a dangerous obsession'. *Foreign Affairs*, 74, 28–44.

Lazonick, W. (1991) *Business Organisation and the Myth of the Market Economy.* New York: Cambridge University Press.

Leung, W.Y. (1988) *Smashing the Iron Rice Pot: Workers and Unions in China's Market Socialism.* Hong Kong: Asia Monitor Resources Center.

Logan, J., Taylor-Gooby, P. and Reuter, M. (1992) 'Poverty and income inequality'. In Susan Fainstein, Ian Gordon and Michael Harloe (eds) *Divided Cities: New York and London in the Contemporary World.* Cambridge, MA: Blackwell, 129–150.

Massey, D. (1984) *Spatial Divisions of Labour.* London: Macmillan.

Mollenkopf, J. and Castells, M. (eds) (1991) *Dual City: Restructuring New York.* New York: Russell Sage Foundation.

Offe, C. (1975) 'The theory of the capitalist state and the problem of policy formation'. In Leon N. Lindberg, Robert Alford, Colin Crouch and Claus Offe (eds) *Stress and Contradiction in Modern Capitalism.* Lexington: D.C. Health, 125–144.

Pfeffer, J. and Baron. J.N. (1988) 'Taking the workers hack out: recent trends in the structuring of employment'. *Research in Organizational Behavior,* 10, 257–303

Porter, M.E. (1985) *Competitive Advantage: Creating and Sustaining Superior Performance.* New York: Free Press.

Porter, M.E. (1990) *The Competitive Advantage of Nations.* London: Macmillan.

Porter, M.E. (1992) 'Capital disadvantage: America's failing capital investment system'. *Harvard Business Review,* September/October: 65–82.

Reich, R.B. (1991) *The Work of Nation:: Preparing Ourselves for 21st Century Capitalism.* New York: Vintage Hooks.

Ross, K. and Trache, K. (1990) *Global Capitalism The New Leviathon.* Albany: SUNY Press.

Runciman, W.G. (1995) 'The "triumph" of capitalism as a topic in the theory of social selection'. *New Left Review,* 210, 33–47.

Sarbanes, P. (1992) *Men At Work: Signs of Trouble.* Washington, D.C.: Joint Economic Committee of Congress.

Sassen, S. (1988) *The Mobility of Labor and Capital: A Study in International Investment and Labor Flow.* New York: Cambridge University Press.

Sassen, S. (1991) *The Global City: New York, London, Tokyo.* Princeton: Princeton University Press.

Sassen, S. (1994) *Cities in a World Economy.* Thousand Oaks, CA: Pine Forge Press.

Sayer, A. (1984) *Method in Social Science.* London: Hutchinson.

Schmitt, H. (1994) 'Collective efficiency: growth path for small scale industry', mimeographed paper, Institute of Development Studies, University of Sussex.

Schoenberger, E. (1988) 'Multinational corporations and the new international division of labour: a critique'. *International Regional Science Review,* 11, 105–119.

Scott, A.J. (1988a) 'Flexible production systems and regional development: the rise of new industrial spaces in North America and Western Europe'. *International Journal of Urban and Regional Research,* 12(2), 171–186.

Scott, A.J. (1988b) *New Industrial Spaces.* London: Pion.

Shapiro, I. and Greenstein, R. (1991) *Selective Prosperity*. Washington, D.C.: Center on Budget and Policy Priorities.

Sheridan, K. (1993) *Governing and Japanese Economy*. Cambridge: Polity Press.

Sklair, L. (1991) *Sociology of the Global System*. London: Harvester Wheatsheaf.

Smith, D.A. and Timberlake, M. (1993) World cities: a political economy/global network approach. *Research in Urban Sociology*, 3, 181–207.

Soja, E. (1991) 'Poles apart: urban restructuring in New York and Los Angeles'. In John Mollenkopf and Manuel Castells (eds) *Dual City: Restructuring New York*. New York: Russell Sage Foundation, 359–376.

Stark, D. (1993) 'Recombinant property in East European capitalism'. *Discussion Paper* FS193–103. Berlin: Wissenschaftszentrum Berlin fur Sozialforschung (WZB).

Storper, M. and Scott, A.J. (1990) 'Work organization and local labour markets in an era of flexible production'. *International Labour Review*, 129(5), 573–577.

Storper, M. and Walker, R. (1989) *The Capitalist Imperative: Territory, Technology and Industrial Growth*. New York: Basil Blackwell.

Thurrow, L. (1992) *Head to Head: The Coming Economic Battle among Japan, Europe and America*. New York: Nicholas Brearly.

Tyson, L. (1992) *Who's Bashing Whom?: Trade Conflict in High Technology Industries*. London: Longman.

Wade, R. (1990) *Governing the Market: Economic Theory and the Role of Government in East Asian Industrialisation*. Princeton: Princeton University Press.

Whitley, R. (1992a) *Business Systems in East Asia: Firms, Markets and Societies*. London: Sage Publications.

Whitley, R. (ed) (1992b) *European Business Systems: Firms and Markets in Their National Contexts*. London: Sage Publications.

Williamson, O. (1973) *Markets and Hierarchies: Analysis and Antitrust Implications*. New York: Free Press.

Williamson, O. (1985) *The Economic Institutions of Capitalism*. New York: Free Press.

Woo, J.E. (1991) *Race to the Swift: State and Finance in South Korean Industrialization*. New York: Columbia University Press.

The World-System Perspective

Alvin So

The Historical Context

When the United States became a superpower after World War II, American social scientists were called upon to study the problems of Third World development. This started the modernization school, which dominated the field of development in the 1950s. However, the failure of modernization programs in Latin America in the 1960s led to the emergence of a neo-Marxist dependency school. This dependency school was highly critical of the modernization school, frequently attacking it as a rationalization of imperialism. From Latin America this dependency school quickly spread to the United States, since it fit nicely with the antiwar sentiments of many American students.

Although the dependency school was unable to "destroy" the modernization school, the modernization school was unable to exclude competing views as illegitimate. The coexistence of contrasting perspectives in the field of development made the 1970s a time of intellectual fertility. By the mid-1970s, the ideological battle between the modernization school and the dependency school began to subside. The debate on Third World development became less ideological and emotional. A group of radical researchers led by Immanuel Wallerstein found that there were many new activities in the capitalist world-economy that could not be explained within the confines of the dependency perspective.

First, East Asia (Japan, Taiwan, South Korea, Hong Kong, and Singapore) continued to experience a remarkable rate of economic growth. It became harder and harder to portray this East Asian economic miracle as "manufacturing imperialism," "dependent development," or "dynamic dependence" because these East

Asian industrial states had begun to challenge the economic superiority of the United States.

Second, there was a crisis among the socialist states. The Sino-Soviet split, the failure of the Cultural Revolution, the economic stagnation in the socialist states, and the gradual opening of the socialist states to capitalist investment have signaled the bankruptcy of revolutionary Marxism. Many radical researchers began to rethink whether delinking from the capitalist world-economy is an appropriate model for Third World countries to apply.

Third, there was a crisis in U.S. capitalism. The Vietnam War, the Watergate crisis, the oil embargo in 1975, and the combination of stagnation and inflation in the late 1970s, as well as the rising sentiment of protectionism, the unprecedented government deficit, and the widening of the trade gap in the 1980s—all signal the demise of American hegemony in the capitalist world-economy. In addition, there has been a steady movement toward a structuring of the alliances in the interstate system. The latest alliance among Washington, D.C., Beijing, and Tokyo makes no ideological sense at all, certainly not in terms of the ideological lines of the Cold War in the 1950s.

In order to rethink the critical issues that emerged out of the changing world-economy over the last two decades, Wallerstein and his followers have developed a new world-system perspective. This school had its genesis at the Fernand Braudel Center for the Study of Economies, Historical Systems, and Civilization at the State University of New York at Binghamton. The Fernand Braudel Center publishes *Review*, a journal that calls for "the primacy of analysis of economies over long historical time and large space, the holism of the socio-historical process, and the transitory (heuristic) nature of theories." The center also publishes a working paper series as well as an annual newsletter on its research activities. In addition, the world-system school holds a professional meeting every year and publishes its conference papers.

According to Chirot and Hall (1982, p. 93), this new world-system perspective has "seized the imagination of a new generation of sociologists" and exerted a profound impact on the discipline of sociology. A new section titled "The Political Economy of the World-System" was established in the American Sociological Association in the1970s. Having originated in sociology, the world-system school has now extended its impact to anthropology, history, political science, and urban planning (Bergesen 1983; Bergquist 1984; Chase-Dunn 1982b; Chirot 1976; Evans et al. 1985; Friedman 1982; Goldfrank 1979; Hechter 1975; Henderson and Castells 1987; Hopkins and Wallerstein 1980, 1982; Kaplan 1978; Moulder 1977; Nash 1981; Rubinson 1981; Thompson 1983).

The Theoretical Heritage

Before presenting an examination of the key concepts and theories of the world-system school, this section retraces its intellectual heritage. According to Kaye (1979), Wallerstein's world-system perspective has drawn on two major intellectual sources—the neo-Marxist literature of development and the French Annales school.

Wallerstein started out as a specialist on Africa. His earlier works present studies of the developmental problems facing Africa after independence (Wallerstein 1964, 1967; see also Ragin and Chirot 1984). Consequently, during his initial stage of formulating the world-system perspective, Wallerstein was strongly influenced by the neo-Marxist literature of development. For example, he has incorporated many concepts from the dependency school—such as unequal exchange, core-periphery exploitation, and the world-market—into his world-system perspective. Wallerstein has also adopted many basic tenets of the dependency school, such as the argument that "the 'feudal' forms of production characteristic of much of American history are not 'persistent from the past' but rather products of Latin America's historical relations with the core' (Kaye 1979, p. 409). In fact, Wallerstein (1979a, p. 53) has included the concepts of Frank, Dos Santos, and Amin as part of his world-system perspective, on the grounds that these concepts have in common a critique of both the modernization school and the Marxist developmentalist perspective.

However, at a later stage, when Wallerstein had fully developed his world-system perspective, it seemed that he moved beyond the domain of the neo-Marxist dependency school. This shift in Wallerstein's orientation may be explained by the strong influence of Fernand Braudel and the French Annales school on Wallerstein's conception of the world-system (see Wallerstein 1978, 1979c, 1982, 1986, 1988a).

The Annales school arose as a protest against the overspecialization of social science disciplines within conventional academic boundaries. Through the works of its long-time leader, Fernand Braudel, the Annales school advanced the following arguments.

First, Braudel sought to develop "total" history or "global" history. Instead of subordinating history to other disciplines, from Braudel's viewpoint history is an all-embracing and catholic discipline. Braudel argues that historians must direct each observation to the totality of the field of social force. As Wallerstein (1988a, p. 5) remarks: "It is indeed this vision of history that emerges in his [Braudel's]

Mediterranean when, not content to stop at the shores of the 'inland sea' . . . , the book starts in the mountains and extends not only to the hot deserts of Africa but to the cold deserts of China, half a world away; and westwards, it extends to Mexico and Lima, to Acapulco and Manila, and back to China."

Second, Braudel argues "for the synthesis of history and social sciences through an emphasis on *la longue duree* (the long-term). In that way, history would move away from the 'uniqueness of events' (eventism), and the social sciences would gain a historical perspective lacking in much of its attempts to formulate trans-historical theory" (Kaye 1979, p. 409). The *longue duree* is a historical process in which all change is slow, a history of constant repetition, even recurring cycles. It is only through the study of the long term that the totality, the deepest layers of social life, the "subterranean history," and the continuing structures of historical reality are revealed.

Third, Braudel was instrumental in shifting the center of concern in historical discourse from the histories of periods to problem-oriented history. As Wallerstein (1988a, p. 7) points out, Braudel's work is characterized by "his willingness to ask 'big' questions: What is capitalism? What accounts for France's failure ever to have dominated the European world? How did 'Europe' grow to global dominance? Why did the center of economic gravity shift from the Mediterranean to the North Atlantic? . . . 'It is the fear of history, of history on the grand scale, which has killed History.'"

In the following sections, we will see how the quest for total history, the *longue duree*, and the "big" questions have provided the foundation on which Wallerstein has formulated his world-system perspective.

Methodology

For Wallerstein (1987, p. 309), world-system perspective is not a theory but a protest—"a protest against the ways in which social scientific inquiry was structured for all of us at its inception in the middle of the nineteenth century." Wallerstein criticizes the prevailing mode of scientific inquiry both for its "closing off rather than opening up" many important research questions and for its inability "to present rationally the real historical alternatives that lie before us." In particular, Wallerstein feels uncomfortable about the following five assumptions of traditional social scientific inquiry that have informed our research process over the past 150 years.

On Social Science Disciplines

In traditional scientific inquiry, "the social sciences are constituted of a number of 'disciplines', which are intellectually-coherent groupings of subject-matter distinct from each other" (Wallerstein 1987, p. 310). The disciplines include anthropology, economics, political science, sociology, and possibly geography, psychology, and history. The disciplines have organizations with boundaries, structures, and personnel to defend their collective interests in the universities as well as in the research world. Based upon this premise, proponents of interdisciplinary research and/or teaching argue that some problem areas can benefit from an approach that combines the perspectives of many disciplines.

But Wallerstein questions whether the disciplines can be separated from one another in the first place. Are the various social scientific disciplines really disciplines? And what exactly constitutes a discipline? Examining the historical origins of social sciences, Wallerstein (1987, p. 311) observes that "there emerged over the course of the nineteenth century a set of names, and then of departments, degrees and associations, that by 1945 (although sometimes earlier) had crystallized into the categories we use today." All these social science divisions are actually derived intellectually from the dominant liberal ideology of the nineteenth century, which argued that state (politics) and market (economics) were analytically separate domains, that sociology was thought to explain the irrational phenomena that economics and political science were unable to account for, and that anthropology specialized in the study of the primitive people beyond the realm of the civilized world. However, according to Wallerstein (1987, p. 312), "as the real world evolved, the contact line between 'primitive' and 'civilized', 'political' and 'economic', blurred. Scholarly poaching became commonplace. The poachers kept moving the fences, without however breaking them down."

From a world-system perspective, Wallerstein (1987, p. 313) rejects this artificial disciplinary boundary because it is a barrier to further knowledge rather than a stimulus to its creation:

> The three presumed arenas of collective human action—the economic, the political and the social or sociocultural—are not autonomous arenas of social action. They do not have separate "logics". More importantly, the intermeshing of constraints, options, decisions, norms, and "rationalities" is such that no useful research model can isolate "factors" according to the categories of economic, political and social, and treat only one kind of variable, implicitly holding the others constant.

> We are arguing that there is a single 'set of rules" or a single "set of con-
> straints" within which these various structures operate.

In short, the various disciplines of social science are actually but a single one.

History and Social Science

In traditional scientific inquiry, "history is the study of, the explanation of, the particular as it really happened in the past. Social science is the statement of the universal set of rules by which human/social behavior is explained" (Wallerstein 1987, p. 313). This is the famous distinction between idiographic and nomothetic modes of analysis, and there is a call to combine the two modes of analysis in the world of scholarship. The historian is said to serve the social scientist by providing the latter with wider, deeper sets of data from which to deduce lawlike generalizations. On the other hand, the social scientist is said to serve the historian by offering reasonably demonstrated generalizations that offer insight into the explication of a particular sequence of events.

Again, Wallerstein questions this "neat division" of intellectual labor—with historical analysis focusing on particular sequences while social scientific analysis examines universal generalizations. Is there a meaningful difference between sequence and universe, between history and social science? Are they two separate activities or one? Wallerstein (1987, p. 314) explains that "all description has time, and . . . , unique sequence is only describable in non-unique categories. All conceptual language presumes comparisons among universes. Just as we cannot literally 'draw' a point, so we cannot literally 'describe' a unique 'event'. The drawing, the description, has thickness or complex generalization."

In response to the arbitrary separation between history and social science analysis, "world-system analysis offers the heuristic value of the *via media* between trans-historical generalizations and particularistic narrations." For Wallerstein (1987, p. 315), the method of world-system perspective

> is to pursue analysis within systemic frameworks, long enough in time
> and large enough in space to contain governing "logics" and "deter-
> mine" the largest part of sequential reality, while simultaneously rec-
> ognizing and taking into account that these systemic frameworks have
> beginnings and ends and are therefore not to be conceived of as "eter-
> nal" phenomena. This implies, then, that at every instant we look both
> for the framework (the "cyclical rhythms" of the system), which we
> describe conceptually, and for the patterns of internal transformation

(the "secular trends" of the system) that will eventually bring about the demise of the system, which we describe sequentially. This implies that the task is singular. There is neither historian nor social scientist, but only a historical social scientist who analyses the general laws of particular systems and the particular sequences through which these systems have gone.

On the Unit of Analysis: Society Versus Historical System

In traditional social scientific inquiry, "human beings are organized in entities we may call societies, which constitute the fundamental social frameworks within which human life is lived" (Wallerstein 1967, p. 315).

In the nineteenth century, the concept of "society" was opposite to that of "state." The key intellectual issue was then the question of how to reconcile society and state. Unlike this formulation, although the state could be observed and analyzed directly through formal institutions, the society was referred to as the manners and customs that represent something more enduring and deeper than the state. Wallerstein states that as time has passed, we have become accustomed to thinking that the boundaries of a society and a state are synonymous, and that sovereign states are the basic entities within which social life is conducted. In traditional social science inquiry, therefore, it has often been assumed that "we live in states. There is a society underlying each state. States have histories and therefore traditions. Above all, since change is normal, it is states that normally change or develop. . . . They have the boundaries, inside of which factors are 'internal' and outside of which they are 'external'. They are 'logically' independent entities such that, for statistical purposes, they can be 'compared'" (Wallerstein 1987, p. 316).

However, Wallerstein questions this treatment of society/state as the unit of analysis. Where and when do the entities within which social life occurs exist? His world-system perspective argues that the basic unit of analysis should be the historical system rather than the state/society. For Wallerstein, this is more than a mere semantic substitution because the term *historical system* rids us of the central connotation that "society" has acquired its link to "state," and therefore of the presupposition about the where and when. Furthermore, *historical system* as a term underlies the unity of historical social science. The entity is systemic and historical simultaneously.

Wallerstein has put forward a set of hypotheses concerning the nature of this historical system. The defining boundaries of a historical system are "those within which the system and the people within it are regularly reproduced by means of some kind of ongoing division of labour." In human history, Wallerstein argues that there have been three known forms of historical systems: *mini-systems, world-empires, and world-economies.*

In the preagricultural era, there were a multiplicity of mini-systems that were small in space and brief in time (a life span of about six generations). The mini-systems were highly homogeneous in terms of cultural and governing structures, and they split up when they became too large. The basic logic was one of reciprocity in exchange.

In the period between 8000 B.C. and 1500 A.D., the world-empires were the dominant form of historical system. The world-empires were vast political structures, encompassing a wide range of cultural patterns. The basic logic was the extraction of tribute from otherwise locally self-administered direct producers that was passed upward to the center and redistributed to a network of officials.

Around 1500, the capitalist world-economies were born. These world-economies were vast, uneven chains of integrated production structures dissected by multiple political structures. The basic logic was that the accumulated surplus was distributed unequally in favor of those able to achieve monopolies in the market networks. By their inner logic, the capitalist world-economies then expanded to cover the entire globe, absorbing in the process all existing mini-systems and world-empires. Hence by the late nineteenth century, for the first time ever, there existed only one historical system on the globe.

On the Definition of Capitalism

In traditional social science inquiry, "capitalism is a system based on competition between free producers using free labour with free commodities, 'free' meaning its availability for sale and purchase on a market" (Wallerstein 1987, p. 318). This definition is adopted because most liberals and Marxists have taken England after the Industrial Revolution as an accurate description of the capitalist norm. In the English model of competitive capitalism, proletarian workers (essentially landless, toolless urban workers) labored in factories owned by bourgeois entrepreneurs (essentially private owners of the capital stocks of these factories). The owners purchased the labor power of (and paid wages to) the workers, who had no real alternative, in terms of survival, but to seek wage work. Wallerstein notes that out of this English model, a degree-of-capitalism scale is constructed in traditional social science inquiry. A state, as the locus of work situation, is classified as more or less capitalist depending on whether it is congruent with the presumed capitalist norm of free wage laborers.

However, Wallerstein (1987, p. 319–320) argues that "the situation of free labourers working for wages in the enterprises of free producers is a minority situation in the modern world. This is certainly true if our unit of analysis is the world economy." If this is true, if a deduced capitalist norm turns out not to be congruent with the reality of the capitalist world-economy, then researchers should wonder whether the prevailing definition of the capitalist norm serves any useful function at all. In other words:

> If we find . . . that the system seems to contain wide areas of wage and non-wage labour, wide areas of commodified and non-commodified goods and wide areas of alienable and non-alienable forms of property and capital, then we should at the very least wonder whether this 'combination' or mixture of the so-called free and the non-free is not itself the defining feature of capitalism as a historical system. (Wallerstein 1987, p. 320)

Wallerstein further argues that if researchers have adopted this new definition of capitalism, it should have opened up new research questions, such as the search for structures that maintain the stability of a particular combination as well as the examination of the underlying pressures that may transform the combination over time. Thus "the anomalies now become not exceptions to be explained away but pattern to be analyzed, so inverting the psychology of the [traditional social] scientific effort."

On Progress

In traditional social science inquiry, "human history is progressive, and inevitably so" (Wallerstein 1987, p. 322). It seems that both liberal evolutionary theorists and Marxist developmentalists have shared this basic assumption of progress. For Wallerstein (1987, p. 322–323), however,

> world-system analysis wants to remove the idea of progress from the status of a trajectory and open it up as an analytical variable. There may be better and there may be worse historical systems (and we can debate the criteria by which to judge). It is not at all certain that there has been a linear trend—upward, downward or straightforward. Perhaps the trend line is uneven, or perhaps indeterminate. Were this conceded to be possible, a whole new arena of intellectual analysis is immediately

opened up. If the world has had multiple instances of, and types of, historical systems, and if all historical systems have beginnings and ends, then we will want to know something about the process by which there occurs a succession (in time-space) of historical system.

Finally, Wallerstein concludes that we are now living in the long moment of transition wherein the contradictions of the capitalist world-economy have made it impossible to continue to adjust its machinery. Thus we are living in a period of real historical choice, and "world-systems analysis is a call for the construction of a historical social science that feels comfortable with the uncertainties of transition, that contributes to the transformation of the world by illuminating the choices without appealing to the crutch of a belief in the inevitable triumph of good."

Equipped with a new methodology, the world-system school has developed a new perspective from which to reexamine the critical issues in the field of development. The following sections address the innovative concept of the semiperiphery as well as how the world-system perspective has provided a new interpretation of the history of the capitalist world-economy during the past four centuries.

The Semiperiphery Countries

Wallerstein (1979b) has criticized the conception of a bimodal system. He argues that the world is too complicated to be classified as a bimodal system, with cores and peripheries only. There are many in-between nations that do not fit into either the core or the periphery category. Consequently, Wallerstein proposes a trimodal system consisting of *core*, *semiperiphery*, and *periphery*.

Wallerstein (1979b, p. 69–70) argues that the present capitalist world-system needs a semiperipheral sector for two reasons. First, a polarized world-system with a small, distinct, high-status sector facing a large low-status sector can lead rapidly to acute disintegration. "The major political means by which such crises are averted is the creation of 'middle' sectors, which tend to think of themselves primarily as better off than the lower sector rather than as worse off than the upper sector." Second, in response to the decline in comparative costs of production in the core countries, individual capitalists must be able to transfer capital from a declining leading sector to a rising sector in order to survive the effects of cyclical shifts in the loci of the leading sectors. As Wallerstein (1979b, p. 70) explains: "There must be sectors able to profit from the wage-productivity squeeze of the leading sector. Such sectors are what we are calling semiperipheral countries. If they weren't there, the capitalist system would as rapidly face an *economic* crisis as it would a *political* crisis."

In Wallerstein's formulation, semiperipheral states have two distinctive features. First, if the exchange between the core and the periphery of a capitalist world-economy is that between highwage products and low-wage products, it would then result in an "unequal exchange," in which a peripheral worker would have to work many hours to obtain a product produced by a core worker in one hour. In reference to this system of unequal exchange, Wallerstein (1979b, p. 71–72) notes:

> The semiperipheral country stands in between in terms of the kinds of products it exports and in terms of the wage levels and profit margins it knows. Furthermore, it trades or seeks to trade in both directions, in one mode with the periphery and in the opposite with the core. . . . it is often in the interests of a semiperipheral country to *reduce* external trade, even if balanced, since one of the major ways in which the aggregate profit margin can be increased is to capture an increasingly large percentage of its *home* market for its *home* products.

This leads to a second distinctive feature of semiperipheral countries; that is, the state has a direct and immediate interest in controlling the domestic market. This politicization of economic decisions can be seen to be most operative for semiperipheral states at the following two moments of active change of status in the capitalist world-economy: (1) the actual breakthrough from peripheral to semiperipheral status, and (2) the strengthening of an already semiperipheral state to the point that it can lay claim to membership in the core.

From Peripheral to Semiperipheral Status

The process of a country's moving from peripheral to semiperipheral status attracts the most attention in the development literature, although it is often treated as though it were a question of shifting from the periphery to the core. Why are some peripheral countries able to achieve semiperipheral status while others are unable to do so? According to Wallerstein, success in moving from periphery to semiperiphery depends on whether the country can adopt one of the following strategies of development: seizing the chance, promotion by invitation, or self-reliance.

First, by *seizing the chance*, Wallerstein (1979b, p. 76) refers to the activity that

> at moments of world-market contraction, where typically the price
> level of primary export from peripheral countries goes down more rap-
> idly than the price level of technologically advanced industrial exports
> from corn countries, the governments of peripheral states are faced
> with balance-of-payments problems, a rise in unemployment, and a
> reduction of state income. One solution is *"import-substitution"*,
> which tends to palliate these difficulties. It is a matter of "seizing the
> chance" because it involves aggressive state action that takes advan-
> tage of the weakened political position of core countries and the weak-
> ened economic position of domestic opponents of such policies.

However, only relatively strong peripheral countries (such as the Latin
American states) with some small industrial bases already established would be
able to expand such bases at a favorable moment; other relatively weaker peripheral countries would not be able to do so. In addition, the strategy of seizing the
chance has certain built-in problems. Instead of importing foreign manufactured
goods, prospective semiperipheral countries are now importing foreign machinery and technologies, thus essentially substituting "technological dependence"
for "manufacturing dependence." Furthermore, the internal market cannot grow
fast enough to absorb domestic industrial products due to the fact that the large
landowners are opposed to the process of full proletarianization of the agricultural sector. Wallerstein notes that a way out of these developmental problems is
to expand outward, to substitute an external market for an internal market, with
the semiperipheral countries serving as purveyors of products that the core countries no longer bother to manufacture.

The second strategy is *semiperipheral development by invitation*.
Wallerstein (1979b, p. 80) observes:

> Direct investment across frontiers grew up in part because of the flow-
> ering of infant industry protectionism and in part because of some
> political limitations to growth of enterprises in core countries (such as
> anti-trust legislation). The multinational corporations quickly realized
> that operating in collaboration with state bureaucracies posed no real
> problems. For these national governments are for the most part weak
> both in terms of what they have to offer and in their ability to affect the
> overall financial position of the outside investor.

The prospective semiperipheral countries have competed with one another for multinational investment because there are distinct advantages in getting it. With the presence of foreign investment In the Ivory Coast, for instance, "in the countryside, the traditional chiefs, transformed into planters, have become richer, as have the immigrant workers from [upper Volta] who come out of traditional, stagnant, very poor milieu; in the town, unemployment remains limited in comparison with what it is already in the large urban centres of older African countries" (translation of Amin, 1971, quoted in Wallerstein 1979b, p. 80).

Wallerstein notes that the strategy of promotion by invitation is different from the strategy of seizing the chance in two ways. Done in more intimate collaboration with external capitalists, promotion by invitation is more a phenomenon of moments of expansion than of moments of contraction in the capitalist world-economy. Thus Wallerstein (1979b, p. 81) argues that "indeed, such collaborative 'development' is readily sacrificed by core countries when they experience any economic difficulties themselves. Second, it is available to countries with less prior industrial development than the first path but then it peaks at a far lower level of import-substitution light industries rather than the intermediate level of heavier industries known in Brazil or South Africa."

The third strategy is *semiperipheral development through self-reliance.* Wallerstein (1979b, p. 81) cites the Tanzania experience as an example showing that "a clearly enunciated and carefully pursued strategy of development including economic independence as a goal can be consistent with an accelerating rate of economic as well as social and political development." However, Wallerstein also cautions that this strategy can be pursued by only a few peripheral countries. In the case of Tanzania, its poverty and "rarity among Africa's regimes stand her in good stead of thus far minimizing the external pressure brought to bear against her economic policies."

From Semiperipheral to Core Status

How have once-semiperipheral countries, such as England, the United States, and Germany, been able to raise their status to that of core countries? According to Wallerstein, the key to a semiperipheral breakthrough is that a country must have a market available that is large enough to justify an advanced technology, and for which it must produce at a lower cost than the existing producers. A semiperipheral country can enlarge a market for its national products in one of the following ways:

1. It can expand its political boundaries by unification with its neighbors or by conquest, thus enlarging the size of its domestic market.
2. It can increase the costs of imported goods through tariffs, prohibitions, and quotas, thus capturing a larger share of its domestic market.
3. It can lower the costs of production by providing subsidies for national products, thus indirectly raising the price of imported goods relative to the subsidized items. The cost of production can also be lowered by reducing wage levels, but this policy would increase external sales at the risk of lowering internal sales.
4. It can increase the internal level of purchasing power by raising wage levels, but this policy may increase internal sales at the risk of lowering external sales.
5. It can, through the state or other social institutions, manipulate the tastes of internal consumers through ideology or propaganda.

Obviously, there are many ways to achieve a perfect combination of the above policies. For example, the strategy that England adopted in the sixteenth century was a medium-wage route, involving

> a combination of a rural textile industry (thus free from the high guild-protection wage costs of traditional centres of textile production such as Flanders, Southern Germany, and Northern Italy), with a process of agricultural improvement of arable land in medium-sized units (thus simultaneously providing a yeoman class of purchasers and an evicted class of vagrants and migrants who provided much of the labor for the textile industry), plus a deliberate decision to push for the new market of low-cost textiles (the "new draperies") to be sold to the new middle stratum of artisans, less wealthy burghers, and richer peasants who had flourished in the expanding cycle of the European world-economy. (Wallerstein 1979b, p. 85–86)

Another perfect combination is the high-wage route undertaken by the white settlers in the United States, Canada, Australia, and New Zealand. In this pattern, high wage levels preceded industrialization, and physical distance from the world centers of production provided the natural protection of high transportation costs for imports.

The Soviet Union provides an example of yet another route to core status. At the turn of the twentieth century, Russia was the fifth industrial producer in the world. The Soviet state kept the industrial wage at a medium level and rural wage at such a low level that there was an extensive urban labor reserve. Last but not least, the Soviet Union is a very large country, which made possible the relatively long period of autarchy that it practiced. However, if the Soviet Union—with its strong prerevolutionacy industrial base, its firm control over external trade and internal wages, and its enormous size—barely made it to the core of the world-economy, Wallerstein ponders what hope there is for semiperipheral countries such as Brazil and Chile to transform their roles in the world-economy.

A Note on the Socialist Semiperipheral Countries

In examining the case of the Soviet Union, it is interesting to note that Wallerstein (1979b, p. 90), as early as 1974, had already proposed a provocative thesis that "establishing a system of state ownership within a capitalist world-economy does not mean establishing a socialist economy." Since the capitalist system is composed of owners who sell for profit, the fact that an owner is a group of individuals (such as a joint-stock company) or a sovereign state (such as a so-called socialist state) rather than a single person makes no essential difference. A state that collectively owns all of the means of production is merely a collective capitalist firm as long as it remains a participant in the market of the capitalist world-economy. In short, Wallerstein argues that "state ownership is not socialism," it is merely a variant of "classical mercantilism" by which the semiperipheral countries are trying to achieve upward mobility in the capitalist world-economy.

Wallerstein (1979b, p. 91) argues that by identifying state ownership with socialism, researchers have contributed to an ideological screen that obscures the reality: "State ownership countries have, in fact, lower standards of living than those countries that have predominantly private enterprises; and, in addition, social inequality in these so-called socialist countries is still manifestly enormous."

What then is socialism? According to Wallerstein (1979b, p. 91):

> A socialist government when it comes will not look anything like the USSR, or China, or Chile, or Tanzania of today. Production for use and not for profit, and rational decision on the cost benefits (in the widest sense of the term) of alternative uses is a different mode of production, one that can only be established within the single division of labor that is the world-economy and one that will require a single government.

From a world-system perspective, Wallerstein therefore contributes by formulating a new concept of semiperipheral states and by identifying the present socialist states as mere semiperipheral countries (or state-owned capitalist enterprises) trying to make it to the core in the capitalist world-economy. Obviously, this new perspective calls for a reinterpretation of the history of the capitalist world-economy over the past four centuries.

History of The Capitalist World-Economy

Wallerstein has discussed the history of the capitalist world-economy in several of his works, but his latest treatment on this subject is quite different from his earlier views. In "Development: Lodestar or Illusion," Wallerstein (1988b) divides the history of the world-economy into two periods: from the sixteenth century to 1945, and from 1945 to the present. In the same study, he also discusses the crisis of the antisystemic movements as well as what should be done in the present era of the transformation of the capitalist world-economy.

Prior to 1945

According to Wallerstein, a capitalist world-economy began to form centered in the European continent in the sixteenth century. This world-economy possessed a set of integrated production processes that Wallerstein calls "commodity chains." The total surplus extracted from these commodity chains was always concentrated to a disproportionate degree in some zones rather than in others. Peripheries are those zones that lost out in the distribution of surplus to the core zones.

What then explains the differentiation of capitalist world-economy into different zones? As Wallerstein (1988b, p. 2018) explains: "Whereas, at the beginning of the historical process, there seemed little difference in the economic wealth of the different geographical areas, a mere one century's flow of surplus was enough to create a visible distinction between core and periphery." The core zones were able to extract surplus from the peripheral zones because the cores had monopolized some segment of the commodity chains to their advantages. "The monopolization could occur because of some technological or organizational advantage which some segment of the producers had or because of some politically-enforced restriction of the market."

Thus, by 1600, the emergent peripheral zones in east-central Europe already exhibited the following traits compared to the emergent core zones in north-west Europe: (1) Per capita consumption was tower, (2) the local production process relied heavily upon coerced labor, and (3) the state structures were less centralized internally and weaker externally. Wallerstein argues that although all of these three comparisons were true by 1600, none was true as of 1450. These comparative differences were the consequence of the operation of the capitalist world-economy.

However, Wallerstein (1988b, p. 2018) further contends, "that a given geographical zone occupies a given role in the world-economy is far from immutable." Whatever the source of the monopolistic advantage of the core zone, it is inherently vulnerable. The advantage can come under attack both within and between the states. For example, mercantilism was a means for the semiperipheral zones to protect their domestic markets in order to overcome the cores zones' monopolistic advantages. Also, some nations could over a period of time copy in one way or another the technological or organizational advantage, or could undermine the politically enforced restrictions of the market. In this respect, Wallerstein (1988b, p. 2018) observes that "every time a major monopoly has been undermined, the pattern of geographical locations of advantage has been subject to reorganization," leading to the so-called interstate mobility in the world-economy. For instance, the undermining of the American monopoly in high-tech industries signals the emergence of Japan as another superpower in the world-economy.

In addition to the accentuation of the polarization of zones, another trait of the capitalist world-economy in the pre-1945 period was *incorporation*, which refers to the constant expansion of the outer boundaries of the world-economy from Europe to the other parts of the world. What explains this expansion of the frontiers of the world-economy? According to Wallerstein, incorporation was a result of the exhaustion of leading monopolies, which led to periodic stagnations in the world-economy (so-called Kondratieff B-phases). In order to restore the overall rate of profit in the world-economy and to ensure its continual uneven distribution, it is necessary to (1) reduce the cost of production by reduction of wage cost (both by further mechanization of production and by site relocation), (2) create new monopolized leading products via innovation, and (3) expand effective demand through further proletarianization of segments of the work force. The expansion of the boundaries of the world-economy, therefore, can be seen as a mode of incorporating new low-cost labor, which in effect compensated for the increase in real wages in the core (in order to promote effective demand) and thereby kept the global average wage down.

Nevertheless, the process of incorporation was not unproblematic. As Wallerstein points out, people everywhere offered resistance, of varying efficacy, to the process of incorporation because it "was so unattractive a proposition in terms both of immediate material interests and the cultural values of those being incorporated." Consequently, only when the core states were technologically advanced in armaments would they be able to conquer the states in the external arena during the long waves of colonialism.

Specifically, incorporation has involved the following major transformations in the external arena. First, there was the transformation of production processes in these areas such that they became integrated into the commodity chains of the world-economy through production of cash crops, mineral products, or food crops. In addition, there was the reconstruction of the existing political structures into states operating within the interstate system of the capitalist world-economy. Wallerstein (1988b, p. 2019) observes that this reconstruction "involved sometimes the remoulding of existing political structures, sometimes their dismemberment, sometimes the fusion of several, and sometimes the creation of entirely new and quite arbitrarily delimited structures." Whatever was the case, the resulting states (sometimes called colonies) had to operate within the rules of the interstate system. These states had to be strong enough to conduct the operation of the commodity chains, but they could not be so strong vis-à-vis the states in the core zone as to threaten the interests of the major existing monopolizers.

The process of incorporation started in the seventeenth century. By the late nineteenth century there was no area on the globe that remained outside the operations of the interstate system. The history of the capitalist world-economy from 1600 to 1945, therefore, was characterized by the polarization of zones and incorporation. As a whole, there was overall growth in the forces of production and levels of wealth in the world-economy during this period. However, Wallerstein argues that although the absolute wealth of 10–20% of the world's population (mostly in the core zones) has risen considerably over the past 400 years, the large majority of the world's population (mostly in the peripheral zones) are probably worse off than their ancestors were. Thus the gap between the rich and the poor has widened enormously over the past four centuries.

Since 1945

Wallerstein notes that the transformation of the capitalist world-economy since 1945 has been remarkable in two respects. First, the absolute expansion of the world-economy since 1945—in terms of population, value produced, forces of production, and accumulated wealth—has probably been as great as that for the entire period of 1500–1945. This remarkable development of the forces of production has meant a massive reduction of the percentage of the world population engaged in producing primary goods, including food products. In the process, nations have come close to exhausting the pool of low-cost labor that has hitherto existed. Virtually all households are now at least semiproletarianized (part peasant and part wageworker), and economic stagnations continue to produce the consequence of transforming segments of these semiproletarianized households into fully proletarianized ones. As such, this proletarianization of households translates into higher-cost wage labor and the decline of profit margins in the capitalist world-economy.

Second, the political strength of the antisystemic forces has increased by an incredible amount. Since 1945 there have been triumphs from all branches of the antisystemic movements, including the creation of socialist countries (due to the military prowess of the Soviet Union or to internal revolutionary forces), the triumph of national liberation movements, and the coming to power of social-democratic/labor parties in the Western world. Despite their differences, these variants of the antisystemic forces all share three elements: Each was the result of the upsurge of popular forces in its own country, each involved parties or movements that aimed at assuming government office, and each set for itself the double policy objective of economic growth and greater internal equality.

However, Wallerstein observes that recently all the above types of antisystemic forces have come under criticism from within their own countries, and often even from within the movements in power, for their failures to achieve the twin goals of economic growth and internal equality. Indeed, the prevailing mood in the 1980s was the disillusionment of the antisystemic movements.

The Crisis of the Antisystemic Movements

According to Wallerstein, the growing disillusionment of the antisystemic movements can be explained by the contradiction embedded in the movements' twin goals. On the one hand, the movements seek greater *internal equality* (which involves fundamental social transformations), and on the other they desire rapid *economic growth* (which involves catching up with the core states). The movements bring together under one organizational roof those who wish to catch up economically and those who search for social change.

Prior to 1945, this contradiction was scarcely a problem. As long as the capitalist world-economy was still in secular expansion, as long as there was a growing pie to ensure that everyone could hope for more, the antisystemic movements remained politically weak. The prospects for upward mobility lured members away from the movements and unwound their sense of collective solidarity in the struggle. Because the antisystemic movements never rose to power, they did not have to confront the contradictions of their ideology.

Since 1945, however, there has been a "weakening of the political carapace of capitalism which, by allowing the anti-systemic movements to arrive at state power in large numbers, exposed the deep internal cleavage of these movements, the rift between those who sought upward mobility and those who sought equality" (Wallerstein 1988b, p. 2021). Since the 1970s, this contradiction in the movements' goals has become a glaring one, and the members of the movements have been asked to make different political choices.

Policy Implications: What Shall Be Done?

What political implications has Wallerstein drawn from his analysis? Given his assumption that the objective is "truly an egalitarian democratic world," Wallerstein argues that we should substitute a new world-level class movement for the prevailing national-level popular movements. First of all, Wallerstein (1988b, p. 2022) asserts that

> national development may well be a pernicious policy objective. This is for two reasons. For most states, it is unrealizable whatever the method adopted. And for those few states which may still realize it, that is transmute radically the location of world-scale production and thereby their location on the interstate ordinal scale, their benefits will perforce be at the expense of some other zone.

This has been especially true since 1945, when the geography of the whole world-economy could no longer expand. As such, development in the world-economy was like a zero-sum game—when a new nation-state comes in, an old nation-state must go out. Wallerstein (1988b, p. 2022) gives an example:

> If in the next 30 years China or India or Brazil were in a true sense to "catch up", a significant segment of the world's population elsewhere in this world-system would have to decline as a locus of capital accumulation. This will be true whether China or India or Brazil "catches up" via delinking or via export-orientation or by any other method.

From this angle, Wallerstein (1988b, p. 2022) thinks that "popularly-organized national movements have found themselves in a dilemma for which there is no easy solution, and which has contributed strongly to the sense of impasse and frustration that has been growing of late." This is because the goal of the national movements was to capture the state power. It was hoped that the nation-state could go against the strong current of unequal exchange flow to the core zones. Nevertheless, Wallerstein argues that the economic self-interest of the state bureaucrats pushed them toward the economic growth and "catching-up" goals. As a result, the goal of internal equality and the interest of the popular strata were sacrificed. Very often, states governed by erstwhile antisystemic movements (such as Poland) may even adopt repressive policies toward their own popular strata (like Solidarity).

Instead of endorsing the national movements that have prevailed in the movement literature since the nineteenth century, Wallerstein advocates a new world-level strategy that requires implementation by a world-level movement. In particular, Wallerstein (1988b, p. 2022) calls for a worldwide attack on the flow of surplus at the point of production: "Suppose that anti-systemic movements concentrated their energies everywhere—in the OECD countries, in the Third World countries, and yes, in the socialist countries as well, on efforts defined as retaining most of the surplus created. One obvious way would be to seek to increase the price of labor or the price of sale by the direct producers." Wallerstein (1988b, p. 2023) further explains that the concern of this world-level movement

> must be how at each point on very long commodity chains a greater percentage of the surplus can be retained. Such a strategy would tend over time to "overload" the system, reducing global rates of profit significantly and evening out distribution. Such a strategy might also be able to mobilize the efforts of all the many varieties of new social movements, all of which are oriented in one way or another more to equality than to growth. . . . [The premise of this strategy is that] global rates of profit are quite open to political attack at a local level. And, as the local victories cumulate, a significant cave-in of political support for the system will occur.

According to Wallerstein, this strategy of surplus retention by the producers could be more effective in the late twentieth century than before, because the world-economy has reached its geographic limit and is in the process of exhausting its reserve labor force. Thus this exhaustion will undermine the capitalist world-economy's ability to maldistribute surplus and to continue its accumulation process.

Finally, Wallerstein stresses that his world-level strategy of promoting surplus retention by the producers is different from the former strategy of national class struggle. In the nineteenth century, the fight against inequality through class struggle took place in the workplace (via trade unions) and in the political arena of the nation-state (via socialist parties). But the capitalists could easily fight back in several ways. They could recruit new workers from the worldwide pool of reserve households, they could use the state to repress such movements, and, if they failed to control the nation-state, they could relocate the locus of their capital to other zones without necessarily losing long-term control over it. In this respect, Wallerstein (1988b, p. 2023) argues that class struggle movements "cannot afford their close links to the state, even to the regimes they have struggled to bring to power." Instead, class struggle movements must be waged at the world level in order to be effective in forcing the pace of the transformation of the capitalist world-economy.

Comparison of the Dependency and World-System Perspectives

In its earlier formulation, the world-system perspective bore traces of the dependency perspective and therefore was frequently cited together with the dependency school (Barrett and Whyte 1982; Chirot and Hall 1982; Koo 1984; Moulder 1977; Petras 1982). However, as the world-system school became more advanced, students of development began to point out differences between the dependency perspective and the world-system perspective (Bach 1982; Chase-Dunn 1982a; So 1981). These differences are discussed in turn in this section (see Table 1 for a summary).

First, the *unit of analysis* for the world-system perspective is, of course, the world-system. Unlike the dependency perspective, which focuses on the national level, the world-system perspective insists that the whole world should be taken as a unit of social science analysis. Wallerstein argues that historical explanation should proceed from the viewpoint of the world-system, and all phenomena are to be explained in terms of their consequences for both the totality of the world-system and its subparts. Thus Wallerstein (1977b, p. 7) calls for the analysis of the holism of the sociohistorical process over a long historical time and large space.

TABLE 1 Comparison of Dependency Perspective and World-System Perspective

	Dependency Perspective	**World-System Perspective**
Unit of analysis	the nation-state	the world-system
Methodology	structural-historical: boom and bust of nation-states	historical dynamics of the world-system: cyclical rhythms and secular trends
Theoretical structure	bimodal: core-periphery	trimodal: core-semiperiphery-periphery
Direction of development	deterministic: dependency is generally harmful	possible upward and downward mobility in the world-economy
Research focus	on the periphery	on the periphery as well as on the core, the semiperiphery, and the world-economy

This world-system perspective may shed new light on many familiar sociological concepts, as Wallerstein (1976, p. xi) explains:

> Once we assume that the unit of analysis is such a world-system and not the state or the nation or the people, then much changes in the outcome of the analysis. Most specifically we shift from a concern with the attributive characteristics of states to concern with the relational characteristics of states. We shift from seeing classes (and status groups) as groups within a state to seeing them as groups within a world-economy.

From the world-system perspective, there is only one world-system in the twentieth century. Even though world-system researchers recognize the profound impact of the socialist revolutions, they argue that the socialist states are still operating within the confines of the capitalist world-economy. Thus the socialist states' policies on economy, politics, and culture are, to a certain extent, constrained by the dynamics of the capitalist world-economy. Unlike classical dependency theorists, who formulate the strategy of socialist delinking as a solution to Third World development, world-system analysts doubt the viability of this delinking strategy.

Second, influenced by French *historical methodology,* Wallerstein (1934, p. 27) perceives social reality as in a state of flux. He points out that "we seek to capture a moving reality in our terminology. We thereby tend to forget that the reality changes as we encapsulate it, and by virtue of that fact." In order to capture this everchanging reality, Wallerstein (1984, p. 27) suggests a study of

> provisional long-term, large-scale wholes within which concepts have meanings. These wholes must have some claim to relative space-time autonomy and integrity. . . . I would call such wholes "historical systems." . . . It is a system which has a history, that is, it has a genesis, an historical development, a close (a destruction, a disintegration, a transformation, an *Aufhebung*).

Unlike the dependency school, which focuses upon the boom and bust of nation-states, the world-system school studies the historical dynamics of the world-economy. Wallerstein (1984, p. 13–26) points out that the capitalist world-economy develops itself through the secular trends of incorporation, commercialization of agriculture, industrialization, and proletarianization. Along with these secular trends, the capitalist world-economy has developed the cyclical rhythms of expansion and stagnation as a result of the imbalance between world effective demand and world supply of goods. When world supply outstrips world demand, when there are too many goods on the market without enough consumers to buy them, factories have to be closed and workers have to be laid off. The world economy then moves into the B-phase of economic stagnation. During this downward phase, the core weakens its control over the periphery, giving the periphery a chance to promote autonomous development and to catch up with the core. The downward phase, therefore, serves as a period of redistribution of world surplus from the core to the periphery. However, after a fairly long period of recession, core production revives as the result of increased demand from the developing periphery and technological breakthrough. When world demand begins to outstrip world supply, this starts another upward A-phase of economic expansion. During an economic boom, the core tries to regain its power and to tighten its control over the periphery in order to dominate the world market. This economic boom, however, cannot last forever and will finally lead to overproduction. At every occurrence of these upward and downward turns in the world-economy, there is ample opportunity for the periphery to catch up and for the core to fall behind. This is a dynamic model, since the nation-states are always put on trial, and are always in the process of transforming to either the core or the periphery at each stage of the cyclical development.

Third, unlike the dependency school, the world-system school has a unique *theoretical structure*. Instead of a simplistic core-periphery model, Wallerstein's capitalist world-economy has three layers: the core, the periphery, and the semiperiphery, which stands between the core and the periphery and exhibits characteristics of both.

The formulation of the semiperiphery concept is a theoretical breakthrough because it enables researchers to examine the complexity and the changing nature of the capitalist world-economy. This three-tiered model allows Wallerstein to entertain the possibilities of upward mobility (a periphery moving into the semiperiphery or a semiperiphery moving into the core) as well as downward mobility (a core moving into the semiperiphery or a semiperiphery moving into the periphery). With this intermediate layer of semiperiphery in the model, the world-system perspective is thus capable of studying the changing locations of the state in relation to the contradictions and crises that are built into the working of the capitalist world-system.

Fourth, with respect to the *direction of development*, Wallerstein's three-tiered model avoids the deterministic statement of the dependency school, namely, that a periphery is bound to have underdevelopment or dependent development because the core always exploits the periphery. With the semiperiphery concept, the world-system perspective no longer needs to explain away the problem of the path of autonomous, independent development in Third World peripheries. Instead, the concept enables researchers to ask such interesting questions as why a few East Asian states are able to transcend their peripheral statuses in the late twentieth century.

Finally, unlike the dependency school, which concentrates on the study of the periphery, the world-system perspective has a much broader *research focus*. The world-system perspective studies not only the backward Third World peripheries but also the advanced capitalist cores, the new socialist states, and the rise, development (the secular trends and the cyclical rhythms), and future demise of the capitalist world-economy.

In sum, the world-system school is different from the dependency school in that it treats the whole world as its unit of analysis, adopts a historical methodology that perceives reality as a state of flux, develops a trimodal theoretical structure, abandons the deterministic point of view on the direction of development, and has a much broader research focus. As will be discussed in the next chapter, these new orientations have led to a series of world-system studies at the global level.

References

List of references is available on the original source.

Ten Myths about Globalization

Sarah Anderson and John Cavanaugh

CLAIM #1

Increased Trade Equals More Jobs at Higher Wages

US government and corporate officials repeatedly claim that jobs in the export sector pay more than jobs on average. Hence, they argue, expanding exports should be a centerpiece of US policy. There are several problems with this rationale. In today's state-of-the-art factories, companies can increase exports without hiring more employees. Caterpillar, for example, had a record $5.5 billion in US exports in 1996, even though it had made significant employment cutbacks during the previous three years.

One gauge of who has been hit hardest by free trade is a NAFTA retraining program for US workers who have lost their jobs because of shifts in production to or increased imports from Mexico or Canada. So far, the Labor Department has certified more than 260,000 workers for this program. The two industries with the most layoffs are apparel and electronics—prime employers of women and people of color. Women make up 66 percent of the work force in the apparel industry, even though they constitute 46 percent of the total work force. African—Americans and Latinos make up about 20 percent of the total work force but constitute 41 percent of apparel workers.

Americans who manage to keep manufacturing jobs contend with employers who often use their increased mobility against workers' interests. A Cornell University study of organizing drives found that in 62 percent of cases studied, management fought the union by threatening to move production to a lower-wage area. The blackmail factor at least partly explains why US wages have been

"Ten Myths About Globalization" by Sarah Anderson and John Cavanaugh. Reprinted with permission from the December 6, 1999 issue of *The Nation*.

stagnant for most of the nineties despite record corporate profits and low unemployment.

CLAIM #2

As Trade Spurs Economic Growth, Governments Invest More in the Environment

Globalization puts multiple pressures on the environment. Some companies deliberately choose production locations where environmental law enforcement is lax and pollute in ways that would be unacceptable in their home countries. Further, the World Bank and International Monetary Fund pressure countries to pay off loans through increased export earnings. This often means cutting down forests for timber exports or plantation expansion, depleting fishing stocks or expanding open-pit mines.

There is little evidence that economic growth linked to exports or foreign investment leads to increased government spending on environmental cleanup. Three of the leading recipients of new investment in the developing world—China, Indonesia and Mexico—are becoming environmental nightmares. China has five of the ten cities with the world's worst air pollution—coal consumption has doubled since 1980, and poor treatment methods have contributed to a lung-disease epidemic. To meet industrial demands, China is ignoring an outcry from environmentalists by building the world's largest hydroelectric dam.

CLAIM #3

Foreign Investment Automatically Raises Living Standards

Most developing-country governments are aggressively pursuing foreign investment by offering low taxes, repressed work forces and lax enforcement of regulations. In a few countries, increased investment has corresponded with rising wages. However, without strong labor protections, there is no guarantee that foreign investment will benefit the average person. In Mexico, for example, direct US investment jumped from $16.9 billion to $25.3 billion in the first four years of NAFTA. And yet the impact on workers has been mixed, at best. Some jobs have been created, but real manufacturing wages have dropped 23 percent. Moreover, overall employment has declined, as locally owned firms are crippled by high interest rates set by the government to attract foreign investors.

CLAIM #4

Free Trade Is the Consumer's Best Friend

Globalization has unquestionably expanded the variety of goods available to consumers. Pristine malls selling the same goods now tower over cityscapes from Manila to Mexico City. It is also true that roughly a third of US imports come from poorer nations where workers earn a fraction of US wages. Hence these goods often enter the United States at prices far below US-made goods. A key question is whether firms sell those goods to consumers at lower prices or hike prices and keep the benefits of trade for themselves.

Evidence suggests that in sectors where a handful of huge global firms dominate the market, such as autos, international trade often does not result in lower prices. For example, General Motors decided after NAFTA passed to increase production of its Suburban sport utility vehicle. But instead of expanding its Suburban plant in Wisconsin, the company built a new facility in Mexico that began producing Suburbans for the US market. GM's labor costs plummeted, as it paid an average of $1.54 an hour to its Mexican workers, compared with $18.96 an hour in the United States. And yet GIVI did not lower the price of the Suburban. The sticker price was $23,500–$31,000 in 1996, up from $21,000–$24,500 in 1994.

CLAIM #5

Globalization Lifts All Boats

The World Bank argues that accelerated globalization has coincided with greater world equality, pointing out that developing countries as a whole are growing faster than the major industrial nations. However, during the period of rapid globalization of the eighties and nineties, the gap between rich and poor within most nations has widened. The gap in per capita income between the industrial and developing worlds tripled from 1960 to 1993. Today the wealth of the world's

200 richest people is greater than the combined incomes of the poorest 41 percent of humanity.

CLAIM #6

What's Good for General Motors Is Good for the Rest of Us

Free-traders often use a version of this old argument to claim that lifting trade and investment barriers will increase corporate profits that will then trickle down to the rest of us. However, this argument carries little weight today, as global firms provide a declining share of government revenues and jobs, and are increasingly difficult for governments to regulate. The top ten US manufacturing corporations employ 33 percent fewer people today than thirty years ago, despite an increase in sales (adjusted for inflation) of 94 percent.

CLAIM #7

It's Fine That Poorer Nations Produce Goods in Sweatshops; The United States Developed That Way

Some economists claim that sweatshops are an essential step toward prosperity for developing countries, pointing to the brutal working conditions that characterized much of early US industrial development. However, there is more evidence that it was the struggles against sweatshops, not the sweatshops themselves, that led to improved US working conditions. Many union activists made tremendous sacrifices to win the struggle for the minimum wage, forty-hour workweek and other protections.

Unfortunately, as clothing retailers roam the globe looking for the most exploited work forces, once again the United States is plagued by sweatshops. The General Accounting Office has estimated that there are as many as 7,000 garment-industry sweatshops in five major US cities alone. Sweatshops can trap workers in a vicious cycle of poor nutrition and poor educational opportunity that leads to more poverty and inequality rather than laying the foundation for a strong middle class and a viable democracy.

CLAIM #8

Immigrants Are a Drain on the US Economy

There are as many misconceptions about the negative impacts of the flow of people across borders as there are myths about the benefits of trade and investment flows. The National Academy of Sciences calculated the taxes a US immigrant and his or her descendants are likely to pay over their lifetimes and then subtracted the cost of the government services they're likely to use. The result: Each additional immigrant and his or her descendants will provide $80,000 in extra tax revenues over a lifetime. The NAS found no negative effects of immigration on US workers, with one important exception: Workers with less than a high school degree earn about 5 percent less than they would without competition from low-skilled immigrants. In terms of overall employment, a number of studies indicate that immigration does not have a significant effect, since new entrants not only fill jobs, they also create jobs through their purchasing power and by starting new businesses.

CLAIM #9

Trade Equals Democracy

A cornerstone of US foreign policy in the nineties is the assertion that free trade will bring prosperity, which is the breeding ground of democracy. In most cases, however, increased trade does not go hand in hand with greater freedom. In its 1997 annual human rights report, the State Department revealed that many countries with export growth rates well above the world average during the nineties are far from free societies. Since free-trade policies often widen the gap between rich and poor, they increase social tensions in countries and poison the ground for democratic development.

CLAIM #10

Superior Productivity Will Protect US Workers from Globalization

Presidential candidate Al Gore once said, "Give us the opportunity to sell our products unimpeded, and we'll knock the socks off the workers of any other country in this world." This argument overlooks the reality that many corporations are in fact already achieving comparable productivity levels in countries where workers' rights are denied but where industrial infrastructure is now quite advanced. China, for example, is becoming increasingly technologically sophisticated. In 1997, 26.5 percent of China's exports to the United States comprised machinery (including consumer electrical goods such as telephones and washing machines, as well as industrial equipment), up from only 1.6 percent in 1985.

Regions

An Overview of Global Regions and Current Issues

The Semiperipheralization of the Newly Industrializing Economies

Alvin So and Steven Wing-Kai Chiu

The rise of the East Asian NIEs (Newly Industrializing Economies) in the postwar world economy, along with Japan's remarkable ascent to the core, has been dubbed the "East Asian miracle." Similar to Japan, the East Asian NIEs also experienced a turbulent period shortly after World War II, as they were confronted with serious political and economic problems. The changing dynamics in the world economy and in the East Asian region laid the foundation for the industrial takeoff of the East Asian NIEs. Nevertheless, this chapter shows that, given a similar opening in the world economy, different links between the state and the capitalist class in the East Asian NIEs have led to their divergent patterns of sociopolitical development in the past 3 decades.

Developmental Problems in the Early Postwar Years

South Korea

The Allied forces defeated Japan on August 15, 1945, and brought Korea's colonial period to an end. The aftermath of World War II, as described by

Henderson (1968, p. 69), was "an entire period of great flux, an era of mass participation virtually unprecedented in Korean history and unequaled since." A dizzying array of mass organizations of workers, peasants, youths, and women mushroomed, thanks to the unprecedented political freedom that accompanied independence. Amidst this atmosphere of exhilaration, the People's Republic of Korea was established in Seoul in late 1945; for a time, it was able to achieve de facto sovereignty throughout the country with the help of numerous local People's Committees.

The destiny of postwar Korea, however, had been determined even before Japan surrendered to the Allied forces. The nation was arbitrarily divided by the interests of two superpowers—the United States and the Soviet Union—thus setting the stage for divided and antagonistic state formation. The North, controlled by the Communists, formed its own government, the Democratic People's Republic of Korea, with Kim Il Sung as its prime minister. South Korea formed south of the 38th parallel under the auspices of the United Nations, which at the time was dominated by the United States.

As Koo (1993) points out, what followed in the South was a forceful demobilization of these mass organizations by the United States Army Military Government in Korea (USAMGIK). In early 1950, after the USAMGIK finally restored order through violent repression, it installed the conservative Syngnam Rhee regime, which was backed by businessmen and local elites, to replace the popular forces. With this development, both the Japanese colonial apparatus of coercion and the former Korean collaborators with the colonial government were revived. However, the Rhee regime was internally undermined by incessant factional fighting, Rhee's autocratic leadership, and his mismanagement of the economy.

In June 1950 North Korean troops crossed the 38th parallel and quickly occupied a large portion of the South. United Nations forces came to the South's rescue, and the Korean War broke out. After more than 6 million casualties, an armistice was finally achieved in July 1953. Koo (1993) remarks that no single event in modern Korean history influenced state formation in Korea more than the Korean War. The war bolstered Rhee's political authority, empowered him to eliminate radical elements and opposition groups, and led to the hypermilitarization of Korean society. The war also led to a firmer U.S. commitment to the security of South Korea as a bulwark against communism.

This U.S. intervention, however, introduced a new element of contradiction in South Korean politics. Although the United States installed a formal democratic government structure in the South, with a public commitment to democracy, in reality it had to support the conservative Rhee regime that blatantly violated such ideals in its daily practices. Had the United States not intervened in the political development of South Korea, the shape of politics in South Korea would have been very different. Rhee's regime would have fallen, and socialism would have become a viable option in the South.

Needless to say, the Korean War caused great damage to the South Korean economy. Vogel (1991) points out that about one fourth of the South Korean population became refugees without homes. Furthermore, when the country was divided, all the industrial facilities built during the Japanese colonial period went to North Korea. Thus, aside from being the nation's breadbasket, South Korea had little industry. In the early 1950s, enormous amounts of resources were spent on healing the wounds of this war.

In the mid-1950s the Rhee regime adopted the strategy of import-substitution. It tried to stimulate industrial production through installing protective tariffs against foreign imports and systems of multiple foreign exchange rates with over-valued *won*. The economy did recover, but its growth was relatively slow. By the late 1950s the Korean economy was besieged by a number of structural weaknesses, such as dependence on foreign aid, a chronic deficit in foreign trade, and exhaustion of the import-substitution industrialization strategy. In the early 1960s, the drop in foreign aid led to a crisis situation. After U.S. aid to South Korea was halved from US$383 million in 1957 to US$199 million in 1961, South Korea's real GNP growth rate quickly dropped from 7.7% to 1.9% in 1959, and wholesale prices increased at a annual rate of 15.6% from 1959 to 1961 (Cathie, 1989, p. 106; Mason et al., 1980, p. 98).

The Rhee regime finally collapsed in the face of a reduction in American aid, serious unemployment and inflation problems, and waves of student protest in the early 1960s (Koo & Kim, 1992). A new government, headed by opposition party politicians, proved unable to consolidate a durable regime and was quickly overthrown by a military coup led by Park Chung Hee.

Taiwan

After the Japanese surrendered in 1945, Taiwan was restored to Chinese sovereignty. Hostility soon developed between the indigenous society and the Guomindang (GMD) state apparatus. This was because Japanese colonialism had heightened the cultural differences between the indigenous Taiwanese and the mainland Chinese. Most Taiwanese spoke not Mandarin, but the Fujianese dialect and Japanese, making communication with the incoming GMD officials difficult and easily engendering misunderstanding (Lai, Myers, & Wou, 1991).

Moreover, there was the misgoverning of the GMD. The Taiwan government was run by mainland officials without any input from local Taiwanese people. Furthermore, the Taiwan government brought with it all the ills of the mainland

GMD regime: lawlessness, corruption, nepotism, and inefficiency (Gold, 1986). Owing to wartime damages and GMD mismanagement, Taiwan's economy was in a crisis situation by 1946, with fallen production, high inflation, and serious shortages of food and other basic commodities.

Conflict eventually broke out in the "February 28 Incident." After a rebellion started in Taipei [Taibei] on February 28, 1947, it quickly spread to all the major cities on the island. It was quelled only after the GMD troops began a brutal crackdown on the Taiwanese resistance. The estimate was that at least 10,000 Taiwanese were killed. This February 28 Incident further widened the cleavage between the mainlanders and the Taiwanese (Meisner, 1964).

In 1949 the GMD retreated to Taiwan after defeat by the Communists on the mainland. The prospect of a resurgence of Taiwanese rebellion continued to haunt the GMD, prompting it to resort to authoritarian and restrictive policies. Stern measures were taken to crack down on anti-GMD movements, especially activities linked to Taiwanese independence. Martial law was declared in May 1949, and independence activists were forced to flee overseas. A two-tier (central and local) government was constructed. The head of state was the president, who enjoyed a wide range of power because of the state of emergency. Mainlanders continued to dominate at the top level of the government and the party; local Taiwanese were restricted to political participation at the local level.

In the early 1950s the GMD adopted the import-substitution strategy to stimulate industrial production. However, due to its small domestic market, there was a pronounced stagnation in the private-sector's real investment after 1954, even though investment by the government continued to grow. Between 1958 and 1960 a series of enterprise failures in the wake of the economic downturn caught public attention. These crises subsided only after the government came forth to rescue some of the enterprises.

More serious was the persistence of the balance-of-payment problem. In the 1950s Taiwan had huge trade deficits because it managed to export only 60% of its imports. Taiwan mostly exported agricultural and handicraft products, and the prospects for such exports were not promising. These trade deficits, therefore, had to be compensated for by a massive inflow of U.S. aid. What had alarmed the Taiwanese government was that it saw South Korea suffer from a deep cut in U.S. aid in the late 1950s. Subsequently, the Taiwanese government pondered what would happen to its economy in the event of complete termination of U.S. aid.

Hong Kong

Before World War II, the GMD government in Nanjing began to recover sovereignty over a number of foreign settlements and treaty ports in China. Hong Kong, however, remained a British colony. Britain was determined to hold on to this Far East colony because Britain conducted a prosperous entrepot trade with China and Southeast Asia through Hong Kong.

The Japanese wartime occupation disrupted the Hong Kong economy momentarily, but the rehabilitation process was swift enough to allow normal entrepot activities to recover in less than a year's time. In 1949, after the Chinese communists defeated the GMD and "liberated" the mainland, there was a sudden influx of refugees to Hong Kong. Subsequently, Hong Kong's population jumped from 1,600,000 in 1941 to more than 2,360,000 in 1950. Hambro (1955, p. 162) estimated that in 1954 there were about 667,000 mainland refugees who came to Hong Kong for political and economic reasons. This massive increase in population subsequently imposed a backbreaking burden on the colony in the early 1950s.

The Korean War dealt another blow to Hong Kong's entrepot economy. The war quickly prompted the United Nations to impose an embargo on Chinese trade, in June 1951. The embargo crippled the Hong Kong economy, because China was the colony's largest trading partner. In 1954 the total value of trade was a meager 60% of the 1948 level (Szczepanik, 1958, p. 45). Apart from the embargo, entrepot trade with China also declined in the 1950s because of the Communist regime's rigid control of foreign investments, imports, and exports. The Communist regime preferred to deal directly with foreign governments and investors, effectively bypassing the traders in Hong Kong. The immediate effects of the embargo and the decline in entrepot trade were disastrous. Taking together the direct loss of earnings from entrepot trade and of indirect earnings through providing warehouses, transport, banking, and insurance services, Hong Kong's real GDP fell by 5.5% in 1951 (Ho, 1979).

In sum, there were serious economic and political problems in South Korea, Taiwan, and Hong Kong in the postwar period. Yet in a short span of about 3 decades, these three states quickly transformed themselves into newly industrializing economies.

The Semiperipheralization of the NIEs

The post-World War II development of South Korea is described by Eckert (1992) as

> a tale whose drama is heightened by breathtaking contrasts: a per capita GNP of about US$ 100 in 1963 versus a figure of nearly US$ 5,000 as the year 1990 began; a war-ravaged Seoul of gutted buildings, rubble,

> beggars, and orphans in 1953 versus the proud, bustling city of the 1988
> Summer Olympics with its skyscrapers, subways, plush restaurants,
> boutiques, first-class hotels, and prosperous middle class; a country
> abjectly dependent on foreign aid in the 1950s versus a 1980s economic
> powerhouse. (p. 289)

Furthermore, Vogel (1991, p. 1) points to the following achievements of East
Asian NIEs in the late 1980s: Hong Kong, South Korea, and Taiwan are among the
world's 17 top trading nations; South Korea is the second-largest shipbuilder in
the world, as well as a formidable producer of steel and automobiles; Hong Kong
joined New York and London as one of the great financial centers of the world;
and the Taiwanese economy has one of the largest foreign currency holdings in
the world.

The above vivid accounts aside, there are five indicators of the semiperipheralization of Hong Kong, South Korea, and Taiwan. First, the East Asian NIEs had
impressive growth rates during the past 3 decades. In the 1960s growth in GDP
was 10% in Hong Kong, 8.6% in Korea, and 9.2% in Taiwan. In the 1970s, even
when the Latin American NIEs' growth rates slowed down, the East Asian NIEs'
GDP still grew at a respectable rate of 9.3% in Hong Kong, 9.5% in Korea, and 8%
in Taiwan (Chiu, 1992).

Second, there was a tremendous expansion in NIEs' exports, which grew at
an average rate of 23.7% in the 1960s. More significant, manufactured goods
accounted for the lion's share of total merchandise exports. By 1970 about 76% of
all exports from South Korea and Taiwan, and about 93% of all exports from Hong
Kong, were manufactured goods (Chiu, 1992; Hirata & Osada, 1990).

Third, there was industrial upgrading among the East Asian NIEs. In the 1960s
the NIEs' economies were dominated by traditional labor-intensive industries,
such as textiles, apparel, and footwear. However, in the 1970s, there were "Heavy
and Chemical Industrialization" programs that focused on steel, machinery, automobiles, shipbuilding, and petrochemicals. In the 1980s there was further upgrading toward skill-intensive, high value-added export industries, whose products
ranged from computers and semiconductors to numerically controlled machine
tools, televisions, videocassette recorders, and sporting goods (Gereffi, 1992).

Fourth, the NIEs largely escaped transnational domination. Whereas the
labor-intensive industries of the Latin American NIEs were mostly owned by foreign transnationals, those of East Asian NIEs were owned by indigenous firms.
As such, East Asian firms had more autonomy in promoting exports than their
Latin American counterparts. East Asian firms could put their products up for
sale to diversified buyers on the world market, and they were famous for finding
export niches (Gereffi, 1992; Haggard, 1990).

Finally, as the East Asian NIEs became semiperipheries, they began to export capital to other East Asian states in order to strengthen their bargaining power in the world market. For instance, Hong Kong's investment in mainland China reached US$26,480 million in 1990; Taiwan's investment in mainland China, started only in the late 1980s, quickly jumped from US$437 million in 1989 to US$1,451 million in 1991; South Korea's investment expanded from nothing to US$269 million in 1991 (Kim, 1993).

What, then, explains the semiperipherization of the East Asian NIEs? How did geopolitics in East Asia in the 1950s lay the preconditions for the NIEs' industrial takeoff? What caused them to shift to export-led industrialization in the 1960s? And why were they able to sustain economic growth, upgrade industrial technology, capture export niches, and export capital in the 1970s and the 1980s? In order to answer these questions, the following sections will examine U.S. hegemony and world-system forces, as well as divergent paths of development among the East Asian NIEs.

U.S. Hegemony and World-System Forces

Geopolitical Preconditions in the 1950s

The global expansion in trade and the United States' free trade policy after World War II had provided an excellent opportunity for developing countries to strive for upward mobility in the world economy. Nevertheless, this favorable postwar environment would benefit any developing country. As such, why were the East Asian NIEs able to seize this favorable opportunity, when other developing countries failed to do so? As the following sections explain, Hong Kong, South Korea, and Taiwan were offered special advantages in promoting development as a result of their unique geopolitical positions in the East Asian interstate system.

To start with, the very existence of the East Asian NIEs was due to the Cold War. Without U.S. intervention and the Cold War, there would not be two Chinas (Communist China and the "Free China" of Taiwan) nor two Koreas (North Korea and South Korea). Though the resumption of Chinese sovereignty over Hong Kong was not yet on the agenda in the immediate postwar period, this would have occurred much more easily without the Cold War. In addition, the separation of Communist China from the capitalist world economy had closed off a more regionalist development trajectory in East Asia. The United Nations' embargo on

Chinese trade caused the trade between mainland China and Hong Kong, South Korea, and Taiwan to come to an abrupt halt, pushing them away from links with the big Chinese hinterland.

Nevertheless, Hong Kong benefited incidentally from the Cold War climate in the 1950s. This was because the "windfall profit" from the Chinese Communist Revolution enabled Hong Kong to take advantage of refugee capital to start its industrial revolution. For example, the "liberation" of Shanghai prompted a large number of Shanghainese textile firms to divert their production to Hong Kong (Wong, 1988). In addition, the massive inflow of refugees from China, many of whom had industrial employment experience, created a pool of potential entrepreneurs. They were willing to work hard and take the risk of setting up manufacturing firms. The result was the mushrooming of small firms with low-level capital investment and technology. Once started, these firms were able to tap into the extensive commercial networks established throughout Hong Kong's entrepot history, as well as into the abundant supply of cheap and diligent refugee workers (Chiu & Lui, unpublished).

The intensive Cold War climate benefited South Korea and Taiwan as well. U.S. interests in East Asia, from the late 1940s to the 1970s, had been political and strategic rather than economic. In order to prevent East Asian states from leaning toward Communist China, the United States provided huge amounts of aid to South Korea and Taiwan to help their military regimes stay in power. From 1946 to 1977, military and economic aid to these two countries (US$18.5 billion) accounted for 10.5% of all American foreign aid, exceeding the totals for all of Africa or Latin America. In both South Korea and Taiwan, foreign economic assistance figured heavily in alleviating huge government budget deficits, financing investment, and paying for imports. In South Korea, foreign aid averaged 9.4% of the GNP, 39.7% of the government budget, 65% of total investment, 70% of imports, and nearly 80% of total fixed capital formation during the period from 1953 to 1961. In Taiwan, U.S. aid financed 95% of its trade deficit in the 1950s; and, through foreign savings, it almost totaled 40% of gross domestic capital formation. Nearly all U.S. aid before 1964 was provided on a grant basis, thus making it possible for South Korea and Taiwan to begin their export-led growth in the 1960s without a backlog of debt (Bello & Rosenfeld, 1990, p. 438; Cumings, 1987, p. 67; Eckert, 1992, p. 295; Kurian, 1979, pp. 64, 79).

If the favorable postwar economy, the huge amount of U.S. aid, and the influx of refugee capital laid the preconditions for the industrial takeoff of East Asian NIEs, what explains the shift of their developmental strategy from import-substitution in the 1950s to export-led industrialization in the 1960s?

Export-Led Industrialization in the 1960s

While Hong Kong pursued export-led industrialization early in the 1950s, the United States still had to take an active role to induce the South Korean and Taiwanese states to adopt such a strategy. In the late 1950s, after making it clear that U.S. aid would not be continued by the mid-1960s, the U.S. AID Mission in Taiwan prodded the Taiwanese state to liberalize its trade regime and reduce its interference in the market. The AID Mission listed areas of economic and financial policies that needed reform, including privatization of public enterprises, liberalization of trade, unification and devaluation of the New Taiwan Dollar, stabilization of the monetary supply, and encouragement of private investment. Upon the proposal of the AID Mission, the Taiwanese planning agencies formulated a 19-Point Program of Reform, encompassing every major aspect of the island's economic, fiscal, monetary, and trade policies (Jacoby, 1966, p. 134; Lin, 1973, p. 83).

South Korea's export-led program was also decided by the United States. Eckert (1992) points out that the U.S. AID Mission

> officials had full access to South Korean government information and personnel. American experts spoke of tutoring President Park in economics and did not hesitate to use aid funds as leverage to force the South Korean government into compliance with their economic suggestions. (p. 295)

Coaxed by U.S. aid officials, the Korean state implemented a series of reforms to promote exports, most notably the currency devaluation in 1964 and the provision of export subsidies (Lim, 1985).

In order to provide more incentives for East Asian NIEs to adopt export-led industrialization, the United States was willing to open its own market to them. Eckes (1992, p. 139) remarks that it was "in the interests of global economic recovery and containment [that] the United States would lower its duties on imported goods while tolerating continued discrimination against dollar exports." That explains why, despite the notorious closed domestic markets of South Korea and Taiwan, their exports still enjoyed unrestricted access to the American market for so long. The U.S. market was critical to the NIEs' economic growth, because it was their largest single market throughout the 1960s and 1970s. Exports to the United States accounted for 30.5% of Hong Kong's exports and 39.5% of Taiwan's exports, respectively (Chiu, in press).

In the late 1960s the East Asian NIEs also reaped important economic benefits from their role as America's chief allies in the Vietnam War. For the NIEs as a whole, their fledgling electronics industry had greatly benefited from the American orders for military radios and radar during the Vietnam War. For Hong Kong, the tourist industry started during the Vietnam War. Wanchi district was a favorite recreational spot for Vietnam soldiers on leave, bringing a huge number of U.S. dollars to the Hong Kong economy. For Taiwan, the war gave an incalculable boost to its economy in the form of U.S. purchases of agricultural and industrial commodities, American spending on "rest and recreation" in Taipei, and U.S. contracts awarded to Taiwanese firms for work performed in Vietnam. For South Korea, the United States not only agreed to equip, train, supply, and pay all the South Korean forces used in Vietnam, but also agreed to modernize its military through new loans and aid in return for South Korea's dispatching 300,000 troops to Vietnam between 1965 and 1973. In 1966 the war accounted for 40% of South Korea's crucial foreign-exchange receipts. Indeed, in the late 1960s, Vietnam War-related revenues accounted for about 4% of South Korea's GNP and up to 58% of total exports in 1967 (Lie, l992b). By 1970 U.S. payments to South Korea totaled nearly US$1 billion. Many South Korean business firms got their first big economic boost from the war. For example, Hanjin established an air and sea transport firm in South Korea, mainly to carry South Korean products and workers to Vietnam (Eckert, 1992).

In sum, the Vietnam War provided a further influx of U.S. money to the East Asian NIEs, and the U.S. market and U.S. planners induced the East Asian NIEs to pursue the strategy of export-led industrialization. Nevertheless, most industries of the NIEs pursued the pattern that Landsberg (1979) labels "international subcontracting." Under such an arrangement, foreign buyers supplied the designs and specifications of the products they wanted to firms of the NIEs, and often supplied the machinery and raw materials as well. Products were then marketed in overseas markets by buyers under a label or brand name owned by the buyers. The manufacturers of the NIEs thus served as no more than subcontractors in the process, responsible for low-skilled assembly work, because they had no direct access to the market and were technologically dependent on the transnationals.

Moreover, the golden era of postwar economic expansion came to an end in the early 1970s. After the oil crisis broke out in 1973, inflation soared and protectionism was on the rise. As a result, many developing countries—including many Latin American NIEs—slipped into recessions by the end of the 1970s. What, then, explains the continuation of economic growth and industrial upgrading among the East Asian NIEs during this period?

Continued Economic Growth in the 1970s

First of all, many South Korean construction companies made use of their Vietnam War contacts and experience to expand into the international construction business, most notably in the Middle East. Eckert (1992) reports that between 1974 and 1979, South Korea's corporations built roads, harbors, and industrial complexes during the oil boom in the Middle East, taking home nearly US$22 billion in construction sales.

Moreover, as a result of the Middle East oil boom in the 1970s, there was a massive increase in the supply of cheap credit and monetary instruments by Western core countries to the East Asian NIEs. As Arrighi et al. (1993) suggest, the inflation of "oil rents" boosted the already overabundant liquidity of these Western financial institutions, so they began outcompeting one another in recycling this liquidity to the NIEs. For example, most of South Korea's foreign loans were made either in the form of supplier's credit or used to finance imports of foreign capital goods, dovetailing with the advanced countries' desire to expand their exports of surplus capital goods. Given a substantially lower nominal interest rate for foreign loans, and also given domestic inflation, the cost for borrowing from abroad was minimal. Subsequently, as the volume of foreign aid inflows declined by the late 1960s, the East Asian NIEs, especially South Korea, came to enjoy a practically unlimited supply of hard currencies and cheap credit to sustain their economic growth in the 1970s.

Furthermore, there was what Bello and Rosenfeld (1990) call "the Japan factor." In the early 1970s, due to the sharp rise of the yen and the rising cost of production in Japan, there was a transborder expansion of Japanese trading companies and small and medium-sized firms to the NIEs. Arrighi et al. (1993) report that only 54 investment projects in the NIEs were authorized by the Japanese government through 1964. But in the early 1970s a total of 1,171 projects were authorized: 581 for South Korea, 400 for Taiwan, 111 for Singapore, and 79 for Hong Kong. Unlike the U.S. transnationals, the Japanese firms preferred minority ownership of these projects, because this approach combined the reach and flexibility of Japanese trading companies and small and medium-sized firms. Moreover, Japanese firms provided a significant portion of the machinery and components that enterprises of the NIEs needed to turn out toys, bicycles, radios, television sets, and personal computer monitors.

What emerged in East Asia, therefore, was an "organic division of labor" between Japan and the NIEs that married Japanese capital and technology to the cheap, relatively docile labor in Hong Kong, South Korea, and Taiwan (Cumings, 1987). The East Asian NIEs became a base for the relocation of Japan's labor-intensive industries as they moved upward through each product cycle and progressively toward high-tech production. In addition, Japan and the NIEs had benefited from their privileged access to the huge U.S. market. Their products were capturing an increasing market share in the United States in the 1970s because of the high U.S. dollar and the high interest rate policy in the United States.

In short, the cheap credit in the 1970s, the arrival of Japanese capital in East Asia, and the access to the U.S. market in this region provided a new space for the states of the NIEs to intervene actively in the industrialization process. Nevertheless, the mode of state intervention and the societal responses to such intervention were quite different in Hong Kong, South Korea, and Taiwan, reflecting divergent paths toward semiperipheralization. The following sections will discuss the authoritarian developmentalism of South Korea and Taiwan, as well as the positive noninterventionist policy of Hong Kong.

South Korea: *Chaebol* and Authoritarian Developmentalism

The Developmental State and *Chaebol*

In South Korea, economic development (in terms of growth, productivity, and competitiveness) was the foremost priority of state action. The state was single-mindedly adherent to economic development, even at the expense of other objectives such as equality and social welfare.

As such, how did the South Korean state upgrade and sustain its industrialization processes in the 1970s? Amsden's (1989) study points to the dual policies of "subsidies" and "discipline." The allocation of subsidies rendered the South Korean government not merely a banker but an entrepreneur, using subsidies to influence what, when, how much to produce, and which strategic industries should be favored. Subsidies were necessary because the long gestation periods and relatively low profitability through adolescence made capital-intensive industries less desirable investments to South Korean firms. Nevertheless, the South Korean government also specified stringent performance requirements (notably in the field of exports) in return for the subsidies it provided. The discipline exercised over private firms involved both rewarding good performers and penalizing poor ones. This carrot-and-stick policy took the form of granting or withholding industrial licensing, government bank loans, advanced technology acquired through government investment in foreign licensing and technical assistance, and so on.

The South Korean state was unusual because it experienced both bureaucratic autonomy and public-private cooperation. On one hand, there was a high degree of bureaucratic autonomy and capacity because of the meritocratic recruitment and a sense of unity and mission among state managers. There was also a strong central planning agency, similar to Japan's MITI, to develop national strategic developmental policies independent of the powerful groups in Korean society.

On the other, there were close institutional links between the developmental state and private-sector conglomerates *(chaebols)* that dominated strategic sectors of the economy. Park (1986) describes the relationship between the postwar Rhee regime and the nascent big capitalist class as one of "alliance for profit." Using this alliance, the Rhee group developed clientele ties with a small number of big capitalists, supported their economic monopolies in exchange for a steady supply of political funding, and prevented the development of anti-Rhee business groups. With the backing from the Rhee regime, the *chaebols* quickly emerged from the ruins of World War II and the Korean War. Then the *chaebols* took advantage of the export-led industrialization programs of the Park regime in the 1960s and the 1970s (Kim, 1979). Having privileged access to bank credit and foreign loan guarantees, the *chaebols* accumulated capital at a rapid rate and achieved dominance in such key sectors as import-export trading, textiles, and electronics industries. Their economic strength can be seen from the fact that top 46 *chaebols* accounted for some 13.4% of South Korea's GOP, and 36.7% of value-added manufacturing by 1975 (Jones & Sakong, 1980, P. 266). Relying heavily upon the state for credits and resources, the *chaebols* were thus highly cooperative with the state's developmental policies.

The developmental state in South Korea, no doubt, played an important role in industrialization. Still, researchers want to know: How could this developmental state emerge within South Korea in the first place? Why was it so autonomous from the private sector and civil society?

Colonial Origins

As Koo (1993) remarks, it is impossible to understand the processes of modern state formation in South Korea apart from its Japanese colonial legacy. In South Korea, the Japanese colonial state possessed a comprehensive, autonomous, and penetrating quality that no previous Korean state could muster. The colonial state modernized the government bureaucracy, built a vast network of police and security forces, introduced modern land taxation, and improved the infrastructure. Subsequently, the Japanese colonial era left behind an "overdeveloped state" and a weak civil society. Moreover, because the indigenous bourgeoisie in South

Korea were tightly controlled by the Japanese colonial state, they remained highly undeveloped and failed to form any strong class organization to protect their interests. Hence, they were too weak to carry out the industrialization projects on their own in the postcolonial era, allowing the state considerable autonomy in planning and implementing its industrial strategies.

In addition, personal relationships formed by Koreans with Japanese during the colonial period were by no means entirely severed after 1945. For many Korean elites who received an education during the colonial period, Japanese newspapers and magazines continued to be a source of the latest information on economic, industrial, and political trends in East Asia. For example, Korean President Park Chung Hee, who was himself an elite product of the colonial military system and was fluent in Japanese and deeply influenced by his training during Japan's period of Asian military industrial supremacy, naturally pushed for a cooperative relationship with Japan and adopted the Japanese developmental state as a model for Korean modernization (Eckert, 1992).

Furthermore, the massive inflow of U.S. aid also buttressed the capacity of the state in South Korea. Foreign aid not only helped solve South Korea's economic problems in the 1950s, but it also presented the state with powerful tools with which to intervene in the economy, enforce compliance in the private sector, and build up a strong military for defense.

Authoritarianism and Ideology

Even so, the developmental state in South Korea still required a strong dose of authoritarianism in order to maintain its control over the civil society. In South Korea, state repression operated to dampen labor militancy (Choi, 1989). In Park's regime, strikes were banned, existing unions were outlawed, and activists were arrested. Under the Yushin Constitution, the terms under which unions could function were restrictive enough to eliminate the possibility of any genuine independent organizing. For example, there was the Korean Labor Union Law, as Bello and Rosenfeld (1992, p. 31) point out, which worked to prevent "unions from cooperating, forming, or contributing to a political party; and another [law] that banned collective bargaining beyond the union local, thus preempting the solidarity, technical cooperation, and strength in numbers that could emerge with industrywide associations." Lie (1991, p. 71) further emphasizes that "the Korean Central Intelligence Agency and the police, aided by goon squads hired by management, intimidated and harassed union organizers and labor leaders." This labor repression served to depress workers' wages, so that the South Korean, labor-intensive industries could remain competitive in the world market.

Aside from labor repression, however, the state also promoted the ideologies of anticommunism, GNPism, and sexism to maintain social control in the South Korean society. Koo (1993) points out that the Korean War helped establish anticommunism as a hegemonic ideology in South Korea. The Korean War experience brought the Cold War's broader ideological conflict down to the level of daily experiences, individual psyches, and social relationships. Because the Korean War never officially ended, the people of South Korea are still subject to a sense of the "constant military threat" from Communist North Korea, making the impact of the war particularly penetrating and enduring.

In addition, there was GNPism. When Park rose to power in the early 1960s, he justified the coup in terms of the urgent need to "rescue the nation from the brink of starvation" as well as defend it from the Communist threat (Koo & Kim, 1992). Export-led industrialization strategy, therefore, was not only a response to the demands of U.S. advisers, but also a means for Park's military regime to establish its political legitimacy and consolidate its power. As a result of this GNPism, social spending by the South Korean government was minimal. In 1973 expenditures on social insurance, public health, public assistance, welfare, and veterans' relief represented only 0.97% of the GNP in South Korea (Cumings, 1987, p. 74).

Furthermore, the enterprise level was infused with the ideology of sexism to exploit and control female workers. Bello and Rosenfeld (1992) argue that the centrality of cheap labor in global competition led South Korean capitalists to prefer women workers in the early years of the industrialization process. The target group was unmarried women aged 16 to 25, with some high school education. In the social organization of these enterprises, patriarchal authority was used as a means of discipline, with few female workers promoted to supervisory positions.

The state structure, the state-capitalist class relationship, and the ideologies in South Korea, however, were quite different from those in Taiwan and Hong Kong.

Taiwan: Small Businesses and Authoritarian Developmentalism

The Developmental State and Small Businesses

Like the South Korean state, the state in Taiwan was highly developmentally oriented. The GMD set up a complex trade regime—such as import quotas, tariff barriers, and export subsidies—to regulate foreign trade. Basic and strategic industries in Taiwan were protected from foreign competition, and export-oriented industries were provided incentives. There were the ingenious tariff and tax rebate systems, through which exporters were qualified to gain refunds on customs duties and other taxes for inputs they imported. In addition, through the control of the financial system, selective credit controls were employed to foster the development of preferred sectors, such as heavy industry, in the 1960s and the 1970s.

However, Taiwan's state-capital link was quite different from its South Korean counterpart in the following aspects. First, the state sector in Taiwan was larger than that in South Korea (Chiu, 1992). The average share of public enterprises in Taiwan's GOP was 15.9% during 1971–1975, which was almost twice the 8.4% share in South Korea (Short, 1984). Whereas South Korean public enterprises mainly served as absorbers of the risk involved in establishing new sectors so private investment could later take over, Taiwan's public enterprises tended to be monopolistic and exclude private participation.

Second, although a few dozen *chaebols* monopolized the South Korean economy and dominated the export sector, it was the small and medium-sized (hereafter abbreviated as SM) firms in Taiwan that filled up the export sector (Shieh, 1992). Of the 260,000 business enterprises in Taiwan, 98% are considered SM firms, and they employ 70% of all employees and account for 65% of exports (Bello & Rosenfeld, 1992, p. 241).

Third, whereas South Korean *chaebols* relied heavily on state credits for export promotions, the SM firms in Taiwan had to rely upon self-financing or informal money markets. The small businessmen in Taiwan complained about the inability to obtain credit from the state, because most credit went to the big enterprises. They also complained that the state failed to supply them with information on trends in international trade, and that they had to pay more than the bigger firms to buy materials from big or state-run companies (Bello & Rosenfeld, 1992).

What, then, made the GMD regime reluctant to fully support SM enterprises in Taiwan?

Ethnic Divisions, Authoritarianism, and Ideology

The GMD regime and the small capitalists in Taiwan were divided by quasi-ethnic schisms and mutual apprehensions after the tragic February 28 Incident. The GMD feared the Taiwanese ambitions for self-sufficiency and independence. As such, the GMD regime maintained a large state sector in order to keep the reins of power in the hands of the mainlanders, and it discouraged the concentration of economic power among the local Taiwanese. Subsequently, after the GMD took over the enterprises belonging to the Japanese colonial government, it staffed the enterprises primarily by mainlanders, especially in the area of management. In this respect, the state sector had safeguarded the GMD's political domination by serving as an economic preserve for the 1.5-million-member retinue of soldiers, bureaucrats, party faithfuls, business people, and family dependents from the mainland. This state sector was used to counter and control the SM sector, which, for the most part, was dominated by indigenous Taiwanese.

Bello and Rosenfeld (1992) suggest that the pattern of state intervention in the economy was influenced by the struggle between mainlander and indigenous Taiwanese economic interests. Power was apparently a major consideration when the GMD government promoted industrial upgrading in the 1970s, which saw the launching of 10 industrial projects, including the state-owned Gao Xiong Shipyards, the government-owned China Steel integrated cold rolling mill, and the state-owned China Petroleum petrochemical project. State control was partly a front for the mainlanders' efforts to continue exercising strategic direction over the economy vis-à-vis the up-and-coming Taiwanese capitalist class.

In order to exercise social control over Taiwan, the GMD's Leninist party deeply penetrated into civil society, so it could curb the development of any organized oppositional forces. Due to martial law, civil liberties—such as freedom of assembly—were severely limited and there was strict censorship of the mass media. Moreover, government surveillance and the strong threat of repression were central mechanisms for GMD's labor control. Its Labor Union Law prohibited unions in workplaces with fewer than 30 employees—or almost 80% of the workforce. For large enterprises, formation of a union had to have the approval of both local government and local GMD committees. Needless to say, strikes were made illegal and banned before the 1980s.

As in South Korea, the GMD promoted the ideologies of anticommunism, GNPism, and sexism. For example, capitalists in Taiwan preferred to hire women workers because they believed "that women were more temperamentally suited to tedious, repetitive work than men; that women had the manual dexterity or nimble fingers required for textile work and electronics assembly; and that women were less likely to rebel than men" (Bello & Rosenfeld, 1992, p. 216). In addition, the GMD promoted the "Three People's Principle" as its state ideology. The Principle of the People's Livelihood, for instance, was used to justify the large state sector in Taiwan, because it ostensibly aimed at establishing a developmental state capable of initiating economic development and preventing capitalist domination.

Hong Kong: Small Businesses and Positive Noninterventionism

Small Businesses and Positive Noninterventionism

There were several distinguishing features that characterized the Hong Kong state and its links with capital. First, it was a liberal colonial state. Because it was a colonial state, the governor of Hong Kong was appointed by the British Parliament and was responsible to the British state. The governor ruled Hong Kong with the help of major British banking capitalists, who were appointed into the Executive Council and the Legislative Council. But unlike other authoritarian states, the state of Hong Kong showed a high degree of political tolerance toward dissent. It is often pointed out that Hong Kong is a free society—its citizens are free to express political opinions, free to criticize the Hong Kong state, free to form political organizations, free to protest, free to travel, and so on (So & Kwitko, 1990).

Second, the Hong Kong state adopted a positive nonintervention policy toward the economy. Although the state in South Korea and in Taiwan intervened extensively in the marketplace to direct industrialization according to state priorities, the colonial state in Hong Kong left investment decisions to the private sector. Certainly the state in Hong Kong has assisted private capital accumulation in a variety of ways, most notably in infrastructure provisions, such as the maintenance of a low-tax business environment, the expansion of the public education system, and the massive public housing program (which houses more than 40% of Hong Kong's population). The public housing program, in particular, had the effect of subsidizing the earnings of low-wage, working-class families, thus socializing the cost of reproduction of labor, keeping down the pressures for wage increases, and increasing the competitive power of Hong Kong products in the world market (Castells, Goh, & Kwok, 1990).

Nevertheless, Hong Kong is still a far cry from the developmental states portrayed in statist literature. In the postwar era, the colonial state deliberately refrained from interfering with the distribution of resources across different sectors, as well as from providing any directions for industrial development. For example, the colonial state failed to support technological innovations, to assist industrial upgrading, to provide bank credits to strategic industries, to promote exports, and to protect domestic markets. Haddon-Cave (1984) thus describes Hong Kong's state-industry relationship as "positive noninterventionism."

Third, like Taiwan, Hong Kong's export sector was composed of predominantly small, local firms which received little help from the colonial government.

The Hong Kong SM firms had to rely upon themselves for self-financing, technological innovation, and securing links to transnational corporations (Chiu & Lui, unpublished).

What, then, explains the emergence of this liberal, laissez-faire state in Hong Kong after World War II?

Colonialism and Communist Origins

First, the Hong Kong state was constrained from pursuing an active developmental strategy or embarking on financially risky intervention because, as a colony, it needed to remain financially solvent and balance its budget or see the British home government step in. In addition, the Hong Kong state also had not benefited from the same soft of geopolitical links with the United States that had endowed the state in South Korea and in Taiwan with large amounts of aid and loans (Chiu, 1992).

Second, the long-standing alliance between the colonial state and the financial-commercial capitalists in Hong Kong, which had evolved during the previous century of entrepot history, served as a social basis for the nonintervention policy. These financial and commercial bourgeoisie were inclined to support the state's hands-off policy in the manufacturing sector. Bankers, for example, opposed the proposal to establish an industrial bank in the late 1950s, because they were afraid that this would cause the state to shift resources away from the commercial and financial sectors to the manufacturing sector.

Third, heightened hostility with the United States during the Cold War explained why socialist China did not take back control of Hong Kong right after the Communist Revolution. Hong Kong was the only port where China could gain the foreign currency to buy necessary foreign equipment. As a result, China was very willing to supply food products, raw materials, and even drinking water to Hong Kong in exchange for much-needed foreign currency. This unequal exchange between cheap Chinese products and Hong Kong currency subsidized the Hong Kong economy, lowered the cost of living, strengthened Hong Kong's competitiveness in the world market, and made the direct intervention of the colonial state less necessary.

Finally, the classic ethnic struggles between the British and the Chinese in Hong Kong were not acute in the late 1970s. The sudden influx of Chinese refugees after World War II did not arouse any tension between the Chinese population and the British ruling class in Hong Kong. Because these refugees were fleeing Communist rule, their refugee mentality made them endure the British monopoly of the colonial government so as not to "rock the boat" (So, 1986a).

The Liberal State and Its Ideology

In sum, Hong Kong's financial constraints as a British colony, the strong links between financial capitalists and the colonial state, the support from the Communist regime in China, and the lack of ethnic struggles against the British help to explain the liberal and noninterventionist policies of the Hong Kong state. Unlike the South Korean and Taiwanese states, the Hong Kong state did not need to militarize in order to stop the spread of communism, or strengthen its police force to suppress local opposition. The Hong Kong state also did not have to involve itself with the promotion of industrialization, because the Hong Kong Chinese capitalists were already getting a head start in exports in the early 1950s, due to their previous experience in conducting entrepot trade.

As a noninterventionist state, the Hong Kong government had not promoted any ideology to enhance its political legitimacy. At the enterprise level, however, the same sexist ideology prevailed in Hong Kong as in South Korea and Taiwan. Salaff's (1981) study of "working daughters" in Hong Kong shows how a traditional sexist ideology compelled young women to leave school early and take up low-paying, unskilled jobs in the fast-expanding manufacturing sector. While forgoing the opportunity to be educated, and hence any hope of upward mobility, these working daughters took home most of their wages. This extra income from the working daughters often enabled the sons in these families to continue their education, in the hope that the status of the family might improve. Therefore, as in South Korea and Taiwan, a sexist ideology was mobilized in Hong Kong to promote the competitiveness of domestic labor-intensive industries in the world market.

Antisystemic Movements

Due to the different state structures and state-capitalist class relationships, there were also different forms of antisystemic movements in South Korea, Taiwan, and Hong Kong.

South Korea

Despite strong state repression, there were robust antisystemic movements in South Korea. The origins of this "contentious society" in South Korea, as Koo (1993) explains, emerged during the colonial period. As a result of the extreme coercive nature of Japanese rule in Korea and the intensive anti-Japanese nationalist struggle among Koreans, civil society became highly politicized and antistatism became a deeply ingrained Korean intellectual orientation during the colonial period, and this antistatist tradition continued in the postwar period. In addition, the intellectuals did not forgive the "original sin" of the Rhee and Park regimes: their secret deals with the *chaebols*, their revival of the colonial coercive apparatus, and their overreliance on the United States for power maintenance. The students and the intellectuals were particularly offended by the contradiction between the ideal of democracy and a military regime that blatantly violated such an ideal in its daily practices, the contradiction between rapid economic growth and the widening gap between the rich and the poor, and the corruption and the conspicuous consumption of the *chaebols*.

Besides students and intellectuals, workers were also getting restless. Despite labor repression, the high concentration of workers in the *chaebols'* large-scale heavy industries provided favorable conditions for a militant labor movement. In the 1970s the Chonggye Garment Workers' Union (CGWU) struggle was marked by a creative combination of tenacity, self-sacrifice, and confrontational tactics that made it the symbolic center of the nascent South Korean labor movement (Bello & Rosenfeld, 1992). Later, the labor movement became explosive when "it developed close linkages with political conflicts outside industry, supported organizationally and ideologically by the larger *minjung* (the people's or the masses') movement, while supplying a major social base and an arena for democratization struggles among students" (Koo, 1993, p. 7). It was this merge between the labor movement and the democratic movement that finally led to the downfall of the Chun regime in 1987.

Taiwan

What distinguished Taiwan from South Korea, however, was the weakness of its labor movement. Whereas South Korea had a robust labor movement that could challenge the military Park regime, the labor movement in Taiwan was weak. First, the GMD was equipped with an elaborate "Three People's Principle" state ideology, and the Leninist party organization was quite effective in controlling labor at the shop-floor level. Second, the docility of the labor force in Taiwan can be explained by its part-time nature. According to Gates (1979), in Taiwan's early phase of industrialization, workers often went from villages to cities to seek work in seasons when their labor was not required in the field. They were willing to accept low wages because they were only temporarily in the cities. Thus, the transient character of the proletariat prevented the growth of a stable working-class community that could buttress collective action. Third, because SM factories accounted for the majority of the manufacturing establishments, the result was a greater organizational dispersion of Taiwan's industrial proletariat (Deyo, 1989).

Small firm size has long been regarded as inimical to labor organization because it increases the cost of organizing. Fourth, although women workers cherished few hopes of upward mobility, male workers often saw their factory work as a stepping-stone to entrepreneurship (Stites, 1982). As a result, male factory workers, mainly skilled workers and supervisors, often identified with their employers and served as disciplinary agents over their female coworkers. The weak labor movement in Taiwan had considerably enhanced the competitiveness of its labor-intensive industries in the world market.

Without a workforce amenable to managerial directives, without workers willing to do boring, repetitive, and exhaustive jobs, and without workers willing to work overtime when necessary and to shift to another product at short notice, the export firms of Taiwan would not be so prompt in their delivery of products to, and so flexible in meeting the deadlines of, transnational corporations.

Nevertheless, despite the peacefulness of industrial relations, there emerged a reform movement among Taiwanese intellectuals in the early 1970s (Chen, 1982). Sparked by the expulsion of Taiwan from the United Nations and the overseas Diaoyutai movement (over the Japanese occupation of the Senkaku Islands), a new generation of indigenous Taiwanese intellectuals began to demand their rights to political participation and representation in the state, freedom of speech, and the lifting of martial law. They complained about violations of human rights by the GMD; they used such new magazines as *China Tide* to resurrect struggles against despotism during the Japanese occupation of Taiwan; they started a native literature focusing upon the lives of indigenous Taiwanese people; and they organized a Dangwai (non-GMD) political group to challenge the GMD in elections. United through their Taiwanese language and culture, this new generation of intellectuals laid the foundation for a middle class and a strong democratic movement in the late 1980s.

Hong Kong

Like Taiwan, Hong Kong also did not possess a strong labor movement. Due to expanding job opportunities and the rise of real income, the Hong Kong working class was fairly satisfied with its existing situation and did not press for structural changes. Whereas Western Marxist critics observed terrible working conditions, immigrant laborers in Hong Kong perceived instead their relatively improved status as compared to their previous work situation in mainland China. Of course, there were unions and there were strikes. But unions tended to be small and ideologically divided between pro-Communist and pro-Nationalist factions, and China was reported to have held back the radical demands of the pro-Communist trade unions so as not to risk any disturbances of its substantial foreign exchange earnings in Hong Kong. Consequently, strikes were few in number, and serious strikes were almost unknown in the 1970s (Levin & Chiu, 1993; Turner et al., 1981).

Instead, the political struggles in Hong Kong in the late 1970s revolved around the new middle class. In the early 1970s many college students participated in pro-China movements, such as the patriotic Diaoyutai protest and the China Week Exhibitions. In the mid-1970s, after the "China heat" died down, this new middle class shifted its attention to the social problems in Hong Kong. Many college students and young professionals formed "pressure groups" to criticize the policies of the Hong Kong state, Through newspaper articles, social protests, and political pressure, they complained about police abuse of power, bureaucratic arrogance, the lack of localization, inadequate services for squatter residents, and soon (Lui & Gong, 1985). These "urban movements," needless to say, proved to be a training ground for new leaders and prepared the new middle class for its forthcoming democratic struggles in the early 1980s (So & Kwitko, 1992).

Conclusion

In the aftermath of World War II, there were serious economic and political problems in South Korea, Taiwan, and Hong Kong. Yet, in a short span of about 3 decades, these three states quickly transformed themselves into newly industrializing economies. This chapter shows that the favorable postwar capitalist world economy, huge amounts of US, aid, and influxes of refugee capital in the 1950s laid the groundwork for the industrial takeoff of the East Asian NIEs. Then, the Vietnam War provided a further influx of U.S. money, and the U.S. market and U.S. planners induced the East Asian NIEs to pursue the strategy of export-led industrialization in the 1960s. Finally, cheap credit in the 1970s, the arrival of Japanese capital in East Asia, and the relative decline of U.S. hegemony in this region provided more space for the NIEs' states to intervene actively in the industrialization process.

However, there were divergent paths of development among the East Asian NIEs. In South Korea, there was a close alliance between the developmental state and a small number of *chaebol* monopolist capitalists. In response to the authoritarianism imposed upon the Korean civil society, there was a robust *minjung* movement by workers and students challenging the military Park regime. In Taiwan, there was an ethnic division between the mainlander-run developmental state and the local Taiwanese small capitalists, who dominated the export sector. Although the GMD was highly effective in exercising authoritarianism over labor, the 1970s saw a new generation of Taiwanese intellectuals rising up to challenge mainland domination. In Hong Kong, because the colonial state adopted a nonintervention policy, small Chinese capitalist firms had to rely upon themselves for survival. Despite the lack of authoritarian control, the labor movement in Hong Kong was weak. Only in the 1970s did a new middle-class generation emerge to challenge colonial rule through urban movements.

These divergent patterns of development among the NIEs, this chapter has argued, resulted from complex interactions among the following factors: colonial heritage (Japanese authoritarianism and nationalist movements in Korea versus British laissez-faire in Hong Kong), historical experiences in the aftermath of World War II (the "original sin" of the Park and Rhee regime, the February 27 Incident in Taiwan, and the influx of refugees in Hong Kong), the general Cold War ideological climate (anticommunism and GNPism in South Korea and Taiwan versus a refugee mentality in Hong Kong), as well as their different industrial structures (concentration of workers in *chaebols* versus organizational dispersion in Taiwan and Hong Kong).

Since the 1980s, the East Asian region has begun to play a more central role in global capital accumulation than before.

References

List of references is available on the original source.

Whose "Model" Failed?

Implications of the Asian Economic Crisis

Linda Y. C. Lim

The Asian economic crisis is cause for rethinking the long-established consensus among mostly Western and Western-trained economists about the causes of the region's "miracle" economic growth and industrial development. Most recently restated in the Asian Development Bank's 1997 study *Emerging Asia: Changes and Challenges*, essentially an update of the World Bank's 1993 study *The East Asian Miracle*, this consensus interpretation among mainstream economists goes as follows:

Asian economic success is the product simply of the application of orthodox Western textbook economic principles—external "openness" to trade and foreign investment on the one hand, and domestic "good government" with small, balanced, or surplus government budgets and conservative monetary policy leading to low inflation and high savings rates, on the other. For these reasons, Asian countries typically rank relatively high on the "economic freedom" indices annually produced by think tanks such as the Fraser Institute in Canada[1] and the Heritage Foundation in Washington, D.C.[2] Of the countries currently in crisis, South Korea has been less open than the various countries of Southeast Asia, but nonetheless has subjected its firms to the discipline of the international marketplace through export manufacturing.

But mainstream economists are not the only Western or Western-trained scholars who have sought to dissect the Asian economic miracle through the lens of their particular discipline. Political scientists and political economists have also had their play with the subject, usually concluding that the "developmental state"—focused on promoting economic development in the national interest—and statist industrial policy-government protection and subsidies targeted at developing specific "strategic" industrial sectors—have been essential to the rapid industrialization of the East Asian newly industrialized economies.[3] South Korea is the classic case, but it is harder to identify "developmental states" and successful statist industrial policy in Southeast Asia outside of Malaysia and Singapore. Rather, state development policy in Thailand, Indonesia, and the Philippines is more likely to be viewed as having been captured by crony capitalists with close personal relations with governments, thereby violating the developmental state principle of state autonomy from special interests.[4]

Notwithstanding this, and despite the contradiction between the economist and the political scientist/political economist views, the Southeast Asian countries are always included as part of the so-called Asian economic miracle or "Asian model" that has been promoted by advocates of free-market economics. These include both conservative Western think tanks like the Heritage Foundation and more liberal multilateral institutions like the World Bank and the International Monetary Fund, whose Washington consensus of liberal economic policies has been foisted on emerging economies around the world.

Although economists like these generally did not care for the industrial policies and microeconomic state interventions pursued by Asian governments, they did praise the latter's practice of conventional macroeconomic policy embracing both openness and fiscal and monetary conservatism. It is not an exaggeration to say that the Asian economies became showcases for the success of a policy prescription that is being peddled to other newly liberalizing emerging economies in Latin America, East Central Europe, Central Asia, and Africa.

When the Philippines, Taiwan, South Korea, and Thailand became politically democratic as well in the late 1980s, this completed the picture of triumph for the Western liberal model of free-markets-with-democracy that Francis Fukuyama proclaimed ushered in The End of History[5] or the end of the ideological political-economic conflict between East and West that defined the Cold War. In Asia, for example, it was proclaimed that the United States "lost the Vietnam war (against communism) but won the peace," as reflected in the economic prosperity and political stability enjoyed by its capitalist allies in the region, and the subsequent embarkation of their socialist neighbors, particularly China and Vietnam, on the path of market-oriented economic reform.[6]

Culture as an element in the Asian economic miracle has largely been neglected or dismissed by both Western economists and political scientists, although the former might occasionally acknowledge that the highly entrepreneurial, economically responsive populations in the region, themselves the product of market forces, might have spurred the development of private-enterprise economies.

The latter sometimes note that Confucian cultures may have lent moral authority and political legitimacy to interventionist developmental states. Western and some Asian anthropologists and sociologists, on the other hand, have identified kin and ethnic networks, or "culturally embedded network capitalisms," as locally efficient means of mobilizing capital and industrial growth in the Asian miracle economies.[7]

Culture has also played a much larger role in explaining the Asian miracle by Asian intellectuals who hail mostly from the political establishment in patriarchal-authoritarian and semi-authoritarian states like Singapore, Malaysia, China, and Indonesia. They argue that "Asian values"—emphasizing the primacy of order over freedom, family and community interests over individual choice, and economic progress over political expression, together with thrift, ambition and hard work—were largely responsible for the fortunate public sector policies and private sector actions that resulted in the Asian miracle.

Whose Model Failed?

The "Asian values" school was unpopular among many Western commentators for suggesting, among other things, that capitalism and democracy need not go hand-in-hand. So it was predictable that when the Asian economic crisis hit during a period of unprecedented economic strength in the United States and economic recovery in Western Europe, opponents of the "Asian values" school were out in full swing (chiefly in the editorial pages of the *Wall Street Journal*), crowing over its assumed demise and the concomitant assumed triumph of the "American way."

The Asian miracle was particularly attacked for its reliance on industrial policy and cronyism, or relationships between big business and government, both of which contributed to moral hazard in the inefficient financial sector and the resultant over-investment in a classic asset bubble. Paul Krugman, the MIT economist who had some years earlier pronounced the Asian miracle a "myth" based on low total factor productivity growth,[8] is one of those who favor the moral hazard argument that "crony capitalism" or Asian reliance on guanxi (relationships) is what caused the crisis, which in this view is essentially a crisis of bad investments in both the public and private sectors.[9] This line of argument directly challenges both the praise of statist industrial policy by mostly Western political scientists and of "culturally embedded networks" favored by mostly Western anthropologists and sociologists.

There is no question that crony capitalism did play a role in the over-inflation and subsequent deflation of economic growth and asset prices in Asia. But this is far from the only or most plausible interpretation for the crisis and it is certainly not the whole story. Indeed, in the affected Asian countries and other emerging economies around the world, another interpretation is taking hold, one that is much less favorable to the liberal orthodoxy favored by Western economists. In this view, it is the Western model of free-markets-with-democracy that has failed along with the collapse of its prime success stories in Asia—or a case of "the West won the Cold War, only to lose the peace."

The Perils of Openness

First, if openness was an essential ingredient of the Asian economic miracle, too much openness too fast was responsible for its downfall. In particular, rapid and sweeping (although not vet complete) capital market liberalization that began in the late 1980s led to a massive influx of foreign capital, especially short-term loan and equity capital, which contributed to the boom economy and over-investment bubble of the 1990s. Without this influx of foreign funds—which in some cases amounted to as much as 75 percent of the equity capital on local stock markets— domestic crony capitalism alone could not have fed a boom and bubble of such proportions. Even without crony capitalism, high growth and the expectation of continued uninterrupted high growth, fed in large part by foreign capital, might have led to excessive risk-taking and overleveraging of local businesses believing that their economies were immune from the business cycle.

High domestic growth and investment in turn contributed to ballooning current account deficits, with imports (mostly of machinery and equipment required by the flood of new investments) constantly exceeding exports by a wide margin. This was further fueled by overvalued exchange rates, the result both of more or less fixed exchange-rate regimes, established to attract foreign capital by removing currency risk, and of large inflows of capital. Open capital markets and capital-account convertibility also increased these economies' vulnerability to currency speculation that could, at the appropriate moment, trigger a sudden massive exit of foreign funds as easily as these funds had previously entered.

Financial market liberalization in Asia also occurred before there were appropriate state or collective institutions to monitor and regulate financial institutions or local expertise to manage them. The region's much-vaunted entrepreneurialism led to the establishment of a horde of new banks and finance companies— Indonesia alone had more than 200 banks—within a short span of time and with inadequate experience in money management. Even without crony capitalism, excess capacity in the financial sector and intense competition to lend and invest among these neophyte institutions would have led to a fair proportion of "bad investments." It was aggravated by the easy availability of cheap capital from abroad, in many cases pressed on local borrowers by overeager foreign lenders who should have known better, but faced intense competition among themselves and were attracted by the returns presented by higher interest rates and by rosy projections of continued rapid growth.

With or without the moral hazard presented by local crony capitalism, the resultant excess supply of capital was bound to lead to some bad investments as capital started flowing to more and more marginal projects. Unlike their local borrowers, foreign lenders and investors from Western countries and Japan possessed the requisite expertise in risk assessment and credit evaluation. But they apparently chose not to apply this knowledge, yielding instead to herd instinct[10] and, as Alan Greenspan characterized the sentiments toward the booming U.S. stockmarket, "irrational exuberance." This exuberance contributed first to the overvaluation of assets, then reversed course and with "irrational pessimism"[11] led to the current undervaluation, as the following quotes indicate.

> All banks are under certain competitive pressure. If the market is attractive, you go with the herd. Even if you have doubts, you don't stop lending.[12]
> —Ernst-Mortiz Lipp, member of the board of managing directors of Dresdner Bank AG
>
> There was a huge euphoria about Asia and Southeast Asia. It was the place to be.[13]
> —Dennis Phillips, Spokesman for Commerzbank
>
> All the banks would be standing in line
> —J.P. Morgan, Deutsche Bank, Dresdner.
>
> We were all standing in line trying to help these countries borrow money. We would all see each other at the same places. We all knew each other.[14]
> —Klaus Friedrich, chief economist, Dresdner Bank AG
>
> There are problems in Asia now because investors and bankers were overly optimistic about the Asian economies, and then they panicked.[15]
> —Anonymous American banker
>
> Openness and the dominance of private enterprise in the Asian economies also severely limited their governments' ability to intervene to control these flows. Given domestic excess demand and external imbalance (huge current account deficits), governments should have allowed their currencies to depreciate or raised taxes and interest rates

and cut government spending to reduce domestic demand and correct the imbalance. But in very open economies such as these, with high import shares of GDP, currency depreciation would increase costs, including offshore loan servicing costs, and cause inflation from higher import prices, while higher domestic interest rates would be ineffective so long as businesses could resort to cheaper borrowing in accessible offshore markets—that is, they may as well have increased rather than reduced external borrowing.

We could have borrowed locally, something like 14 percent per annum, or borrowed overseas, where we could get (dollar) loans for 8 percent or 9 percent. If I had borrowed locally, the analysts would be saying that we were being foolish for not taking advantage of lower rates overseas. . . . We could have bought insurance, but that would only be adding to the cost. Our government, our bankers, economists, even foreigners were telling us that the baht was stable. . . . We never imagined that the baht would be devalued.[16]

—Chumpol Nalamlieng, CEO of Siam Cement, a blue-chip Thai company on their $4.2 billion dollar debt

At the same time, public sectors were small and mostly in balance, and governments had little control over overborrowing in the private sector. This reduced the effectiveness of raising taxes and cutting expenditures as is typically required, for example, in IMF programs in countries that have large fiscal deficits and loose money policies. In short, the dominance of private enterprise reduced the influence that governments had over the macroeconomy.

The Perils of Democracy

The nascent democracies that since the late 1980s had taken hold in Korea, Thailand, and the Philippines also caused a loss of government control over the macroeconomy. Whereas previous authoritarian regimes could impose higher interest and taxation costs on local business communities almost at will, and had done so to maintain currency stability for decades prior, this became difficult with the increased political influence of businesses over elected legislatures whose members were either business persons themselves, or required business support to get elected.

As *Wall Street Journal* reporter George Melloan commented on the American political process,

> Practicing politics costs money, and all politicians, unless they are fabulously wealthy, depend on campaign contributions. The more generous donors usually would like a favor or two. Quid pro quo, dating back at least to the steps of the Roman Forum, is alive and well in the U.S., as in most other corners of the world.[17]

Thailand's short-lived coalition governments (five in six years), frequent general elections, and extensive vote-buying ($1.1 billion in the November 1996 general election alone) made it particularly vulnerable to vested interest opposition to the fiscal and monetary contraction necessary to correct an external imbalance—as suggested by the parade of four finance ministers and three central bank governors in the year before the July 2, 1997, devaluation of the baht. Democracy has also contributed to the expansion of crony capitalism, as exemplified by the favoring of businesses with ruling political party connections in Malaysia's joint public-private sector infrastructure projects, who naturally would oppose both interest rate increases and cuts in public expenditures from which they benefit.

By contrast, Hong Kong—which does not have an elected government—and Singapore—which has a single-party-dominated parliament—have done relatively well through the economic crisis. Like the authoritarian governments of the past in Korea and Thailand, both administrations maintain strong central economic control and can impose economic hardship on their populations or take politically unpopular measures when necessary for economic stabilization. Thus the Singapore government cooled off the domestic property market when it was still booming in 1996, and the Hong Kong authorities were able to ignore domestic business leaders' complaints about the currency peg hurting their businesses and were able to raise local interest rates to beat back an attack by currency speculators in 1997. In the terminology of political scientists, both states have an autonomy from business interests that their newly democratic neighbors do not have.

In Defense of the Western Model

Proponents of the Western liberal model do not, of course, see things this way. Instead, they assert that open markets and democracy have worked and that instead it is the "Asian" parts of the Asian economic model that have failed—

particularly statist industrial policy in Korea (beloved though it is of some Western political scientists); crony capitalism in Thailand, Malaysia, and Indonesia (a reflection of both statist industrial policy and culturally embedded networks); and political mismanagement everywhere—from the virtual absence of government in Thailand, to persistent authoritarianism in Indonesia, and an idiosyncratic strong leader in Malaysia. They further argue that the excessive lending and investment by domestic and foreign financial institutions resulted from information gaps caused by inadequate local government regulation, monitoring, and disclosure requirements, not from mistakes made by financial markets. They believe that financial restructuring along Western lines and the takeover of troubled local financial institutions by more experienced and expert foreign counterparts would increase efficiency in the channeling of local savings to investments, reduce the risk of bad investments, and forestall a recurrence of the present crisis.

The IMF occupies a peculiar position in the Western economic policy canon. On the one hand, the multilateral agency is seen and has operated as an instrument of Western policy orthodoxy that advocates free trade and capital flows together with fiscal austerity and monetary conservatism. The IMF typically requires policy deregulation and liberal economic reforms, including financial sector liberalization and restructuring, in exchange for low-interest emergency loans of foreign exchange for client countries facing balance of payments difficulties and inability to meet their external liabilities. At the same time, it is recognized that the availability of IMF "bailouts" creates another moral hazard problem, by encouraging governments and private borrowers, lenders and investors to take excessive risks in emerging markets, secure in the knowledge that their risk is minimized by the likelihood of an IMF rescue should things go really bad. The result is periodic overinvestment and overlending bubbles such as characterized Mexico in 1994 and Southeast Asia and Korea in 1997.

The Asian Response

For Asians, disillusionment with market openness has set in. At worst, they see themselves as the victims of a massive conspiracy of Western governments, the IMF, financial markets, and industrial corporations to first deliberately inflate and then deflate the asset values of Asian banks and corporations, and then to subsequently take control of them at post-crisis fire sale prices under forced liberalization by the IMF.[18] At best, Asians view the current crisis as a case of massive market failure, particularly on the part of globally unregulated foreign financial market actors who, despite their greater expertise and global experience, still indulge in excess lending and investment to Asian markets and so cannot be trusted to better manage the local financial institutions that they may take over.

One of Thailand's most respected economists, Ammar Siamwalla, former president of the Thailand Development Research Institute, has been very critical of his own government's errors that led to the crisis, but still expresses extreme doubts about the policy of financial liberalization.

> The currency market is really crazy . . . we are receiving all the punishment because we have opened our currency markets to the forces of globalization (which) in retrospect has been far too rapid.[19]

Others share his views:

> The West has pushed us to open our markets, but what are we getting in return? Through globalization we have created a monster.[20]
> —Park Yung Chul, President of Korea Institute of Finance

Already, China and Vietnam have postponed capital market liberalization that would expose their currencies to speculation, and there have been calls for regional and global cooperation in the monitoring and possibly regulation of international capital flows. This idea was first raised by Malaysian prime minister Mahathir and supported by his nemesis, currency trader George Soros, who has said:

> Financial markets are inherently unstable, and international financial markets are especially so. International capital movements are notorious for their boom-bust pattern. . . . The recent turmoil in Asian markets raises difficult questions about currency pegs, asset bubbles, inadequate banking supervision, and the lack of financial information which cannot be ignored. Markets cannot be left to correct their own mistakes, because they are likely to overreact and to behave in an indiscriminate fashion.[21]

Today, even the World Bank has lent its support to some forms of capital controls for small open economies that can be severely disrupted by massive inflows and outflows of foreign capital. There is a growing consensus that, at a minimum, some international monitoring and perhaps risk-insuring agency is necessary to oversee these currently largely unregulated flows.

At the same time, some Asians may also lose their enthusiasm for the chaos, corruption, and weak and unstable government that political democracy has ushered in to different degrees, in countries like Korea, Thailand, and the Philippines, which contributed to the crisis both by weakening government macroeconomic control in some cases and by increasing financial markets' perception and punishment of political risk in these countries.

Conclusion

Clearly, both the Western economists' and Western political scientists' competing open and statist models have, in some sense, failed with the crisis in their showcase economies in Asia. On the one hand, market openness without the requisite institutional infrastructure and expertise—including political infrastructure and managerial expertise—to manage it can be a recipe for economic disaster. Even the normal workings of global financial markets themselves can be disruptive to small open economies. On the other hand, statist industrial policy can lead to crony capitalism, excess capacity, overleverage, and bad investments (as can Western sociologists' "culturally embedded networks" of ethnic business relationships or guanxi). Both openness and statism have contributed not only to the Asian miracle, but also to the Asian meltdown.

What about "Asian values"? At first glance, the indictment of openness and democracy in the crisis, and the evident need for more state-led institution building, state monitoring if not control of private sector financial transactions, and state autonomy from private interests in the political sphere, might seem to be a confirmation of the wisdom of the Asian values school. Too much freedom too fast in both markets and politics can lead to downfall, suggesting a continued need for a strong, benevolent, central state authority.

But at the same time, Asian government involvement in industrial policy and Asian cultural networks may also be indicted for fostering the crony capitalism that led to overinvestment in bad projects—ranging from Indonesia's Timor "national car" project[22] (of President Suharto's son), to Malaysia's privatization of huge public infrastructure projects favoring politically well-connected businesses and individuals, and the overextension of credit by overseas Chinese-owned banks to overseas Chinese industrial conglomerates with the presumed security of "relationships" substituting for modern risk assessment. The fact that the authoritarian regime and Indonesia's policy errors have compounded both the economic crisis and its adverse social and political consequences also under-mines the belief of some Asian values advocates that authoritarianism might be superior to democracy in economic policy management. The Indonesian case contrasts vividly with the market confidence inspired, at time of writing, by the policy statements and actions of newly elected President Kim Dae Jung of Korea.

In short, the Asian economic crisis does not provide unqualified support for either the Western open-markets and-democracy model or the Asian strong-government-and-cultural-values model. Both need some adjustment for global and national capitalisms to work smoothly. Certainly, the paths to capital market liberalization and democracy should be carefully planned, and perhaps staged to occur only in line with the concomitant development of supportive state and civil institutions. At the same time, governments need to resist the pressures of would-be crony capitalists to interfere with their fiscal, monetary, and regulatory auton-omy, while private sector business networks need to be adjusted to adequately account for risk and to reduce purely rent-seeking behavior.

The Asian crisis does expose the futility of applying simplistic and essentially ideological models to the messy practical business of public and private sector economic management in developing countries whose political, economic, and business systems are not only diverse and complexly intertwined, but also still evolving. Far from yet another presaging of the end of history—in this case the presumed triumph of "Western" over "Asian" models—the crisis suggests that it is time to return to history, that is, to each country's particular configuration of economic, political, social, and cultural forces, to discern both the complex, mul-tifaceted causes of the crisis and its eventual solutions. This is a task too impor-tant to allow to be jeopardized by those who would approach it only through the limited lenses of partial, monocausal theories and models of one or the other cultural-ideological predilection.

Endnotes

1.   James Gwartney, Robert Lawson, and Walter Block, *Economic Freedom of the World 1975–1995* (Canada: Fraser Institute, 1996).

2.   Bryan T. Johnson, Kim R. Holmes, and Melanie Kirkpatrick, eds., *1998 Index of Economic Freedom* (Washington, D.C.: Heritage Foundation and the *Wall Street Journal*, 1998).

3.   Frederic C. Deyo, *The Political Economy of the New Asian Industrialism* (Ithaca, NY: Cornell University Press, 1987); Alice Amsden, *Asia's Next Giant: South Korea and Late Industrialization* (New York: Oxford University Press, 1989); Stephen Haggard, *Pathways from the Periphery: The Politics of Growth in Newly Industrialized Countries* (Ithaca: Cornell University Press, 1990); Robert Wade,

Governing the Market: Economic Theory and the Role of Government in East Asian Industrialization (Princeton, N.J.: Princeton University Press, 1990); Karl Fields, "Strong States and Business Organization in Korea and Taiwan," in Sylvia Maxfield and Ben Ross Schneider, eds., *Business and the State in Developing Countries*, (Ithaca, N.Y.: Cornell University Press, 1997), pp. 122–151.

4. Andrew MacIntyre, ed., *Business and Government in Industrializing Asia* (Ithaca: Cornell University Press, 1994); K. S. Jomo, ed. *Southeast Asia's Misunderstood Miracle* (Boulder, Colo.: Westview Press, 1997).

5. Francis Fukuyama. *The End of History and the Last Man* (New York: The Free Press, 1992).

6. About the only sour note in this triumph was sounded by Samuel Huntington's *Clash or Civilizations*, which warned that the cessation of the Cold War's ideological conflicts would usher in an era of mounting cultural conflict between the West on one side and the competing civilizations of Islam and Confucianism on the other. See Samuel Huntington, *The Clash of Civilizations* (New York: Simon and Schuster, 1996).

7. S. Gordon Redding, *The Spirit of Chinese Capitalism* (Berlin: Walter de Gruyter, 1990); Gary G. Hamilton, ed., *Business Networks and Economic Development in East and Southeast Asia* (Hong Kong: Center of Asian Studies, University of Hong Kong, 1991); Robert W. Hefner, *Market Cultures: Society and Morality in the New Asian Capitalism* (Boulder Colo.: Westview, 1998). Richard Whitley, *Business Systems in East Asia: Firms, Markets and Societies* (London: Sage Publications, 1992); World Bank, *The East Asian Miracle: Economic Growth and Public Policy* (New York: Oxford University Press, 1993).

8. Paul Krugman, "The Myth of Asia's Miracle," *Foreign Affairs* 73 (November/ December 1994)pp. 62–78.

9. Paul Krugman, "What Happened to Asia?" (mimeo, January 1998).

10. Jeffrey A. Frankel, "How Well Do Foreign Exchange Markets Function?" in Mahbub ul-Haq, Inge Kaul, and Isabelle Grunberg, eds., *The Tobin Tax: Coping with Financial Volability* (New York: Oxford University Press, 1996), pp. 41–81.

11. "Irrational pessimism" is how Japanese finance ministry official Eisuke Sakakibara's characterized sentiment toward the depressed Japanese stockmarket.

12. Nayan Chanda, "Rebuilding Asia." *Far Eastern Economic Review*, February 12, 1998, pp. 46–50.

13. Timothy O'Brien, "Covering Asia with Cash, Banks Poured Money into Region Despite Warning Signs," *New York Times*, January 28, 1998, p. D1.

14. Ibid.

15. Ibid.

16. Assif Shameen, "Biting the Bullet: Siam Cement Tackles its Debts," *Asiaweek*, October 24, 1997, p. 62.

17. George Melloan, "Influence Peddlers Have a Growing Global Clientele," *Wall Street Journal*. February 17, 1998, p. A23.

18. I have analyzed and dismissed such "conspiracy theory" in Linda Lim, "Economic Crisis and Conspiracy Theory in Asia" (mimeo, February 1998).

19. Paul Scherer, "Distrust of Western Economics Grows in Thailand Amid Crisis," *Wall Street Journal*, January 20, 1998, p. A14.

20. Brian Bremmer, Pete Engardio et al., "What to Do about Asia," *Business Week*, January 26, 1998, pp. 26–30.

21. George Soros, "Toward a Global Open Society, *Atlantic Monthly*, January 1998, pp. 20–24.

22. This project gave special tariff privileges to a new car company started by Tommy Suharto in a joint venture with Kia Motors of Korea, enabling their product, the Timor, to be sold on the local market for a price far below that of established competitors (mainly Japanese) and aspiring new entrants (from U.S. and European carmakers).

Latin American Society in Transition

Benjamin Keen

Crises in the Twentieth Century

By the early 1990s, Latin America's economic, social, and political problems had reached explosive proportions. The neoliberal economic model imposed on the area by the International Monetary Fund and the World Bank sharpened all the old problems of dependency and created new ones. Those lending agencies used the area's gigantic foreign debt as a weapon to pressure the countries of the region into accepting neoliberal policies—privatization, lower tariffs, cuts in social programs, and emphasis on exports instead of production for internal consumption and development—in return for easier repayment terms and new loans. Agreements under the much ballyhooed Brady Plan, which was supposed to ease the burden of the debtor nations, had failed to provide significant or lasting relief. From 1980 to 1992 Latin America had a net negative transfer of capital of $220 billion, meaning that $220 more billion left the region than came in. Most of this exported capital was in the form of debt payments. Despite this immense drain, the foreign debt did not decrease; from $250 billion in 1980 it rose to $425 billion in 1990 and $478 billion in 1993 and was projected by the World Bank to reach $547 billion in 1994. Deals made with debtor countries under the Brady Plan continued to siphon off enormous sums in interest, while their debt-swap provisions enabled foreign corporations and their domestic partners to acquire profitable Latin American state enterprises in exchange for depreciated debt for a fraction of their worth.

Latin America's unequal terms of trade also caused immense losses to the region. Latin America exported cheap primary goods that suffered from declining demand and prices but had to pay exorbitantly high prices for imported technology, machinery, and other finished products. The volume of Latin American exports in 1992 was 86 percent more than in 1980, but the value of the exports was only 24 percent higher because of a 42 percent decline in export prices. Latin America, in other words, had to export much more in order to earn as much as before.

These and other economic and social indicators suggested that the nineties might become another "lost" decade, like the eighties. The per capita Gross Domestic Product (GDP), for example, dropped from a base of 100 in 1980 to 92.7 in 1992. Unemployment hovers about 10 percent in most countries, and if the underemployment of the "informal sector" is included, the figure could reach 50 percent or more. Inflation, averaging 1,185 percent in 1990, still registered 410 percent in 1992. Between 1980 and 1992 wages lost 40 percent of their purchasing power. After a decade of neoliberal "structural adjustment," poverty has increased, with 41 percent of the population, or 183 million, living below the poverty line, and 21 percent, or 88 million, described as living in extreme poverty.

The harmful effects of the neoliberal economic program reached into every area of Latin American life, including its political institutions. Politicians like Menem in Argentina, Fujimori in Peru, and Collor in Brazil have resorted to populist demagoguery to gain power and conceal the antipopular essence of their neoliberal projects. This politics of deceit served to discredit democracy and promote cynicism and abstentionism.

Economic Problems

By 1990 the population of Latin America was estimated to be 433 million. It was growing at a rate of about 2 percent a year and was projected to reach 515 million by the end of the century. In order to achieve even a modest improvement in Latin American living standards, per capita staple food production should grow considerably faster than population. In fact, Latin American agricultural production has greatly increased in recent decades due to the expansion of acreage and the "green revolution," which has dramatically raised crop yields through increased use of tractors, fertilizers, and new hybrids. But the bulk of this increase is accounted for by increased production of such export crops as sugar, coffee, and soybeans. Meanwhile, there has been a sharp increase in the importation of grains. Countries that once were self-sufficient now suffer from food shortages. Mexico, which as late as 1969–1971 was a net exporter of grain, had to import one-third of its food needs in 1992. In 1988–1989 Mexican food imports consumed more than half of the foreign exchange obtained from oil exports. The dependence on food imports is reflected in the price of staple foods, which has risen more rapidly than wages in most Latin American countries. The consumption of foods of high nutritive content has declined in recent decades in some of the most favored countries of the area, such as Argentina and Uruguay. The growing dependency in Latin America on imports of basic grains, purchased at international market prices, means that large sectors of the population find these imports prohibitively expensive. Approval by the United States, Canada, and Mexico of the North American Free Trade Agreement (NAFTA) foreshadows similar agreements with other Latin American countries that would open their markets to imports of U.S. grain. Recent changes in the General Agreement on Tariffs and Trade (GATT) that would reduce or eliminate tariffs within five to ten years, opening Latin American markets to unlimited imports, also increase the likelihood of increased Latin American dependence on grain imports. The dangers of such extreme dependency on foreign grain producers are obvious.

Population pressure on limited land resources is not a major cause of the food problem. In 1980, of the total area of 570 million hectares suitable for cultivation, only 143 million hectares, or 28 percent, were actually worked. A major cause of the food crisis is an agricultural strategy, vigorously promoted by the IMP, the World Bank, and the U.S. Agency for International Development, that emphasizes export crops at the expense of internal consumption. A closely related cause of the problem is an unjust system of land tenure and use, the latifundio. The new capitalist highly mechanized type of latifundio in particular sharply limits employment and absorbs by legal or illegal means many small plots previously devoted to staple food productions, forcing many small farmers to move into rugged hillsides, rain forests, or other land of poor agricultural quality or to migrate to the cities and plantations in search of employment

Along with Latin America's food crisis there has arisen an ecological crisis of unprecedented proportions caused by reckless, profit-driven exploitation of the area's natural and human resources. Central America again provides a prime example. More than two-thirds of the region's rain forests have been destroyed, resulting in the loss of many valuable plants and animal species. Deforestation and watershed destruction cause massive soil erosion, undermining the basis for continued subsistence farming. Dangerous pesticides, banned in the United States, poison thousands of workers. About 50 percent of all Central Americans lack access to safe drinking water. As a result infant diarrhea, malaria, and chronic parasitosis remain among the leading causes of death in the region.

There is a direct link between the food and ecological crises and the debt crisis. In Central America, for example, the debt crisis pressures governments to exploit their reserves of natural resources as quickly as possible to pay principal, interest and interest-on-interest to the international lending agencies. Moreover, in Central America, as in other parts of Latin America, the international banks dictate to debtor governments certain changes in economic policy, innocuously called "structural adjustments," that are designed to make more foreign exchange available to service the foreign debt In addition to "austerity" measures—meaning reductions in government spending, especially in the realm of social services, education, health, and the like—the debtor states are required to increase production of traditional and nontraditional exports in order to boost foreign exchange earnings. The immense, unpayable foreign debt weighs like a nightmare on Latin America, draining resources that should be used for sustainable development, imposing economic and social policies that make impossible sound development. Recognition that the debt is unpayable should lead to negotiations between debtors and creditors that result in forgiveness of all or the greater part of the debt. Liberation from the debt is a prior condition for the solution of the food and ecological crises of the area.

Freed from the burdens of the debt and the associated corporate control of economic policy, Latin Americans can adopt a new agricultural strategy based on different priorities that would place meeting the area's nutritional needs ahead of generating foreign exchange to make interest payments or extracting wealth for agribusinesses from the production of industrial crops, livestock feed crops, and luxury fruits and vegetables. Such a shift would have to take place within the context of thorough, democratically controlled agrarian reforms. It would be naive, however, to expect that most Latin American governments, currently controlled by and representing elite interests, will willingly adopt such new policies, which should include strict monitoring and control of the activities of foreign corporations that in the past have practiced "garbage imperialism," using Latin America as a dumping ground for toxic waste, freely polluting its soil and rivers as they have done in the Mexican-U.S. border zone. Sound environmental policies must also recognize the relation between poverty and environmental degradation. Much of the deforestation taking place in the Amazonian rain forest, for example, is the result of the exodus of landless peasants to the region, where they make clearings for planting, firewood, and other uses. That is why agrarian reform must occupy a central place in the solution of both the food and ecological crises.

The obstacles in the path of realizing such reforms are very great since they run counter to the current trend of "globalization" of the world economy, favored by the United States and other major capitalist powers and reflected in the recently approved NAFTA and the amended GATT. The leading international environmental organization Greenpeace claimed, "Many of NAFTA's provisions . . . are simply impossible to reconcile with the principles of environmental protection and resource conservation." What makes these agreements especially dangerous is that they create organisms with supranational powers, including the right to nullify or make changes in domestic laws. "They augur," observed *Latin-america Press*, "an Orwellian world ruled by commerce, with secret tribunals guaranteeing the right to trade freely, to exploit natural resources and to produce products at the lowest possible cost regardless of the environmental consequences."

Social Problems

The area's social problems have reached gigantic proportions in recent years. The main causes are growing poverty and reductions in social programs (social-sector spending has declined by more than 50 percent over the last decade). Both developments are directly linked to the ongoing debt crisis and the neoliberal "structural adjustment" programs adopted by most Latin American governments in response to that crisis.

Housing is one of the area's worst social problems. Throughout the area, much of it is improvised, ranging from thatched huts and caves to tin and plywood shacks, and lacks proper sanitary facilities. The absence of adequate drinking water and sewage services contributes to a high incidence of parasitic and infectious diseases.

Rising health problems are clearly related to the present economic crisis, the worst since the Great Depression of the 1930s. Purchasing power has declined by 40 percent or more in many nations in recent years; in some countries half the working force is unemployed or underemployed. Many Latin American governments have sharply reduced health services as part of austerity programs designed to meet interest payments on foreign debt These cutbacks are reflected in the deterioration of hospital care, fewer pharmaceutical imports, and reduced government support for medical schools.

The reappearance of diseases that had apparently been eradicated in the area provides other evidence that the health situation in Latin America is deteriorating. In 1991 Peru had its first cholera epidemic in more than 100 years. In its first three months the epidemic took over 1,000 lives and infected 150,000 others. From Peru it spread to Colombia, Brazil, Chile, and Ecuador and soon reached the suburbs of Buenos Aires. Like the upsurge in the incidence of malaria that accompanied it, the cholera epidemic was linked to the absence of clean drinking water, inadequate sanitation, and poor health facilities, conditions that are also major causes of such infections as typhoid, hepatitis, and the great killer diarrhea.

Children are the principal victims of malnutrition, the greatest health problem. Recent UNICEF statistics indicate that in Latin America, 3,000 children under the age of five die every day; malnutrition is believed to account for half of these deaths. Commercial infant formulas, aggressively promoted in Latin America by such transnational corporations as Nestlé and Bristol Myers, have contributed to infant malnutrition because poor women have been persuaded to substitute bottled formula for breast milk. In areas without clean water, the mothers' frequent practice of watering the milk to save money on formula makes bottle feeding especially dangerous for newborns, resulting in repeated epidemics of diarrhea and a vicious cycle of diarrhea-malnutrition that brings early death. Latin American infant mortality rates declined in the 1970s but increased in the 1980s as a result of deteriorating economic conditions.

Hunger, neglect, and disease are not the only threats millions of Latin American children and young adults face. There is a frightening indifference on the part of the authorities to the killing of thousands of street urchins by death squads, often composed of off-duty policemen. These "children of chaos" have been forced into the streets to fend for themselves or as street vendors to help out their parents. Some become petty criminals and a source of annoyance to businessmen and conservative middle-class groups who wish to "cleanse" the streets by any means and hire off-duty policemen to assassinate the offending children. A study by the human rights group Americas Watch and the University of São Paulo confirmed that 5,644 teenagers between the ages of fifteen and seventeen were murdered in Brazil between 1988 and 1991. Violence against children is most common in Brazil and Guatemala but occurs elsewhere.

Latin America suffers from a tremendous shortage of educational facilities. In Brazil, for example, a majority of school-age children do not attend school because there are not enough schools and teachers or because the poverty of their parents forces them to join the work force. Almost everywhere the dropout rate is very high. Only socialist Cuba and more recently Nicaragua (until the effects of the contra war and the rightist electoral victory in 1990 reversed that trend) showed dramatic improvement in this area. Cuba's nationwide campaign to wipe out illiteracy had achieved its goal by 1982.

An accelerated urbanization, caused by a massive migration of rural dwellers to the city, has sharpened all social problems. The rural exodus results from the interplay of two forces: the "pull" of the city, which attracts rural people with the frequently illusory prospect of factory work and a better life, and the "push" of the countryside, where concentration of land and the mechanization of agriculture are expelling millions of peasants from their farms and jobs. "Poverty and despair," writes Jorge E. Hardoy, a leading student of urban problems, "are behind many of these massive displacements." The urban population is increasing at more than twice the rate of the population as a whole. A United Nations estimate foresaw that by the year 2000 the urban population (*urban* here refers to a settlement of more than 2,000) would form some 80 percent of the total population of the area.

Most striking, however, has been the growth in the number of cities with over 1 million inhabitants. Between 1950 and 1970 the number of such cities rose from six to seventeen, and their total population increased from 15 to 55 million. If these trends continue, in the year 2000 the cities will contain about 220 million inhabitants, or about 37 percent of the total Latin American population at that time. In the same period the number of people living below the poverty line is expected to increase from 40 percent in 1985 to 66 percent in 2000.

Industrialization and the rural exodus have produced the phenomenon of hyperurbanization—the rise of vast urban agglomerations or zones of urban sprawl. About 80 percent of Brazil's industrial production is located in the metropolitan zones of São Paulo, Rio de Janeiro, and Belo Horizonte. Two-thirds of Argentine production is concentrated in the area between Buenos Aires and Rosario. More than half of the industrial production of Chile and Fern is located in the metropolitan zones of Santiago and LimaCallao, respectively. Caracas accounts for 40 percent of the industrial production of Venezuela. Between 25 and 50 percent of the populations of Uruguay, Mexico, and Argentina now live in the capitals of these countries.

As these vast urban concentrations increase, life becomes more and more difficult for their inhabitants. All the urban problems—food, housing, transportation, schools, drinking water, and sanitation—are immensely aggravated. Mexico City is a case in point. At the present rate of growth, the population will reach 30 million by the end of the century. The pollution caused by toxic agents generated by the city's 35,000 industrial establishments and 3 million cars has been denounced by medical specialists as a major danger to health and life; half of all infants have unacceptable toxic levels in their blood, which, specialists warn, could reduce IQs by as much as 10 percent. Shantytowns cover almost 40 percent of the urban area and house approximately 4 million people, a large proportion of whom are unemployed or underemployed; in 1978, 1.2 million persons lacked potable water. "The Latin American metropolis," writes city planner Thomas Angotti, "is characterized by mass poverty and severe environmental pollution on a scale generally unparalleled in the North."

In Europe and North America, urbanization, industry, and the demand for labor grew at a fairly even pace, but in Latin America, industrial growth and demand for labor lag far behind the explosive growth of the urban population. Much of the new industry, especially its foreign-owned sector, is highly mechanized and automated; it therefore generates relatively little new employment. In such a traditional Latin American industry as textiles, mechanization has actually produced a net loss of jobs. The low purchasing power of the masses also hinders the creation of new jobs, for the market for goods is quickly saturated and industry chronically operates below capacity. Finally, many of the rural migrants are illiterate and lack the skills required by modern industry. Perhaps as many as 50 percent of the area's labor force are completely or partly unemployed.

Industry's inability to absorb the supply of labor has produced an exaggerated growth of the so-called service or informal sector. The growth of this sector considerably exceeds that of the industrial labor force, which grew from 20 to 24 percent of the labor force from 1960 to 1980, while the service sector rose from 33 to 45 percent in the same period. The service sector includes a great number of poorly paid domestic servants and a mass of individuals who eke out a precarious living as lottery ticket vendors, car watchers and washers, shoeshiners, and street peddlers of all kinds. As a result of the economic crisis of the 1980s and 1990s, this informal sector of the economy has grown considerably in the past decade.

Cuba alone has made a serious effort to check and reverse the hypertrophy of the city. Almost from the day it took power, the revolutionary government undertook to redress the balance by shifting the bulk of its investments to the countryside and by raising rural living standards through the provision of adequate medical, educational, and social services; a more rational geographic distribution of the economic infrastructure; and the creation of the planned new cities. Thanks to these policies, aided by the departure of thousands of middle-class dissidents for the United States, the growth of Havana's population had begun to decline by 1965 and a reverse current of migration began from the capital to a countryside that was itself becoming urbanized.

The New Class Structure

In the middle decades of the twentieth century, industrialization, urbanization, and the commercialization of agriculture significantly altered the Latin American social structure and the relative weight of the various classes. These changes included the transformation of the old landed elite into a new latifundista class with a capitalist character, the emergence of a big industrial and financial bourgeoisie with close ties to foreign capital, an enormous growth of the so-called urban middle sectors, and the rise of a small but militant industrial working class. More recently, the neoliberal economic policies adopted by most Latin American governments, favoring multinationals and their local allies, have caused a sharp decline in the number and influence of small and medium national manufacturers; they have also caused growing impoverishment and unemployment among the middle class and the working class as a result of the privatization or dismantling of many state enterprises, reduction of social services, and a general downsizing of the state as part of "structural adjustment" programs demanded by the

IMF and the World Bank. A survey of these and other developments suggests the complexity of modern Latin American class alignments and the possible direction of future social and political change.

The Great Landowners

Although they have had to yield first place economically and politically to the big bourgeoisie, with which they maintain close links, the great landowners, Latin America's oldest ruling class, retain immense power, thanks to their control over the land and water resources of the area. Over the last few decades, as earlier chapters have shown, there has been a major expansion of the latifundio, especially of the new agribusiness type, which produces industrial and export crops with the aid of improved technology and wage labor. More recently, the dominant policies of free trade and open doors to foreign investment have further spurred the trend toward concentration of landownership and penetration of Latin American agriculture by foreign capital. Chile, whose civilian government has made no effort to restore the agrarian reform destroyed by the Pinochet dictatorship, and Mexico, where Congress recently approved an agrarian law that ends land redistribution and legalizes the sale or rental of communally owned ejido land, illustrate the shift toward policies favoring the rise of a new latifundio.

The traditional hacendado is a vanishing breed. His successor is often a cosmopolitan, university-trained type who combines agribusiness with industrial and financial interests. But the arbitrary and predatory spirit of the old hacendados survives in the new latifundistas. The great landowners continue to be the most reactionary class in Latin American society.

The New Bourgeoisie

A native commercial bourgeoisie arose in Latin America after independence and consolidated its position with the rise of the neocolonial order after mid-century. In the second half of the nineteenth century, an industrialist class, largely of immigrant stock, appeared in response to the demand of a growing urban population for consumer goods. World War I further stimulated the movement for export-import substitution industrialization. But the day of the industrial entrepreneur did not arrive until the great economic crisis of 1930 disrupted the trading patterns of the area. Aided by favorable international and domestic background conditions and massive state intervention, the native industrial bourgeoisie quickly gained strength and in many countries displaced the landed elite as the dominant social and economic force. As a rule, however, the new bourgeoisie avoided frontal collision with the latifundistas, preferring to form bonds of kinship and interest with the landed elite.

Meanwhile, foreign capital, attracted by the potential of the growing Latin American market, began to pour into the area, particularly after 1945. Possessing immensely superior capital and technological resources, foreign firms absorbed many small- and middle-sized national companies and came to dominate key sectors of the economy of the host countries. Aware, however, that the survival of a national bourgeoisie was essential to their own security, foreign capitalists endeavored to form close ties with the largest, most powerful national firms through the formation of mixed companies and other devices. This dependence on and linkage with foreign corporations explains why the Latin American big bourgeoisie lacks nationalist sentiment.

In its youth, some sections of the Latin American national bourgeoisie supported the efforts of such nationalist, populist chieftains as Cardenas, Perón, and Vargas to restrict foreign economic influence and accepted, though with misgivings, their concessions to labor. But soon the big bourgeoisie adopted the hostility of its foreign allies to restrictions on foreign capital and independent trade unionism. With rare exceptions, the big capitalists supported repressive military regimes in such countries as Brazil, Argentina, Uruguay, and Chile until, convinced that the policies of those regimes threatened the stability of capitalism itself, they became converts to democracy.

The neoliberal policies currently in vogue have given an immense stimulus to the alliance of foreign multinationals and local big capitalists, an alliance in which foreign capital plays the dominant role. The process has been under way in many countries, but particularly in Brazil, Argentina, Mexico, Chile, and Venezuela. Privatization has become a major instrument for denationalizing the Latin American economy through auctions and debt-equity swaps that virtually donate valuable state companies to foreign firms. The privatization and liberalization programs under way enjoy the overwhelming support of the big Latin American industrial bourgeoisie. This surrender of the Latin American state and economic elite to foreign capital represents a transition to a new, more completely dependent relationship.

The Urban Middle Sectors

The urban middle sectors are that great mass of urban dwellers who occupy an intermediate position between the bourgeoisie and the landed elite, on the one hand, and the peasantry and the industrial working class, on the other. The boundaries of this intermediate group with other classes are vague and overlapping. At one end, for example, the group includes highly paid business managers whose lifestyle and attitudes identify them with the big bourgeoisie; at the other, it takes in store clerks and lower-echelon government servants whose incomes are often lower than those of skilled workers.

The oldest urban middle sector consists of self-employed craftsmen, shop-keepers, and owners of innumerable small enterprises. The great number of small workshops in which the owner both works and employs other workers suggests the importance of this sector.

White-collar employees form another large urban intermediate sector. Urbanization, the growth of commercial capitalism, and the vast expansion of the state in the middle decades of the century contributed to an inflation of both public and private bureaucracies. Until recently, public employees made up about one-fifth of the economically active population of the area

University students compose a sizable urban middle sector. Between 1960 and 1970 their number rose from 250,000 to over 1 million. The great majority come from middle-class backgrounds, and many must combine work and study. Student discontent with inadequate curricula and teaching methods and the injustices of the social and political order have made the university a focal point of dissidence and protest. But the students are in the end transients, in Latin America as elsewhere; their radical or reformist zeal often subsides after they enter a professional career.

Because of their great size, the ideology of the urban middle sectors and their actual and potential role in social change are issues of crucial importance. Following World War II, many foreign experts on Latin America, especially in the United States, pinned great hopes on the "emerging middle sectors" (to which they assigned the new industrialist class), as agents of progressive social and economic change. The history of the following decades did not confirm these expectations. The urban middle sectors mushroomed, but with the exception of many students and intellectual workers—teachers, writers, scientists—they were not a force for social change.

The error of the foreign experts consisted in confusing the Latin American middle sectors with their counterparts in Europe and North America. Unlike the European and North American middle classes, the Latin American middle sectors did not arise from a process of dynamic industrial development. They arose in the protective shadow of a neocolonial export-import economy that was gradually transformed into a dependent, deformed capitalism with strong ties to the lati-fundia. Very few self-made men came from their ranks. Their ideology mirrored that of the ruling class, whose lifestyle they tried to copy by keeping one or two servants and in other ways. They regarded manual labor as degrading, resented forced contact with the lower orders in buses and trolleys, and looked down on Indians and blacks. Confused and misinformed on economic and political issues, they were easy prey to rightist demagogy and anticommunist propaganda. These groups provided the mass base for the right-wing military coups in Brazil and Chile. But, the urban middle sectors should not be written off as hopeless reactionaries. By their very intermediate nature, they are capable of strong political oscillations, especially in response to the movement of the economy. The "savage capitalism" implanted in many Latin American countries in recent decades by both military and civilian governments is playing havoc with middle-class living standards and expectations. In the process it is also transforming the traditionally conservative, complacent thought patterns of the urban middle sectors.

The Peasantry

The term *peasantry* refers here to all small landowners, tenants, and landless rural laborers. As documented in previous chapters, the current expansion of the new type of latifundio is creating an unparalleled crisis for the Latin American peasantry. The increased use of tractors and other kinds of mechanized farm equipment has already displaced millions of farmworkers and the process is accelerating. The current movement toward the removal of trade barriers, opening national markets to the competition of foreign grain producers with immensely superior resources, threatens the existence of large groups of small farmers. Meanwhile, the trend is not to adopt land reforms but to reverse them; in Mexico, for example, the recent passage of legislation making communally owned ejido land alienable is removing the last obstacles to the concentration of land in a few hands. Contrary to some earlier assumptions, however, despite the exodus to the cities the countryside is not becoming depopulated; the number of small tanners is actually growing, but in most areas they are becoming increasingly marginalized and pauperized, reduced to subsistence fanning or compelled to combine farming with wage labor.

The Industrial Working Class

The rapid growth of capitalism in Latin America since about 1930 has been accompanied by a parallel growth of the industrial working class. Although miners and factory workers form the best-organized and most class-conscious detachments of the army of labor, they are a minority of the labor force. Artisans, self-employed or working in shops employing less than five persons, constitute the largest group. The predominance of the artisan shop, whose labor relations are marked by paternalism and individual bargaining, hinders the development of workers' class consciousness and solidarity.

Despite its small size, the industrial working class has played a key role in major recent movements for social and political democracy in Latin America. Armed Bolivian tin miners helped achieve the victory of the 1952 revolution and its program of land reform and nationalization of mines. Cuban workers gave decisive support to the guerrilla struggle against the Batista dictatorship, and their general strike in 1959 helped topple it. The working class of Buenos Aires intervened at a critical moment (October 1945) to save Juan Perón from being overthrown by a reactionary coup, and its pressure broadened his reform program. In Chile the working class led the Popular Unity coalition that brought Salvador Allende to the presidency, ushering in a three-year effort (1970–1973) to achieve socialism by peaceful means.

These advances—particularly the Cuban and Chilean revolutions—provoked a counterrevolutionary reaction that until recently was still ascendant. In many countries under personal or military dictatorships, all working-class parties were banned, trade unions were abolished or placed under strict government control, and many labor leaders were murdered or forced into exile. The effects of this repression of the Latin American labor movement continue to be felt today.

The gradual restoration of formal democracy in the region did not bring full recognition of labor's right to organize and other basic rights. In Chile, for example, the new civilian government retained major features of the Pinochet labor code. In Mexico, workers may not freely join unions of their choice, and most union members have been forced to join unions affiliated with the ruling PRI. In the export-processing or free trade zones, like Mexico's *maquila* sector, union rights are routinely ignored. A major threat to trade unionism, particularly in Central America and the Caribbean, is the spread of *Solidarismo*—an ideology promoting company unions that withdraw growing numbers of workers from the collective bargaining process.

Today there are about 40 million union members in Latin America, comprising about 20 percent of the labor force. Despite continuing repression and restrictive legislation, labor is waging increasingly effective strike battles, like the 1993 general strike in Ecuador against the neoliberal economic policies of President Durán-Ballén, and in some countries it is forming coalitions with various grassroots organizations for joint struggle against the devastating social consequences of the "structural adjustment" programs. It is increasingly turning, too, to political action to achieve its goals. The large advances of the Workers' party in Brazil and the December 1993 election of Rafael Caldera to the presidency of Venezuela with the support of a coalition that included socialist and workers' parties illustrate the potential of this approach for changing the direction of economic and social policy in Latin America.

The Service or Informal Sector

Earlier in this chapter we noted that this sector, the largest of all,[1] arose as a result of industry's inability to absorb the supply of labor, we also said that it included "a great number of poorly paid domestic servants and a mass of individuals who eke out a precarious living as lottery ticket vendors, car watchers and washers, shoeshiners and street peddlers." But the meaning of "informal sector" is extremely elastic and the list of occupations that fit the category almost endless. It includes, for example, workers for manufacturing and repair operations who subcontract work they do in their own homes or small workshops, prostitutes, beggars, and garbage pickers who sell various types of wastepaper, bottles, and the like. Its main defining elements are self-employment and the irregular and precarious nature of the work. "Informal sector," observes sociologist Tessa Cubitt, Implies a dualist interpretation of the urban economy, since it proposes a dichotomy between a formal modern capitalist sector in which big businesses and multinationals flourish, and the mass of the poor who are unable to benefit from participation in this sector."

In fact, many of the activities of the informal sector are integrated into the modern capitalist sector, and the links between them are exploitative. The garbage pickers of Cali, Colombia, collect wastepaper, which they sell to warehouses, which in turn sell it to the giant paper company Cartón de Colombia, whose main shareholder is the Mobil Oil Company. "Why," asks Cubitt, "do Cartón de Colombia not directly employ the garbage pickers? Clearly, it is cheaper for them to operate like this because they do not have regular wage bills to pay. The income the garbage pickers receive for each item is extremely low and reduced even further by the competition between them, which is encouraged by the system that is very much a buyer's market." In effect, the low income of the garbage pickers subsidizes the multinational Cartón de Colombia. Similar exploitive relations exist between manufacturers and workers who subcontract to do work in their own homes and are paid for each completed piece. In all such cases the companies save on wages and the costs of social security benefits; there is the additional benefit of keeping workers weak and divided, unable to present a common front to employers.

Attitudes and Mentalities: Change and Resistance to Change

Change was in the air of Latin America as it entered the last quarter of the twentieth century. Economic modernization demanded changes in family life, race relations, education, and the whole superstructure of society, but the old attitudes and mentalities struggled hard to survive. As a result, Latin America presented dramatic contrasts between customs and mores that were as new as the Space Age and others that recalled the age of Cortés and Pizarro.

Women's Place

The status of women was a case in point. In some ways that status had improved; the struggle to obtain the vote, for example, began around World War I and ended successfully when Paraguay granted women suffrage in 1961. More and more Latin American women held appointive and electoral offices, and in increasing numbers they entered factories, offices, and the professions. By 1970, in some countries, notably Brazil and Argentina, the number of women classified as professionals was higher than the number of men, a significant fact because the proportion of economically active women was much lower than that of men. In Brazil, out of every 100 women working in nonagricultural services in 1970, eighteen were engaged in professional and technical operations, whereas for men the figure was only six out of every 100. The ratios were reversed, however, for positions of higher responsibility, reflecting the persistence of discriminatory attitudes.

The small movement for women's rights could claim much less progress in such areas as family patterns, divorce laws, and sexual codes. The traditions of the patriarchal family, of closely supervised courtship and marriage, continued strong among the upper and middle classes. The ideology of machismo, the cult of male superiority, with its corollary of a sexual double standard, continued to reign almost everywhere in the continent. "The Mexican family," wrote sociologist Rogelio Díaz-Guerrero in 1967, "is founded upon two fundamental propositions: (a) the unquestioned and absolute supremacy of the father and (b) the necessary and absolute self-sacrifice of the mother." The flood of economic, political, and social change of almost three decades has weakened the force of this statement, but with some qualifications it still holds for most Latin American republics.

Socialist Cuba has made great advances in abolishing sexual discrimination in law and practice; in 1976 it introduced the Family Code, which gave the force of law to the division of household labor. Working men and women are required to share housework and child care equally, and a recalcitrant spouse can be taken by the other to court. But Vilma Espín, head of the Cuban women's movement, admitted that the law was one thing and the way people lived was another: "Tradition is very strong. But we have advanced. Before, the machismo was terrible. Before, the men on the streets would brag about how their wives took care of them and did all the work at home. They were very proud of that. At least now we have reached the point where they don't dare say that. That's an advance. And now with young people you can see the difference."

Nicaragua is another country where a liberating revolution transformed the lives and roles of many women. Women, both rural and urban, took part in the struggle against the Somoza tyranny and made an immense contribution to its final triumph in July 1979. Women prepared for the final offensive by stockpiling food, gathering medical supplies, and organizing communications networks to send messages to Sandinista fighters and their families. By the time of the final victory, from one-quarter to one-third of the Sandinista People's Army were female—some as young as thirteen. Three women were guerrilla commanders; two served on the general staff of the People's Army. Following the triumph of the revolution, women assumed responsible positions at all levels of the Sandinista government. A similar process of women's liberation took place as part of the revolutionary struggle in neighboring El Salvador.

In the Southern Cone, women took the lead in the struggle against the military dictatorships that arose in Chile (1973), Uruguay (1973), and Argentina (1976). That role was thrust upon them as a result of the repressive policies of the dictatorships, the banning of trade unions and political parties, and the murder or disappearance of thousands of activists. Women paid a price for their sacrifices. Thirteen members of the Argentine human rights movement, including the president of the Mothers of the Plaza de Mayo, who demanded an accounting for their disappeared children, vanished into the death camps.

Despite their services, women in Cuba, Nicaragua, and the countries of the Southern Cone have not achieved full consciousness of themselves as equals or full recognition of their equality by males. Gioconda Betti, a former Nicaraguan guerrilla leader, complains: "We'd led troops into baffle, we'd done all sorts of things, and then as soon as the Sandinistas took office we were displaced from the important posts. We'd had to content ourselves with intermediate-level positions for the most part." Her complaint is echoed by an Uruguayan trade unionist who had taken part in the struggle against the military dictatorship: "When the men came out of prison or returned from exile, they took up all the spaces, sat down in the same chairs, and expected the women to go back home." And Rosa, one of the Chilean working-class women who played key roles in the resistance to the military dictatorship, wryly remembers: "When the democratic government took over, the men around here said, 'It's okay, Rosa, you can leave it to us now.' We thought, 'Have they forgotten everything we did during the dictatorship?'" Consciously or unconsciously, the old prejudices persist in the thought patterns of men—even radicals and revolutionaries—from one end of the area to the other.

Women have responded to the continuing challenge of machismo by forming a multitude of groups that, whether or not they call themselves feminist, have as their essential goal the end of the old unequal relations between the sexes. One *encuentro* or meeting in Nicaragua in March 1992 brought together some five-hundred Central American women "who talked about the power Central American women have in their 'public' and 'private' lives, the kind of power they would like to have, and how to go about getting that power." But women are divided among themselves by class, and Latin American working-class women often criticize traditional feminist organizations as middle-class and indifferent to their own practical needs. "We have things in common with middle-class women, but we also have other problems that middle-class women don't have, like the housing shortage, debt problems, unemployment," said one Chilean woman activist, "and we're not going to advance as women if the two things aren't closely linked."

Economic forces, in particular the disastrous impact of neoliberal economic policies on household incomes and living standards, are silently helping transform gender and familial relations in many parts of the area. It is becoming increasingly difficult for one wage to support a family. From sheer necessity, women are entering industry in record numbers. According to the Inter-American Development Bank, the proportion of women in the labor force rose 50 percent, from almost 18 percent in 1950 to just under 27 percent in 1990.

The results are particularly evident in an area like the Caribbean Basin, where declining traditional exports such as sugar, coffee, and bananas, industries that employ a predominantly male labor force, have given way to export manufacturing, typically employing poorly paid woman workers. Similar economic trends, challenging male dominance in the household, are under way in other countries of the region.

Race Prejudice

Notions of black and Indian inferiority are everywhere officially disapproved, but race prejudice remains strong, especially among upper- and middle-class whites. In Brazil, often touted as a model of racial democracy, sociologist Florestan Fernandes found that the white man clung to "the *prejudice of having no prejudice*, limiting himself to treating the Negro with tolerance, maintaining the old ceremonial politeness in inter-racial relationships, arid excluding from this tolerance any true egalitarian feeling or content."

In Brazil, Venezuela, Colombia, and most other Latin American countries with large black populations, unlike the situation in the United States, where people are categorized as either white or black, prejudice and discrimination against blacks tend to vary according to the shade of their skin color. Mulattos are usually favored over dark blacks. As a rule, the higher occupations, such as medicine, law, upper-level government posts, and the officer and diplomatic corps, are closed to both categories. But mulattos can aspire to become schoolteachers, journalists, bank tellers, low-level municipal officials, and the like. The lowest-paying jobs are reserved to dark-skinned people. Even in black Haiti, a vast economic and social gulf separates an urban mulatto elite from the rural black masses of poor people and the "black ghetto" of downtown Port-au-Prince. In the neighboring Dominican Republic, octogenarian President Joaquín Balaguer preaches an overt racism, claiming that his "white and Christian" country is threatened by the "biological imperialism" of Haitian immigrants. Only revolutionary Cuba has virtually eliminated racism in both theory and practice, and blacks hold high positions in government, the armed forces, and the professions.

The Indian remains the principal victim of racist exploitation and violence. In Brazil, according to one recent estimate, the number of Indians has dropped from 1 million to 180,000 since the beginning of the century. The process of destroying the Indians in the interests of economic progress continues. Since 1975 some 1,000 Yanomamis, of the 9,000 living in Brazil and 12,000 in Venezuela, have been murdered, mostly by gold miners. Wanton killings of Indians have been reported from the jungle lowlands of Colombia, and murders of Indians by landgrabbing hacendados or their *pistoleros* (gunmen) have occurred in Mexico, Guatemala, and other countries with sizable Indian populations. In Guatemala, military regimes have practiced systematic genocide against the Maya Indian population and attempted to eradicate their culture.

In some countries, the Indian peasantry is subjected to a many-sided economic, social, and cultural exploitation. "The Indian problem," writes Mexican sociologist Pablo González Casanova, "is essentially one of internal colonialism. The Indian communities are Mexico's internal colonies. . . . Here we find prejudice, discrimination, colonial forms of exploitation, dictatorial forms, and the separation of a dominant population, with a different race and culture." That the legendary Indian patience has its limits is shown by the explosion of revolt in the Mexican state of Chiapas in January 1994.

Today the Indians of the Americas are on the move, fighting back against old and new forms of exploitation. One milestone in that struggle was the decision of the United Nations to declare 1993 the International Year of the Indigenous Peoples of the World. Another was the award of the Nobel Peace Prize to the Guatemalan indigenous leader Rigoberta Menchú (October 1992) in recognition of her work in behalf of the Indian peoples of America.

The Catholic Church

The ideological crisis of Latin America is illustrated by the rifts that have emerged in two of the area's oldest and most conservative institutions, the Catholic church and the armed forces.

The new reformist and revolutionary currents that have emerged within the Catholic church since about 1960 have different sources. One is a more liberal climate of opinion within the church since the Second Vatican Council, convened in 1962 under Pope John XXIII Another is concern on the part of some elements of the hierarchy that the church's traditional collusion with the elites risked a loss of the masses to Marxism. Still another is a crisis of conscience on the part of some clergy, especially working clergy whose experiences convinced them that the area's desperate dilemmas required drastic solutions.

The new ferment within the Latin American church found dramatic expression in the life and death of the famous Colombian priest and sociologist Camilo Torres. Born into an aristocratic Colombian family, a brilliant scholar and teacher, Tortes, who became convinced of the futility of seeking to achieve reform by peaceful means, joined the communist-led guerrilla National Liberation Army. He was killed in a clash with counterinsurgency forces in February 1966.

The proper stand for the church to take in the face of Latin America's structural crisis was hotly debated at the second conference of Latin American bishops, held at Medellín, Colombia, in 1968. The presence of Pope Paul VI at its opening session underlined the meeting's importance. Reflecting the leftward shift of portions of the clergy, the bishops at Medellín affirmed the commitment of the church to the task of liberating the people of Latin America from neocolonialism and "institutionalized violence." This violence, declared the bishops, was inherent in the economic, social, and political structures of the continent, dependent on what Pope Paul called "the international imperialism of money."

Even before Medellín, a group of Latin American bishops had taken a position in favor of socialism. Their leader was Helder Câmara, archbishop of Recife (Brazil). He and seven other Brazilian bishops had signed a pastoral letter issued by seventeen bishops of the Third World that called on the church to avoid identification of religion "with the oppression of the poor and the workers, with feudalism, capitalism, imperialism." Rejecting violence as an instrument of revolutionary change, Helder Câmara expressed sympathy and understanding for those who felt that violence was the only effective tactic.

These developments were accompanied by the emergence and growing acceptance by many clergy of the so-called theology of liberation, the product of the study and reflection of leading church scholars in various Latin American countries. This doctrine taught that the church, returning to its roots, must again become a Church of the Poor. It must cease to be an ally of the rich and powerful and commit itself to the struggle for social justice, to raising the consciousness of the masses, to making them aware of the abuses from which they suffered and of the need to unite in order to change an oppressive economic and political system.

Liberation theology rejected Marxism's atheist world view but drew heavily on the Marxist analysis of the causes of the poverty and oppression in the Third World. On the subject of revolution, while deploring all violence, liberation theologians taught that revolution, or counterviolence, was justified as a last resort against the greater violence of tyrants, an orthodox Catholic teaching that goes back to St. Thomas Aquinas. It was in this spirit that Archbishop Oscar Arnulfo Romero of San Salvador, in one of the last sermons he gave before he was murdered by a right-wing assassin in March 1980, declared: "When all peaceful means have been exhausted, the Church considers insurrection moral and justified."

In order to implement the teachings of liberation theology, progressive clergy set about developing a new type of Christian organization, the *comunidad de base*, or Christian grassroots organization. Composed of poor people in the countryside and the barrios of cities, assisted and advised by priests and students, these communities combined religious study and reflection with efforts to define and solve the practical social problems of their localities. The great landowners and the authorities frequently branded their activities as subversive, and both laity and priests were subjected to severe repression. This led to a growing politicization and radicalization of many communities and their involvement in revolutionary movements. In Nicaragua, the Christian communities were integrated into the revolutionary struggle led by the Sandinista Front for National Liberation to a degree not found elsewhere in Latin America.

This unity of rank-and-file Catholic clergy and laity with the revolution continued alter the Sandinista triumph in July 1979. Five priests held high office in the revolutionary government and defied a 1980 Vatican ruling barring direct priestly involvement in political life. Many priests and nuns enthusiastically supported and participated in the literacy campaign and other reconstruction projects of the new regime.

The church hierarchy, headed by Archbishop Miguel Obando y Bravo, grew increasingly critical of the Sandinist government, however. Before the revolution, the hierarchy, historically aligned with the wealthy class, gradually moved toward anti-Somoza positions, but never became pro-Sandinist. The bishops may have feared the gradual growth of atheism among the people and the loss of their influence over the faithful. The Sandinist government claimed that the hierarchy was again aligning itself with the rich and playing the game of the Reagan administration by trying to destabilize the revolutionary regime.

The conflict between traditionalists and progressives concerning the role of the church was high on the agenda of the third conference of Latin American bishops, convened at Puebla, Mexico, in March 1979. Unlike Medellín, where the progressives had the upper hand, a conservative faction controlled the preparations for the Puebla conference and clearly intended to put down the troublesome liberation theology and its supporters. The dominant conservative faction prepared a working paper that urged resignation on the part of the poor in the hope of a better hereafter and placed its trust for the solution of Latin America's great social problems in the failed reformist models of the 1960s. This document raised a storm of criticism among progressive bishops and other clergy.

The unknown element in the equation at Puebla was the position of the new pope, John Paul II, who was to inaugurate the conference. Despite their ambiguity, the pope's statements in general tended to reinforce the position of progressives and moderates at the Puebla conference. Its final document continued the line of Medellín, especially in its expression of overwhelming concern for the poor: "We identify as the most devastating and humiliating scourge, the situation of inhuman poverty in which millions of Latin Americans live, with starvation wages, unemployment and underemployment, malnutrition, infant mortality, lack of adequate housing, health problems, and labor unrest."

Since 1982 the pope's opposition to liberation theology and the so-called popular church has hardened. He expressed this opposition during his visit to Nicaragua in 1983, a visit that produced an extraordinary confrontation between the pope and the mass of the faithful who came to hear his homily. Brazil—where many bishops accept the basic tenets of liberation theology, actively engage in the struggle for land reform and other reforms, and enjoy the support of many thousands of grass-roots communities—became another target of the pope's attack on the supposed subversive or heretical teachings of liberation theology. This attack took the form of sanctions against a very popular theologian, Leonardo Boff, and of efforts to weaken the majority of progressive Brazilian bishops by naming more conservative bishops. More recently, the Vatican joined the Mexican government in efforts to force Bishop Samuel Ruiz of San Cristóbal de las Casas in Chiapas, to resign. Ruiz, a champion of the poor Maya campesinos of his diocese, was accused of having a Marxist interpretation of the Gospel and "incorrect theological reflection." The effort apparently collapsed when the Salinas administration asked Ruiz to mediate between the government and the Indian rebels after the outbreak of a revolt in Chiapas in January 1994.

The recent rapid growth in membership and influence of Protestant evangelical or fundamentalist sects poses a major challenge to the religious supremacy of the Catholic church in Latin America. Between 1981 and 1987 the membership of these sects had doubled to 50 million. In Guatemala they claim 30 percent of the population; the most recent figures for Chile and Brazil are 15 and 10 percent of the population. The dramatic economic and social changes taking place throughout the continent have much to do with the phenomena] growth of these new churches. Their revivalist preaching and "pie-in-the-sky" message bring color, excitement, and hope to the lives of the uprooted rural immigrants of the shantytowns that ring every Latin American city. The churches' support networks often provide these "marginal" people with material assistance as well.

The fervently right-wing, anticommunist teachings of the fundamentalist sects have gained them the approval and support of sections of the Latin American oligarchy, who find in these teachings a useful foil for the radical social doctrines of Catholic liberation theology. In Guatemala, Efraín Ríos Montt, the general who directed the brutal suppression of Maya highland Indians, is a born-again Christian, as is Jorge Serrano, elected president in the 1991 election. President Alberto Fujimori of Peru, who has implemented a harsh free-market "shock therapy" for the country's economic problems, also belongs to a fundamentalist sect. But not all evangelicals are accomplices of the ruling classes; in Nicaragua, Ecuador, and other countries, mainstream Protestant churches and spin-offs from evangelical groups have found common ground with Catholic base communities in supporting agrarian reform and other progressive changes.

The Military

Within the Latin American armed forces, as within the church, a differentiation is taking place. The phenomenon of the reformist or even social revolutionary military officer is older than is sometimes supposed. In Brazil, we recall, the tenente revolts of the 1920s paved the way for the triumph of Getúlio Vargas's reformist revolution of 1930. Juan Perón and other members of the Group of United Officers exemplified a similar tendency within the Argentine officer corps in the 1930s. In Guatemala in 1944, a group of progressive officers led by Colonel Jacob Arbenz overthrew the Ubico dictatorship and installed a government that enacted a sweeping land reform and other democratic changes.

The massive influx of North American capital into Latin America after 1945, accompanied by the growing political influence of the United States in the area, altered the balance of forces between conservatives and progressives within the Latin American military. Many high-ranking officers became fervent converts to the North American system of free enterprise and accepted the inevitability of a mortal struggle between "atheistical communism" and the "free world." By the Treaty of Rio de Janeiro (1947), the Latin American republics committed themselves to join the United States in the defense of the Western Hemisphere. In the context of the cold war, this commitment entailed collaboration with the United States in a global anticommunist strategy, to the extent of justifying military intervention in any country threatened or conquered by "communist penetration." Under the cover of this doctrine, in 1965 Brazilian troops joined United States forces in intervening in the Dominican Republic to crush the progressive revolutionary government of Colonel Francisco Caamaño. The integration of Latin American armies into the strategic plans of the Pentagon converted many into appendages of the North American military machine.

This integration was accompanied by the establishment of the technical and ideological tutelage of the Pentagon over the Latin American military, aimed particularly at the destruction of Latin American revolutionary movements. After the victory of the Cuban Revolution in 1959, this program of training and indoctrination was greatly expanded. Thousands of Latin American officers were sent to take courses in counterinsurgency warfare at Fort Bragg, Fort Knox, Fort Monmouth, and other installations in the United States and in the Panama Canal Zone. An especially important role continues to be played by the School of the Americas (S.O.A.), run by the United States Army for the training of Latin American officers. Founded in 1946 in Panama, it was moved in 1984 to Fort Benning, Georgia, when the Panama Canal Zone Treaty forced its removal from Panama. Since its inception more than 56,000 Latin American personnel have received training at the S.O.A. in the art of waging a "dirty little war." Dubbed by *Newsweek* "a school for dictators," S.O.A.'s graduates include General Augusto Pinochet, until lately head of the Chilean fascist junta; Manuel Noriega, dictator of Panama and US. protégé until an imprudent display of independence caused his downfall, now serving forty years in a U.S. prison for drug trafficking; and the late Roberto D'Aubuisson, organizer of death squad activities and charged with responsibility for the assassination of Archbishop Oscar Romero in El Salvador. According to the United Nations Truth Commission in El Salvador, S.O.A. graduates directed many of the massacres and atrocities committed by the military in that country; nineteen of the twenty-seven officers implicated in the Jesuit priest killings in 1989 were S.O.A. alumni, as were eight of the twelve officers charged with responsibility for the El Mozote massacre. Among documents recently discovered in Paraguay's so-called "Horror Archives" was a folder labeled "Confidential" containing a torture manual used at the S.O.A. The manual taught "interrogators" how to keep electric shock victims alive and responsive by methods that included dousing their heads and bodies with salt water.

The formation of dose ties between high-ranking officers and large foreign and domestic firms contributed to the making of a reactionary military mentality. In Argentina in the 1960s, 143 retired officers of the highest ranks held 177 of the leading posts in the country's largest industrial and financial enterprises, mostly foreign-controlled. Latin America thus developed its own military-industrial complex. Through all these means, the United States acquired an enormous influence over the Latin American military.

Pentagon influence over the Latin American military engendered not only an obsessive anticommunism but an implacable hostility to even moderate programs of social and economic reform. North American ideological influence undoubtedly played an important role in creating a favorable climate of military opinion for the wave of counterrevolutionary coups that swept over Latin America in the 1960s and 1970s.

Not all Latin American military, however, are reactionaries of the Pinochet type. In some countries, the military seized power not to preserve the status quo but to change it. Although the military regimes in Peru (1968), Panama (1968), and Ecuador (1972) differed considerably in the scope and depth of their reforms, they demonstrated the existence of a reformist or even revolutionary officer class. In Panama, a group of officers of the Panamanian National Guard organized a revolt in 1968 that overthrew President Arnulfo Arias, a representative of the traditional oligarchy. The rebels formed a military junta, headed by General Omar Torrijos, which soon displayed an unexpected reformist and nationalist fervor: it demanded the liquidation of the American military presence in Panama and a revision of the ancient Treaty of 1902 that would restore Panamanian sovereignty over the Canal Zone.

Endnote

1. According to the International Labor Organization, from 1980 to 1992 employment in the informal sector rose from 40.2 percent to 54.4 percent of the total.

Growing Pains

Industrialisation, the Debt Crisis and Neoliberalism

Duncan Green

São Paulo is made of cheap concrete. Millions of tons, poured in a hurry, spewed forth to make houses, tower blocks, factories and flyovers. Within a few years rain and sun leave it stained and crumbling, but quantity matters more than quality, for dilapidated buildings can always be replaced by bigger and newer constructions, using yet more concrete. The flood of concrete that created the great megalopolis of São Paulo is past of Brazil's rush for industrialisation, a titanic effort which has turned a relatively primitive coffee-exporter into a great industrial power, the tenth largest economy in the world. However, like the concrete, Brazil's industrial development is flawed and vulnerable. To pay for it, the national economy ran up huge debts in the 1970s, driving the country to the verge of bankruptcy during the debt crisis of the 1980s. State-led industrialisation has also failed the Brazilian people. In the main thoroughfares of São Paulo, the rush-hour is a stampede of the well-heeled, the manicured and beautiful beneficiaries of Brazil's growth. On the street corners the losers, the old and unemployed, earn a pittance working as human billboards. Standing in bored clumps all day, they wear T-shirts saying 'I buy gold', with a phone number.

For a half century after the Great Depression of the 1930s, Latin Americans saw industrialisation as the path to development. The satanic mills whose fumes now choke Caracas or Mexico City may seem unlikely saviours, but the region's planners pointed to the experience of the rich countries, like the UK, US or Japan, where the growth of industry had led to a rise both in political power and the standard of living. Industrialisation, they argued, offered Latin America a way out of its crippling dependence on commodity exports, and its humiliating reliance on foreign governments and multinational companies for aid and manufactured goods. In recent years, the failings of Latin America's industrialisation efforts have forced a rethink, and industrialisation in many cases has gone into reverse as governments have abandoned local industries to sink or swim in the global economy, in many cases reverting to commodity exports as the path to economic growth.

Latin America's industrial quest started late. During the colonial period, the Spanish and Portuguese governments did everything they could to prevent the growth of domestic industry, which they feared would disrupt the continent's dependence on commodity exports which provided a lucrative trade for the colonial powers. In 1785 a royal decree from the Portuguese crown banned all industry in its Brazilian colony, ordering all textile looms to be burnt. When independence arrived in the early 19th century, Britain's cheap manufactures soon undercut what little local industry had arisen as the colonial ties had weakened. Nevertheless, most countries managed to achieve a first stage of industrialisation; they semi-processed agricultural crops and minerals for export, and local industries produced simple goods like soap, clothing and bottled drinks. European immigrants set up many of the first local industries—in Argentina and Uruguay, British immigrants built slaughter-houses, freezer plants and tanneries to serve the beef export industry, while Germans set up Peru's beer industry and controlled ninety per cent of Brazil's textile production by 1916.

Despite these primitive local industries, Latin America remained a commodity exporter, dependent on manufactured imports, until the late 1920s. By then, the cattle and grain trade had made Argentina the fifth richest country in the world, and coffee had established São Paulo as Brazil's economic powerhouse. In 1929 the Wall Street Crash and the ensuing depression in the industrialised world rudely awoke Latin American governments to the perils of commodity-dependence. Brazil's exports fell by sixty per cent between 1929–32, and the country suddenly had no hard currency with which to import manufactured goods.

Latin America learned its lesson. Just like the US government under Roosevelt's 'New Deal', or the followers of John Maynard Keynes in the UK, they concluded that the state had to play a much greater role in running the economy if future crashes were to be avoided. In Latin America, as local entrepreneurs moved in to start producing simple manufactured goods to plug the gap left by the import collapse, several governments began looking at ways to encourage 'import substitution'. By the late 1930s they were taking the first steps to improve transport, electricity and water supplies for local factories. When the Second World War came, the dilemma of the Great Depression was reversed; the industrialised nations were now desperate for Latin America's exports, but had fewer manufactures to spare as factories were converted to war production. The largest Latin American economies accumulated great wealth during the war, and afterwards used it to begin import substitution in earnest.

Besides improving national infrastructure, countries such as Argentina, Brazil and Mexico set up state-owned companies in strategic industries such as iron and steel and raised taxes on imported manufactured goods. These tariff barriers were essential to protect fledgling local industries from being undercut by cheap imports. At the same time, governments encouraged multinational companies to set up factories on Latin American soil, arguing that this would create jobs, while providing the technology and capital that the region lacked. Volkswagen built its first factory in Brazil in 1949, with other car producers from the US, Germany and Japan hot on its heels. By 1970, eighty per cent of the country's cars were assembled in Brazil itself.

The initial results of import substitution were impressive. From 1950–70 Latin America's Gross Domestic Product (GDP, a measure of all the goods and services produced by a country) tripled, and even in per capita terms it rose by two-thirds. In the mid- 1950s, Latin America's economies were growing faster than those of the industrialised West. By the early 1960s, domestic industry supplied 95 per cent of Mexico's and 98 per cent of Brazil's consumer goods. By this time, however, there were already clear signs that the model was approaching exhaustion, as state-led development in Latin America began to suffer much the same fate as the state-run economies in Eastern Europe. Protected industries had no need to invest or innovate, and fell behind the rest of the world in technology and productivity; political interference encouraged corruption and incompetence, as people were appointed to run state companies on the basis of political favouritism rather than merit. The ever-growing state sector began to outspend meagre revenues (rich Latin Americans have always been adept at avoiding taxes), generating growing inflation.

In social terms, import substitution also failed. Latin America and the Caribbean have always had hugely unequal societies and import substitution further aggravated the situation. In order to keep wage costs down in industry, governments held down food prices, penalising the peasant farmers who grew the food and creating growing poverty in the countryside. Millions of peasants gave up hope of earning a living from the land and drifted to the cities, where they joined the armies of hopeful job-seekers in the shanty towns that sprang up on the edges of the continent's cities. Some achieved their ambition of a steady, waged job, but most ended up as street sellers, domestic servants or doing odd jobs.

The local market for manufactured goods was limited because most people in Latin America were too poor to buy more than the most basic necessities. This prevented industry from growing and reducing costs through mass production. Even Brazil, the most populous country in the region, faced this problem, although among its 140 million people, there was at least a significant middle class to buy locally-produced goods, enabling Brazilian industry to outperform its Spanish American counterparts. The problem of a small domestic market could have been solved if wealth were redistributed to allow more people to buy goods, an option ruled out by the wealthy elite.

Initially, governments responded to the lack of an internal market by establishing a variety of free trade agreements with other Latin American nations. Organisations like the Latin American Free Trade Association and the Central American Common Market, both established in 1960, soon foundered, however, because the smaller countries opened their markets to the more industrialised nations in the agreement, but received little in return.

The Dance of the Millions

Many Latin American governments were forced to adopt austerity programmes to cope with the slowdown in growth. In Brazil and Argentina, military governments seized power in order to implement such unpopular policies. They used both the law and brute force to suppress trade unions and lower the living standards of the poor majority. The major economies then set off in pursuit of the elusive third stage of industrialisation, the move from import substitution to becoming an exporter of manufactured goods. This meant large-scale investments, which had to be funded by foreign capital. Latin America turned to the international loan sharks. The initial results were astonishing. In just thirteen years, from 1967 to 1980, Latin America's manufactured exports increased in value forty-fold, from US$1 billion a year to US$40 billion.

Brazil led the field in both industrialisation and the race for foreign loans. In 1958, it overtook Argentina as the region's leading industrial power. By 1961 it was self-sufficient in electric stoves, refrigerators and television sets. Vehicle production boomed from 31,000 in 1957 to 514,000 in 1971. In 1968 Brazilian industry finally outstripped agriculture as the major wealth producer in the country. By 1994 Brazil's industrial output was over twice that of Mexico, and nearly three times greater than Argentina's, and by 1996 four out of Latin America's top five companies were Brazilian. The one-time coffee producer has become the region's superpower.

As the factories multiplied, so did the foreign debt. The big borrowers were the state corporations which dominated the politically vital areas of steel, petroleum and electricity production. By the early 1980s, Mexico's petroleum corporation, Pemex, had run up a debt of US$15 billion. State and private banks also borrowed heavily abroad, in order to re-lend to local businesses.

TABLE 1 Industrialisation in Latin America

Country	A	B	C
Brazil	555	39	23
Mexico	377	28	24
Argentina	282	30	32
Colombia	67	32	23
Venezuela	58	42	27
Chile	52	-	25
Peru	50	37	18
Ecuador	17	38	19
Uruguay	16	23	27
Guatemala	13	19	17
Dominican Republic	10	22	29
Paraguay	8	22	22
Costa Rica	8	24	27
El Salvador	8	24	21
Panama	7	16	16
Bolivia	6	-	18
Honduras	3	32	20
Nicaragua	2	20	26
Haiti	2	12	9

A: Gross Domestic Product (US$billion), 1994
B: Industrial output as % of GDP, 1994
C: Percentage of the workforce employed in industry, 1990

Sources: UNDP *Human Development Report 1996*, World Bank *World Development Report*, 1996

The 'dance of the millions', as the round of frenzied foreign borrowing became known, took off after the oil price rise decreed by the Organisation of Petroleum Exporting Countries (OPEC) in 1973–74. OPEC oil producers recycled their new wealth to western banks, who in turn were anxious to find outlets for their 'petrodollars'. Latin America seemed the ideal borrower; it had decades of steady growth and industrialisation already behind it, and countries such as Mexico and Venezuela were sitting on huge oil reserves. Foreign bankers fell over themselves to lend as much as possible, as fast as possible. Since they assumed that governments could not go bankrupt, they paid little attention to where the money was actually going. In practice, it went into a number of unproductive areas, such as capital flight, where government officials and business leaders siphoned billions of dollars back out of the country into US bank accounts; on prestige 'megaprojects' such as hydroelectric dams and roads, and on arms, as military governments splashed out on the latest hardware for their troops.

In all, US$60 billion in foreign loans entered Latin America between 1975 and 1982. Sixty per cent of the money went to Brazil and Mexico, as they and Argentina became the Third World's top three debtors. In Mexico, the rain of dollars funded exploration and development of the oil industry; in Brazil it fuelled the country's further rise as an industrial power. Brazil was the only country successfully to make the leap to the third stage of industrialisation as an exporter of manufactured goods. From 1970–78 it doubled its proportion of the region's exports, becoming a producer of everything from computers to aircraft.

The dance of the millions ended abruptly in August 1982, when the Mexican government announced it could no longer pay the interest due on its foreign debt. Many US and other banks suddenly realised that what had seemed a safe and lucrative loans business in Latin America could drive them into bankruptcy, if other countries followed Mexico's lead. The announcement sent a shudder through the international banking community, raising fears of a run on the banks and a possible collapse of the world financial system. The following weeks established the pattern for years to come. The banks and creditor governments worked together to find a solution—not to the problem of Mexico's excessive debt repayments, but to remove the threat to the global banking system. The initial remedy was a band-aid affair whereby the banks rescheduled debt repayments and lent Mexico new money, purely so that it could give it straight back as interest payments. This avoided the banks having to write off Mexico's loans as bad debts, which would have damaged their profits and sent their shares plunging on the stock market.

By early 1984, every Latin American nation except Venezuela, Colombia and Paraguay had been forced into similar rescheduling deals. Cuba and Nicaragua also avoided such agreements, since Washington was imposing an effective financial boycott on both left-leaning governments. In every case the creditors stuck together, but insisted on negotiating with each debtor nation separately. Rescheduling was good business for the banks, since they could exact particularly high interest rates in exchange for deferring repayments. In return for rescheduling US$49.5 billion in loans, the banks earned an extra US$1.7 billion. At the same time, they ended virtually all new lending to Latin American nations, other than that needed to enable them to keep up with interest payments on the original loans.

The immediate cause of the debt crisis was the sudden rise in US interest rates announced by newly-elected President Reagan in 1981. Since Latin America's debts had been largely contracted at floating interest rates, this meant a massive increase in its interest payments. Each time the international interest rate rose by one per cent, it added nearly US$2 billion a year to the developing countries' bills. At the same time the austerity policies of 'Reaganomics' and the second OPEC price rise of 1979 produced a sharp recession in the industrialised nations which cut demand for Latin America's manufactured exports and sent commodity prices tumbling. Latin America earned less hard currency for its exports, just as it needed to pay more interest on its debt.

For Sir William Ryrie, a top World Bank official, the debt crisis was 'a blessing in disguise'. It forced Latin America into a constant round of debt negotiations, providing the Reagan government, along with the International Monetary Fund (IMF) and the other international financial institutions controlled by the wealthy industrialised countries, with all the leverage they needed to overhaul the region's economy, in alliance with northern commercial creditor banks and the region's home-grown free-marketeers. The state-led model was discredited, monetarism was in the ascendant with champions in the White House and 10 Downing Street—Latin America was ripe for a free market revolution.

Since then, almost all of Latin America and the Caribbean has followed a similar path. In the initial stage of reform, known as 'stabilisation', the IMF and banks pressured governments both to crack down on inflation by cutting spending, and to keep up their debt repayments by cutting their imports and generating a trade surplus. At the same time, commercial banks decided Latin America had become a bad risk, and stopped lending. Throughout the 1980s, capital flowed out of Latin America, destined for the rich countries of the north. This perverse flow of wealth from the poor to the wealthy squeezed out US$218.6 billion, over US$500 for every man, woman and child in the region.

With time, reforms have moved on to a broader process known as 'structural adjustment', involving a relentless assault on the state's role in the economy, including cuts in social spending, privatisation, and deregulation of everything from trade to banking to employers' abilities to hire and fire at will. The aim of such measures is to move Latin America and the Caribbean rapidly to a dynamic market-based economy, but up to now, the panorama has largely been one of recession and austerity.

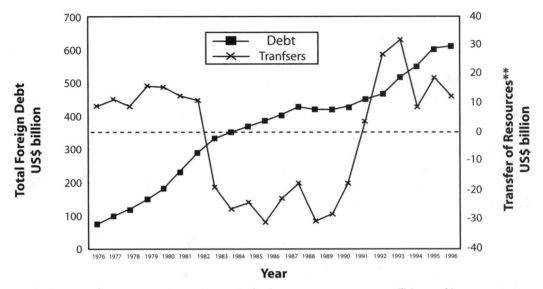

*Preliminary figures ** Net incoming capital minus net payments on utilities and interest

Figure 1 Total Foreign Debt and Capital Flows To and From Latin America and the Caribbean, 1975–96
Source: UN Economic Commission for Latin America and the Caribbean

Silent Revolution

The slump in Latin America's economy which followed the Mexican collapse contributed to one war and several bloody 'IMF riots'. Argentina's military leaders invaded the Falklands/Malvinas islands to divert attention from a collapsing economy, while riots, protests and looting afflicted cities across the continent. Prior to the 1980s, Latin Americans were accustomed to a growing economy. In every year between 1964 and 1980, the regional economy grew by more than four per cent, making the recession that hit in 1982 all the more painful. In 1982 Latin America's economy shrank in real terms for the first time since the Second World War. Chile was the worst hit, with per capita GDP falling by 14.5 per cent in a single year. The despair of Chile's unemployed workforce was captured in the lyrics of one of its top rock bands in the late 1980s, *Los Prisioneros*

> They're idle, waiting for the hands
> that decide to make them run again
> The mist surrounds and rusts them . . . .

> I drag myself along the damp cement,
> remembering a thousand laments.
> Of when the misery came, when they said
> don't come back, don't come back, don't come back
> The factories, all the factories have gone.

The cause of the collapse was the austerity programmes implemented under IMF pressure to keep debt repayments flowing. The extraction of wealth from the region left a large hole in the economy, in the form of an investment collapse. Governments forced to adopt IMF austerity measures found it less politically costly to cut public investment than to sack employees in the middle of a recession, (although many did that as well), while the private sector was deterred from investing both by the impossibility of borrowing abroad and the recession and high interest rates at home, as governments lifted interest rates to fight inflation. Foreign investors also took fright. Across the region, gross domestic investment (which includes both local and foreign investment) collapsed from US$213 billion in 1980 to just US$136 billion in 1983. The level of investment is crucial to any economy's prospects; Latin America was mortgaging its people's future to pay its debts.

Falling investment and the domestic recession brought about by austerity programmes provoked an industrial collapse. By 1983, the degree of industrial development in Latin America had regressed to the levels of 1966. In Argentina and Peru it was back to 1960 levels, while in Chile and Uruguay it was more like 1950.

The 1980s was a period of recession and false starts, as governments desperately sought a way out of the debt crisis and continued to send billions of dollars to overseas creditors. By 1991, the capital tide had turned. Although debt repayments continued, foreign investors rediscovered the region, and started pouring money in again. Partly, they did so because pickings were thin elsewhere, partly they were lured in by the latest component of Latin America's structural adjustment programme: from the late 1980s, governments have been privatising the state assets built up over fifty years of import substitution.

The pressures on governments to privatise seem irresistible. The growing fiscal crisis of the state sector, provoked by both foreign and domestic debt payments, has forced governments to increase revenue or cut expenditure; privatisation achieves both, shedding loss-making companies while raising substantial amounts of cash. In Argentina, President Carlos Menem's selling spree raised US$9.8 billion in cash, and enabled the government to lop a further US$15.6 billion off its foreign debt between 1989 and 1993 as multinational corporations bought up debt paper and swapped it for a stake in the newly privatised companies (a process known as 'debt for equity swaps'). In Mexico, the family silver raised a total of US$13.7 billion in 1990–91, during which time privatisation receipts provided just under a tenth of government revenues.

Privatisation is also part of a broader ideological shift, since neoliberals believe in cutting back the state and passing ever-larger chunks of the economy over to the private sector. Once privatised, they argue, management will be able to take decisions based on economic efficiency rather than politics and a company's performance is bound to improve. The rhetoric employed is the same as in Mrs. Thatcher's Britain, the only country to surpass the large Latin American economies in its privatising zeal. In Latin America, privatisation provides a juicy carrot with which to attract foreign investment back into the region after the capital famine of the debt crisis. Multinational corporations are expected to introduce capital and new technology into a region starved of both.

State airlines and telecommunications companies have gone on the block throughout the region, but so far only Argentina and Bolivia have allowed the rush to market to sweep away their state oil companies. Elsewhere, governments have been reluctant to hand over such strategic or highly profitable companies, preferring instead to encourage joint ventures with multinational corporations to attract technology and investment while retaining some degree of overall control. The track record of privatisations has varied enormously. Areas which urgently required injections of capital and cutting-edge technology, such as telecommunications, have clearly benefited, but critics of the privatisation process argue that governments have missed the chance to divide up giant companies and introduce competition, and have been lax in regulating the newly-privatised companies. Privatisation programmes are, however, extremely good news for the local business class with the capital (often through joint ventures with foreign companies) to snap up the bargains. Mexico's stock of billionaires rose from 2 to 24 during the privatising presidency of Carlos Salinas de Gortari (1988–94), all of them with close ties to the ruling Institutional Revolutionary Party (PRI). In another echo of the British experience, Chile's pioneering privatisers in the 1970s operated a highly questionable revolving door system, moving from government posts in which they oversaw the privatisations to top jobs in the big conglomerates who cashed in on the sell-offs.

In Mexico and Argentina, the sudden inflows of dollars produced a shortlived rerun of the 'dance of the millions', as governments abandoned austerity in favour of reducing inflation by using the exchange rate. Overvalued currencies made imports artificially cheap, keeping prices down at home. Not surprisingly, imports boomed, but governments were able to use the incoming capital, as long as it lasted, to cover the resulting trade gap. It lasted until 1994, when a series of political crises, including the Zapatista uprising in Chiapas and the assassination of the PRI's anointed successor to Carlos Salinas, made foreign investors reassess Mexican risk. Capital flows to Mexico fell away, producing a run on the peso, a devaluation, and a devastating recession, costing two million jobs over the course of 1995. In the so-called 'tequila effect', foreign investors also pulled out of Argentina which was pursuing a similar policy to that of Mexico, provoking massive recession and unemployment there during 1995. By 1997, capital inflows had still not recovered their pre-tequila levels, and for the time being, governments had little option but to return to the 1980s-style, more painful form of adjustment.

By disposing of loss-making companies and pulling in one-off windfalls, the privatisation bonanza has played a crucial part in curbing governments' spending deficits and getting inflation down in many Latin American countries in the early 1990s. Inflation in the region as a whole peaked at around 1,200 per cent in 1989 and 1990. Since then, privatisations, further government cutbacks in spending and investment and improved tax collection have all helped to get fiscal deficits down, reducing inflation to a regional average of 19 per cent in 1996.

Trade

Under the new neoliberal regime, countries are encouraged to trade on the basis of their 'comparative advantage'—economic jargon for sticking to what you are good at. In the case of Latin America, this means raw materials and cheap labour. In a return to the course of development followed since the conquest, Latin America has gone back to exporting commodities, both traditional products such a minerals and oil, and a whole range of new, non-traditional exports, covering everything from cut flowers to fresh salmon. The other side of the export drive is an attempt to increase the exports of manufactured goods, usually low-tech products such as shoes or textiles, or the output of assembly plants, such as the *maquiladoras* strung along the US-Mexican border, where imported components are assembled by cheap Latin American labour. By 1997, these were employing close to a million people in Mexico, and many more factories were dotted around Central America and the Caribbean.

Although exports have boomed in the 1990s, Latin America's attempt to get in on the ground floor of the global economy as a purveyor of raw materials risks confining it to one of the most sluggish areas of world trade, continuing its traditional reliance on the fickle prices of the commodity markets. The recovery in its exports has been matched by a flood of imports, following blanket trade liberalisation, bankrupting potentially competitive local producers and raising fears that the 'opening' has undermined the region's industrial future. Furthermore, the boom in non-traditional exports has been achieved at a high social cost, exacerbating inequality and undermining the region's food security, while both assembly plants and pesticide-intensive agriculture have damaged the environment.

Regional Integration

The region's shift away from import substitution towards the merits of 'export-led growth' has also seen a renewed interest in free trade agreements. Within Latin America dozens of bilateral and multilateral agreements have been signed since the late 1980s, the largest being the Southern Cone Common Market (Mercosur). Mercosur, which came into operation in 1995, brings together Argentina, Brazil, Uruguay and Paraguay.

The best-known free trade agreement in the region is the North American Free Trade Agreement, NAFTA, between Mexico, the US and Canada, which came into force in 1994. Over a period of 15 years, NAFTA will phase out all trade tariffs and restrictions on foreign investment between the three countries. Its many critics argue that it is little more than a 'charter of corporate rights', working to the benefit of large corporations, at the expense of the poor. Big companies in the US can relocate to Mexico in order to cut wages, thereby increasing unemployment in the US; although some Mexicans will find jobs in the new factories, far more will suffer the impact of ending tariffs on imported maize, which is produced on commercial US farms at a fraction of the cost of Mexican-grown maize. By the Mexican government's own admission, over a million Mexican farmers and their families will be put out of business by the flood of cheap imports.

Those hoping to extend NAFTA to the rest of the region received a boost in December 1994, when President Clinton went to Miami to host the 'Summit of the Americas' with every Latin American head of state bar Fidel Castro. The summit agreed to establish a 'Free Trade Area of the Americas' by the year 2006. However, two years later, domestic opposition to further free trade agreements within the US has effectively stalled progress. Into the vacuum has stepped Brazil, which is keen to expand Mercosur into a Latin American counterweight to US economic might in the hemisphere. Mercosur has already added Chile to its ranks (after Chile was rebuffed by NAFTA) and is currently negotiating free trade agreements with Bolivia and Venezuela.

Soft Fruit, Hard Labour

Orchards fill the Aconcagua valley north-east of Santiago de Chile. Parallel rows of peach trees stretch off to infinity, playing tricks with the eye. The monotony is punctuated by the occasional fat-trunked palm tree or weeping willow, shining with new leaf on a cold and dusty spring day.

Carlos Vidal is a union leader, president of the local *temporeros,* the temporary farm labourers who plant, pick and pack the peaches, kiwi fruit and grapes for the tables of Europe, Asia and North America. A shock of black curls streaked with grey fringe his round, gap-toothed face. A freezing wind off the nearby Andes blows across the vineyards as Carlos tells his story.

'On this land there were 48 families who got land under [former President] Allende. We grew vegetables, maize and beans together, as an *asentamiento* [farming co-operative]. There were a few fruit farms then, but we planned them. After the coup the land was divided up between 38 families—the others had to leave. Then it started to get difficult, we got the land but nothing else—the military auctioned off the machinery.

Then the *empresarios* started to arrive, especially an Argentine guy called Melton Moreno. The bank started taking people's land—foreclosing on loans—and Moreno bought it up. Three *compañeros* committed suicide here because they lost their farms. Melitón got bank loans and bought yet more land and machinery. He planted nothing but fruit—grapes at first, then others.

My father was a leader of the asentamiento. The first year after the coup we were hungry, lunch was a sad time. We began to sell everything in the house, then we looked for a *patrón* to sell us seeds and plough our land for us, and we paid him with part of the harvest. Next year we got a bank loan and managed to pay it off, but the following year they sold us bad seed. We lost all the maize and the whole thing collapsed. We had to sell the land and Melitón Moreno bought it.

Of the 38 families, most are now temporeros. We all sold our land but kept our houses and a small garden to grow food. Trouble is, even the gardens are no good, the water's full of pesticides from the fruit. This area used to be famous for water melons and now they don't grow properly any more. They chuck fertiliser and pesticide everywhere, it doesn't matterthat the earth is dead because the fruit trees live artificially. No one grows potatoes or maize any more—it's cheaper to buy the imported ones from Argentina.'

Duncan Green, *Silent Revolution: The Rise of Market Economics in Latin America*, London 1995

The Lost Decade

The Third World War has already started—a silent war, not for that reason any the less sinister. This war is tearing down Brazil, Latin America and practically all the Third World. Instead of soldiers dying there are children, instead of millions of wounded there are millions of unemployed; instead of destruction of bridges there is the tearing down of factories, schools, hospitals, and entire economies.
Luís Inácio da Silva (Lula), Brazilian labour leader, 1985

Such a profound economic transformation has only been achieved at enormous social cost. Throughout the region, after decades in which the percentage of Latin Americans living in poverty had been falling (though not their actual number), poverty is once again on the rise. By the end of the 1980s, sixty million new names had joined the grim rollcall of the poor, leaving 46 per cent of the population, nearly 200 million people, living in poverty. Almost half of them were indigent, barely existing on an income of less than a dollar a day. As the poor got poorer, the rich got richer, especially the very rich: according to *Forbes* magazine, the number of Latin American billionaires rose from six in 1987 to 42 in 1994.

The problem of rising poverty in Latin America is one of political will, not resources—there *is* enough money to go round. Latin American inequality is on such a scale that a comparatively minor move towards a fairer distribution of income could eradicate poverty overnight. According to the World Bank's 1990 *World Development Report*, 'Raising all the poor in the continent to just above the poverty line would cost only 0.7 per cent of regional GDP—the approximate equivalent of a 2 per cent income tax on the wealthiest fifth of the population.'

Structural adjustment programmes have exacerbated poverty and inequality in numerous ways. According to the UN, the main cause of increasing poverty and inequality has been the 'massive decline in real wages, . . . the rise in unemployment and . . . the number of people employed in very low-productivity jobs.' State cutbacks, recession and unemployment have all combined to suppress wages, as have adjustment policies to 'flexibilise' the labour market. In practice, this has meant cracking down on trade unions and making it easier for managers to hire and fire employees, shift to part-time work and to cut costs by subcontracting work to smaller companies, often little more than sweatshops. By the early 1990s, 23 per cent of wage-earners in the manufacturing sector were living below the poverty line, whereas before the debt crisis a job in a factory virtually guaranteed a pay packet big enough to keep a family out of poverty.

Although curbing inflation has undoubtedly improved the quality of life of the poor, adjustment policies have also exacerbated poverty by removing food subsidies and other price controls. The combined impact of changes to prices and the labour market under adjustment has shifted poverty away from the rural to urban areas. From 1980 to 1990 the number of poor Latin Americans in rural areas increased from 73 million to 80 million, but was overtaken for the first time by the battalions of the urban poor, which jumped from 63 million people to 116 million.

Women have borne the brunt of adjustment. Many of the new, low-waged or part-time jobs generated by adjustment go to women, while many men have lost their role as family breadwinner as full-time waged jobs disappear, or wages fall so far that a single income becomes insufficient to feed a family. On top of this 'double day' of work and running the home, the deterioration of social services, especially in urban areas, has forced women into a third role, taking responsibility for running their communities, fighting or substituting for inadequate state services in schools, health, drainage, water supply, or roads.

Adjustment has made all these tasks more vital to the family's survival and more exhausting: 'flexibilisation' often means lower wages, longer hours and greater insecurity, just as cuts in state subsidies have brought steep price rises in basics like food and public transport. One study of women in a shanty town in Guayaquil, Ecuador gives a graphic picture of the impact of adjustment on women. The research found that the women were affected differently by adjustment. About thirty per cent of the women were coping, juggling the competing demands of their three roles in the workplace, home and community. They were more likely to be in stable relationships with partners who had steady jobs. Another group, about 15 per cent of the women, were simply 'burnt out', no longer able to be superwomen 24 hours a day. They were most likely to be single mothers or the main breadwinners and were often older women, physically and mentally exhausted after the effort of bringing up a family against such heavy odds. They tried to hand over all household responsibilities to their oldest daughter, while their younger children frequently dropped out of school and roamed the streets. The remaining 55 per cent were described as simply 'hanging on', sacrificing their families by sending sons out to work or keeping daughters home from school to help with the housework. If nothing is done to change the impact of adjustment policies, many of these women will also 'burn out', swelling the number of families broken by the impact of Latin America's silent revolution.

Latin America is still searching for a development model which benefits all its people. Import substitution failed because it produced uncompetitive industries and an ineffectual and corrupt state bureaucracy while aggravating social inequality. Now Latin America's renewed infatuation with the market is needlessly destroying local industry and ratcheting up inequality still further, although admittedly it has got inflation under control, and produced a return to fitful growth. Across the region, the search is on for a new, more genuinely Latin American economic model of development which can combine the elusive goals of growth and economic equity. But the search is taking place under heavy constraints, not least because the flawed neoliberal model has such powerful allies—the United States, the IMF, the World Bank and the World Trade Organisation, in alliance with foreign investors and the global money markets will all resist any move away from neoliberal orthodoxy. For the foreseeable future, Latin America seems destined to sink or swim in a Darwinian free-market world order.

PART III

Global Issues

The Emerging World Economy

Commodity Chains and Marketing Strategies: Nike and the Global Athletic Footwear Industry

Miguel Korzeniewicz

The world-economic trends and cycles of the past two decades have made it increasingly apparent that the production and distribution of goods take place in complex global networks that tie together groups, organizations, and regions. The concept of commodity chains is helpful in mapping these emerging forms of capitalist organization. Most often, analysts depict global commodity chains (GCCs) by focusing primarily on production processes and their immediate backward and forward linkages. Less attention has been paid to the crucial role played by the design, distribution, and marketing nodes within a GCC. These nodes are important because they often constitute the epicenter of innovative strategies that allow enterprises to capture greater shares of wealth within a chain. Furthermore, a GCC perspective helps us understand how marketing and consumption patterns in core areas of the world shape production patterns in peripheral and semiperipheral countries. Thus an analysis of the design, distribution, and marketing segments within a commodity chain can provide unique insights into the processes through which core-like activities are created, and competitive pressures are transferred elsewhere in the world-economy.

To provide such an analysis, this chapter focuses on the distribution segment of a particular commodity chain: athletic footwear. In particular, this chapter examines the marketing strategy of one corporation within the global athletic shoe industry (Nike) to refine our understanding of the dynamic nature of global commodity chains. The example of athletic footwear is useful in exploring how commodity chains are embedded in cultural trends. The social organization of advertising, fashion, and consumption shapes the networks and nodes of global commodity chains. The athletic footwear case shows that the organization of culture itself is an innovative process that unevenly shapes patterns of production and consumption in core, semiperipheral, and peripheral areas of the world-economy.

The first section of the chapter highlights the phenomenal growth of the athletic shoe industry, and its economic and cultural importance in our society. Athletic footwear has experienced explosive growth over the past two decades. The meteoric popularity and success of athletic shoes as a consumer good is explained by a complex interaction of cultural and organizational innovations. The analysis of these innovations within a commodity chain's framework can help produce a more refined theoretical understanding of the relationship between economics and culture.

The second section examines the historical trajectory and organizational strategies of Nike Corporation. Nike provides a particularly clear example of how successful growth strategies by core enterprises generally entail constant upgrading, or a shift within the commodity chain toward control over more sophisticated and value-added service activities. This process of upgrading or innovation can best be appreciated by examining three periods that reflect different environmental constraints and response strategies on the part of Nike Corporation. This section examines each of these periods.

Trends in the US Athletic Shoe Market

The athletic footwear market in the United States has been characterized over the past two decades by phenomenal rates of growth. As indicated by Table 1 and Figure 1, wholesale revenues of athletic shoes in the United States it tripled between 1980 and 1990. In the past six years, consumers in the United States more than doubled their expenditures on athletic shoes: In 1985 they spent $5 billion and bought 250 million pairs of shoes, whereas by the end of 1991 retail sales totaled $12 billion for nearly 400 million pairs of shoes. Three-fourths of all Americans bought athletic shoes in 1991, compared with two-thirds in 1988. In 1990, athletic shoes accounted for about a third of all shoes sold. The athletic footwear industry today generates $12 billion in retail sales, with at least twenty-five companies earning $20 million or more in annual sales. From the point of

TABLE 1 Wholesale revenues in the US athletic footwear market, 1981–1990 (in millions of US dollars)

	All firms	*Nike*	*Reebok*
1981	1,785	458	1
1982	1,900	694	4
1983	2,189	867	13
1984	2,381	920	66
1985	2,989	946	307
1986	3,128	1,069	919
1987	3,524	877	1,389
1988	3,772	1,203	1,785
1989	5,763	1,711	1,822
1990	6,437	2,235	2,159

Source: NSGA, 1990.

view of Schumpeterian innovations, the trajectory of the athletic footwear commodity chain over recent times provides valuable insights into the creation of a modern consumer market.

Retail markets for athletic shoes are highly segmented according to consumer age groups. Teenagers are the most important consumers of athletic shoes. A study sponsored by the Athletic Footwear Association found that the average American over twelve years of age owns at least two pairs of athletic shoes, worn for both athletic and casual purposes. As experienced by many parents and youngsters during the 1980s and 1990s, athletic shoes have been constructed and often promoted among teenagers as an important and visible symbol of social status and identity.

The products in this commodity chain also are highly differentiated according to models and the particular sport for which they are purportedly designed. By 1989, Nike was producing shoes in 24 footwear categories, encompassing 300 models and 900 styles. Reebok sold 175 models of shoes in 450 colors, and planned to add 250 new designs. Adidas and LA Gear sell 500 different styles each. The two fastest-growing segments of athletic shoes in the late 1980s were basketball shoes and walking shoes, while the volume of sales for tennis and running shoes declined. In 1991, basketball shoes accounted for 22 percent of sales, and cross

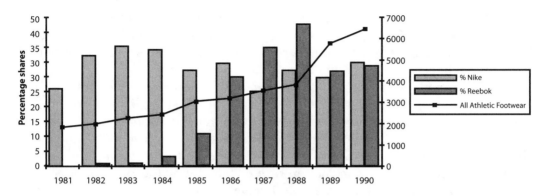

Figure 1. Total wholesale revenues of athletic footwear and Nike's and Reebok's shares, 1981–90
Source: NSGA

trainers for 14 percent of sales. Product differentiation provides an important vehicle both for competition among enterprises and price stratification.

Finally, the sports footwear market is highly segmented according to price. Indicative of this segmentation, the price distribution of athletic shoes has a very wide range. In 1989 the average cost of basketball, walking, and running shoes was between $40 and $47, while top-of-the-line shoes cost about $175. The bulk of production is oriented toward sales of the lower priced shoes, while the market for the higher-priced commodities is substantially smaller. In 1990, more than 80 percent of athletic shoe purchases were priced under $35, with only 1.4 percent of shoes bought costing more than $65. Price rather than appearance or functionality often constitutes the primary matrix differentiating athletic shoes as status symbols.

Since displacing Adidas in the early 1980s, and after falling behind Reebok in the mid-1980s (see Table 1), Nike Corporation has become the largest and most important athletic shoe company in the United States. Nike's sales have grown from $2 million in 1972 to $270 million in 1980, and to over $3 billion in 1991. Reebok, the number two brand in the United States today, experienced similar rates of growth—in fact, Reebok has been the fastest-growing company in the history of American business. Between 1981 and 1987, Reebok's sales grew from $1.5 million to $1.4 billion, experiencing an average annual growth rate of 155 percent. Similarly, LA Gear grew at a dazzling rate, from $11 million in 1985 to $535 million in 1989. Between 1985 and 1990, Nike's share of the athletic footwear marker in the United States declined from 30 to 25 percent, Reebok's rose from 14 to 24 percent; LA Gear's increased from a minimal share to 11 percent, and

Converse's share declined from 9 to 5 percent. These data suggest that a limited number of large firms compete within the athletic footwear market in the United States, but also that the organization of the market provides considerable permeability for successful entry and competition by new enterprises.

What are the factors that explain the enormous growth of the athletic shoe industry? The evidence suggests, in part, that the most important enterprises within this commodity chain have grown by increasing their control over the nodes involved in the material production of athletic shoes. The most fundamental innovation of these enterprises, however, has been the *creation* of a market, and this has entailed the construction of a convincing world of symbols, ideas, and values harnessing the desires of individuals to the consumption of athletic shoes. By focusing on the marketing and circulation nodes of a commodity chain, greater analytical precision can be gained in identifying the crucial features of these innovations.

Rather than analyzing the athletic footwear chain as a whole, the next section focuses on a single enterprise, Nike Corporation. Although a comparative analysis of other enterprises would yield greater insights into possible differences in organizational trajectories, the focus on a single firm allows a more detailed exploration of the innovative strategies that have characterized the athletic footwear commodity chain. This approach also highlights the relevance of world-systems theory, and the concept of commodity chains, to the study of economic and social processes at a microlevel of observation. Nike's rise to prominence has been based on its ability to capture a succession of nodes along the commodity chain, increasing its expertise and control over the critical areas of design, distribution, marketing, and advertising. This strategy also involved a fundamental reshaping of production and consumption, hence contributing to the recent transformation of the athletic footwear commodity chain.

Nike Corporation: Competition, Upgrading and Innovation in a Commodity Chain

The activities of Nike Corporation created a quintessential American product that has captured a large share of the giant US athletic footwear market. Nike Corporation increased its revenues tenfold in the past ten years, from $270 million in 1980 to an estimated $3 billion in 1991. Nike sells tens of millions of athletic shoes in the United States every year, yet all of the firm's manufacturing operations are conducted overseas, making the company an archetype of a global sourcing strategy. Nike Corporation never relocated domestic production abroad, as many American companies have done, because the firm actually originated by importing shoes from Japan. It has subcontracted nearly all of its production overseas ever since: currently, "all but 1 percent of the millions of shoes Nike makes each year are manufactured in Asia." In the United States, Nike has developed essentially as a design, distribution, and marketing enterprise.

Nike's successful implementation of its overseas sourcing strategy can best be understood as part of the firm's effort to retain control over highly profitable nodes in the athletic footwear commodity chain, while avoiding the rigidity and pressures that characterize the more competitive nodes of the chain. "We don't know the first thing about manufacturing," says Neal Lauridsen, Nike's vice-president for Asia-Pacific. "We are marketers and designers." Nike's practice of overseas sourcing provides strategic and geographical mobility to the firm by developing a complex division of labor among the components of a global subcontracting network. The way these characteristics are linked to consumer demand and marketing strategies helps explain the tremendous growth and success of Nike.

Imports and Distribution as a Competitive Strategy (1962–1975)

Nike Corporation originated in an enterprise called Blue Ribbon Sports. A founding member of the company was Philip Knight, who visited Japan in 1962 and claimed to represent an American distribution network for shoes that didn't really exist. In Japan, Philip Knight contacted the Onitsuka Company, manufacturers of a brand of athletic shoes (Tiger) whose image had been enhanced by the 1964 Tokyo Olympics. The timing of Knight's travel to Japan was fortunate because executives at the Onitsuka Company were beginning to realize the enormous potential of the US market. After preliminary contacts, and upon returning to the United States, Phil Knight and Bill Bowerman (an Oregon track and field coach) contributed $500 each to start a new enterprise, the Blue Ribbon Sports Company (BRS). In February of 1964, Phil Knight placed his first order for BRS, totaling $1,107, and a few months later they sold their first pairs of Tiger shoes at a state high-school track meet. By the end of 1967, the total revenues of Blue Ribbon Sports were $300,000. The company successfully developed a competitive market niche by targeting a small market of dedicated athletes, runners, and sports enthusiasts.

Tiger's marketing advantage in this early stage was based first and foremost on price competitiveness. The retail price of the very first shipment of Tiger shoes sold was $9.95, a few dollars below the price of the shoes made by Adidas. Later, when BRS began to market Nike shoes, the company's target once again was to undercut their main competitors (Adidas and now Tiger) by a few dollars. The distribution network of these early years centered mostly on a few BRS outlet stores and a painstakingly constructed network of contacts with independent spotting goods retailers. Shoes were promoted primarily at track meets and marathons through word of mouth and very elementary forms of athletic endorsements.

Through the 1960s and early 1970s, Blue Ribbon Sports remained a distribution company in charge of importing and distributing Tiger shoes. During the first few years of the partnership between Onitsuka company and BRS, the Japanese firm clearly held the upper hand because it was able to negotiate and bargain among several athletic footwear distributors in the United States. Trying to enhance its own bargaining position, BRS struggled to attain a contract granting it exclusive tights to distribute Tiger shoes in thirteen western states. Over time, a successful distribution strategy allowed BRS to enhance its leverage, and in 1966 Onitsuka Company granted BRS exclusive rights for the distribution of Tiger's shoes in the United States. Already in this partnership, BRS began to contribute design and performance innovations to Tiger's basic models. Within this arrangement, BRS remained vulnerable because of its financial dependence on Onitsuka Company. But until the late 1960s, the partnership worked as originally conceived: Onitsuka Company manufactured and delivered Tiger shoes, and BRS distributed them in the United States.

By 1968, as the market for athletic shoes underwent rapid growth, strains began to develop in the partnership between BRS and Onitsuka Company. Each of the two firms sought to enhance its share of profits by affirming greater control over new nodes in the commodity chain. Seeking to exploit new market opportunities, Onitsuka Company expanded its volume of shoe production, and apparently began to explore alternative distribution networks. BRS, doubting Onitsuka's commitment to maintaining exclusive arrangements, began identifying alternative supply sources. For this latter purpose, Phil Knight enlisted the services of Nissho Iwai, one of the largest Japanese trading companies, which offered to finance shipments of shoes for a 2 percent commission. Eventually Nissho Iwai became the importer of record, receiving a commission on all shipments, and BRS enjoyed financial backing. As tensions between Onitsuka and BRS simmered, the former attempted to take over BRS in 1971 by extending an ultimatum proposal that would in effect give Onitsuka control over SI percent of the company.

In 1971 Knight went to Japan and placed his first independent order for 20,000 shoes, which included 6,000 pairs with the Nike "swoosh" pattern. Eventually, BRS entered into a longstanding relationship with two Japanese shoe manufacturers: Nippon Rubber and Nihon-Koyo. in 1971, BRS split with Onitsuka. In 1972

Onitsuka decided to stop shipments of shoes to BRS after finding shoes with Nike brands in one of BRS's stockrooms. Soon thereafter, both parties began lawsuits against each other. Onitsuka Company sued BRS in Japan for breach of contract. BRS sued for breach of contract, unfair competition, trademark infringement, and violation of the antitrust Clayton Act. In July of 1975, Phil Knight agreed to receive an out-of-court settlement of $400,000 after Onitsuka finally succumbed to pressure from the Tiger distributors to settle. By making a decision to design its own logo and produce its own brand of shoes, Nike Corporation emerged out of this conflict with greater control *vis-á-vis* its overseas suppliers in Japan. Its corporate image was enhanced as well, so that by the end of the 1970s the Nike Corporation had superseded BRS.

During this initial period in the history of BRS/Nike, the company also began to delineate an innovative strategy regarding product design and promotion. Perhaps the one promotional idea that had the longest-lasting effect on the future of Nike Corporation was the choice of both the company's name (Nike is the name of the winged goddess of victory in Greek mythology) and the distinctive "swoosh" design on the side of the shoes. Although they later became promotional, the distinctive three stripes in the athletic shoes made by Adidas had primarily a functional purpose (additional bond between the upper and the sole). Nike's "swoosh," on the other hand, was designed solely on the basis of aesthetics. From that point on, anybody wearing Nike products was also advertising Nike shoes. Marketing and product design, in this sense, were closely related from the very beginning.

The Eugene, Oregon track and field Olympic trials in 1968 became the first major event where Nike developed its promotional efforts. Through its association with some of the best track and field athletes, who wore the company's newest models, Nike began to build a reputation as a new, specialized firm that focused on high-performance athletic shoes. The event convinced Nike that associating product promotion with athletes was a very effective form of advertising athletic shoes. For this reason, Blue Ribbon Sports initiated and maintained a program of subsidies for athletes and sponsorship of track meets throughout the 1970s. Later, Nike's strategy of associating its name with track and field athletes allowed the company's products to be viewed by consumers as associated with the development of first-class competitors for the 1980 Olympics, providing high visibility for Nike shoes.

Marketing as an Upgrading Strategy (1976–1984)

During this second period, Nike Corporation introduced major innovations in marketing, distribution, and subcontracting for the production of athletic footwear. First, between 1976 and 1984, Nike was shaped by (and helped to shape) the "fitness boom"—the phenomenal growth of jogging, running, and exercise as a common activity by millions of Americans. Nike was part of this phenomenon by implementing a marketing strategy that involved the development of a vast and visible network of endorsement contracts with basketball, baseball, and football players and coaches. Second, Nike's distribution network was enhanced by the establishment of a strategic alliance with Foot Locker, a rapidly growing chain of retail stores marketing athletic products. Finally, Nike Corporation sought to further enhance its control over subcontractors and lower production costs by shifting most manufacturing activities from Japan to South Korea and (to a lesser extent) Taiwan. Combined, these innovations provided a significant competitive edge to Nike Corporation.

Beginning in the mid-1970s, running, jogging, and exercise in general became part of mainstream American culture. Nike Corporation was in the right place at the right time to capitalize on this phenomenon by outperforming competing brands and becoming the most important athletic shoe company in the United States. But the ability to gain from this phenomenon required a major reorientation in the marketing of the company's products: Nike Corporation's main customer base had to shift, as one observer puts it, from "running geeks to yuppies." To achieve this shift, Nike's promotional efforts in the 1970s moved slowly but consistently away from amateur sports to professional sports, and from lesser-known track and field runners to highly visible sports figures. In 1977 and 1978 Nike developed a strategy to sign visible college basketball coaches; by 1979 it had signed over fifty college coaches. One measure of Nike's promotional success was the cover of *Sports Illustrated* of March 26, 1979, which showed Larry Bird (at the time a player in the NCAA tournament) wearing Nike shoes. In the late 1970s, Nike also began to promote heavily in baseball, and by 1980 a Nike representative had signed over fifty players in different baseball teams—as well as eight players in the Tampa Bay team that made it to the 1980 Super Bowl. This new marketing strategy enhanced Nike's image in its new market niche.

Nike's rise as the largest athletic shoe company in the United States also involved creating a more effective distribution network. Foot Locker, an emerging chain of sport equipment retailers, became the most important distributor of Nike shoes. As a way to solve inventory and financial bottlenecks, Nike people devised an advance-order purchase system they called "futures." The system required major distributors to commit themselves to large orders six months in advance, in return for a 5–7 percent discount and a guaranteed delivery schedule. Foot Locker was one of the first dealers to try the futures contracts, and to benefit from them, eventually becoming Nike's most important retailer. Another reason for Foot Locker's close relationship with Nike was the latter's flexibility, and its willingness to change design specifications on request from dealers. This responsiveness of Nike contrasted with Adidas' generally inflexible approach to their supply of shoes, and further extended the company's competitive edge.

Finally, the phenomenal growth in the demand for athletic shoes changed Nike's subcontracting patterns. Nike now needed larger outputs, lower labor prices, and more control over the manufacturing process. In 1974 the great bulk of BRS's $4.8 million in sales was still coming from Japan. Phil Knight, aware of rising labor costs in Japan, began to look for sourcing alternatives. One of these alternatives was the United States. In early 1974, BRS rented space in an empty old factory in Exeter, New Hampshire, and later opened a second factory in Saco, New Hampshire. Domestic facilities also fulfilled a critical R&D function that Nike would later use to gain greater control over production processes abroad. However, by 1984 imported shoes (mostly from Korea and Taiwan) rose to 72 percent of the US shoe market, and US-based factories were forced to close. The collapse of the US production base was due primarily to its limited manufacturing capacity and its economic implausibility. Product timelines lagged and American-based manufacturing found itself unable to compete with lower Asian labor costs.

While Nippon Rubber (Nike's Japanese supplier) reportedly made the decision to relocate part of its production to South Korea and Taiwan, Nike also began to look for new sources of its own. In October 1975, Phil Knight flew to Asia to search for alternative supply sources to lessen his dependency on both Nissho Iwai and Nippon Rubber without losing either company. In Japan, Knight met a Chinese trader who agreed to set up a Nike-controlled corporation called Athena Corporation that established production facilities in Taiwan. In South Korea the Sam Hwa factory of Pusan became the main partner, which began 1977 making 10,000 pairs of Nike shoes a month, and ending the year by making about 100,000 pairs a month. By 1980, nearly 90 percent of Nike's shoe production was located in Korea and Taiwan.

The consolidation of South Korea and Taiwan as the main geographical centers of manufacturing also involved the emergence of a complex system of stratification among Nike's Suppliers. Donaghu and Barff identify three main classes of factories supplying Nike: developed partners, volume producers, and developing sources. "Developed partners" are the upper tier of Nike suppliers, responsible for the most innovative and sophisticated shoes. "Volume producers" are those that manufacture a specific type of product in large quantities. These factories are typically less flexible than developed partners in their manufacturing organization. Finally, "developing sources" are the newer factories that attracted Nike because of their low labor costs, entering into a series of tutelary arrangements both with Nike and the more experienced Nike suppliers.

The geographical dynamism of Nike's shifts in subcontracting arrangements interacted with this complex stratification system in interesting ways. As labor costs in Japan rose in the 1970s, Nike Corporation shifted production to emerging semiperipheral countries such as South Korea and Taiwan. As labor costs in the established semiperipheral supply locations began to rise in the 1980s, Nike tried to shift some of the labor-intensive, technologically less advanced segments of its production to new locations in peripheral areas (such as China). It is interesting to note, however, that linkages with developed partners remained critical for two reasons. First, several of Nike's more sophisticated models required the expertise and flexibility of older, more reliable partners. Second, the technological expertise and capital of the older partners was often necessary to bring newer production facilities up to Nike standards, leading to joint ventures between the older, more established sources and the newer ones. From this point of view, centralization and decentralization of subcontracting arrangements were constrained by marketing requirements.

Design, Advertising, and the Return to the Semiperiphery (post–1985)

After 1985, Nike entered into another period of high growth, based on innovations in product design (the creation of the "Air Nike" models, which quickly became immensely popular) and advertising strategies (signing its most popular endorser, Michael Jordan). Also, Nike Corporation continued to target new market niches, entering the aerobics segment of the market, where Reebok had become increasingly dominant, and the growing and profitable athletic apparel markers. Finally, Nike Corporation altered its subcontracting arrangements, shifting important segments in the manufacture of Nike's athletic shoes to the People's Republic of China, Thailand, and Indonesia. However, the need for specialized and sophisticated production runs once again forced Nike to return to more experienced manufacturers in South Korea and Taiwan.

The ability to produce high-performance, sophisticated footwear models became critical to Nike because the company was able to pull out of its early 1980s stagnation through its "Nike Air" technological innovation. By 1984 the phenomenal growth of a mass market for jogging shoes began to stabilize, particularly in the men's segment of the market. Other companies, like Reebok and LA Gear, were becoming more effective in selling to the female and aerobics segments of the market. Nike Corporation, accustomed to years of high growth, was in crisis. Many endorsement contracts were canceled, the Athletics West program cut down its sponsored athletes from 88 to 50, and by the end of 1984, Nike had laid off 10 percent of its 4,000-person work force. Another indication of Nike's bad fortunes was its declining influence among sports coaches and agents. To reverse this decline, Nike Corporation once again turned toward introducing a drastic product innovation.

Nike's declining fortunes in the mid-1980s (see table 1) were reversed by the introduction of Air Nike (a new technology that allowed a type of gas to be compressed and stored within the sole) and by the phenomenal success of its "Air Jordan" line of basketball shoes, as well as the success of the endorser they were named after, Michael Jordan. In Nike's Los Angeles store, the first two shipments of Air Jordans sold out in three days. By 1985 it was clear that Air Jordan shoes were a huge success. Nike sold in three months what had been projected for the entire year. The first contract between Nike Corporation and Michael Jordan was worth $2.5 million over five years, and it included (among other things) a royalty to the athlete on all Air Jordan models sold by the company.

The several advertising campaigns featuring Michael Jordan highlight Nike's capacity to influence market demand for its shoes. Nike's video and print advertisements have been among the most innovative and controversial in recent years, adding to Nike's visibility and undoubtedly contributing to its phenomenal growth. Part of the appeal of Nike advertising is its success in tapping and communicating a consistent set of values that many people in the 1970s and 1980s identified with: hipness, irreverence, individualism, narcissism, self-improvement, gender equality, racial equality, competitiveness, and health.

But there also have been several allegations made that by targeting inner-city youths in its advertising and marketing campaigns, Nike has profited substantially from sales directly related to drug and gang money, showing little concern for the social and financial stability of the predominantly black, poor communities, where sales account for 20 percent of the total athletic footwear market. The relationship between the athletic footwear industry and drug money has become increasingly evident by the alarming rate of robberies and killings over expensive sports shoes. Some store owners claim that Nike is not only aware that drug money contributes heavily to its sales, but that Nike representatives adamantly encourage distributors in the inner cities to specifically target and cater to this market.

Nike commercials tend to be subtle. The trademark "swoosh" logo is often far more prominent than dialogue or a straightforward pitch. They are also controversial. Nike's use of the Beatles' song "Revolution" to advertise its new "Nike Air" was startling, and so has been its recent use of John Lennon's song "Instant Karma." Some of the most distinctive Nike advertisements contain themes that can best be described as postmodern: the rapid succession of images, image self-consciousness, and "ads-within-ads" themes. The "Heritage" Nike commercial, showing a white adult runner training in an urban downtown area while images of sports heroes are projected on the sides of buildings, is particularly striking because it seeks to identify the viewer with all idealized figure (the runner) who is in turn identifying with idealized figures (the sports heroes). This ninety-second advertisement cost over $800,000 to run once in its entirety during the 1991 Superbowl. Though there is no dialogue, the product is identifiable (it is seen almost subliminally several times), and the message of the commercial is clear. Postmodern theory, given its sensitivity to new cultural phenomena, can be helpful in understanding advertising as a crucial element in the athletic footwear global commodity chain. An understanding of consumption must be based on commodity aesthetics because consumption is increasingly the consumption of signs. Similarly, Featherstone has noted the increasing importance of the production of symbolic goods and images. In a sense, Nike represents an archetype of a firm selling to emerging postmodern consumer markers that rest on segmented, specialized, and dynamic features.

As in the previous periods, these drastic changes in marketing and distribution strategies were accompanied by shifts in the firm's subcontracting strategy. In 1980 Nike began a process of relocation to the periphery (particularly China, Indonesia, and Thailand) that most other companies would gradually follow in the course of the decade. This relocation was driven by cost advantages: "a mid-priced shoe made in South Korea which costs Nike US $20 when it leaves the docks of Pusan will only cost about US $15 to make in Indonesia or China." Nike Corporation was one of the very first companies to enter the People's Republic of China. In 1980, Phil Knight began to set up a manufacturing base in China. Soon an agreement between Nike Corporation and the Chinese government was finalized, and shoes began to be produced in the PRC. This rapid success can be explained by the fact that Nike used a Chinese-born representative (David Chang) who was thoroughly familiar with the local environment, which meant that proposals were quickly translated into Chinese and attuned to the negotiating style and objectives of the Chinese government. Also, Nike's objectives were long-term and the volumes of production being negotiated were significant, which coincided with the development priorities of the Chinese government at the time.

Just as Nike led the trend of entry into China, later in the mid-1980s it led a reevaluation of the benefits and disadvantages of associating directly with developing partners. By late 1984, production in Chinese factories totaled 150,000 pairs a month, one-seventh of the originally projected 1 million pairs a mouth. The early 1980s also signaled a slowdown in the rapid growth of conventional athletic footwear markets at a time when competition from other athletic footwear firms (LA Gear, Reebok) was increasing. By 1983 Nike terminated its subcontracting arrangement with the Shanghai factory, and in 1984 negotiated an early termination of its contract with the Tianjin factory.

In the mid-1980s Nike briefly considered shifting production back to established manufacturing sources in South Korea and Taiwan. The advantages of lower labor costs in the developing manufacturing areas had to be weighed against disadvantages in production flexibility, quality, raw material sourcing, and transportation. The development of a new shoe model from technical specifications to shoe production was four months in South Korea, compared to eight months in China. The ratio of perfect-quality (A-grade) shoes to aesthetically flawed, but structurally sound (B-grade) shoes was 99 : 1 in Korea, 98 : 2 in Taiwan, and 80 : 20 in China. While Taiwan and South Korea sourced 100 percent of the raw materials needed for production, China was only able to source 30 percent. Finally, shipping from Taiwan and South Korea was 20–25 days; from Shanghai it was 35–40 days.

The mid-1980s also marked the introduction of the "Nike Air" technology and especially the "Air Jordan" model. Being more sophisticated, secretive, and expensive, this model required more experienced and trustworthy suppliers of the "developed partners" type that had been developed in South Korea over the years. One Reebok executive argued that "as the complexity of our product increases, it continues to go to [South Korea]. The primary reason is that product development out of Korean factories is quick and accurate for athletic footwear, better than any place in the world." An observer concluded in the mid-1980s that after the trend of relocation to low-wage locations like Thailand, Indonesia, and China, "buyers are starting to return [to Pusan] after finding that the extra cost of doing business in South Korea is offset by reliability and the large capacity of its factories." This need for more established suppliers coincided with the adjustments that the Korean shoe producers themselves made in an effort to adapt to rising labor costs and the migration of many firms to other countries. Many Pusan firms shrunk in size but also increased the unit value of their production.

However, the relative importance of South Korean firms has continued to decline. Thus, "at least one-third of the lines in Pusan have shut down in the past three years. Only a handful of South Korean companies are expected to remain significant shoe exporters in a couple of years." Similar changes have affected shoe-producing firms in Taiwan, where "since 1988, the number of footwear companies has fallen from 1,245 to 745. Athletic shoe exports slipped from US$1.5 billion in 1988 to US$ 1 billion (in 1991)." Taiwanese and South Korean-based firms, on the other hand, are used for managing and mediating the relocation of production facilities to the periphery.

The shift of Nike's production to the periphery has become significant. "In the fiscal year to 31 May 1988, Nike bought 68 percent of its shoes from South Korea but only 42 percent in 1991–92. China, Indonesia and Thailand produced 44 percent of Nike's shoes last fiscal year; against less than 10 percent in 1987–88." This same trend is expected to continue in the future: "now, Vietnam looks like the next country on the list. Two major Taiwanese suppliers, Feng Tay and Adi Corporation, are interested in starring production in Vietnam if and when the U.S. trade embargo of its old adversary is lifted."

The advantages of Nike Corporation that have enabled it to become a powerful and profitable link in the athletic footwear commodity chain are the expertise of its designers in finding technological advances in shoe comfort and performance, the distribution networks built over the past twenty-five years, and the effectiveness of its marketing, promotion and advertising campaigns.

Overall Assessment

To summarize the arguments made in this section, Nike's development of its twin strategies of overseas subcontracting and domestic marketing can best be understood as involving three distinct periods, each corresponding to different patterns of market demand, geographical locus of production, and marketing strategies. In the first period, between 1962 and 1975, Nike Corporation emphasized control over the import and distribution nodes of its commodity chain. Between 1976 and 1984, Nike Corporation enhanced its relative competitive position by extending control no marketing, and by redesigning its subcontracting strategy to take advantage of new opportunities in Southeast Asia (in South Korea and Taiwan initially, later in China, Thailand, and Indonesia). Finally, beginning in the mid-1980s, Nike Corporation successfully extended control to product design and advertising, further upgrading the firm's organizational structure. As a whole, these three periods suggest that Nike Corporation has sustained and enhanced its competitive edge through the implementation of frequent innovations in the nodes and networks of its commodity chain.

Conclusions

This chapter has examined the organizational strategies of Nike Corporation within the global athletic shoe industry. Nike's uncommon success and growth is due in part to social and cultural trends that have made leisure and fitness more important in our contemporary society. It is also the outcome of Nike's strategy of responding to these trends by accumulating expertise and control over the increasingly important service nodes of the athletic footwear commodity chain: import, distribution, marketing, and advertising.

Nike Corporation (and the athletic footwear industry in general) are excellent case studies of how goods emerge from complex, transnational linkages at different stages of production and distribution. Nike Corporation was born a globalized company. The study confirms a division of labor between core or postindustrial societies (that will presumably specialize in services over time) and noncore societies at different levels of industrialization (that will increasingly specialize in manufacturing). While Korean and Chinese firms are producing the actual shoe, US-based Nike promotes the symbolic nature of the shoe and appropriates the greater share of the value resulting from its sales.

Nike and the athletic shoe industry show that there are emerging patterns of consumption that have enormous consequences for social and economic organization. Linkages between consumption and production must be explored in greater detail. While a consensus has been building for some time that there are new patterns in the organization of production (alternatively called flexible specialization, flexible production, or post-Fordist production), we also need a better understanding of what may be called "post-Fordist consumption"—that is, the emerging patterns of consumption and distribution that are the counterpart to transformations in the realm of production.

Women in Poverty
A New Global Underclass

Mayra Buvinić

To understand the plight of poor women around the world, consider the stories of Ade, Runa, and Reina. On the outskirts of Ibadan, Nigeria, Ade cultivates a small, sparsely planted plot with a baby on her back and other visibly under-nourished children nearby. Her efforts to grow an improved soybean variety, which could have improved her children's diet, failed because she lacked the extra time to tend the new crop, did not have a spouse who would help her, and could not afford hired labor. Runa, a young woman with boundless energy, piercing eyes, and a warm smile, founded and runs the Self-Employed Women's Association in the Indian city of Lucknow, one of the country's most disadvantaged regions. Until a year ago, she had been unable to obtain credit from local banks for her impressively well-organized business, which now employs about 5,000 women homeworkers who sell *chikan* embroidery in national and international markets. Reina is a former guerrilla fighter in El Salvador who is being taught how to bake bread under a post-civil war reconstruction program. But as she says, "The only thing I have is this training and I don't want to be just a baker. I have other dreams for my life."

A farmer, an entrepreneur, and a former guerrilla—the working lives of these three women have little in common, except that they, along with most women worldwide, face similar obstacles to increasing their economic power: no "slack" time to invest in additional work that could bring in needed income; lack of access to commercial credit; and training in traditionally female—and mostly low-wage—skills. These obstacles differentiate the work experiences of men and women, exacerbate women's poverty, and sustain a vicious cycle of impoverishment from one generation to the next.

They also help to account for a disturbing global trend: the "feminization" of poverty. When the yardstick used to measure the degree of people's poverty is their level of well-being, women are traditionally found to be more impoverished than men. But poverty is more commonly defined according to income, and today, although the gap between the two sexes is decreasing in terms of well-being, it is increasing in terms of income. The evidence is imperfect, but current trends suggest that women account for a growing proportion of those people who are considered poor on the basis of income, not only in industrial countries such as the United States, but also in the developing world.

Poor Women, Poor World

This feminization of poverty should be considered a legitimate foreign policy concern. Because women are increasingly economic actors and heads of households as well as mothers, their poverty slows global economic growth. Moreover, in poor countries, their disadvantage feeds a destructive spiral of poverty, population growth, and environmental degradation. In a world of blurring borders, women's poverty creates enclaves of want in the midst of wealth and puts rising pressures on the developed world, whether by fueling costly humanitarian crises or by unleashing—for the first time—waves of females who migrate without spouses to seek work in richer countries.

The United States and other industrial countries have much to gain by reducing the impoverishment of women in developing countries. Not only can there be no substantial easing of world poverty until the international community focuses on female well-being as a goal and widens women's economic opportunities, but in this age of shrinking foreign aid budgets, investing in women offers policymakers the highest economic and social returns at the lowest cost.

Poverty has many dimensions and is difficult to measure. Calculated in dollars and cents, it is inadequacy of income. But measured in terms of the human condition, it is inadequacy of health and nutrition, education, and other components of well-being, including leisure time.

There is broad evidence that women in developing countries seem to bear the brunt of this latter type of "capability-based" poverty. In 1996, the United Nations Development Programme (UNDP) introduced a new index in their annual *Human Development Report* that reflects the percentage of people who lack three basic, or minimally essential, capabilities: to be well nourished and healthy (measured by the proportion of children under five who are underweight); to reproduce healthily (assessed by the proportion of births unattended by trained

TABLE 1   Four Key Indicators of Women's Quality of Life

Region	Life Expectancy[a] (years)		Fertility[b] (births per woman)		Girls Enrolled in Primary School[c] (percent)		Women Aged 15–44 Using Modern Contraception (percent)	
	1970	1990	1970	1990	1970	1990	1970	1990
Arab States	57	65	6.1	4.7	46	92	29	52
East Asia	65	72	4.4	2.2	95[d]	113[d]	69	81
Latin America and the Caribbean	64	70	5.0	3.2	89	103	39	52
OECD	75	79	2.1	1.8	104	102	68	73
South Asia	49	57	5.8	4.5	53	75	30	39
Southeast Asia and Oceania	54	63	5.3	3.6	—	—	33	51
Sub-Saharan Africa	47	52	6.7	6.5	36	67	14	19

[a]Regional average weighted by each country's total female population.

[b]Regional average weighted by each country's total female population aged 15–44.

[c]Girls aged 6–11. The gross enrollment ratio may exceed 100 if the actual age distribution of pupils goes outside the official school ages, e.g., because of early age at enrollment, repetition of grades, etc. Data for 1970 from UNESCO *World Education Report 1991* (Paris: UNESCO, 1991); 1986–92 data from UNICEF 1995 *State of the World's Children* (New York: Oxford University Press, 1995); all other data from WISTAT Database, version 3, United Nations, New York.

[d]Includes figures for East Asia, Southeast Asia, and Oceania.

Source: International Center for Research on Women, Washington, D.C. 1995.

health personnel); and to be educated (represented by rates of illiteracy). This index primarily gauges women's deprivation since two of the three measures pick up disadvantages that are specific to women. Calculations show that 37 percent of the population in developing countries, or 1.6 billion people, lack these three essentials of well-being, while only 21 percent of them, or 900 million people, are "income poor," with incomes below the poverty line defined by the World Bank. Most of the "extra" 700 million poor are women.

Statistics that show women lagging behind men in terms of well-being support the idea that women bear more than their fair share of capability-based poverty.

- Global literacy statistics show that in 1990 there were only 74 literate women for every 100 literate men. Schooling statistics reveal a similar trend. Worldwide, 77 million girls of primary school age (6–11 years) are out of school, compared with 52 million boys—a gap that becomes even larger when girls' higher overall dropout rates, absenteeism, and repetition levels are taken into account.
- Contrary to the biological advantage in survival that females have over males at all ages, men outnumber women in some regions, especially in South Asia, which is home to about one-half of the world's poor. Using vital statistics on the actual ratio of women to men in a society and contrasting them with those figures on the ratio expected if there were no female disadvantage in survival, economist and philosopher Amartya Sen of Harvard University has estimated that more than 100 million females are "missing" globally—a stark figure that he attributes to the comparative neglect of female health and nutrition, especially, but not exclusively, during childhood.
- Time is perhaps the one resource that the poor have available to them, and study after study shows that in poor families males have more leisure time than their female kin. To take care of their families, women farmers wake up before dawn in Honduras to grind the corn for tortillas, in Nigeria to process cassava, and in Nepal to fetch water and firewood. Put simply, women in poor households work more hours than men, and the poorer the household, the longer women work.
- While statistics on female reproductive health tell little about gender differences in poverty levels, they help to reveal women's disadvantage in poor countries, where high fertility and maternal mortality rates are the norm. About one-half million women die every year from complications related to pregnancy and delivery, the majority in poor countries. In some countries in sub-Saharan Africa, approximately one woman in 50 dies during childbirth—a grim contrast to Scandinavia where the rate is one per 20,000. At a total fertility rate of seven or more children per woman, the odds of such a woman surviving her reproductive years is one in six. As economist Partha Dasgupta of Cambridge University observes, for these women producing children is like playing Russian roulette.

The good news is that two decades ago, the proportion of women lacking the basics of well-being would have been much higher. Between 1970 and 1990, the life expectancy at birth of the average woman in the developing world rose by as much as five to nine years. She had substantially more schooling than she had in 1970, especially in the poorest countries where the school-age population of girls almost doubled. She also had greater access to modern contraception. As a result, global fertility rates fell by 40 percent. Unfortunately, international statistics on women are not disaggregated by levels of income, and it is likely that the quality of life of better-off women improved more than that of poor ones. Still, there is evidence of substantial gains in well-being, even for women in the most impoverished countries.

The bad news, however, is that while poor women have made gains in their overall well-being, they are falling behind in terms of income. Measuring household income or consumption is intrinsically difficult; even more so is apportioning this household income by gender, or separating women's income from men's. One way to gauge gender differences in poverty levels is to compare the situation of female-headed households with that of male-headed ones in developing countries. Looking at female-headed households also makes sense because in industrial countries such as the United States, where information on individuals and households is more reliable, the feminization of poverty has been closely linked with the rise in poor households headed by women.

Using information on female-headed households, the International Fund for Agricultural Development estimated the extent of rural poverty in 41 developing countries, which together account for 84 percent of the total rural developing country population. They found that between 1965–70 and 1988, the number of women in rural communities living below the poverty line rose more than the number of rural men living below the poverty line—increasing by 47 percent for women versus 30 percent for men. While in 1965–70 women made up 57 percent of the rural poor, by 1988 they accounted for 60 percent.

Female-headed households used to be the exception in developing societies, but no longer. In recent decades, the percentage of households headed by women has risen. Women everywhere are shouldering households' economic burdens. They are farmers in southern Botswana and Uttar Pradesh, India, left behind to mind farm and family by migrant husbands who sometimes do, and sometimes do not, send remittances back home. They are abandoned wives and young widows in Bangladesh and Egypt; unwed mothers in Latin American and sub-Saharan African cities; and refugee women with children throughout the world. Data compiled by the Population Council show a rise in female-headed households in 18 out of 26 censuses and surveys reviewed globally. Tabulations by the U.N.

Economic Commission for Latin America and the Caribbean (ECLAC) find this trend in 8 out of 13 countries in the region.

Another new phenomenon in some countries is households maintained by wives. Two Argentine researchers, Rosa Geldstein and Nena Delpino, report that the number of households maintained by women in Buenos Aires rose from 19 percent in 1980 to 27 percent in 1992—one in every 3.7 households. Almost one-half of these female heads of household were wives who became main earners. Wife-householders were more prevalent in the middle-income groups, and their earnings helped families through economic downturns. Unpartnered females with children were more typical of low-income households. Where wives were the main earners and had small children, one-half of the households were poor; this figure rose to two-thirds for households with unpartnered female heads (while for all Buenos Aires households the figure was 40 percent).

The available evidence suggests that most female-headed families, especially those with younger children, are overrepresented among the poor. Data from ECLAC show that they are more numerous in the lowest income (indigent) category in 9 out of 13 countries. The International Center for Research on Women reviewed 61 headship studies conducted in developing countries over the last decade and in 53 of them found greater poverty in female-headed families. And if anything, the deficiencies in how we measure poverty (including the fact that leisure time is not computed as a household resource) suggest that the poverty of female-headed households is underreported.

A main reason for the greater poverty of these families is the lower earnings of the women heading them. Trends such as lower fertility and increased female schooling, combined with the economic downturns that many countries suffered during the 1980s and 1990s, have led to more women working in both low-paid market activities and in nonmarket production. In developing countries, we have seen a feminization of agricultural work, a sector characterized by low earnings. Women seek market work to "weather" the effects of economic and environmental crises and tend to spend more time participating in unpaid activities such as community kitchens and in providing primary health care to compensate for reduced government services.

Research on the economics of poor households and families has shown that increased family burdens, including declining household income or additional children, tend to change women's and children's—but not men's—allocation of time between work and leisure. That women respond to increased external demands on the family by sacrificing more of their leisure time is a gender feature in poor families. Poor women can be caught in a vicious cycle of deprivation: Unable to cope with too much work, they hand over child-care responsibilities to

Planting Seeds of Hope

Despite the important role that women in developing countries play in agriculture, they have often been denied the attention and assistance given to their male colleagues. For example, predominantly male agricultural extension agents (the primary purveyors of everything from fertilizer to new farming techniques) have generally failed to seek out or assist female farmers.

To help bridge this gap in Zambia, where 75 percent of the labor force engages in agricultural work, the United Nations Food and Agricultural Organization began an effort in 1983 to help organize poor rural women and men into small groups devoted to farming, trading, and craftsmaking. The People's Participation Programme (PPP) aims to improve living conditions by increasing access to rural services, encouraging group savings, and fostering self-reliance, with a special emphasis on the needs of women. Locally recruited group promoters—all women—help the groups to grow and serve as links to other groups and external agencies.

By 1995, the program had created 230 small groups in Zambia's Western Province. Of the 2,550 people directly affected, 73 percent were women, 32 percent of whom represented female-headed households. As a result of the PPP, access to agricultural extension services increased for 67 percent of the groups engaged in farming. The increase was particularly large for women, many of whom had never before been visited by an extension agent. Research showed that from 1983 to 1994, the average land under cultivation in three districts participating in the program had increased between 30 and 90 percent. A group-based savings program also began to show results, leading to the establishment of an informal village banking system that mainly serves female clients. For many women, the program also offered the first chance to be involved in decision-making, in some cases deepening their involvement in village affairs.

Today the Zambian PPP encompasses 386 groups serving 4,402 members (indirectly reaching about 22,500 household members), and similar PPPs reach out to poor rural men and women in other parts of Africa, Asia, and Central America. One sign of the program's success is the widespread adoption of its small-group approach in Zambia by other aid groups. More revealing, perhaps, is that 55 percent of the Zambian PPP members are now men.

older daughters, who then must drop out of school. Thus, deprivation carries from one generation of women to the next, leading to the feminization of income poverty.

It is widely known that women's access to paid employment has drastically increased in recent decades, as has their social equality in many countries. Why, then, are more and more women finding themselves in poverty? Mahbub ul Haq, principal coordinator of the 1995 UNDP *Human Development Report*, which carried a special section on women, summarized women's achievements in the last decades as "a story of expanding capabilities and limited opportunities." Social and economic progress, including the contributions of development assistance and the international women's movement, have improved the well-being of women and better equipped them for the world of paid work and public life. Women have left their homes and their farms. A few have broken barriers and risen to the top, but most have encountered limited opportunities.

The majority of women obtain low-wage work because of persistent sexual discrimination in terms of employment and wages. In Honduras, for example, coffee and tobacco farmers prefer to hire girls and women as laborers because they are willing to accept lower wages and are more reliable workers. Especially in poor countries, female labor is primarily sought for low-paid positions in services, agriculture, small-scale commerce, and in the growing, unregulated manufacturing and agribusiness industries, which pay their workers individual rather than family wages, offer seasonal or part-time employment, and carry few or no benefits. Hence, this explains the seemingly contradictory trends of women's increased economic participation alongside their growing impoverishment.

Breaking the Vicious Cycle

The vicious cycle of poverty that unfolds when women work more and earn less and children, as a result, get less food and maternal time, is both commonplace and hard to break. But recent studies have also made clear that while households headed or maintained by women may lack resources, they are generally more "resourceful" than their male counterparts. In Brazil, for instance, economist Duncan Thomas has found that income in the hands of mothers has an effect on child health that is almost 20 times greater than income that is controlled by the father. Similar results have been reported in Chile, Guatemala, Kenya, and Malawi. The key appears to be that in households where women control resources, they prefer (whether for reasons of nature or nurture) to invest scarce resources in child well-being. In Jamaica, for instance, studies have found that female-headed households spend more on food and other family-oriented goods than male-headed households.

These differences in the way that men and women prefer to spend scarce resources in poor households suggest that the income that poor women earn can yield higher health or social benefits than that earned by men. They are a strong argument for the desirability of expanding poor women's economic opportunities—precisely the area where there has been little, if any, advancement in recent decades.

In short, the question before individual nations and the international community at large is not why they should invest more in women, but how. Nations need to take measures that reinforce the virtuous cycle between poor women's and children's well-being. They also need to avoid actions that aggravate the obstacles that women and children already face.

A good place to start would be avoiding the unintended consequences of social and economic policies that can increase women's work burdens—such as reducing those public services that cushion the impact of negative economic shocks. Taking such measures without providing complementary policies that adequately "protect" poor women in their multiple roles as producers and reproducers is likely to set in motion, or intensify, the poverty cycle. Enlightened approaches such as providing women with access to reliable credit and savings can have multiplier effects that raise poor women's productivity in the home, as well as productivity and earnings in the market.

With that in mind, policymakers should also stop promoting well-meaning programs that ignore women's traditional productive roles, the economic value of their time, and their domestic time constraints. One project, for example, established a cooperative for rural women in western Kenya that produced potholders for sale in Nairobi at a price lower than the cost of the banana fiber that was used to make them.

There are several other specific areas of national and international policy where changes and improvements could yield great dividends for poor women and for the developing world in general. Governments should take the following measures:

- Expand substantially the access of poor women to family-planning and reproductive health services. Many successful reproductive health programs offer women a package of health services for themselves—and sometimes their children—bundled into one visit, in one location, which saves them both time and transportation costs. Boosting women's capacities to generate income will also increase their access to higher quality health services that may be purchased through private providers.

- Adopt education reform agendas designed to increase the quantity and quality of, first primary, and then secondary, schooling for girls. With the support of international agencies, innovative efforts to increase girls' access to schools are under way in Bangladesh, Pakistan, and other countries. These include giving scholarships and engaging families and communities in the task of getting and keeping girls enrolled. As World Bank vice president Mieko Nishimizu has said, "If you educate a boy you educate a human being. If you educate a girl, you educate generations."

- Create incentives for the private sector to expand women's access to agencies that offer credit and savings services. Microfinance operations, like the well-known Grameen Bank in Bangladesh, have succeeded in providing access to reliable credit and savings services to more than 3 million female borrowers in developing countries, but such operations still reach only about 5 percent of those in need of their services. They also provide benefits in other areas. One female microcredit client in Bangladesh, for example, mentioned that the profits from her expanded business had enabled her to buy a rickshaw for her unemployed husband to use as a taxi. As a result, she mentioned in passing, he had stopped beating her.

- Increase rural women's access to agricultural extension services by modifying existing ones or by establishing separate services for them. Currently, women farmers receive fewer farm extension services than men. In western Kenya, the lack of these services accounted for about 30 percent of the productivity loss in food crops grown by women.

- Expand women's access to productive infrastructure, especially in rural areas. This requires shifting government investment priorities to favor rural roads, improving women's access to water and electricity, and designing infrastructure that will support rural women as well as men.

- Adopt labor-intensive "pro-poor" economic growth policies that expand employment opportunities. Invest in upgrading women's skills in both traditional and nontraditional occupations that can compete in national as well as export markets.

- Overhaul social security systems as a complement to pro-poor growth policies, establishing gender-friendly regulatory frameworks for industrial and agricultural growth, and legislating childcare options.

TABLE 2 Costs and Benefits of One Additional Year of Schooling for 1,000 Women in Pakistan (Estimated)

	Costs
Schooling:	Cost of 1,000 = $30,000

	Benefits
Female Earnings:	Increase in Wages = 20%
Child Mortality:	Child Deaths Averted = 60
	Alternative Health Intervention to Save 60 Lives = $48,000
Fertility:	Total Births Averted = 500
	Alternative Family Planning
	Costs Per 500 Births Averted = $33,000
Maternal Mortality:	Total Merternal Deaths Averted = 3
	Alternative Costs Per 3 Averted
	Maternal Deaths = $7,500

Source: Lawrence H. Summers, *Investing in All the People*, World Bank Policy Research working paper 905. (Washington, D.C.: The World Bank, May 1992).

- Target agricultural policies at impoverished farmers and give women farmers access to land titles; financial policies should promote the growth of small enterprises and foster entrepreneurship among women.
- Change statistical collection systems—that which is not counted is not valued. Much of the poor's productive work worldwide takes place in the informal sector, in home-based production, petty trading, and small-holder agriculture. Such work is still mostly invisible in labor force and employment statistics. Globalization, export promotion, and deregulation have all dramatically changed the nature of labor markets, and women's participation in them, while employment statistics have lagged behind. If women are not counted as working in productive activities, and employment trends are not disaggregated by gender, it will be hard to justify the implementation of public policies designed to increase women's productivity and wages.

Show Me the Money

Poor, often illiterate women without any collateral do not exactly rank high among banks' traditional list of preferred customers. However microfinance institutions—which offer small loans usually secured by peer pressure rather than property—are rapidly emerging as an alternative to help women break the cycle of poverty.

One of the forerunners in the microcredit industry is Bolivia's Banco Solidario, S.A., better known as BancoSol. In 1992, after operating for several years as a nonprofit joint venture between members of the business community and Acción International, a Boston-based nongovernmental organization, BancoSol became the first private commercial bank dedicated to microlending. Now it serves over 76,000 borrowers—70 percent of whom are women—through 33 branch offices, making it the largest Bolivian bank in terms of number of borrowers. In 1996, the bank loaned slightly more than $100 million.

To be eligible for credit, would-be borrowers must form "solidarity groups" of four to seven entrepreneurs. Each group member is responsible for the loan, a division of responsibility that helps to guarantee it will be repaid. The average loan is $600, although first loans are typically much smaller, averaging around $150. After groups demonstrate their ability to be responsible borrowers by paying back their initial loans, they become eligible for more credit At the end of 1996, default rates were only 2.6 percent—much lower than in the financial system as a whole.

BancoSol's typical clients are urban artisans and merchants for whom even a small line of credit can mean the difference between self-sufficiency and brutal poverty. As the *Wall Street Journal* recently reported, one Bolivian woman, Gloria Quintanilla, went from selling clothes on the street to owning her own shop, mainly due to the loans she received from BancoSol. Teresa Montano used a $ 125 loan to transform her one-woman bakery into a business that employs 14 people, according to the *Minneapolis Star Tribune*. Microlending programs around the world have spawned similar successes, from Uganda and Indonesia to Bangladesh and the Philippines. Indeed, microcredit lending is growing at an annual rate of 30 percent and, by the end of 1997, it is expected to total as much as $12 billion.

Women's issues are becoming more visible in U.S. foreign policy. But although Secretary of State Madeleine K. Albright has legitimized a concern for women in foreign policy, she has done so primarily within a human rights framework. A growing body of statistical evidence shows that for developing countries what makes sense in terms of human rights also makes sense in terms of economics.

If not out of altruism, then for reasons of bald self-interest, developed countries should work to expand the economic opportunities of poor women. Once upon a time, women like Reina, the former guerrilla fighter in El Salvador, only migrated to follow or find a husband. This is no longer the case. It is likely that Reina, with few opportunities in her own country, will sooner or later join the rising number of female migrants who leave families and children behind to seek better paying work in the United States and other industrial countries. Wisely spent foreign aid can give Reina the chance to realize her dreams in her *own* country.

I have not met Reina but I have met Runa and Ade, and I am convinced that they represent some of the wisest and safest investments available in the developing world today.

In Pursuit of Labor Rights

Anita Chan

Today, there is growing recognition that the objectives of development go beyond simply an increase in GDP: we are concerned with promoting democratic, equitable, sustainable development. If that is our objective, then it is natural that we should pay particular attention to the issue of how the plight of workers changes in the course of development; and we should look not only at their incomes, but broader measures— at their health and safety, and even at their democratic participation, both at the workplace, and within the broader political arena. Workers' rights should be a central focus of a development institution such as the World Bank.

Joseph E. Stiglitz January 8, 2000[1]

From the point four years ago when I first thought about writing this book to the time of penning this conclusion, the Western mass media's attitude toward sweatshop labor in developing countries has changed enormously. The expression "labor standards" was once used almost exclusively within labor and government circles. I, for one, had never heard the expression, nor had it appeared in print in academic writings about China. But the term has now found its rightful place in ordinary conversations, in political speeches, and in the mainstream press. The impact of globalization on nations and on the world economy is now recognized to be integrally related to labor, and to labor rights. The above quote from Joseph Stiglitz, the World Bank's former vice-president and chief economist, symbolizes this shift in the views of a number of senior policymakers in the international arena.

Four years ago, it was also unthinkable that the rights of Chinese workers could become a controversial issue in the United States, yet this became a factor in the 2000 Congressional debate over whether to grant China permanent normal trade relations (PNTR). The U.S. government and international public opinion have long been critical of China's human-rights record, but the concerns had always focused on the rights of a few political dissidents, the existence of prison labor, and the suppression of Tibetans. Times have changed. When the Democratic whip in the House of Representatives, David Bonior, a leading opponent of granting China PNTR, ordered his list of rights in his Congressional debate speech, labor rights came first: "That is what this debate is about today: labor rights, human rights, environmental concerns, religious rights."[2]

This increased recognition among American politicians of the important relationship between labor rights and trade owes much to the publicity generated by vocal critics of the exploitation of third-world labor from nongovernmental organizations (NGOs), labor unions, students, and consumer groups. The anti-Nike campaign in particular has attracted considerable media attention. But it was the massive protests in Seattle in November 1999 at the World Trade Organization (WTO) Ministerial Conference that forcefully brought the world's attention to the link between globalization and the exploitation of labor and destruction of the environment.[3]

The close timing of three controversial issues—China's accession to the WTO, the Seattle protests, and the PNTR vote in Congress—suddenly made the exploitative working conditions faced by many Chinese workers, especially workers in foreign and joint-venture enterprises, highly relevant. A book project that began without an international context in mind ended up with a global dimension. This is highly appropriate, given that Chinese workers produce vast quantities of products for export to the developed world, particularly the United States. As shown in this book, most workers producing products for export are migrants from the poorer provinces, at times working under degrading and even slave-like conditions. Their plight has set in motion a "race to the bottom," in which low wages and high unemployment among the unskilled have spread to Chinese workers in other sectors, as well as depressing wage levels in other countries. It is therefore fitting that this concluding chapter should explore possible ways to help alleviate the conditions faced by Chinese workers in a global economy.

The Five Core Labor Rights

Five core labor rights were enshrined in the International Labor Organization (ILO) Conventions, and reaffirmed in the ILO Declaration of Fundamental Principles at Work in 1998,[4] and have been championed by the international trade union movement:

1. freedom of association;
2. the rights to organize and bargain collectively;
3. a minimum age of employment;
4. no forced or slave labor; and
5. a prohibition against discrimination.[5]

Inasmuch as the ILO is a tripartite organization made up of government, employer, and labor representatives, this means that even governments and employers endorse these rights as core rights. The first two—freedom of association and freedom to organize and collectively bargain—are the most fundamental of these rights[6] (henceforth, they will be referred to as the two main core rights). What is truly ironic is that the United States has only ratified one of the core rights, the one on forced labor.[7]

In contrast, the chapter titles of this book highlight other labor standards, sometimes known as non-core labor standards, such as wages and work hours.[8] I would debate the pertinence of merely pushing for compliance with the five core rights in a country like China. I hope that readers will become convinced by the end of this chapter that violations of the non-core labor rights of Chinese workers should be considered no less serious than violations of the five core rights.

The chapters are organized to highlight the violations that daily affect workers most immediately and directly. Although not all are violations of core rights, all have been guaranteed in ILO conventions, and some are rights contained in articles of the United Nations' Universal Declaration of Human Rights. Only two chapters pertain to the core rights: chapter 6, on violations of the right to take collective action and organize unions; and chapter 7, on indentured labor abroad (which can be considered as within the parameters of forced labor). Thus far, international concern regarding forced Chinese labor has been limited to prison labor.[9]

The book does not have a chapter on industrial child labor because this is a less serious problem than in many other developing countries. In a country the size of China, it does of course exist in pockets, but hiring children as wage labor is not pervasive in China, unlike in India and Pakistan.

International organizations have almost completely focused on the two main core rights, of freedom of association and of collective bargaining. They are rights that all workers should enjoy, but they are not the overriding focus of this book because these issues are not at the forefront of Chinese workers' concerns and grievances, especially among migrant workers.[10] Miserable wages, very long work hours, and dangerous working conditions are the problems that most directly affect workers' physical well-being and are in need of immediate solution. To this end, this chapter will make three main arguments:

1. To improve the conditions of Chinese workers, we need to expand our focus from the five core rights to include a range of other labor rights.
2. Labor rights, including the non-core rights, should be seen as human rights and should be fully integrated into the international human-rights discourses and practices.
3. NGOs should apply pressure on the Chinese government, which professes to champion the cause of labor, to persuade it to play a more positive role in regulating labor conditions.

The Historical Relationships between Core Rights and Non-Core Rights

It may surprise those who are unfamiliar with international labor history that this history at one time was centrally concerned with the adoption of what we today classify as non-core rights. Industrialization in the West in the nineteenth century created a new class of industrial laborers who worked in horrific conditions. There were efforts made across the political spectrum to alleviate the onerous conditions of workers. Thus, "at the Paris Congress of 1890 that led to the formation of the Second International, considerable attention was given to the problem of achieving an eight-hour day."[11] Even the conservative political establishment was aware of an international need to improve working conditions, and, in 1905, the Swiss government convened an intergovernmental conference in Berne—the first international labor conference. At this and a later conference, the first two international labor conventions were adopted, dealing with "the limitation of night work for women in industry and the prohibition of the manufacture of and trade in matches containing white phosphorus."[12]

At Versailles in 1919, a Labor Charter of nineteen principles was drawn up, nine of which obtained a two-thirds majority vote, were adopted, and were embodied in the Peace Treaty:

i. that labor should not be regarded merely as a commodity or article of commerce;
ii. the right of association;
iii. the payment of an adequate wage to maintain a reasonable standard of living;
iv. an eight-hour day or forty-eight-hour week;
v. a weekly rest of at least twenty-four hours;
vi. the abolition of child labor;
vii. equal pay for equal work;
viii. equitable economic treatment of all workers in a country (i.e., immigrants as well as nationals); and
ix. an inspection system to ensure the enforcement of the laws for worker protection.[13]

It can be said that these nine principles were the core labor rights of that era in history. Of these nine, principles ii, vi, and viii were precursors of today's five core rights. Of the six remaining principles, three—a living wage, limited work hours, and a right to rest—had a direct impact on workers' physical well-being and were agreed to be of prime importance.

After World War I, the ILO was established as the first international tripartite institution in which governments, employers, and workers had equal voting power. In October 1919, the first ILO Conference was held in Washington, D.C., and its first conventions were adopted.[14] The work of the conference was dominated by two themes: hours of work and unemployment. Employment was a major issue because of the massive unemployment after the war, while reining in long work hours was a traditional aim of labor. It was held at the time that this:

> would prolong the useful life of the worker. If he worked for ten to twelve hours a day his useful life would only last some ten years. Second, reduction of working hours increased the time available for leisure, family life and education. Third, during the war the workers had been sustained by the belief that they would be rewarded by a reduction of hours in the peace.[15]

It was only after World War II that the international trade-union movement was able to better establish itself, and in 1948, Convention 87 on the right to freedom of association was passed, followed a year later by Convention 98 on the right to organize and collectively bargain.

In short, international labor history from the second half of the nineteenth century to the end of World War II focused largely on so-called industrial labor problems rather than on the freedom to form trade unions. One could argue that this was because the international trade-union movement was still weak, and in a tripartite arrangement, was not able to force attention to matters of greatest organizational interest to itself.[16] But it can also be argued that prior to World War II, precisely because organized labor was still weak, the "sweating" of labor was the biggest problem—wages were too low to provide a minimally decent livelihood, and work hours were sometimes so long that they endangered health and safety. The international trade-union movement agitated for these "industrial" rights, and they were not alone. The conditions endured by so many workers aroused humanitarian concerns, and even governments recognized their role in regulating working conditions.

After World War II, when human rights began to become a focus of international covenants, labor rights were included among them. In 1947, the ILO and the United Nations concluded an agreement on "the inclusion in their respective agendas of items proposed by the other."[17] Many of the issues debated, principles adopted, and conventions passed in the ILO were precursors of articles in the 1948 Universal Declaration of Human Rights (UDHR).[18] A number of these articles directly concern workers as human beings. It is also important to note that many of these overlapping articles embody both civil-political rights and social, economic, and cultural rights. The five core labor rights fall within the rubric of civil and political rights, whereas the non-core rights are considered economic and social rights. Those that specifically relate to the so-called non-core rights of workers are contained in article 22 (a right to social security); article 23 (a right to work, no discrimination, equal pay for equal work, and reasonable remuneration); article 24 (a right to rest and leisure, including a reasonable limitation of work hours and periodic holidays with pay); article 25 (a right to a standard of living adequate for the health and well-being of the worker and his or her family); and article 26 (a right to education). In other words, what today are not regarded as important enough to be classified as core labor rights occupied a prominent place in the UDHR in 1948. In particular, the right to rest and leisure (which we have seen is of paramount importance to Chinese workers today) occupied a full article.[19]

However, as time passed, these rights concerning the physical well-being of workers became less important to the ILO and human-rights organizations. As welfare states were established, and as legislation was passed to limit maximum working hours and to provide overtime rates—successes due in part to the effectiveness of the international trade-union movement—the movement shifted its priorities toward matters that remained of immediate concern to Western trade unions in their own organizing efforts; that is, Conventions 87 and 98, sanctifying freedom of worker association, a right to organize workers, and a right to collective bargaining.

During these same years, the onset of the Cold War also undermined the status of the economic and social rights that had been included in the Universal Declaration of Human Rights. These rights became casualties of the antagonism between the capitalist camp led by the United States and the communist camp led by the Soviet Union, partly because the latter emphasized these rights in its attacks on capitalism and proclamations of the superiority of socialism.[20] The United States developed an "aversion" to mentioning social and economic rights[21] and, as the most powerful country, it set the agenda of the international rights discourse.

The lack of commitment to this set of rights in the UN is clearly demonstrated in institutional negligence. In the UN Center for Human Rights, according to Philip Alston, an authority on international human-rights law, "Special rapporteurs, country rapporteurs, advisory services experts, members of treaty bodies, officials of other UN agencies, and nongovernmental experts have not even one person within the Centre to whom they can turn for expert advice or assistance in relation to these [social and economic] rights. The Centre has no meaningful collection of materials, books or documents relating to these issues."[22] The United Nations Committee on Economic, Social, and Cultural Rights receives very few resources. Its members meet annually for a single session and do not even have borrowing privileges at the United Nations library in Geneva.[23] Such is the sorry state of economic and social rights within the international human-rights arena.

The Relationship between Labor Rights and Human Rights

Readers introduced by this book to the harsh lives endured by many Chinese workers probably have unwittingly—and correctly—associated the violations of their labor rights with violations of human rights. But there are many reasons—theoretical, practical, historical, political, institutional—why the non-core labor rights have not always been regarded as human rights[24] or, if recognized, why they have been situated far down in the hierarchy of human rights. The examples in this book show how imperative it is that labor rights are put on an equal footing with other kinds of human rights. It is ironic that we need to belabor this point, as it was recognized more than fifty years ago.

Yet between 1948 and 1999, the internationally agreed-upon recognition of what I call the "non-core labor rights" lost their importance in international discourse and have been short-changed in international human-rights diplomacy.[25] In the accusations and counter-accusations about human rights violations, there has been silence on issues of excessively low wages, extremely long working hours, and dangerous and degrading labor conditions. References to Chinese labor rights over the past two decades have generally been restricted to complaints about barriers to forming trade unions, the imprisonment of specific labor activists, or prison labor. For instance, the U.S. government, one of the most vehement critics of China's human-rights record, issues annual Country Reports on Human-Rights Practices, which include a section called "Reporting on Worker Rights."[26] Although, in principle, the American government recognizes labor rights as human rights, when China's human-rights violations were raised, labor-rights violations were barely mentioned.[27]

The Chinese government has countered criticism of its human rights record by refusing to recognize that it violates political and civil rights. It argues that the U.S. government is picking on China, which, as an erstwhile victim of imperialism and as a developing country, needs to place its emphasis on social, economic, and cultural rights. China claims to honor what it calls "socialist human rights with Chinese characteristics."[28] Amidst this verbal jousting, Beijing strategically released dissidents from jail like trump cards—one at a time, each time international pressure mounted too high or when it wanted something in return, such as to host the 2000 Olympic Games.[29]

China is not the only Asian country to claim "special characteristics" in interpreting human rights. In 1993, several Asian countries issued the Bangkok Declaration as a counteroffensive to Western criticisms, arguing that there exists an "Asian conception of human rights."[30] The argument was posed in terms of cultural and historical specificities rather than universality in the application of human rights.[31]

In addition to pointing to its "excellent" record of honoring social and economic rights, in 1996, the Chinese government issued a report that included a section entitled "Protection of Workers' Rights." It stated that China had instituted a minimum-wage system and provided employment and social security to its people. The report made no mention of the widespread violations of non-core rights such as illegally low wages and long work hours that have been widely reported in China's own news media and documented in this book.[32] China subsequently signed the International Convention on Economic, Social, and Cultural Rights in 1997.[33] But the timing of China's signing was particularly ironic. Prior to the 1990s, Beijing could have prided itself for providing secure employment and a range of benefits to state-sector workers. But in 1997, the labor rights of many of its workers, and in particular their social and economic rights, were increasingly being systematically abused.

Western human-rights NGOs have traditionally addressed a very narrow range of rights that are mainly civil and political in nature,[34] and within this range, the concern is directed toward political dissidents jailed for their beliefs. Workers locked up in factories toiling day and night for low wages and given inadequate food and little rest do not come within the purview of human rights. This downgrading of the rights of ordinary workers is a universal problem, and not limited to China.

One of the many causes of this problem involves semantics. Let us look again at Representative Bonior's statement quoted above. When Bonior listed "labor rights, human rights, environmental concerns, religious rights," what was on his mind? Are labor rights a kind of human rights? Do labor rights differ in kind from human rights? Or are they a form of human rights, but superior (only recently) to what he called "human rights?" From this quote it can be seen that the status of labor rights as human rights is confusing and elusive. In this instance, Bonior did not seem to be thinking of labor rights as human rights or as a kind of human right. He most likely was equating human rights with civil and political rights only, which is generally how the term is understood in the United States.

During the past several years, human-rights NGOs have become more inclusive in their human-rights concerns. Amnesty International, for example, has begun urging companies to uphold human-rights standards in their operations.[35] While freeing prisoners of conscience continues to be its priority, in early 1998 Amnesty drew up a document called "Human Rights Principles for Companies."[36] The issue has also been pressed by smaller human-rights groups such as Human Rights Watch/Asia[37] and Human Rights in China. But these are only initial efforts, and it will be some time before the labor rights of the ordinary worker will become an integral part of the discourse of international human-rights organizations.

The loudest, most energetic, and most visible critiques of labor rights have emanated from labor NGOs, trade unions, consumer groups, church groups, community groups, and, within the past three years, American university students.[38] These loosely coordinated groups have formed an anti-sweatshop movement. This movement started as a one-person campaign in the early 1990s by Jeffrey Ballinger against Nike's exploitative labor practices in Indonesia, and now, linked by e-mail, it has developed into an international protest movement.[39] The protests have attracted considerable media coverage and put enormous

pressure on a few multinationals to improve their labor standards in the factories from which they outsource their products, a large volume of which derives
from China. The multinationals have been embarrassed by the exposure of low
wages, long working hours, poor health and safety conditions, and the existence
of corporal punishment in these plants. An increasing number of multinationals
seek to preempt criticism by drawing up their own corporate codes of conduct.[40]
About 90 percent of American multinationals had developed their own codes by
1999.[41] Some created new labor-relations departments, which also double as
public-relations departments to stave off criticism. A small number have hired
the equivalent of labor inspectors to internally monitor conditions in their subcontractors' factories.[42] Even the most vocal NGO critics have to admit that the
unrelenting pressure from the anti-sweatshop campaign has improved conditions for workers in the factories of a few of the multinationals' suppliers.

The anti-sweatshop campaign also prompted President Clinton to commission the establishment of an Apparel Industry Partnership in which multinationals and their critics negotiated the terms for the formation of a Fair Labor
Association (FLA). Signatories to the FLA are required to abide by the association's rules to improve workers' conditions.[43] As of September 2000, twelve companies had joined the FLA, and 141 colleges and universities had become
affiliates. The founding NGO members are the International Labor Rights Fund,
the Lawyers Committee for Human Rights, the National Consumers League, and
the Robert F. Kennedy Memorial Center for Human Rights.[44] Most multinationals
find the FLA's terms too restrictive for their management practices, while trade
unions and a number of NGOs would not participate, mainly because the multinationals refused to agree to an effective system of independent external monitoring of factories. American campus protests, including student sit-ins, continue
to dog corporations such as Nike, whose owner has retaliated by withdrawing
multimillion-dollar donations to universities. Students, university administrations, and corporate donors remain locked in an unending series of protests and
negotiations.[45]

There is a difference in emphasis between trade-union organizations, especially at the international level, and the anti-sweatshop NGOs and student groups.
Trade-union organizations hold the five core labor rights sacrosanct. The
International Confederation of Free Trade Unions (ICFTU), the umbrella trade-
union organization that claims to represent 125 million members of 215 affiliated
unions in 145 countries, and the International Trades Secretariat, which is the
umbrella organization for international trade-sector unions, are the driving forces
for the inclusion of a "social clause" in WTO trade negotiations.[46] This social
clause basically amounts to the five core labor rights.[47]

In comparison, the labor-rights NGOs and grass-roots trade unions that work
closely with grass-roots associations in the developing world tend to have a

broader and more flexible stand on the social clause than the international trade-union organizations.[48] Although they see the importance of the five core labor rights, they campaign mostly for standards regarding a minimum living wage, occupational safety and health, maximum length of working hours, social security, and environmental protection.

In sum, whether or not labor rights are recognized as human rights varies from arena to arena. The arena of international politics dominates the discourse, and the peak international organizations in this arena, such as the WTO, the International Monetary Fund, and the World Bank, have refused to consider labor rights as a factor in their agendas. On the other end of the spectrum are the labor-rights advocates, who vehemently attack these world organizations for ignoring labor rights.

Balancing Priorities

The question we need to ask: Is the strategy of prioritizing the two main core labor rights necessarily the most appropriate one for working people in the developing world? Over the past twenty years, globalization has accelerated, with investors scouring poor countries to find the best and cheapest labor. We have seen the return with a vengeance of the "sweating" of labor in developing countries, especially in Asia. In China, where the political system renders it nigh impossible to organize independent unions, but where working conditions urgently need alleviation, what role can outsiders play?

For migrant workers in China, for instance, what rights are the most concrete and most urgent to them? They want to be paid regularly, on time, and to be paid at least U.S.$2 a day (not $2 an hour) rather than $1.50 a day. Workers want to retain their human dignity, to have some leisure time (not the luxury of paid vacations as stipulated by the Universal Declaration of Human Rights), to be free of occupational hazards that threaten their lives and limbs, and to be free from fear of being put into detention centers for not having the right residential (*hukou*) papers. Their wants are concrete and tangible. A small handful of Chinese intellectuals such as Li Wenming and Goo Baosheng (case 17) have tried to organize workers at great personal risk, but this has only invited suppression and incarceration—a picture that is not likely to change soon.

Even for urban state workers, independent trade unionism seems far from their most pressing demand. The immediate need is to eke out a livelihood the right to a job, to wages, and to a pension. Even when not paid for months, they take to the streets only as a last resort.[49] Head-on confrontation spells upheaval, something Chinese workers try to avoid, preferring to work through existing structures and, sometimes, their official workplace union, which may show some sympathy. Thus, even Han Dongfang, who tried to organize fellow workers during the 1989 Tiananmen protests and now works for Chinese worker rights from Hong Kong, today advises Chinese workers to initially go to the official trade unions for help.[50] In a similar vein, our role as outsiders should be to campaign for the protection of the economic and social rights of Chinese workers in light of the present realities, in addition to their civil and political rights.

The Tactics of the Anti-Sweatshop Movement

The anti-sweatshop coalition has targeted specific multinationals, largely for violating three types of rights (in the following order of priority): paying workers less than a living wage, long mandatory overtime work, and occupational health and safety issues. But activists have not been self-consciously aware that they are championing issues that have not historically been deemed "core" rights, in part because the activists are unaware of the artificial divide that has been made between these two sets of rights. Although the anti-sweatshop campaign also calls for honoring the five core rights, some of the people who prioritize trade-union rights feel uncomfortable about or even opposed to the campaign's call for independent workplace monitors, as they feel external monitoring does not lead to a situation whore the workers can self-consciously protect their own rights.[51]

Efforts to fight for a living wage for workers in developing countries have absorbed much of the campaigners' energy. How to define a living wage and set one for each country has become both an academic and a practical issue. The movement conducts research to compare wages against the minimum-wage standards. They gather workers' pay slips, calculate the cost of food baskets, measure with great precision the workers' wages against their expenditures and against inflation, and calculate the workers' wages as a percentage of the retail price of the products the workers manufacture. Conferences have been held to determine a conceptual and working definition of a living wage, and findings of the research have been circulated through the news media and organizational channels.[52] Citations of incredibly low wages paid to workers in the producing countries tend to draw more sympathy from consumers and the general public in high-income countries than any other violations of labor standards.

The movement and the multinationals come into conflict over monitoring. The anti-sweatshop activists demand to be free to enter factories to conduct independent monitoring, a request that many multinationals try to preempt by saying they are conducting their own internal monitoring. In a historical perspective, the movement is trying to revive an inspection system that was contained in one of the principles adopted by the first ILO conference in 1919. The difference here is that instead of being monitored by government, the system today would be monitored by the NGOs.

The anti-sweatshop movement needs to explicitly frame the campaign as one to upgrade the status of economic and social rights in the international labor-rights and human-rights communities. This is the thrust of their movement and it should be portrayed as such. With time and effort, they might be able to help redress what is now an unbalanced approach to labor rights, and increase the awareness that labor rights should also include rights concerning the survival and well-being of workers.

The Role of the State

The anti-sweatshop campaign, in my view, would further its cause if it reoriented its strategy toward the role of the state. Currently, the movement does not apply any pressure on the governments of the developing countries where the products are produced. Yet they are important players. These governments today are the main opponents to the inclusion of a social clause in WTO agreements.[53] Many such governments, far from representing the interests of their workers, are instead preoccupied with competing with other poor countries to sell cheap labor. This is of course shortsighted, in that a race to the bottom has emerged in the developing countries to the detriment of all, especially workers. Instead of rejecting the social clause while undercutting each other's price to sell their labor in the international labor market, the developing countries should form a bloc to collectively bargain with the industrialized nations, much as some of the developing countries have organized, at times successfully, to protect commodity prices such as coffee and oil. They should set a floor price for the labor they are selling in the world labor market and join hands with international labor activists to protect against exploitation by foreign investors. Not only will their workers benefit, this will also aid economic development. The anti-sweatshop movement would do well to divert some of its efforts into pressuring and persuading these governments to accept the social clause and other non-core-rights standards as the best way to stem the downward spiral in wages.

The movement has to understand that its current targets are only a handful of the many thousands of firms outsourcing in developing countries. Locking a few multinationals into high-profile confrontations can spotlight the issues, but the impact in terms of improving the conditions of the masses of workers in the developing countries can only be limited. In China, for example, a relatively small number of workers are directly employed by giant multinationals; by contrast, far more are employed by enterprises owned by small and medium-sized firms. By comparison to the impact of the movement, in many of these countries, the state's capacity to change the situation for workers is far reaching. A government that enforces good labor laws can accomplish far more than the movement's campaign against individual manufacturers.

A professedly "socialist" state, China is vulnerable to pressures to live up to its own rhetorical claims that it champions the cause of workers. As we have seen in previous chapters, the Chinese state, including one of its arms, the official trade union, might be drafted into playing a more active role in protecting labor rights. The legacy of an official socialist ideology may yet be used to good ends. According to Jude Howell, a British specialist on Chinese labor issues, the anti-sweatshop activists "need to work with the [Chinese] government at the national, provincial and municipal levels." Athar Hussain, another expert, notes, "I would strongly support the inclusion of government. You would find allies there."[54]

Recent measures adopted by Guangzhou city in southern China illustrate how the state, where it has the will, can intervene positively to enforce labor laws. One of the city's districts is pioneering a wage-inspection system to ensure workers are being paid. More than a thousand local officials have been assigned to oversee the district's 2,000 mostly Asian-funded enterprises. Local government bodies that rent out buildings and land to factories are responsible for paying any unpaid wages for factories that default." Another innovation in Guangzhou city is a scheme to ensure that companies and factories contribute to social-security funds for their employees, with the funds collected by the local tax department.[56] Before the scheme, only 33 percent of the Hong Kong-owned and Taiwanese-owned enterprises and 24 percent of the private enterprises in the district made social-security contributions, as opposed to 97 percent of the state enterprises.

Conclusion

I believe that the non-core rights should have the same status as the core rights. The right to a living wage, the right to rest, and the right to an intact body are all fundamental. International dialogue may be on the verge of recognizing these non-core rights as essential human rights. Among other things, the international labor movement has begun to see that workers in the developing world have different circumstances and needs from those of organized labor in the industrialized countries. In light of these differences, the international labor movement now needs to shift its priorities and campaign for the very basic rights that were the foundation of the labor movement at the start of the twentieth century. There are causes for optimism. As an example, in a 1997 report on "The ILO, Standard Setting and Globalization," the ILO director-general recognized that the ILO needed to shift course. He suggested that "workers' clauses" ought to be internationally implemented to cover such areas as minimum wages, working hours, weekly hours of rest, and occupational safety and health standards.[57] These critical labor standards had long been neglected by the ILO.

The international labor movement, as represented by the International Confederation of Free Trade Unions (ICFTU), is now searching for new strategies and solutions. While continuing to press the international community to honor the five core rights, at the ICFTU World Congress held in Durban, South Africa, in April 2000, the organization's general secretary declared:

> The new thing is that our movement will seek to establish a global social safety net and will expand far beyond traditional collective bargaining to encompass hundreds of millions of workers and their families to end once and for all the scourge of poverty which deprives billions of people of a decent life in dignity.

The AFL-CIO president, John Sweeney, concurred that the ICFTU, "which has fought for political democracy for the past fifty years," needs to fight for "economic democracy." To promote this aim, a resolution to form coalitions with NGOs on a case-by-ease basis was adopted.[58] And, with the anti-sweatshop movement gathering momentum, this book ends on a more optimistic note than I believed possible when I first thought about drafting it four years ago.

Endnotes

1. Joseph F. Stiglitz, "Democratic Development as the Fruits of Labor," keynote address to the Industrial Relations Research Association, American Economic Association Meeting, January 8, 2000. See *http:/www.worldbank.org/knowledge/chiefecon/articles/boston/htm*
2. "Transcript: Democrats in House Argue Against China PNTR, May 16," United States Information Service, EPF308 5/17/00, p. 1. In the academic field of China studies, Andrew Nathan, longtime China human-rights advocate, used the expression "labor standard" in his discussion of Chinese human rights for the first time (Andrew J. Nathan, "WTO Is Not a Human Rights Policy—Neither Granting nor Withholding PNTR Is Likely to Have a Clear Net Effect on Human Rights in China," *Asian Wall Street Journal*, April 12, 2000).

3. There was an enormous amount of reporting on the "Battle in Seattle." The following selections present different sides to the issue. Richard Lacayo, "Rage Against the Machine: Despite, and Because of Violence, Anti-WTO Protesters were Heard," *Time*, December 31, 1999, pp. 24–29; "After Seattle: A Global Disaster," *The Economist*, December 11, 1999, pp. 17–19; David Moberg, "After Seattle," *In These Times*, No. 15 (January 10, 2000), pp. 15–17.

4. The Declaration was passed by the 86th session, international Labor Conference, Geneva, June 1998. The four principles adopted were basically the five core labor standards with freedom of association and freedom to organize collapsed into one. *http://ilo.org/public/English/10ile)ilc86/com-dtxt.htm.*

5. David Chin, *A Social Clause for Labour's Cause—a Challenge for the New Millennium*, London: Institute of Employment Rights, 1998, p. 8; Erika de Wet, "Labor Standards in the Globalized Economy: The Inclusion of a Social Clause in the General Agreement on Tariffs and Trade/World Trade Organization," *Human Rights Quarterly*, No. 17 (1995), pp. 443–452.

6. For articles emphasizing these two rights, see, "Introduction" to special issue: Labor Rights, Human Rights, *International Labour Review*, Vol. 137, No. 2 1998, pp. 127–133; Lance Compa, "Labor Rights and Labor Standards in International Trade," *Law and Policy in International Business*, Vol. 25, No. 1 (Fall 1993), pp, 165–191.

7. In fact, the ICFTU report of July 1999 called on the United States to ratify the other core ILO conventions. Cited in a message "Campaign Against Deregulation and for Labor Rights for All!" issued by the Open World Conference in Defense of Trade Union Independence and Democratic Rights, owc@energy-net.org; September 28, 2000.

8. Ibid., pp. 169–191.

9. The attention the West has paid to Chinese prison labor has resulted from a successful anti-*laogai* (prison camp) campaign launched by Harry Wu, a former prison-camp inmate. See the Laogai Research Foundation website *http://www.laogai.org/welcome.htm*

10. Not even one out of some sixty private letters of migrant workers that I have analyzed contained any reference to trade unionism. See Anita Chan, "Culture of Survival: Lives of Migrant Workers Through the Prism of Private Letters," in Perry Link, Richard Madsen, and Paul Pickowicz (eds.), *Popular Thought in Post-Socialist China*, Boulder: Rowman and Littlefield, forthcoming.

11. Antony Alcock, *History of the International Labor Organization*, London: Macmillan, 1971, p. 9.

12. Harold Dunning, "The Origins of Convention 87 on Freedom of Association and the Right to Organize," *Industrial Labour Review*, Vol. 137, No. 2, 1998, p. 153.

13. Alcock, *History of the International Labor Organization*, p. 35.

14. Nicolas Valticos and Geraldo W. von Potobsky, *International Labour Law*, Boston: Kluwer Law and Taxation Publishers, 1995, p. 19.

15. Alcock, *History of the International Labor Organization*, p. 42.

16. Ibid., p. 9.

17. Dunning, "The Origins of Convention No. 87," p. 159.

18. Universal Declaration of Human Rights (thereafter, UDHR), adopted December 10, 1948. Reprinted in *The United Nations and Human Rights, 1945–1995*, New York: United Nations, Blue Books Series, Volume VII, 1995, pp. 153–155.
19. Ibid.
20. Philip Alston, "Economic and Social Rights," in Louis Henkin and John Lawrence Hargrove (eds.), *Human Rights: An Agenda for the Next Century*, Washington, D.C.: The American Society of International Law, Studies in Transnational Legal Policy, No. 26, 1994, p. 152.
21. Ibid., p. 137.
22. Ibid., pp. 156–157.
23. Ibid., p. 162.
24. This is pointed out, for example, in Roy Adams and Sheldon Friedman, "The Emerging International Consensus on Human Rights in Employment," *Perspectives on Work*, Vol. 2, No. 2, 1998, pp. 24–27.
25. See Peter Van Ness, "Asia and Human Rights Diplomacy," *Current Affairs Bulletin*, December 1993, pp, 27–29; see also Ann Kent, "Human Rights in Australia-China Relations, 1985–95," in Cohn Mackerras (ed.), *Australia and China: Partners in Asia*, Melbourne: Macmillan Education Australia, 1996, pp. 57–68.
26. For example, see the 1,376-page report of 1996. For China, listed under "Section 6, Workers Rights," are subsections on: the right of association, the right to organize and bargain collectively, the prohibition of forced and compulsory labor, a minimum age for the employment of children, and acceptable conditions of work (pp. 591–594).
27. See Hilary K. Josephs, "Labor Law in a 'Socialist Market Economy': The Case of China," *Columbia Journal of Transnational Law*, No. 33, 1995, pp. 577–578. Josephs thinks that China's labor record has not been addressed because the United States has ratified fewer ILO conventions than China, and because the United States' own labor record is tarnished.
28. Information Office of State Council (China's Cabinet), "Progress in China's Human Rights Cause in 1996" (March 31, 1997), in *Beijing Review*, Vol. 40, No. 16 (April 21, 1997), p. 15. Within China, the term "labor rights" is politically sensitive, however, and as yet, the term and concept have not appeared at all in China's mass media. I was told in China that those who want to use the term, even in specialized publications, are warned by their superiors about the personal risks involved. One of the rare books published with the term "labor rights" in the title is Chang Kai, *Laodong guanxi, laodongzhe, laoquan* (Labor Relations, Laborers, Labor Rights), Beijing: Chinese Labor Press, 1995.
29. For a discussion of this tactic of the Chinese government toward well-known political activists, see Anita Chan, "The Changing Ruling Elite and Political Opposition in China," in Garry Rodan (ed.), *Political Oppositions in Industrializing Asia*, London: Routledge, 1996, pp. 161–187. This government tactic was confirmed by John Kamm, Executive Director of an NGO called the Dui Hua Foundation, who, as a private individual, has been negotiating with various bureaucracies of the Chinese government since 1989 for the release or reduction of the sentences of Chinese

political prisoners. This information is based on a talk he presented at The Australian National University in June 2000.

30. See, for example, Christian M. Cera, "Universality of Human Rights and Cultural Diversity: Implementation of Human Rights in Different Social-Cultural Contexts," *Human Rights Quarterly*, Vol. 16 (1994), pp. 740–752.

31. Marina Svensson, *The Chinese Conception of Human Rights: The Debate on Human Rights in China, 1998–1949*, Lund: University of Land Press, 1996, pp. 10–11.

32. Information Office of State Council, "Progress in China's Human Rights Cause in 1996," *Beijing Review*, Vol. 40, No. 16 (April 21–27, 1997), pp. 11–16.

33. *China Rights Forum*, Winter 1997–98, p. 6.

34. Alston, "Economic and Social Rights," pp. 159–160.

35. See, for instance, the speech by Pierre Sane, Secretary General of Amnesty International, "Does Human Rights Make Business Sense?" presented at the One World Conference: Companies Caught in Conflict, March 18, 1997, London.

36. Amnesty International, "Human Rights Principles for Companies," January 1998 (AI Index: ACT 70/01/98).

37. The introduction to the *World Report 1997: Events of 1996* includes two pages on "Labor Rights and the Global Economy," pp. xxi–xxii.

38. Steven Greenhouse, "Activism Surges at Campuses Nationwide, and Labor is at Issue," *New York Times*, March 29, 1999; Duncan Campbell, "U.S. Students Leave Shopping Malls to Sign up for Protests," *The Guardian Weekly*, November 25–December 1, 1999. No such student activism has flared up on university campuses in other Western countries.

39. Harvard Business School, "Hitting the Wall: Nike and International Labor Practices," unpublished manuscript N1–700–047k, January 19, 2000, pp. 3–4.

40. Celia Mather, "Do It Just—Campaigning on Company Codes of Conduct," *IRENE*, Nos. 24 and 25 (February 1997), pp. 6–13.

41. "Hong Kong NGO Seminar on Codes of Conduct, 15 July 1999," *Labor Rights in China Seminar Report*, Hong Kong, unpublished, 1999, p. 2.

42. Robert Collier, "Some U.S. Firms Work to Cut Abuses in Chinese Factories," *San Francisco Chronicle*, May 17, 2000.

43. *Washington Post*, April 10, 1997.

44. The companies participating in the FLA include Adidas-Saloman, Eddie Bauer, Gear for Sports, Kathie Lee Gifford, Levi Strauss, Liz Claiborne, L.L. Bean, Nicole Miller, Nike, Patagonia, Phillip-Van Heusen, and Reebok.

45. Martin Van Der Werf, "Miffed by Sweatshop Code, Nike Moves to End Agreement to Supply Sports Equipment to Brown University," *The Chronicle of Higher Education*, March 31, 2000; Associated Press, "Nike Kills University of Michigan Talks," April 27, 2000.

46. But even within this arena, there is no consensus over including a social clause. See *Asian Labor Update* (November 1995–March 1996), an issue specially devoted to the debate over the social clause.

47. "Workers in Global Economy Project," International Labor Rights Fund website, http://www.laborrights.org/projects/globalecon/index.html.

48. For example, a Workers' Relations Branch of the ILO observed that non-core standards are of less concern to ILO than the core standards. Statement made at the Sixth World Congress of the International Textile, Garment, and Leather Workers Federation, published in the "Sixth World Congress Summary of Proceedings," distributed at the Seventh World Congress of the ITGLWF held in April 1996 in Melbourne, p. 81.

49. Feng Chen, "Subsistence Crises, Managerial Corruption and Labour Protests in China," *The China Journal*, No. 44 (July 2000), pp. 41–63.

50. Han Dongfang, *Reform, Corruption and Livelihood—Recorded Conversation Between Han Dongfang and Chinese Workers, Vol. 1* (Gaige, wubi, minsheng—Han Dongfang yu Zhongguo gongren duihualu, di yi ij), Hong Kong: Chinese Labor Bulletin, 1998, pp. vii, 4–5.

51. Trini Leung. "Labor Rights Without Labor—Not Only Impossible, But Unacceptable," *China Rights Forum*, Spring 2000, pp. 30–33. For a different position advocating that NGOs work with corporations to monitor their codes of conduct, see Bama Athreya, "Governing the Ungovernable? Corporations and Human Rights," ibid., pp. 36–39, 52. For a debate among labor advocates on this controversial issue, see Labor Rights in China (LARIC), "Hong Kong NGO Seminar on Codes of Conduct, 15 July 1999," Seminar Report, 1999.

52. For an example of such research, see Melissa Connor, Tara Gruzen, Larry Sacks, Jude Sunderland, Darcy Tromanhauser, Faculty Advisor: Shubham Chaudhuri, "The Case for Corporate Responsibility: Paying a Living Wage to Maquila Workers in El Salvador" unpublished report for the National Labor Committee, New York, Columbia University, Program in Economic and Political Development, School of International Public Affairs, May 14, 1999.

53. "After Seattle: A Global Disaster," *The Economist*, December 11, 1999, pp. 17–18; Leif Pagrostsky (Sweden's Trade Minister), "Put All Workers' Rights On the Trade Agenda," *International Herald Tribune*, February 16, 2000.

54. Ethical Trading Initiative Seminar Report 4, "Governance in China: What are the Implications for Ethical Trading?" September 1999, at http://www.eti.org.uk/_html/events/seminar_04/ framesets/f_page.shtml.

55. *Nanfang ribao* (Southern Daily), March 31, 2000.

56. *Nanfang ribao*, April 19, 2000.

57. International Labour Conference, 85th Session 1997, *Report of the Director General: Executive Summary, The ILO, Standard Setting and Globalization*, June 3, 1997, available at http://www.ilo.org/public/english/10i1c/ilc85dg.rep.htm (visited September 22, 1998).

58. "All About the ICFTU World Congress, Durban, 3–7 April 2000: The Future Shape of the Trade Union Movement," ICFTU Online, 0810000510/LD.

Dying of Thirst

How the Global Water Crisis Threatens Humanity

Maude Barlow and Tony Clark

The world's water crisis is having a devastating impact on quality of life for billions of the world's citizens caught between the twin realities of water scarcity and water pollution. In fact, the world's intensifying water crisis is literally the arbiter of life and death for a growing number of people. It is also becoming a matter of fierce competition and struggle within societies and social classes and between nations.

The 3,400-kilometer *maquiladora*, or export-processing zones, on the border between Mexico and the United States are toxic cesspools. Rivers and streams in the region are so polluted that only 12 percent of the people living there have reliable access to clean water, and many residents live in homes with no sewage systems whatsoever. In the shantytowns and cardboard shacks that surround the free trade zones, where precious drinking water is delivered by truck once a week, the absence of fresh water has become a symbol of the poverty of the more than one million people who have flocked to the area in the last five years. And the filthy water of the region carries disease and causes severe diarrhea. Though residents drink the trucked-in water, they use local water for cooking and bathing and for irrigating crops, which then become dangerous to eat.

The filth of the *maquiladora*, its lethal water, and its squalid poverty push thousands of young Mexicans away from their home country. Every night, they head for the border, trying to enter the United States illegally to seek a better life. The strips at the crossings are notoriously dirty and dangerous. Six-lane highways divide cities like Tijuana and Juárez from the desolate belts of dirt where the men gather at dusk. A steep cement drop leads to a slow-moving river of chemical sludge and raw sewage about two feet deep. On the other side, the cement wall inclines at a 90-degree angle, fenced in at the top by a huge barbed-wire electric fence and lit by floodlights. The stench along the strip is unbearable; human and animal excrement, used condoms and needles, and piles of garbage mix with the stinking little river of sludge the men must run through to get to the other side. The chemicals and sewage get on their feet and into their shoes. Whether they reach the U.S. or are caught by American security patrols and sent back, they have had to pass through this deadly, filthy river and may have to do so again.

Also at the crossing are the people who can find no work in the *maquiladora*. They hang around the border at night, peddling fried tacos, condoms, and drugs—and plastic bags. Even the poorest of the would-be illegal immigrants will shell out the little they have to wrap plastic bags around their feet, for protection from the poisoned water.

Lethal Waters

Half the people on this planet lack basic sanitation services. Every time they take a drink of water, they are ingesting what Anne Platt of the Worldwatch Institute calls water-borne killers. So it is not surprising that 80 percent of all disease in the poor countries of the South is spread by consuming unsafe water. The statistics are sobering: 90 percent of the Third World's wastewater is still discharged untreated into local rivers and streams; water-borne pathogens and pollution kill 25 million people every year; every eight seconds, a child dies from drinking contaminated water; and every year, diarrhea kills nearly three million children, a full quarter of the deaths in this age group. The declining quality of the world's water has also caused malaria, cholera, and typhoid to occur more frequently in many places where they had been all but wiped out. They proliferate in conditions of dense population, poor sanitation, and poverty. Between 1990 and 1992, the number of people suffering from cholera worldwide rose from one hundred thousand to six hundred thousand, and these numbers continued to rise throughout the decade, though not so sharply.

In 1991, a pollution crisis caused a particularly bad cholera outbreak. In that year, a Chinese ship dumped its sewage into a bay in Lima, Peru, and within three weeks, cholera had spread up and down the coast, causing acute diarrhea, severe dehydration, and sometimes death. In the first year alone, nearly three thousand Peruvians died. Over the next two years, this one outbreak gradually contaminated the water supply of all but two countries in Latin America, infecting five hundred thousand people.

People living in Africa are afflicted by many different water-borne diseases. As many as two hundred thousand are thought to suffer from schistosomiasis, or bilharzia, a disease borne by water snails often found in irrigated water taken from dams. It causes cirrhosis of the liver and intestinal damage. Some 18 million Africans have onchocerciasis, or river blindness, carried by a blackfly that breeds in dirty rivers. And during the Sudan civil war of 1997, thousands of people fleeing from the war drank putrid water in refugee camps and became infected with sleeping sickness, a brutal illness carried by the water-bred tsetse fly.

Some disease-causing organisms—*cryptosporidium, E. coli, giardia*—are directly linked to poor or nonexistent sewage treatment and are also making a comeback. They are caused by too much human and animal sewage leaking into drinking water. In some cases, these afflictions are a result of too many people living in too little space, right near their sources of untreated drinking water. A family in Africa may have to defecate in a place not far from their well, and if they have livestock, the animals may have to do the same. A child in a shantytown in the Philippines might have no choice but to defecate near the family's water tank, and whole villages may drink water from a river that also carries raw sewage.

In other cases, government cutbacks are affecting the quality of drinking water. In Canada, the Ontario provincial government massively cut the budget of the Ministry of the Environment, gutted the water protection infrastructure, and laid off many trained water-testing experts. Some of the testing previously done by government workers was farmed out to private testing labs. Then, in 1999, a Canadian federal government study revealed that a third of Ontario's rural wells were contaminated with *E. coil*, and in June 2000 at least seven people, one of them a baby, died from drinking the water in the little town of Walkerton.

Back in Africa, mounting debt repayments during the 1980s and 1990s forced many countries to cut down on water and sanitation services to their citizens. These are only some of the Third World countries that are still paying as much as 70 percent of their national budgets to repay their debts to the International Monetary Fund and the World Bank. The tragedy that ensued was documented by Peter Gleick of the Pacific Institute for Studies in Development, Environment, and Security, a highly respected think tank on water issues based in California. In Nairobi, capital expenditures for water fell by a factor of ten in just five years during the 1980s. In Zimbabwe, 25 percent of village water pumps failed when the government cut maintenance funds by more than half. Dysentery rates in Kinshasha soared in 1995 when funds for water chlorination ran out, and cholera cases and deaths rose dramatically.

* * *

In South Africa, a recent cholera outbreak has been directly linked to the government's decision to cut off water supplies to those who could not pay their water bills. More than 100,000 people in KwaZulu-Natal province became ill with cholera, and 220 died in the course of ten months beginning in August 2000, after the South African government, urged by the World Bank, implemented a "cost recovery" program and denied water and sanitation services to many thousands of citizens who had been getting their water free of charge.

Some diseases are linked to modern pollution and afflict people living in the industrialized nations of the North as much as or more than those living in the Third World. Lead has been linked to loss of intelligence and behavioral problems in children in both the South and the North. Sixty billion people on the Indian subcontinent have been poisoned by fluoride. The combination of household and industrial disinfection by-products, along with chlorine added to water, has been implicated in cancer deaths. Arsenic has been associated with bladder, skin, and lung cancers. Over the last decade, high levels of this poison were found in Bangladesh, where one in five water pumps was contaminated with high levels of arsenic. Although in these cases, the arsenic occurred naturally, rather than being the result of toxic dumping, people were forced to dig deep into wells because of severe groundwater shortages and pollution. If they had not had to dig so deeply, they could have avoided the arsenic.

The U.S. Environmental Protection Agency (EPA) estimates that more than half the wells in the United States are contaminated with pesticides and nitrates. Pesticides and chemicals such as perchloroethylene, or "perc"; PCBs; and dioxins accumulate in the body fat of animals, fish, and humans and are linked to cancer. In infants, reports the U.S. group Physicians for Social Responsibility, ingestion of high concentrations of nitrates from well water results in methemoglobinemia, which carries an 8 percent fatality rate. The Women's Environmental Network in Britain claims that as many as 8 percent of the country's children have sustained some nervous-system damage and memory loss as a result of exposure to dioxins and PCBs, and the World Health Organization has said that the increasing use of pesticides is killing forty thousand people every year.

Some diseases are even related to poor maintenance of water infrastructure. Half the people in the industrialized nations of the North, and more in poor countries, carry the stomach bacterium *helicobacter pylori*, usually caused by slime build-up in water pipes. The bacterium causes stomach ulcers and cancer and is particularly prevalent in unchlorinated well water and water supplies in Third World countries.

Unequal Access

There is nowhere on earth to go to escape the global water crisis. For instance, in the wealthy United States, says the Natural Resources Defense Council, some 53 million Americans—nearly one-fifth of the population—drink tap water contaminated with lead, fecal bacteria, or other serious pollutants. Alarmingly, according to the Environmental Protection Agency, outbreaks associated with groundwater sources grew by almost 30 percent between 1995 and 1998 in the United States.

However, it is also very clear that the world's poor are taking the brunt of the crisis, whether we are talking about water-borne diseases or outright scarcity. A report from the United Nations Economic and Social Council to the UN's Commission on Sustainable Development says that fully three-quarters of the population living under conditions of water stress—amounting to 26 percent of the total world population—are located in Third World countries. By 2025, the commission projects, the citizens of low-income countries experiencing water stress will amount to 47 percent of the total world population. Furthermore, the great majority of the megalopolises in which more than 50 percent of the population has no access to clean water are located in the Third World, and the highest rate of growth within these cities is in the slums. By 2030, says the UN, more than half the population of these huge urban centers will be slum dwellers with no access to water or sanitation services whatsoever.

It is often said that the population explosion is a "water bomb" about to be detonated. There is no question that there is truth in this concern. Every year the world population grows by another 80 million people who have to share dwindling fresh water supplies. But as water expert Riccardo Petrella points out, that argument alone may encourage some to lay all the blame on the Third World, where the majority of the population explosion is taking place, and to overlook the fact that people living in the countries of the North consume much more water—among other goods—than people living in Third World countries.

The richest fifth of the world accounts for 86 percent of consumption of all goods. As Petrella explains, a newborn baby in the West, or a rich one in the South, consumes between 40 and 70 times more water, on average, than one in the South who has no access to water. North Americans use 1,280 cubic meters (about 45,000 cubic feet) of water per person every year; Europeans use 694; Asians use 535; South Americans use 311; and Africans use 186. Although the average European consumes only about half as much water as the average North American, their consumption levels are still high compared to citizens of nonindustrialized countries. And ironically, as the United Nations reports, Europeans spend US$11 billion a year on ice cream—US$2 billion more than the estimated amount needed to provide clean water and safe sewers for the world's population.

The disparity in consumption levels of North and South is partly a reflection of the fact that some parts of the planet have more fresh water supplies than others, but this is not the full explanation. For instance, Australians, who occupy the driest land mass on earth, use 694 cubic meters (about 24,500 cubic feet) per year—the same amount as Europeans—because their consumer-based culture results in high volumes of water wastage. Conversely, China has almost as much fresh water as Canada, but because of population demands and pollution of its surface waters, that country is considered an area of crisis.

The countries of the North are responsible for a disproportionate amount of the world's water consumption, partly because of individual habits and lifestyles. Citizens of the most privileged countries simply take water for granted or are able to buy it, even if it is expensive. And their lifestyles—SUVs, lawns and golf courses that are watered and sprinklered, swimming pools, and toilets that consume 18 liters (about 4.8 US gallons) of water per flush—use vast amounts of water. Another important factor in the consumption disparity is the use of water by industry. While globalization is spreading industrialization all over the planet, most industries are still located in the North. And where there is industry, water consumption is rampant. While agriculture still accounts for the vast majority of water use in the Third World, industry uses as much water as agriculture in North America and almost twice as much as agriculture in Europe. The water resources of the so-called Developed Nations are not yet as scarce as those of the Third World, but they are being wasted by a lifestyle based on water-depleting consumerism.

* * *

North Americans and Europeans have set themselves on a path that is leading to water scarcity. So far, resources in these nations appear to be abundant, but they are not infinite, and current rates of consumption will lead to depletion—especially as nonindustrialized nations try to emulate North American lifestyles. If these trends continue, we will, in time, be living on a water-scarce planet. To get a glimpse of what that future will look like, we can go to the Third World today. In crowded Asian, African, and Latin American countries, massive increases in animal and human waste, intensified by the establishment of factory farms, are exposing more and more people to cholera and deadly diseases caused by the *E. coli* bacterium. Most local governments cannot even afford basic chlorine to treat their water. And where local communities once turned to aquifers and hand pumps to avoid the problem of polluted surface water, chemical and human waste seeping into these sources has now made groundwater dangerous as well. In China, 80 percent of the population drinks contaminated water. In Papua New Guinea, one-quarter of the inhabitants live in critical conditions because they lack clean water, even though the country is water rich. And in India, 70 percent of the population has no proper drainage system. In Manila, in the Philippines, water shortages affect 40 percent of the residents, and in most Third World cities, water is often rationed to neighborhoods for only a few hours a day or a few days a week.

The people of Africa have suffered more than many as a result of bad water. Of the 25 countries that the UN lists as having the least access to safe water, 19 are in Africa, and people living on that continent have the highest rate of death from diarrhea, as well as a high incidence of malaria and other water-related diseases. Water in Nairobi is so scarce that slum dwellers have started to tap into wastewater mains, and for about 15 million South Africans, the nearest source of water is at least one kilometer away. According to Water Policy International, South African women collectively walk the equivalent of going to the moon and back 16 times a day just to fetch water.

Elite Privilege

Although water inequality parallels the inequities that exist between the industrialized and nonindustrialized countries of the world, disparities also occur within individual societies. Surprisingly, the poorest people in poor countries pay much more for their water than the rich of their society. Municipal water, subsidized by governments, is delivered to the wealthy, and people in the middle class can install a small water tank for trucked-in water or dig a well. (The richer among the middle class can afford to sink deeper boreholes when the well water starts to dry up.) But the poor buy water by the can from private water carriers who may charge as much as one hundred times the rate of municipally delivered water. Anne Platt of Worldwatch Institute reports that a family in the top fifth income groups in Peru, the Dominican Republic, or Ghana is, respectively, three, six, or twelve times more likely to have water connected to their home by pipe than a family in the bottom fifth in those countries. Because they lack access to publicly subsidized utilities, says Platt, the poor often end up paying more for their water than do the rich because they must obtain it from illegal sources or private vendors.

In Lima, Peru, for instance, poor people may pay a private vendor as much as three dollars for a cubic meter of water, which they must then collect by bucket and which is often contaminated. The more affluent, on the other hand, pay 30 cents per cubic meter (about 35 cubic feet) for treated water provided through the taps in their houses. Hillside slum dwellers in Tegucigalpa, the capital of Honduras, pay substantially more for water supplied by private tankers than they would even if they paid for the government to install a water pipe. In Dhaka, Bangladesh, squatters pay water rates that are 12 times higher than what the local utility charges. And in Lusaka, Zambia, low-income families spend, on average, half their household income on water.

The elite of a nation and wealthy tourists also have special water access. In 1994, when Indonesia was hit with a major drought, residents' wells ran dry, but Jakarta's golf courses, which cater to wealthy tourists, continued to receive one thousand cubic meters (about 35,000 cubic feet) per course per day. In 1998, in the midst of a three-year drought that dried up river systems and further depleted aquifers, the government of Cyprus cut the water supply to farmers by 50 percent while guaranteeing the country's two million tourists a year all the water they needed. And where race and class come together, water privilege can be startling. In South Africa, six hundred thousand white farmers consume 60 percent of the country's water supplies for irrigation, while 15 million blacks have no direct access to water.

In Mexico, the situation is not much better. In the *maquiladora* zones near the U.S. border, clean water is so scarce that babies and children drink Coke and Pepsi instead. And during a drought crisis in the northern part of the country in 1995, the government cut water supplies to local farmers while ensuring emergency supplies to the mostly foreign-controlled industries of the region.

Food Scarcity

As societies all over the world have become more dependent on irrigated land to grow their food, the lack of fresh water sources also threatens their food supplies. Simply put, many of the world's most important food-producing regions are running out of water for irrigation. Humans obtain 40 percent of their food from irrigated land, and the amount of irrigated land has grown exponentially in the last several decades.

This change in the basis of humanity's food production has put a profound strain on the world's groundwater supplies. The global harvest of fruit, vegetable, and grain crops uses an enormous quantity of water—so much that author Sandra Postel of the Global Water Policy Project in Amherst, Massachusetts, notes in her book *Pillar of Sand* that many important food-producing regions are sustained by the hydrological equivalent of deficit financing. As irrigators draw on water reserves to support current production, they are racking up large water deficits that will one day have to be balanced. Annual depletion (that is, net water loss) in India, China, the United States, North Africa, and the Arabian Peninsula alone adds up to about 160 billion cubic meters (about 5,650 billion cubic feet) a year.

Postel estimates that about 180 million tons of grain—approximately 10 percent of the global harvest—is being produced by using water supplies that are not being replenished. To feed the world's population by 2025, an additional two thousand cubic kilometers (about 476 cubic miles) of irrigation water will be needed. But since agricultural operations are already creating water deficits, Postel points out, where are farmers going to find the additional irrigation water needed to satisfy the food demands of the more than two billion people expected to join humanity's ranks in the next several decades?

Dam Fallout

The human suffering caused by big dam projects (linked, of course, to the massive increase in irrigation practices around the world) is as serious as their environmental fallout. An estimated 60 to 80 million people have been displaced by the building of dams around the world in the last six decades. These legions of "oustees," as they are called in India, have been culturally, economically, and emotionally devastated by the loss of community, livelihood, and links to their ancestral homes. This situation is familiar to the International Rivers Network, a U.S.-based group that was instrumental in convincing the United Nations to set up a commission investigating dams. According to Patrick McCully of this organization, families have often been flooded out with minimal or no compensation, and millions of independent farm families have ended up as slum dwellers on the edges of the Third World's burgeoning cities. These numbers do not even take into account the untold millions who are also negatively affected by massive diversion projects, but who still live on the land or rivers nearby.

India and China have created the largest number of oustees and have used brutal tactics to enforce their evictions. As an average of more than six hundred large dams were built every year in the three decades following the Chinese Revolution of 1949, at least ten million people were displaced, according to the Chinese government. But other observers put the number much higher. Chinese dam critic Dai Qing puts the total at more than 40 million. And many of the evictions have been carried out brutally. In 1958, for instance, hundreds of thousands of people were evicted to make way for China's Xinanjiang Dam. Officials, who ordered that the resettlement be carried out "like a battle action," sent in laborers to tear down houses, and traumatized peasants were forced to walk for days to resettlement sites. And more recently, nearly two hundred thousand people have been displaced for the massive US$4billion Xiaolangdi Dam now being built on the Yellow River. Observers fear a repeat of the failure of the Sanmenxia Dam built upstream on the same river in the 1950s. That dam deposited massive amounts of sediment and flooded riverbanks. Mao ordered it to be bombed when it threatened the ancient city of Xian. It had to be redesigned, and this fortified construction flooded 66,000 hectares (about 163,000 acres) of fertile farmland. According to a World Bank report, the majority of the 410,000 people displaced by the Sanmenxia Dam still live in abject poverty, without any means of livelihood.

Violence and intimidation face those objecting to evacuation to make way for the internationally contentious US$50 billion Three Gorges Dam. Probe International reports that in August 2000, residents living in a local resettlement village were beaten and put under house arrest by soldiers because they were voicing peaceful protests against the submergence of their ancestral homeland. Altogether, the Three Gorges Dam will displace 1,100,000 people, who may also face brutal methods of resettlement. One villager displaced by the dam had this to say to Probe International: "Officials can decide whether people live or die. Without the survival rights, we dare not tell anyone our real names. We will face terrible disasters if the county government knows we talk to you. We are being watched by people assigned by the county government. If found out, the outsiders [environmentalists and journalists] will be beaten up first and then inspected."

According to the World Commission on Dams, between 16 and 38 million people have been displaced by dams in post-Independence India. In 1981, for instance, one hundred thousand people living in the submergence zone of the Srisailam Dam in Andhra Pradesh were driven out of their homes in what authorities called "Operation Demolition." And over four hundred thousand have been directly evicted in the construction of the Sardar Sarovar (formerly the Narmada), now stopped by a court injunction. Like China, India has taken a brutal approach to dam evictions. In 1961, the Indian finance minister spoke to local farmers at a meeting in the submergence zone of the Pong Dam. He was blunt: "We will request you to move from your houses after the dam comes up. If you move, it will be good, otherwise we shall release the waters and drown you all."

Other evictions around the world have included acts of unspeakable barbarity. In the Soviet Union, evictees were often forced to take part in the burning and destruction of their own houses, orchards, and churches and the exhuming of relatives' coffins. But even worse was a case cited by Patrick McCully of International Rivers Network involving the murder of 378 Maya Achi Aboriginal people in Guatemala. In the early 1980s, a European consortium threatened to displace 3,400 people in order to build Guatemala's Chixoy Dam. In spite of the obvious presence of thousands of residents, the consortium's feasibility study claimed that the land held "almost no population." The Maya Achi from the village of Rio Negro objected and asked for a fairer resettlement payment. But instead of receiving better compensation, on three separate and horrific occasions, Guatemalan soldiers appeared and massacred the Maya Achi men, women, and children.

This story is symbolic of how Indigenous peoples have traditionally been shoved aside to make way for dam projects. All over the world, their livelihoods have been disproportionately affected. In India, 40 percent of all those who have been displaced by dams are *adivasis*—low-caste Indigenous peoples who represent just 6 percent of the population. Almost all the large dams built in the Philippines are on land where Indigenous peoples live. In 1948, the Garrison Dam in the U.S. flooded most of the North Dakota Native reservation and displaced the majority of the people living there. More recently, the Innu peoples of northern Quebec suffered loss of habitat and traditional fish-spawning grounds when rivers near James Bay were inundated as part of a hydro project in northern Quebec in the 1970s.

Dams create the habitat for the parasites that cause schistosomiasis and other water-borne diseases, and the victims are often the oustees or people living downstream from the reservoir. After the construction of the High Aswan Dam in Egypt, schistosomiasis became endemic. After the Akosombo Dam in Ghana was flooded in 1964, displacing eighty-four thousand people, 90 percent of the children living near the reservoir became afflicted with the disease. Similarly, reports Patrick McCully, onchocerciasis, or river blindness, is carried by the irrigated waters from dams. So is malaria, a disease that is on the rise again after intensive eradication programs. Malaria breeds in the billions of mosquitoes found in stagnant water in hot, humid climates, but the ecological changes caused by dams and irrigation projects in arid and semi-arid areas also create the ideal breeding grounds for the disease. Malaria kills over one million people worldwide every year. In the area of Sri Lanka's five-dam Mahaweli project, stagnant water pools became a breeding ground for malaria-carrying mosquitoes, and in 1986, the first-ever case of malaria was reported in the region. Similarly, an epidemic of malaria, a disease which had been eradicated in southern Brazil, followed the construction of the Itaipú Dam in 1989.

Water Conflicts

Given the reality of shrinking fresh water supplies, the pollution of existing sources, and the growing demand for water, it is inevitable that conflicts will arise over access. All over the world, communities in water-stressed countries are beginning to compete with one another for prior use of this precious resource. Tensions are growing across nation-state borders and between cities and rural communities, ethnic groups and tribes, industrialized and nonindustrialized nations, people and Nature, corporations and citizens, and different socio-economic classes.

Urbanization is also adding pressure to the already uneasy situation. As people move or are displaced to growing urban centers, demand for water will also rise in those places. So water is being diverted from rural and wilderness areas to meet urban demand, but farmers, already stretched to feed a burgeoning population, are understandably reluctant to let those precious water allocations go. As described in Chapter 1, this transfer is well under way in China, where the urban migration is just beginning in earnest. Cities and industry are favored openly by the Chinese government, and farmers are having their water taken from them without consent or even prior knowledge. The same situation is occurring in India. Some farmers are making more money selling their groundwater to urban and industrial users than they once made from growing food.

In *Pillar of Sand*, Sandra Postel reports that rice farmers in parts of the Indonesian island of Java are losing water supplies to textile factories, even though the law requires priority to be given to agriculture. To make matters worse, the factories sometimes take more than their permits allow, leaving farmers high and dry. They have also polluted local water supplies, which has a damaging effect on crops. In South Korea, farmers south of Seoul recently armed themselves with hoes and blocked municipal water trucks from pumping water for city dwellers, for fear of having too little water left for their crops. And in the American Pacific Northwest, farmers in the Columbia River Basin were paid forty dollars an acre in the summer of 2001 not to irrigate their crops, so the massive hydroelectric generators along the river could supply power to California.

In some cases, rural dwellers are pitted against other rural dwellers. In Brazil's Northeast, prolonged drought is fomenting strife between water haves and have-nots. The powerful São Francisco River has been diverted for irrigation, and what remains of it now snakes its way through what was formerly some of Brazil's bleakest terrain. As reported by Joelle Diderich for Reuters News Agency, this irrigation program has transformed 300,000 hectares (about 740,000 acres) of the dry river valley into orchards growing tropical fruits such as coconuts and guava for export. The state-run project is also financing roads, sewage systems, and an airport. Some might defend this gargantuan enterprise by pointing out that it has become a magnet for farmers seeking work and has created a wealthy few. The handful of farmers who came to the project first have become prosperous, but there are a limited number of lots, and farm workers have no job security. This has heightened inequities within the region. Drought also threatens more than 10 million people—the vast majority of the area—with starvation. This reflects the situation throughout Central America, where drought endangers more than half the 35 million citizens—some of it caused when huge quantities of water are used up by large, corporate-run, farm-for-export operations, leaving little for local family farmers to raise their crops.

Water scarcity has also pitted farmers against Indigenous peoples and those defending endangered species. In Klamath Falls, Oregon, for example, during the long, hot summer of 2001, farmers took the law into their own hands and repeatedly reopened reservoir gates for irrigation water that the Federal Bureau of Investigation had ordered closed, to protect endangered bottom-feeding sucker-fish and threatened coho salmon during a year of record drought. Local Native tribes also had treaty rights to these fish and had demanded government protection of the fish and for water to be diverted back to their natural habitat. The Native people and commercial salmon fishermen farther downstream say that favoring farmers with massive irrigation for decades has deprived them of their livelihood and cultural rights.

For the farmers, however, the order was devastating. It cut off water to about 1,400 family farmers and ranchers in the Klamath Basin, and about two hundred thousand acres (about eighty thousand hectares) that grow water-thirsty alfalfa—normally kept green through irrigation—are now parched. The local community was so supportive of the farmers that the sheriff wouldn't arrest the trespassers who reopened the reservoir gates, and local prosecutors refused to prosecute. In a similar dispute involving farmers in California, a precedent-setting federal claims court decision determined that the redirection of water supplies to help endangered species in that state in the early 1990s constituted a taking of property and ordered compensation to the farmers.

Once more, the demands of the so-called free market placed farmers in the awkward position of entering into large-scale, water-hungry enterprises in order to increase volume of production and make up for the paltry prices they are paid for their crops. Once invested in highly mechanized, large-scale operations, farmers cannot continue to operate without depending on massive use of resources such as fossil fuels and water. Ironically, they are then placed in a position where they can do considerable damage to ecosystems and contravene Native rights. If farmers were encouraged and enabled to switch to more drought-resistant crops and less fuel-intensive farming, water conflicts like the ones just described would be less frequent. But for this to happen, the American government—like other governments around the world—will have to stop subsidizing industrial, resource-depleting agriculture and support sustainable, smaller-scale farming and encourage the cultivation of more drought-resistant crops.

Nature and Power

Unemployed people can also be used as pawns in schemes that do damage to Nature. In Canada's easternmost province, Newfoundland, unemployment is chronically high, but many wilderness areas still abound with life. On the province's south shore, for instance, is a lake full of pristine water, 16 kilometers long by 10 kilometers wide (about 10 by 6 miles). Starting in 1997, a local businessman has applied to the province for an export licence, so he can sell Gisborne Lake water to thirsty consumers around the world. Not surprisingly, the proposal is extremely contentious. On one side are many Canadians concerned about the ecological effects of massive water removals and about losing control of the water supplies Canada needs to support its growing population—including future immigrants from water-starved countries. These concerns are heightened by the fact that Canada has short-sightedly signed trade agreements in which water is described as a tradable commodity. On the other side of the argument are the residents of Grand Le Pierre, a small fishing community of 350 located near Gisborne Lake, which was impoverished when the cod they depended on were overfished almost to extinction. With unemployment rampant, the community leapt at the opportunity to create jobs associated with the proposed project. The former premier, Brian Tobin, closed the door on water exports, but the new premier, Roger Grimes, has reopened it and the issue is being hotly contested.

Water disputes have also broken out between small farmers and the interests of agribusiness. In Ecuador, for instance, a new law on water is currently on the table and two opposing agricultural groups are working to shape it in quite different ways. As reported by water expert Riccardo Petrella, one of these proposals has been advanced by the Agricultural Chambers of Commerce and defends the interests of the big farmer and agribusiness. They tend to support privatization of water services and want water to be used for greater industrial productivity. The other proposal is offered by CONAIE (the Ecuadorian Indigenous Nationalities Confederation) on behalf of small farmers and workers. This statement maintains that water is a public asset that should be used mainly to serve the equitable development of the country's entire population. CONAIE contends that the food and water security of the local population should be the number one priority.

In many countries in the world, the elite of society are gaining privileged access to water, to greater and greater degrees. Throughout southeast Asia, for instance, golf tourism is on the rise, but this is creating a strong backlash from local residents who believe that the water-guzzling courses are "water-favored" by governments because of the tourism dollars they bring in. Nevertheless, golf courses continue to spring up all over this part of the world: Malaysia, Thailand, Indonesia, South Korea, and the Philippines maintain 550 golf courses, and they are building another 530.

The disparity of water access between rich and poor was violently dramatized in Bangladesh in 1999, when hundreds of residents of the capital city, Dhaka, attacked a power supply office, barricaded roads, and burned vehicles in the spring of that year to protest the scarcity of running water. The Dhaka Water and Sewage Authority admits that more than 30 percent of the city's nine million residents have no access to drinking water. The residents contend that the poor have been left by governments to fend for themselves.

Water strife can also be based on historic struggles of racism and power. Under apartheid, South Africa was openly discriminatory in its distribution of water. So the country's first democratic government inherited a serious set of water problems: water scarcity, unequal distribution of water based on race and class, severe pollution of water sources, heavily dammed rivers, and substandard or nonexistent sanitation for the black majority. At first it seemed that the new government understood these deep-seated social inequities and were prepared to eliminate water discrimination. In fact, South Africa's majority party set out to remedy the inequality by guaranteeing every person basic water rights in the new constitution. The African National Congress's Reconstruction and Development Programme declared that household water access as a human right was the "fundamental principle of our water resources policy."

However, in a study of post-apartheid water distribution, water scholars Patrick Bond and Greg Ruiters found that the African National Congress had also adopted a market-oriented approach to water management, thereby building in continued water shortages for the poor majority and water privilege for those who could pay. The government emphasized that water was a "scarce" good, requiring marginal cost pricing, even for the poor. Bond and Ruiters also discovered that the new government retained the apartheid-era hydrological bias toward supply enhancement through building expensive dams, while failing to charge a sufficient price to those who were wasting water. "The result was drought for those most in need of water and excess liquidity for those most prone to abuse it." And worse, water access and sanitation services to the majority of South Africans had actually declined during the first half-decade of democracy. A lower percentage of South Africans now enjoyed access to affordable water in their homes and yards than they had in 1994, and hundreds of thousands of water consumers had had their taps shut off in the late 1990s.

As a result, the distribution of South Africa's water throughout the population is even more inequitable, measured in class, race, and gender terms, than the distribution of income. More than half of South Africa's raw water is used for white-dominated commercial agriculture, and half of that water is wasted in poor irrigation practices. Another quarter is used in mining and industry. About 12 percent of South Africa's water is consumed by households, but of that amount, more than half goes into white households, including water for gardens and swimming pools. And, as stated earlier, 16 million South African women still have to travel by foot at least one kilometer to supply their families with basic water needs. In September 2001, police shot 15 people, one a five-year-old child, when residents resisted the cutting off of water to 1,800 people in Cape Town's Unicity. Private workers and protection services, guarded by hundreds of police, succeeded in cutting the water lines, leaving behind a devastated community. Fires broke out as local people, weeping openly, set up burning barricades to prevent retaliation.

Border Struggles

About 40 percent of the world's population relies on the 214 major river systems shared by two or more countries. As water travels from its source, it is diverted for drinking, irrigation, and hydro power—putting downstream countries in a vulnerable position. Many countries in water-scarce areas also share lake waters and aquifers. With more people chasing less water, the social, political, and economic impact of water scarcity is becoming a destabilizing force between countries. Even within a country, disputes can break out between political jurisdictions. The mayor of Mexico City, for example, has predicted that conflicts will break out in the Mexican Valley in the foreseeable future if a solution to his city's water crisis is not found soon. And in the United States, a dispute between Nebraska and Kansas over the use of water from the Republican River has been taken all the way to the Supreme Court. Kansas has alleged that Nebraska has allowed unregulated and unrestricted well drilling and pumping in the river basin, which depleted the flow of water into Kansas.

Most border disputes, however, are between countries. In 1997, for instance, Malaysia, which supplies about half of Singapore's water, threatened to cut off that supply after Singapore criticized its government policies. In Africa, relations between Botswana and Namibia have been severely strained by Namibian plans to construct a pipeline to divert water from the shared Okavango River to eastern Namibia. Farther north, Ethiopia plans to divert more water from the Nile—although Egypt depends heavily on that river for irrigation and power. Other tensions have arisen because of Turkey's plan to dam the Euphrates River, which it shares with Syria and Iraq, and Bangladesh suffered greatly when India diverted water from its borders. Bangladesh actually depends on river water that flows from or through India, but in the 1970s, when India was faced with increasing food security problems, it diverted the flow of these rivers into its irrigation systems. Bangladesh was left dry. It took over 20 years for the two countries to sign a water-sharing treaty to end their dispute.

* * *

In 1992, Slovakia, then a province of Czechoslovakia, ignored objections from environmentalists and started operations on the Gabcikova Dam on the Danube River along the border with Hungary. The Hungarians had been participants in the project, but pulled out in 1989 in response to that country's growing environmental movement. In 1993, the opposing sides agreed to refer the case to the International Court of Justice in The Hague, but much damage had already been done. The water table in the Danube had seriously dropped, drying out thousands of hectares of forest and wetlands and reducing fish catches in the lower Danube by 80 percent.

Back in North America, disputes over the control and use of groundwater beneath the U.S.-Mexican border threaten to create major tensions between the two countries. First, the Hueco Bolson, an aquifer that serves municipal water use from Las Cruces to El Paso to Ciudad Juarez, Mexico, is trending toward depletion. In addition, the U.S. has proposed building a major irrigation canal that would serve California's Imperial Valley. These and many other water-extraction projects threaten to deplete groundwater along the border. Though there is a treaty between the two countries covering surface water, there is unfortunately no agreement covering groundwater, so the disagreements between the countries will have to be settled without benefit of a covenant between the two parties.

At the northern border, conflicts over water use are bound to grow among the 40 million people from eight U.S. states and two Canadian provinces who share the Great Lakes Basin. With water tables falling, the new demands of hundreds of new sprawling communities that lie just outside the basin area (whose demand has outstripped local supply) are straining the Great Lakes system to capacity. William Ruoff, the mayor of Webster, New York (population 2,500), learned just how contentious water issues can be when he placed an ad in the *Wall Street Journal* and the *New York Times,* offering to sell 2 million gallons (about 7.5 million liters) of "crystal clear" well water to the highest bidder. Ruoff backed off when the Great Lakes Governors and Premiers Association informed him that he was offering to sell Lake Ontario water and had no business doing so.

Fears in Canada about U.S. interest in its water are deep and longstanding. In the mid-19th century, the United States first began following a policy of Manifest Destiny, or continental expansion—an obvious threat to Canadian sovereignty. Today, Canadians are more concerned about the inclusion of water in the North American Free Trade Agreement (NAFTA) as a tradable commodity. Many Canadians believe that American politicians and business leaders view Canadian resources, including water, as continental resources, to be shared as if there were no border. Although Canadians have sovereignty over their land, some fear that if the U.S. runs short of water and Canadians refuse to divert their resources south of the border, Americans might view this as tantamount to a declaration of war. Canadian concerns were not allayed when President George W. Bush remarked in July 2001—just before the famous G-8 meeting in Genoa, Italy—that he saw Canadian water as an extension of Canada's energy reserves, to be shared with the U.S. by pipeline in the near future.

Tensions that are only potential in North America have already resulted in conflict in the Middle East, where water is perhaps as precious, and as contentious, an issue as anywhere else on earth. Forty percent of Israel's groundwater supply originates in occupied territories and water scarcity has been an issue in past Arab-Israeli wars. In 1965, Syria tried to divert the Jordan River from Israel, provoking Israeli airstrikes that forced Syria to abandon the attempt. Israel diverts water from the Jordan River, leaving the country of Jordan itself with depleted resources. Although armed conflict over water has not arisen between Jordan and Israel, the late King Hussein once said that he would never go to war with Israel *unless* it was over water.

Water scarcity has also increased tensions between Israel and the 2.3 million Palestinians living in the Occupied Territories. Even in recent times of drought,

Israel has kept its parks green and grown thirsty crops like cotton by limiting supplies to the 2.3 million Palestinians in the Occupied Territories. While some Israelis refuse to give up their watered lawns and swimming pools, many Palestinians are forced to get their drinking water from tankers, and Israeli per capita consumption of water is three times that of the Palestinians. "They cannot make peace with thirsty people," said Fadel Kaawash, deputy director of the Palestinian Water Authority.

Water can be used as a target in war as well. During the 1991 Gulf War, the United States considered bombing dams in the Euphrates and Tigris rivers north of Baghdad but backed off for fear of high casualties. The Allies also discussed asking Turkey to reduce the Euphrates flow at the Ataturk Dam upstream from Iraq. As it was, they targeted Baghdad's water-supply system while the Iraqis destroyed Kuwait's desalination plants.

In Yugoslavia a 1999 NATO bombing contaminated the massive aquifer that supplies most of eastern Europe with fresh water. Targets included a petro-chemical factory making artificial fertilizers, a chlorine-producing factory, a factory for the chemical production of rocket fuel, the municipality of Grocka where a nuclear reactor is situated, and four national parks. Chemicals released into the water table as a result of these bombings will be there for decades, perhaps centuries.

Private vs. Public Control of Water

Perhaps the most important dispute over fresh water supplies has to do with the increasing role of the private sector in deciding who gets it and why. No sector in the world has become ore conscous of the worth of water than the private sector, which sees a profit to be made from scarcity. The result is a fairly new phenomenon: water trading for profit.

Informal, small-scale water trading among farmers is common throughout the nonindustrialized nations of the South and was once frequent the North as well. These arrangements are made between local farmers and local communities and are based on principles that view water a common heritage, to be shared on the basis of need. But today, water trading, as carried out by large transnational corporations, is based on principles of profit, which are driving the price of water out of reach of the poor. In addition, when large corporations enter the game, they typically buy up block water rights, deplete water resources in an area, and move on. When Chile privatized water, for instance, mining companies were given nearly all the water rights in that country, free of charge. Today, they control Chile's water market and the shortage of water has served to push up prices.

In California, water rights trading is becoming a very big business. In 1992, the U.S. Congress passed a bill allowing farmers, for the first time in U.S. history, to sell their water rights to cities. Then, in 1997, Interior Secretary Bruce Babbitt announced plans to open a major water mark among the users of the Colorado River. The new system would allow interstate sales of Colorado River water between Arizona, Nevada, and California.

Wade Graham of *Harper's Magazine* calls this development "the large deregulation of a national resource since the *Homestead Act* of 1862" and adds that the only measure that could have topped it would have been the privatization of all U.S. federal lands. Babbitt was counting on the free market to do what politicians and the courts have not been able to do—act as a referee between the many parties laying claims to the Colorado's water. The deals are expected to be small at first, like the arrangement already reached between Nevada and Arizona, with Arizona storing water for Nevada to use in the future. In the long run, the fast-growing areas where the high-tech industry is concentrated will be able to obtain vast quantities of reasonably priced water from what is misconstrued as virtually limitless source.

A similar experiment in water privatization has already taken place in the Sacramento Valley, and Graham points to it as a warning. For the first time, in the early 1990s, southern California cities and farmers were no longer prevented from buying water directly from farmers in northern California, hoarding it, and selling it on the open market. Large-scale operators helped themselves to huge amounts of water and stored it with the Drought Water Bank until the price was right to sell. A small handful of sellers walked away with huge profits, while other farmers found their wells running dry for the first time in their lives. The results were disastrous: the water table dropped and the land sank in some places.

Graham compares this incident with the Owens Valley tragedy at the turn of the century. The once lush, water-rich Owens Valley was bled dry when water officials from Los Angeles devised a scheme to divert Owens Valley water to southern California. "The Owens Valley scam," writes Graham, "demonstrated that although only a few individuals or corporate entities hold registered water rights, the entire community depends upon those rights . . . Water in California is prosperity, and if the legal right to use it can be privatized and transferred away, then the prosperity of the community may go with it." No portion of the private sector knows this better than the computer industry, which is claiming unfair shares of local water supplies. Computer manufacturers use massive quantities of de-ionized fresh water to produce their goods and are constantly searching for new sources. Increasingly, this search is pitting giant high-tech corporations against economically and socially marginalized peoples in a battle for local water.

Electronics is the world's fastest-growing manufacturing industry according to the Silicon Valley Toxics Coalition. Giants such as IBM, AT&T, Intel, NEC, Fujitsu, Siemans, Philips, Sumitomo, Honeywell, and Samsung have annual net sales exceeding the gross domestic product of many countries. There are currently about 900 semiconductor fabrication facilities (fabs) around the world, where the computer wafers used in computer chips are manufactured. Another 140 plants are now under construction. These plants consume a staggering amount of water. The question is: Where will the water come from? It will have to be derived from the limited amounts available, and that will not happen without conflict. As the Southwest Network for Economic justice explains: "In an arena of such limited resources, a struggle ensues between those who have traditionally enjoyed these resources and those newcomers who look at these resources with covetous eyes."

* * *

High-tech companies are engaging in mechanisms to capture traditional water rights at low cost, without having to pay for cleaning up contaminated water. These include *water pricing*, whereby industry pressures governments for subsidies and circumvents city utility equipment to directly pump water, thus paying much less than residential water users; *water mining*, whereby companies gain rights to deplete aquifers while driving up the access costs to smaller users such as family farmers; *water ranching*, whereby industry buys up water rights of ranches and farmers: and *waste dumping*, whereby industry contaminates the local water sources and leaves the community with polluted water or a costly cleanup bill.

Despite increasing industrial demand, conservation programs aimed at ordinary people are not applied to industry. *The Albuquerque Tribune* pointed out this irony in a description of a city conservation project: "While some residents tore out their lawns last year (1996) to save water," the newspaper said, "it poured with increasing volume through the spigots of industry." While residents were required to decrease their use by 30 percent, Intel Corporation, a software company based in Albuquerque, was allowed to increase its use by the same amount. In addition, Intel pays only a quarter of what the city's residents pay for their water. Perhaps the most disturbing trend, however, is the deliberate destruction of a local traditional pueblo *acequia*—a collective system of agricultural water distribution—to feed the voracious appetite of the high-tech giants.

Under the new commercial system, water is separated from the land it belongs to and transported great distances. This is anathema to the local Indigenous ways and makes no long-term economic or ecological sense. Says John Carangelo, a mayordomo of the La Joya Acequia Association, "In New Mexico, where the total finite supply of water is allegedly fully appropriated, the location of a high-tech industry is dependent on the purchase of existing water rights. This high demand for water and their vast financial resources makes water a valuable commercial product." He warns that water trading could hollow out rural America.

* * *

As the planet dries up and water supplies are bought up by private interests, we have begun moving into a new economic configuration, where sprawling cities and agribusiness operations thrive and the wells of private citizens and local farmers run dry. Old ways of wasting water—like the rights trading that benefited a few but devastated the Owens Valley in southern California—are being revived, though they were demonstrated failures in the past. Meanwhile, in Third World countries, where children are already dying of thirst, the World Bank and the International Monetary Fund make privatization of water services a condition of debt rescheduling, and the poor soon find they are unable to pay for the sky-rocketing costs of water and sanitation services. What lies ahead is a world where resources are not conserved, but hoarded, to raise prices and enhance corporate profits and where military conflicts could arise over water scarcity in places like the Mexican Valley and the Middle East. It's a world where everything will be for sale.

PART IV

Global Issues

A New World Order?

Has Globalization Gone Too Far?

Dani Rodrik

The process that has come to be called "globalization" is exposing a deep fault line between groups who have the skills and mobility to flourish in global markets and those who either don't have these advantages or perceive the expansion of unregulated markets as inimical to social stability and deeply held norms. The result is severe tension between the market and social groups such as workers, pensioners, and environmentalists, with governments stuck in the middle. [. . .]

While I share the idea that much of the opposition to trade is based on faulty premises, I also believe that economists have tended to take an excessively narrow view of the issues. To understand the impact of globalization on domestic social arrangements, we have to go beyond the question of what trade does to the skill premium. And even if we focus more narrowly on labor-market outcomes, there are additional channels, which have not yet come under close empirical scrutiny, through which increased economic integration works to the disadvantage of labor, and particularly of unskilled labor. This book attempts to offer such a broadened perspective. As we shall see, this perspective leads to a less benign outlook than the one economists commonly adopt. One side benefit, therefore, is that it serves to reduce the yawning gap that separates the views of most economists from the gut instincts of many laypeople.

Sources of Tension

I focus on three sources of tension between the global market and social stability and offer a brief overview of them here.

First, reduced barriers to trade and investment accentuate the asymmetry between groups that can cross international borders (either directly or indirectly, say through outsourcing) and those that cannot. In the first category are owners of capital, highly skilled workers, and many professionals, who are free to take their resources where they are most in demand. Unskilled and semiskilled workers and most middle managers belong in the second category. Putting the same point in more technical terms, globalization makes the demand for the services of individuals in the second category *more elastic*—that is, the services of large segments of the working population can be more easily substituted by the services of other people across national boundaries. Globalization therefore fundamentally transforms the employment relationship.

The fact that "workers" can be more easily substituted for each other across national boundaries undermines what many conceive to be a postwar social bargain between workers and employers, under which the former would receive a steady increase in wages and benefits in return for labor peace. This is because increased substitutability results in the following concrete consequences:

- Workers now have to pay a larger share of the cost of improvements in work conditions and benefits (that is, they hear a greater incidence of non-wage costs).
- They have to incur greater instability in earnings and hours worked in response to shocks to labor demand or labor productivity (that is, volatility and insecurity increase).
- Their bargaining power erodes, so they receive lower wages and benefits whenever bargaining is an element in setting the terms of employment.

These considerations have received insufficient attention in the recent academic literature on trade and wages, which has focused on the downward shift in demand for unskilled workers rather than the increase in the elasticity of that demand.

Second, globalization engenders conflicts within and between nations over domestic norms and the social institutions that embody them. As the technology for manufactured goods becomes standardized and diffused internationally, nations with very different sets of values, norms, institutions, and collective preferences begin to compete head on in markets for similar goods. And the spread of globalization creates opportunities for trade between countries at very different levels of development.

This is of no consequence under traditional multilateral trade policy of the WTO and the General Agreement on Tariffs and Trade (GATT): the "process" or "technology" through which goods are produced is immaterial, and so are the social institutions of the trading partners. Differences in national practices are treated just like differences in factor endowments or any other determinant of comparative advantage. However, introspection and empirical evidence both reveal that most people attach values to processes as well as outcomes. This is reflected in the norms that shape and constrain the domestic environment in which goods and services are produced—for example, workplace practices, legal rules, and social safety nets.

Trade becomes contentious when it unleashes forces that undermine the norms implicit in domestic practices. Many residents of advanced industrial countries are uncomfortable with the weakening of domestic institutions through the forces of trade, as when, for example, child labor in Honduras displaces workers in South Carolina or when pension benefits are cut in Europe in response to the requirements of the Maastricht treaty. This sense of unease is one way of interpreting the demands for "fair trade." Much of the discussion surrounding the "new" issues in trade policy—that is, labor standards, environment, competition policy, corruption—can be cast in this light of procedural fairness.

We cannot understand what is happening in these new areas until we take individual preferences for processes and the social arrangements that embody them seriously. In particular, by doing so we can start to make sense of people's uneasiness about the consequences of international economic integration and avoid the trap of automatically branding all concerned groups as self-interested protectionists. Indeed, since trade policy almost always has redistributive consequences (among sectors, income groups, and individuals), one cannot produce a principled defense of free trade without confronting the question of the fairness and legitimacy of the practices that generate these consequences. By the same token, one should not expect broad popular support for trade when trade involves exchanges that clash with (and erode) prevailing domestic social arrangements.

Third, globalization has made it exceedingly difficult for governments to provide social insurance—one of their central functions and one that has helped maintain social cohesion and domestic political support for ongoing liberalization throughout the postwar period. In essence, governments have used their fiscal powers to insulate domestic groups from excessive market risks, particularly those having an external origin. In fact, there is a striking correlation between an economy's exposure to foreign trade and the size of its welfare state. It is in the most open countries, such as Sweden, Denmark, and the Netherlands, that spending on income transfers has expanded the most. This is not to say that the government is the sole, or the best, provider of social insurance. The extended family, religious groups, and local communities often play similar roles. My point is that it is a hallmark of the postwar period that governments in the advanced countries have been expected to provide such insurance.

At the present, however, international economic integration is taking place against the background of receding governments and diminished social obligations. The welfare state has been under attack for two decades. Moreover, the increasing mobility of capital has rendered an important segment of the tax base footloose, leaving governments with the unappetizing option of increasing tax rates disproportionately on labor income. Yet the need for social insurance for the vast majority of the population that remains internationally immobile has not diminished. If anything, this need has become greater as a consequence of increased integration. The question therefore is how the tension between globalization and the pressures for socialization of risk can be eased. If the tension is not managed intelligently and creatively, the danger is that the domestic consensus in favor of open markets will ultimately erode to the point where a generalized resurgence of protectionism becomes a serious possibility.

Each of these arguments points to an important weakness in the manner in which advanced societies are handling—or are equipped to handle—the consequences of globalization. Collectively, they point to what is perhaps the greatest risk of all, namely that the cumulative consequence of the tensions mentioned above will be the solidifying of a new set of class divisions—between those who prosper in the globalized economy and those who do not, between those who share its values and those who would rather not, and between those who can diversify away its risks and those who cannot. This is not a pleasing prospect, even for individuals on the winning side of the divide who have little empathy for the other side. Social disintegration is not a spectator sport—those on the sidelines also get splashed with mud from the field. Ultimately, the deepening of social fissures can harm all. [. . .]

The Role of National Governments

Policymakers have to steer a difficult middle course between responding to the concerns discussed here and sheltering groups from foreign competition through protectionism. I can offer no hard-and-fast rules here, only some guiding principles.

Strike a Balance between Openness and Domestic Needs

There is often a trade-off between maintaining open borders to trade and maintaining social cohesion. When the conflict arises—when new liberalization initiatives are under discussion, for example—it makes little sense to sacrifice social concerns completely for the sake of liberalization. Put differently, as policymakers sort out economic and social objectives, free trade policies are not automatically entitled to first priority.

Thanks to many rounds of multilateral trade liberalization, tariff and nontariff restrictions on goods and many services are now at extremely low levels in the industrial countries. Most major developing countries have also slashed their trade barriers, often unilaterally and in conformity with their own domestic reforms. Most economists would agree that the efficiency benefits of further reductions in these existing barriers are unlikely to be large. Indeed, the ditty little secret of international economics is that a tiny bit of protection reduces efficiency only a tiny bit. A logical implication is that the case for further liberalization in the traditional area of manufactured goods is rather weak.

Moreover, there is a case for taking greater advantage of the World Trade Organization's existing escape clause, which allows countries to institute otherwise-illegal trade restrictions under specified conditions, as well as for broadening the scope of these multilateral safeguard actions. In recent years, trade policy in the United States and the European Union has gone in a rather different direction, with increased use of antidumping measures and limited recourse to escape clause actions. This is likely because WTO rules and domestic legislation make the petitioning industry's job much easier in antidumping cases: there are lower evidentiary hurdles than in escape clause actions, no determinate time limit, and no requirement for compensation for affected trade partners, as the escape clause provides. Also, escape clause actions, unlike antidumping duties, require presidential approval in the United Stares. This is an undesirable situation because antidumping rules are, on the whole, consistent neither with economics principles nor, as discussed below, with fairness. Tightening the rules on antidumping in conjunction with a reconsideration and reinvigoration of the escape clause mechanism would make a lot of sense.

Do Not Neglect Social Insurance

Policymakers have to bear in mind the important role that the provision of social insurance, through social programs, has played historically in enabling multilateral liberalization and an explosion of world trade. As the welfare state is being pruned, there is a real danger that this contribution will be forgotten.

This does not mean that fiscal policy has to be profligate and budget deficits large. Nor does it mean a bigger government role. Enhanced levels of social insurance, for better labor-market outcomes, can be provided in most countries within existing levels of spending. This can be done, for example, by shifting the composition of income transfers from old-age insurance (i.e., social security) to labor-market insurance (i.e., unemployment compensation, trade adjustment assistance, training programs). Because pensions typically constitute the largest item of social spending in the advanced industrial countries, better targeting of this sort is highly compatible with responsible fiscal policies. Gearing social insurance more directly toward labor markets, without increasing the overall tax burden, would be one key step toward alleviating the insecurities associated with globalization.

There is a widespread feeling in many countries that, in the words of Tanzi and Schuknecht, "[s]ocial safety nets have . . . been transformed into universal benefits with widespread free-riding behavior, and social insurance has frequently become an income support system with special interests making any effective reform very difficult." Further, "various government performance indicators suggest that the growth in spending after 1960 may not have brought about significantly improved economic performance or greater social progress." However, social spending has had the important function of buying social peace. Without disagreeing about the need to eliminate waste and reform in the welfare state more broadly, I would argue that the need for social insurance does not decline but rather increases as global integration increases. So the message to reformers of the social welfare system is, don't throw the baby out with the bath water.

Do Not Use "Competitiveness" as an Excuse for Domestic Reform

One of the reasons globalization gets a bad rap is that policymakers often fall into the trap of using "competitiveness" as an excuse for needed domestic reforms. Large fiscal deficits or lagging domestic productivity are problems that drag living standards down in many industrial countries and would do so even in closed economies. Indeed, the term "competitiveness" itself is largely meaningless when applied to whole economies, unless it is used to refer to things that already have a proper name—such as productivity, investment, and economic growth. Too often, however, the need to resolve fiscal or productivity problems is presented to the electorate as the consequence of global competitive pressures. This not only makes the required policies a harder sell—why should we adjust just for the sake of becoming better competitors against the Koreans or the Mexicans?—it also erodes the domestic support for international trade—if we have to do all these painful things because of trade, maybe trade isn't such a wonderful thing anyhow!

The French strikes of 1995 are a good case in point. What made the opposition to the proposed fiscal and pension reforms particularly salient was the perception that fundamental changes in the French way of life were being imposed for the sake of international economic integration. The French government presented the reforms as required by the Maastricht criteria, which they were. But presumably, the Maastricht criteria themselves reflected the policymakers' belief that a smaller welfare state would serve their economies better in the longer run. By and large, the French government did not make the case for reform on its own strengths. By using the Maastricht card, it turned the discussion into a debate on European economic integration. Hence the widespread public reaction, which extended beyond just those workers whose fates would be immediately affected.

The lesson for policymakers is, do not sell reforms that are good for the economy and the citizenry as reforms that are dictated by international economic integration.

Do Not Abuse "Fairness" Claims in Trade

The notion of fairness in trade is not as vacuous as many economists think. Consequently, nations have the right—and should be allowed—to restrict trade when it conflicts with *widely held* norms at home or undermines domestic social arrangements that enjoy *broad* support.

But there is much that is done in the name of "fair trade" that falls far short of this criterion. There are two sets of practices in particular that should be immediately suspect. One concerns complaints made against other nations when very similar practices abound at home. Antidumping proceedings are a clear example: standard business practices, such as pricing over the life of a product or pricing over the business cycle, can result in duties being imposed on an exporting firm. There is nothing "unfair" about these business practices, as is made abundantly clear by the fact that domestic firms engage in them as well.

The second category concerns cases in which other nations are unilaterally asked to change *their* domestic practices so as to equalize competitive conditions. Japan is frequently at the receiving end of such demands from the United States and the European Union. A more recent example concerns the declaration by the US Trade Representative that corruption in foreign countries will henceforth be considered as unfair trade. While considerations of fairness and legitimacy will guide a country's own social arrangements, even by restricting imports if need be, such considerations should not allow one country to impose its own institutions on others. Proponents of fair trade must bear this key distinction in mind. Thus, it is perfectly legitimate for the United States to make it illegal for domestic firms to engage in corrupt practices abroad (as was done with the Foreign Corrupt Practices Act of 1977). It is also legitimate to negotiate a multilateral set of principles with other countries in the Organization for Economic Cooperation and Development (OECD) with broadly similar norms. It may also be legitimate to restrict imports from a country whose labor practices broad segments of the domestic population deem offensive. But it is not acceptable to unilaterally threaten retaliation against other countries because their business practices do not comply with domestic standards at home *in order to force these countries to alter their own standards.* Using claims of fairness to advance competitive aims is coercive and inherently contradictory. Trying to "export" norms by asking other countries to alter their social arrangements to match domestic ones is inappropriate for the same reason. [. . .]

The Free-Trade Fix

Tina Rosenberg

Globalization is a phenomenon that has remade the economy of virtually every nation, reshaped almost every industry and touched billions of lives, often in surprising and ambiguous ways. The stories filling the front pages in recent weeks—about economic crisis and contagion in Argentina, Uruguay and Brazil, about President Bush getting the trade bill he wanted—are all part of the same story, the largest story of our times: what globalization has done, or has failed to do.

Globalization is meant to signify integration and unity—yet it has proved, in its way, to be no less polarizing than the cold-war divisions it has supplanted. The lines between globalization's supporters and its critics run not only between countries but also through them, as people struggle to come to terms with the defining economic force shaping the planet today. The two sides in the discussion—a shouting match, really—describe what seem to be two completely different forces. Is the globe being knit together by the Nikes and Microsofts and Citigroups in a dynamic new system that will eventually lift the have-nots of the world up from medieval misery? Or are ordinary people now victims of ruthless corporate domination, as the Nikes and Microsofts and Citigroups roll over the poor in nation after nation in search of new profits?

The debate over globalization's true nature has divided people in third-world countries since the phenomenon arose. It is now an issue in the United States as well, and many Americans—those who neither make the deals inside World Trade Organization meetings nor man the barricades outside—are perplexed.

When I first set out to see for myself whether globalization has been for better or for worse, I was perplexed, too. I had sympathy for some of the issues raised by the protesters, especially their outrage over sweatshops. But I have also spent many years in Latin America, and I have seen firsthand how protected economies became corrupt systems that helped only those with clout. In general,

I thought the protesters were simply being sentimental; after all, the masters of the universe must know what they are doing. But that was before I studied the agreements that regulate global trade—including this month's new law granting President Bush a free hand to negotiate trade agreements, a document redolent of corporate lobbying. And it was before looking at globalization up close in Chile and Mexico, two nations that have embraced globalization especially ardently in the region of the third world that has done the most to follow the accepted rules. I no longer think the masters of the universe know what they are doing.

The architects of globalization are right that international economic integration is not only good for the poor; it is essential. To embrace self-sufficiency or to deride growth, as some protesters do, is to glamorize poverty. No nation has ever developed over the long term without trade. East Asia is the most recent example. Since the mid-1970's, Japan, Korea, Taiwan, China and their neighbors have lifted 300 million people out of poverty, chiefly through trade.

But the protesters are also right—no nation has ever developed over the long term under the rules being imposed today on third-world countries by the institutions controlling globalization. The United States, Germany, France and Japan all became wealthy and powerful nations behind the barriers of protectionism. East Asia built its export industry by protecting its markets and banks from foreign competition and requiring investors to buy local products and build local know-how. These are all practices discouraged or made illegal by the rules of trade today.

The World Trade Organization was designed as a meeting place where willing nations could sit in equality and negotiate rules of trade for their mutual advantage, in the service of sustainable international development. Instead, it has become an unbalanced institution largely controlled by the United States and the nations of Europe, and especially the agribusiness, pharmaceutical and financial-services industries in these countries. At W.T.O. meetings, important deals are hammered out in negotiations attended by the trade ministers of a couple dozen powerful nations, while those of poor countries wait in the bar outside for news.

The International Monetary Fund was created to prevent future Great Depressions in part by lending countries in recession money and pressing them to adopt expansionary policies, like deficit spending and low interest rates, so they would continue to buy their neighbors' products. Over time, its mission has evolved into the reverse: it has become a long-term manager of the economies of developing countries, blindly committed to the bitter medicine of contraction no matter what the illness. Its formation was an acknowledgment that markets sometimes work imperfectly, but it has become a champion of market supremacy in all situations, echoing the voice of Wall Street and the United States Treasury Department, more interested in getting wealthy creditors repaid than in serving the poor.

It is often said that globalization is a force of nature, as unstoppable and difficult to contain as a storm. This is untrue and misleading. Globalization is a powerful phenomenon—but it is not irreversible, and indeed the previous wave of globalization, at the turn of the last century, was stopped dead by World War I. Today it would be more likely for globalization to be sabotaged by its own inequities, as disillusioned nations withdraw from a system they see as indifferent or harmful to the poor.

Globalization's supporters portray it as the peeling away of distortions to reveal a clean and elegant system of international commerce, the one nature intended. It is anything but. The accord creating the W.T.O. is 22,500 pages long—not exactly a *free* trade agreement. All globalization, it seems, is local, the rules drawn up by, and written to benefit, powerful nations and powerful interests within those nations. Globalization has been good for the United States, but even in this country, the gains go disproportionately to the wealthy and to big business.

It's not too late for globalization to work. But the system is in need of serious reform. More equitable rules would spread its benefits to the ordinary citizens of wealthy countries. They would also help to preserve globalization by giving the poor of the world a stake in the system—and, not incidentally, improve the lives of hundreds of millions of people. Here, then, are nine new rules for the global economy—a prescription to save globalization from itself.

1. Make the State a Partner

If there is any place in Latin America where the poor have thrived because of globalization, it is Chile. Between 1987 and 1998, Chile cut poverty by more than half. Its success shows that poor nations can take advantage of globalization—if they have governments that actively make it happen.

Chile reduced poverty by growing its economy—6.6 percent a year from 1985 to 2000. One of the few points economists can agree on is that growth is the most important thing a nation can do for its poor. They can't agree on basics like whether poverty in the world is up or down in the last 15 years—the number of people who live on less than $1 a day is slightly down, but the number who live on less than $2 is slightly up. Inequality has soared during the last 15 years, but economists cannot agree on whether globalization is mainly at fault or whether other forces, like the uneven spread of technology, are responsible. They can't agree on how to reduce inequality—growth tends not to change it. They can't agree on whether the poor who have not been helped are victims of globalization or have simply not yet enjoyed access to its benefits—in other words, whether the solution is more globalization or less. But economists agree on one thing: to help the poor, you'd better grow.

For the rest of Latin America, and most of the developing world except China (and to a lesser extent India), globalization as practiced today is failing, and it is failing because it has not produced growth. Excluding China, the growth rate of poor countries was 2 percent a year lower in the 1990's than in the 1970's, when closed economies were the norm and the world was in a recession brought on in part by oil-price shocks. Latin American economies in the 1990's grew at an average annual rate of 2.9 percent—about half the rate of the 1960's. By the end of the 1990's, 11 million more Latin Americans lived in poverty than at the beginning of the decade. And in country after country, Latin America's poor are suffering—either from economic crises and market panics or from the day-to-day deprivations that globalization was supposed to relieve. The surprise is not that Latin Americans are once again voting for populist candidates but that the revolt against globalization took so long.

When I visited Eastern Europe after the end of Communism, a time when democracy was mainly bringing poverty, I heard over and over again that the reason for Chile's success was Augusto Pinochet. Only a dictator with a strong hand can put his country through the pain of economic reform, went the popular wisdom. In truth, we now know that inflicting pain is the easy part; governments democratic and dictatorial are all instituting free-market austerity. The point is not to inflict pain but to lessen it. In this Pinochet failed, and the democratic governments that followed him beginning in 1990 have succeeded.

What Pinochet did was to shut down sectors of Chile's economy that produced goods for the domestic market, like subsistence farming and appliance manufacturing, and point the economy toward exports. Here he was following the standard advice that economists give developing countries—but there are different ways to do it, and Pinochet's were disastrous. Instead of helping the losers, he dismantled the social safety net and much of the regulatory apparatus that might have kept privatization honest. When the world economy went into recession in 1982, Chile's integration into the global marketplace and its dependence on foreign capital magnified the crash. Poverty soared, and unemployment reached 20 percent.

Pinochet's second wave of globalization, in the late 1980's, worked better, because the state did not stand on the side. It regulated the changes effectively and aggressively promoted exports. But Pinochet created a time bomb in Chile: the country's exports were, and still are, nonrenewable natural resources. Chile began subsidizing companies that cut down native forests for wood chips, for example, and the industry is rapidly deforesting the nation.

Chile began to grow, but inequality soared—the other problem with Pinochet's globalization was that it left out the poor. While the democratic governments that succeeded Pinochet have not yet been able to reduce inequality, at least it is no longer increasing, and they have been able to use the fruits of Chile's growth to help the poor.

Chile's democratic governments have spread the benefits of economic integration by designing effective social programs and aiming them at the poor. Chile has sunk money into revitalizing the 900 worst primary schools. It now leads Latin America in computers in schools, along with Costa Rica. It provides the very low-income with housing subsidies, child care and income support. Open economy or closed, these are good things. But Chile's government is also taking action to mitigate one of the most dangerous aspects of global integration: the violent ups and downs that come from linking your economy to the rest of the world. This year it created unemployment insurance. And it was the first nation to institute what is essentially a tax on short-term capital, to discourage the kind of investment that can flood out during a market panic.

The conventional wisdom among economists today is that successful globalizers must be like Chile. This was not always the thinking. In the 1980's, the Washington Consensus—the master-of-the-universe ideology at the time, highly influenced by the Reagan and Thatcher administrations—held that government was in the way. Globalizers' tasks included privatization, deregulation, fiscal austerity and financial liberalization. "In the 1980's and up to 1996 or 1997, the state was considered the devil," says Juan Martin, an Argentine economist at the United Nations' Economic Commission for Latin America and the Caribbean. "Now we know you need infrastructure, institutions, education. In fact, when the economy opens, you need *more* control mechanisms from the state, not fewer."

And what if you don't have these things? Bolivia carried out extensive reforms beginning in 1985—a year in which it had inflation of 23,000 percent—to make the economy more stable and efficient. But in the words of the World Bank, "It is a good example of a country that has achieved successful stabilization and implemented innovative market reforms, yet made only limited progress in the fight against poverty." Latin America is full of nations that cannot make globalization work. The saddest example is Haiti, an excellent student of the rules of globalization, ranked at the top of the I.M.F.'s index of trade openness. Yet over the 1990's, Haiti's economy contracted; annual per capita income is now $250. No surprise—if you are a corrupt and misgoverned nation with a closed economy, becoming a corrupt and misgoverned nation with an open economy is not going to solve your problems.

2. Import Know-How Along with the Assembly Line

If there is a showcase for globalization in Latin America, it lies on the outskirts of Puebla, Mexico, at Volkswagen Mexico. Every New Beetle in the world is made here, 440 a day, in a factory so sparkling and clean that you could have a baby on the floor, so high-tech that in some halls it is not evident that human beings work here. Volkswagen Mexico also makes Jettas and, in a special hall, 80 classic Beetles a day to sell in Mexico, one of the last places in the world where the old Bug still chugs.

The Volkswagen factory is the biggest single industrial plant in Mexico. Humans do work here—11,000 people in assembly-line jobs, 4,000 more in the rest of the factory—with 11,000 more jobs in the industrial park of VW suppliers across the street making parts, seats, dashboards and other components. Perhaps 50,000 more people work in other companies around Mexico that supply VW. The average monthly wage in the plant is $760, among the highest in the country's industrial sector. The factory is the equal of any in Germany, the product of a billion-dollar investment in 1995, when VW chose Puebla as the exclusive site for the New Beetle.

Ahhh, globalization.

Except . . . this plant is not here because Mexico has an open economy, but because it had a *closed* one. In 1962, Mexico decreed that any automaker that wanted to sell cars here had to produce them here. Five years later, VW opened the factory. Mexico's local content requirement is now illegal, except for very limited exceptions, under W.T.O. rules; in Mexico the local content requirement for automobiles is being phased out and will disappear entirely in January 2004.

The Puebla factory, for all the jobs and foreign exchange it brings Mexico, also refutes the argument that foreign technology automatically rubs off on the local host. Despite 40 years here, the auto industry has not created much local business or know-how. VW makes the point that it buys 60 percent of its parts in Mexico, but the "local" suppliers are virtually all foreign-owned and import most of the materials they use. The value Mexico adds to the Beetles it exports is mainly labor. Technology transfer—the transmission of know-how from foreign companies to local ones—is limited in part because most foreign trade today is intracompany; Ford Hermosillo, for example, is a stamping and assembly plant shipping exclusively to Ford plants in the United States. Trade like this is particularly impenetrable to outsiders. "In spite of the fact that Mexico has been host to many car plants, we don't know how to build a car," says Huberto Juarez, an economist at the Autonomous University of Puebla.

Volkswagen Mexico is the epitome of the strategy Mexico has chosen for globalization—assembly of imported parts. It is a strategy that makes perfect sense given Mexico's proximity to the world's largest market, and it has given rise to the *maquila* industry, which uses Mexican labor to assemble foreign parts and then re-export the finished products. Although the economic slowdown in the United States is hurting the maquila industry, it still employs a million people and brings the country $10 billion a year in foreign exchange. The factories have turned Mexico into one of the developing world's biggest exporters of medium- and high-technology products. But the maquila sector remains an island and has failed to stimulate Mexican industries—one reason Mexico's globalization has brought disappointing growth, averaging only 3 percent a year during the 1990's.

In countries as varied as South Korea, China and Mauritius, however, assembly work has been the crucible of wider development. Jeffrey Sachs, the development economist who now directs Columbia University's Earth Institute, says that the maquila industry is "magnificent." "I could cite 10 success stories," he says, "and every one started with a maquila sector." When Korea opened its export-processing zone in Masan in the early 1970's, local inputs were 3 percent of the export value, according to the British development group Oxfam. Ten years later they were almost 50 percent. General Motors took a Korean textile company called Daewoo and helped shape it into a conglomerate making cars, electronic goods, ships and dozens of other products. Daewoo calls itself "a locomotive for national economic development since its founding in 1967." And despite the company's recent troubles, it's true—because Korea made it true. G.M. did not tutor Daewoo because it welcomed competition but because Korea demanded it. Korea wanted to build high-tech industry, and it did so by requiring technology transfer and by closing markets to imports.

Maquilas first appeared in Mexico in 1966. Although the country has gone from assembling clothing to assembling high-tech goods, nearly 40 years later 97 percent of the components used in Mexican maquilas are still imported, and the value that Mexico adds to its exports has actually declined sharply since the mid-1970's.

Mexico has never required companies to transfer technology to locals, and indeed, under the rules of the North American Free Trade Agreement, it cannot. "We should have included a technical component in NAFTA," says Luis de la Calle, one of the treaty's negotiators and later Mexico's under secretary of economy for foreign trade. "We should be getting a significant transfer of technology from the United States, and we didn't really try."

Without technology transfer, maquila work is marked for extinction. As transport costs become less important, Mexico is increasingly competing with China and Bangladesh—where labor goes for as little as 9 cents an hour. This is one reason that real wages for the lowest-paid workers in Mexico dropped by 50 percent from 1985 to 2000. Businesses, in fact, are already leaving to go to China.

3. Sweat the Sweatshops— But Sweat Other Problems More

When Americans think about globalization, they often think about sweatshops— one aspect of globalization that ordinary people believe they can influence through their buying choices. In many of the factories in Mexico, Central America and Asia producing American-brand toys, clothes, sneakers and other goods, exploitation is the norm. The young women who work in them—almost all sweat- shop workers are young women—endure starvation wages, forced overtime and dangerous working conditions.

In Chile, I met a man who works at a chicken-processing plant in a small town. The plant is owned by Chileans and processes chicken for the domestic market and for export to Europe, Asia and other countries in Latin America. His job is to stand in a freezing room and crack open chickens as they come down an assembly line at the rate of 41 per minute. When visitors arrive at the factory (the owners did not return my phone calls requesting a visit or an interview), the workers get a respite, as the line slows down to half-speed for show. His work uniform does not protect him from the cold, the man said, and after a few min- utes of work he loses feeling in his hands. Some of his colleagues, he said, are no longer able to raise their arms. If he misses a day he is docked $30. He earns less than $200 a month.

Is this man a victim of globalization? The protesters say that he is, and at one point I would have said so, too. He—and all workers—should have dignified con- ditions and the right to organize. All companies should follow local labor laws, and activists should pressure companies to pay their workers decent wages.

But today if I were to picket globalization, I would protest other inequities. In a way, the chicken worker, who came to the factory when driving a taxi ceased to be profitable, is a beneficiary of globalization. So are the millions of young women who have left rural villages to be exploited gluing tennis shoes or assem- bling computer keyboards. The losers are those who get laid off when companies move to low-wage countries, or those forced off their land when imports under- cut their crop prices, or those who can no longer afford life-saving medicine— people whose choices in life *diminish* because of global trade. Globalization has offered this man a hellish job, but it is a choice he did not have before, and he took it; I don't name him because he is afraid of being fired. When this chicken company is hiring, the lines go around the block.

4. Get Rid of the Lobbyists

The argument that open economies help the poor rests to a large extent on the evidence that closed economies do not. While South Korea and other East Asian countries successfully used trade barriers to create export industries, this is rare; most protected economies are disasters. "The main tendency in a sheltered market is to goof off," says Jagdish Bhagwati, a prominent free-trader who is the Arthur Lehman professor of economics at Columbia University. "A crutch becomes a permanent crutch. Infant-industry protection should be for infant industries."

Anyone who has lived or traveled in the third world can attest that while controlled economies theoretically allow governments to help the poor, in practice it's usually a different story. In Latin America, spending on social programs largely goes to the urban middle class. Attention goes to people who can organize, strike, lobby and contribute money. And in a closed economy, the "state" car factory is often owned by the dictator's son and the country's forests can be chopped down by his golf partner.

Free trade, its proponents argue, takes these decisions away from the government and leaves them to the market, which punishes corruption. And it's true that a system that took corruption and undue political influence out of economic decision-making could indeed benefit the poor. But humans have not yet invented such a system—and if they did, it would certainly not be the current system of globalization, which is soiled with the footprints of special interests. In every country that negotiates at the W.T.O. or cuts a free-trade deal, trade ministers fall under heavy pressure from powerful business groups. Lobbyists have learned that they can often quietly slip provisions that pay big dividends into complex trade deals. None have been more successful at getting what they want than those from America.

The most egregious example of a special-interest provision is the W.T.O.'s rules on intellectual property. The ability of poor nations to make or import cheap copies of drugs still under patent in rich countries has been a boon to world public health. But the W.T.O. will require most of its poor members to accept patents on medicine by 2005, with the very poorest nations following in 2016. This regime does nothing for the poor. Medicine prices will probably double, but poor countries will never offer enough of a market to persuade the pharmaceutical industry to invent cures for their diseases.

The intellectual-property rules have won worldwide notoriety for the obstacles they pose to cheap AIDS medicine. They are also the provision of the W.T.O. that economists respect the least. They were rammed into the W.T.O. by Washington in response to the industry groups who control United States trade policy on the subject. "This is not a trade issue," Bhagwati says. "It's a royalty-collection issue. It's pharmaceuticals and software throwing their weight around." The World Bank calculated that the intellectual-property rules will result in a transfer of $40 billion a year from poor countries to corporations in the developed world.

5. No Dumping

Manuel de Jesús Gómez is a corn farmer in the hills of Puebla State, 72 years old and less than five feet tall. I met him in his field of six acres, where he was trudging behind a plow pulled by a burro. He farms the same way *campesinos* in these hills have been farming for thousands of years. In Puebla, and in the poverty belt of Mexico's southern states—Chiapas, Oaxaca, Guerrero—corn growers plow with animals and irrigate by praying for rain.

Before NAFTA, corn covered 60 percent of Mexico's cultivated land. This is where corn was born, and it remains a symbol of the nation and daily bread for most Mexicans. But in the NAFTA negotiations, Mexico agreed to open itself to subsidized American corn, a policy that has crushed small corn farmers. "Before, we could make a living, but now sometimes what we sell our corn for doesn't even cover our costs," Gómez says. With NAFTA, he suddenly had to compete with American corn—raised with the most modern methods, but more important, subsidized to sell overseas at 20 percent less than the cost of production. Subsidized American corn now makes up almost half of the world's stock, effectively setting the world price so low that local small farmers can no longer survive. This competition helped cut the price paid to Gómez for his corn by half.

Because of corn's importance to Mexico, when it negotiated NAFTA it was promised 15 years to gradually raise the amount of corn that could enter the country without tariffs. But Mexico voluntarily lifted the quotas in less than three years—to help the chicken and pork industry, Mexican negotiators told me unabashedly. (Eduardo Bours, a member of the family that owns Mexico's largest chicken processor, was one of Mexico's NAFTA negotiators.) The state lost some $2 billion in tariffs it could have charged, and farmers were instantly exposed to competition from the north. According to ANEC, a national association of campesino cooperatives, half a million corn farmers have left their land and moved to Mexican cities or to America. If it were not for a weak peso, which keeps the price of imports relatively high, far more farmers would be forced off their land.

The toll on small farmers is particularly bitter because cheaper corn has not translated into cheaper food for Mexicans. As part of its economic reforms,

Mexico has gradually removed price controls on tortillas and tortilla flour. Tortilla prices have nearly tripled in real terms even as the price of corn has dropped.

Is this how it was supposed to be? I asked Andres Rosenzweig, a longtime Mexican agriculture official who helped negotiate the agricultural sections of NAFTA. He was silent for a minute. "The problems of rural poverty in Mexico did not start with NAFTA," he said. "The size of our farms is not viable, and they get smaller each generation because farmers have many children, who divide the land. A family in Puebla with five hectares could raise 10, maybe 15, tons of corn each year. That was an annual income of 16,000 pesos," the equivalent of $1,600 today. "Double it and you still die of hunger. This has nothing to do with NAFTA.

"The solution for small corn farmers," he went on, "is to educate their children and find them jobs outside agriculture. But Mexico was not growing, not generating jobs. Who's going to employ them? NAFTA."

One prominent antiglobalization report keeps referring to farms like Gómez's as "small-scale, diversified, self-reliant, community-based agriculture systems." You could call them that, I guess; you could also use words like "malnourished," "undereducated" and "miserable" to describe their inhabitants. Rosenzweig is right—this is not a life to be romanticized.

But to turn the farm families' malnutrition into starvation makes no sense. Mexico spends foreign exchange to buy corn. Instead, it could be spending money to bring farmers irrigation, technical help and credit. A system in which the government purchased farmers' corn at a guaranteed price—done away with in states like Puebla during the free-market reforms of the mid-1990's—has now been replaced by direct payments to farmers. The program is focused on the poor, but the payments are symbolic—$36 an acre. In addition, rural credit has disappeared, as the government has effectively shut down the rural bank, which was badly run, and other banks won't lend to small farmers. There is a program— understaffed and poorly publicized—to help small producers, but the farmers I met didn't know about it.

Free trade is a religion, and with religion comes hypocrisy. Rich nations press other countries to open their agricultural markets. At the urging of the I.M.F. and Washington, Haiti slashed its tariffs on rice in 1995. Prices paid to rice farmers fell by 25 percent, which has devastated Haiti's rural poor. In China, the tariff demands of W.T.O. membership will cost tens of millions of peasants their livelihoods. But European farmers get 35 percent of their income from government subsidies, and American farmers get 20 percent. Farm subsidies in the United States, moreover, are a huge corporate-welfare program, with nearly 70 percent of payments going to the largest 10 percent of producers. Subsidies also depress crop prices abroad by encouraging overproduction. The farm bill President Bush signed in May—with substantial Democratic support—provides about $57 billion in subsidies for American corn and other commodities over the next 10 years.

Wealthy nations justify pressure on small countries to open markets by arguing that these countries cannot grow rice and corn efficiently—that American crops are cheap food for the world's hungry. But with subsidies this large, it takes chutzpah to question other nations' efficiency. And in fact, the poor suffer when America is the supermarket to the world, even at bargain prices. There is plenty of food in the world, and even many countries with severe malnutrition are food exporters. The problem is that poor people can't afford it. The poor are the small farmers. Three-quarters of the world's poor are rural. If they are forced off their land by subsidized grain imports, they starve.

6. Help Countries Break the Coffee Habit

Back in the 1950's, Latin American economists made a simple calculation. The products their nations exported—copper, tin, coffee, rice and other commodities—were buying less and less of the high-value-added goods they wanted to import. In effect, they were getting poorer each day. Their solution was to close their markets and develop domestic industries to produce their own appliances and other goods for their citizens.

The strategy, which became known as import substitution, produced high growth—for a while. But these closed economies ultimately proved unsustainable. Latin American governments made their consumers buy inferior and expensive products—remember the Brazilian computer of the 1970's? Growth depended on heavy borrowing and high deficits. When they could no longer roll over their debts, Latin American economies crashed, and a decade of stagnation resulted.

At the time, the architects of import substitution could not imagine that it was possible to export anything but commodities. But East Asia—as poor or poorer than Latin America in the 1960's—showed in the 1980's and 1990's that it can be done. Unfortunately, the rules of global trade now prohibit countries from using the strategies successfully employed to develop export industries in East Asia.

American trade officials argue that they are not using tariffs to block poor countries from exporting, and they are right—the average tariff charged by the United States is a negligible 1.7 percent, much lower than other nations. But the rules rich nations have set—on technology transfer, local content and government aid to their infant industries, among other things—are destroying poor nations' abilities to move beyond commodities. "We are pulling up the ladder on policies the developed countries used to become rich," says Lori Wallach, the director of Public Citizen's Global Trade Watch.

The commodities that poor countries are left to export are even more of a dead end today than in the 1950's. Because of oversupply, prices for coffee, cocoa, rice, sugar and tin dropped by more than 60 percent between 1980 and 2000. Because of the price collapse of commodities and sub-Saharan Africa's failure to move beyond them, the region's share of world trade dropped by two-thirds during that time. If it had the same share of exports today that it had at the start of the 1980's, per capita income in sub-Saharan Africa would be almost twice as high.

7. Let the People Go

Probably the single most important change for the developing world would be to legalize the export of the one thing they have in abundance—people. Earlier waves of globalization were kinder to the poor because not only capital, but also labor, was free to move. Dani Rodrik, an economist at Harvard's Kennedy School of Government and a leading academic critic of the rules of globalization, argues for a scheme of legal short-term migration. If rich nations opened 3 percent of their work forces to temporary migrants, who then had to return home, Rodrik says, it would generate $200 billion annually in wages, and a lot of technology transfer for poor countries.

8. Free the I.M.F.

Globalization means risk. By opening its economy, a nation makes itself vulnerable to contagion from abroad. Countries that have liberalized their capital markets are especially susceptible, as short-term capital that has whooshed into a country on investor whim whooshes out just as fast when investors panic. This is how a real-estate crisis in Thailand in 1997 touched off one of the biggest global conflagrations since the Depression.

The desire to keep money from rushing out inspired Chile to install speed bumps discouraging short-term capital inflows. But Chile's policy runs counter to the standard advice of the I.M.F., which has required many countries to open their capital markets. "There were so many obstacles to capital-market integration that it was hard to err on the side of pushing countries to liberalize too much," says Ken Rogoff, the I.M.F.'s director of research.

Prudent nations are wary of capital liberalization, and rightly so. Joseph Stiglitz, the Nobel Prize-winning economist who has become the most influential critic of globalization's rules, writes that in December 1997, when he was chief economist at the World Bank, he met with South Korean officials who were balking at the I.M.F.'s advice to open their capital markets. They were scared of the hot money, but they could not disagree with the I.M.F., lest they be seen as irresponsible. If the I.M.F. expressed disapproval, it would drive away other donors and private investors as well.

In the wake of the Asian collapse, Prime Minister Mahathir Mohamad imposed capital controls in Malaysia—to worldwide condemnation. But his policy is now widely considered to be the reason that Malaysia stayed stable while its neighbors did not. "It turned out to be a brilliant decision," Bhagwati says.

Post-crash, the I.M.F. prescribed its standard advice for nations—making loan arrangements contingent on spending cuts, interest-rate hikes and other contractionary measures. But balancing a budget in recession is, as Stiglitz puts it in his new book, "Globalization and Its Discontents," a recommendation last taken seriously in the days of Herbert Hoover. The I.M.F.'s recommendations deepened the crisis and forced governments to reduce much of the cushion that was left for the poor. Indonesia had to cut subsidies on food. "While the I.M.F. had provided some $23 billion to be used to support the exchange rate and bail out creditors," Stiglitz writes, "the far, far, smaller sums required to help the poor were not forthcoming."

Is your international financial infrastructure breeding Bolsheviks? If it does create a backlash, one reason is the standard Bolshevik explanation—the I.M.F. really is controlled by the epicenter of international capital. Formal influence in the I.M.F. depends on a nation's financial contribution, and America is the only country with enough shares to have a veto. It is striking how many economists think the I.M.F. is part of the "Wall Street-Treasury complex," in the words of Bhagwati. The fund serves "the interests of global finance," Stiglitz says. It listens to the "voice of the markets," says Nancy Birdsall, president of the Center for Global Development in Washington and a former executive vice president of the Inter-American Development Bank. "The I.M.F. is a front for the U.S. government—keep the masses away from our taxpayers," Sachs says.

I.M.F. officials argue that their advice is completely equitable—they tell even wealthy countries to open their markets and contract their economies. In fact, Stiglitz writes, the I.M.F. told the Clinton administration to hike interest rates to lower the danger of inflation—at a time when inflation was the lowest it had been in decades. But the White House fortunately had the luxury of ignoring the I.M.F.: Washington will only have to take the organization's advice the next time it turns to the I.M.F. for a loan. And that will be never.

9. Let the Poor Get Rich the Way the Rich Have

The idea that free trade maximizes benefits for all is one of the few tenets economists agree on. But the power of the idea has led to the overly credulous acceptance of much of what is put forward in its name. Stiglitz writes that there is simply no support for many I.M.F. policies, and in some cases the I.M.F. has ignored clear evidence that what it advocated was harmful. You can always argue—and American and I.M.F. officials do—that countries that follow the I.M.F.'s line but still fail to grow either didn't follow the openness recipe precisely enough or didn't check off other items on the to-do list, like expanding education.

Policy makers also seem to be skipping the fine print on supposedly congenial studies. An influential recent paper by the World Bank economists David Dollar and Aart Kraay is a case in point. It finds a strong correlation between globalization and growth and is widely cited to support the standard rules of openness. But in fact, on close reading, it does not support them. Among successful "globalizers," Dollar and Kraay count countries like China, India and Malaysia, all of whom are trading and growing but still have protected economies and could not be doing more to misbehave by the received wisdom of globalization.

Dani Rodrik of Harvard used Dollar and Kraay's data to look at whether the single-best measure of openness—a country's tariff levels—correlates with growth. They do, he found—but not the way they are supposed to. High-tariff countries grew faster. Rodrik argues that the countries in the study may have begun to trade more because they had grown and gotten richer, not the other way around. China and India, he points out, began trade reforms about 10 years after they began high growth.

When economists talk about many of the policies associated with free trade today, they are talking about national averages and ignoring questions of distribution and inequality. They are talking about equations, not what works in messy third-world economies. What economic model taught in school takes into account a government ministry that stops work because it has run out of pens? The I.M.F. and the World Bank—which recommends many of the same austerity measures as the I.M.F. and frequently conditions its loans on I.M.F.-advocated reforms—often tell countries to cut subsidies, including many that do help the poor, and impose user fees on services like water. The argument is that subsidies are an inefficient way to help poor people—because they help rich people too—and instead, countries should aid the poor directly with vouchers or social programs. As an equation, it adds up. But in the real world, the subsidies disappear, and the vouchers never materialize.

The I.M.F. argues that it often saves countries from even more budget cuts. "Countries come to us when they are in severe distress and no one will lend to them," Rogoff says. "They may even have to run surpluses because their loans are being called in. Being in an I.M.F. program means less austerity." But a third of the developing world is under I.M.F. tutelage, some countries for decades, during which they must remodel their economies according to the standard I.M.F. blueprint. In March 2000, a panel appointed to advise Congress on international financial institutions, named for its head, Allan Meltzer of Carnegie Mellon University, recommended unanimously that the I.M.F. should undertake only short-term crisis assistance and get out of the business of long-term economic micromanagement altogether.

The standard reforms deprive countries of flexibility, the power to get rich the way we know can work. "Most Latin American countries have had deep reforms, have gone much further than India or China and haven't gotten much return for their effort," Birdsall says. "Many of the reforms were about creating an efficient economy, but the economic technicalities are not addressing the fundamental question of why countries are not growing, or the constraint that all these people are being left out. Economists are way too allergic to the wishy-washy concept of fairness."

The protesters in the street, the Asian financial crisis, criticism from respected economists like Stiglitz and Rodrik and those on the Meltzer Commission and particularly the growing realization in the circles of power that globalization is sustainable for wealthy nations only if it is acceptable to the poor ones are all combining to change the rules—slightly. The debt-forgiveness initiative for the poorest nations, for all its limitations, is one example. The Asian crisis has modified the I.M.F.'s view on capital markets, and it is beginning to apply less pressure on countries in crisis to cut government spending. It is also debating whether it should be encouraging countries to adopt Chile's speed bumps. The incoming director of the W.T.O. is from Thailand, and third-world countries are beginning to assert themselves more and more.

But the changes do not alter the underlying idea of globalization, that openness is the universal prescription for all ills. "Belt-tightening is not a development strategy," Sachs says. "The I.M.F. has no sense that its job is to help countries climb a ladder."

Sachs says that for many developing nations, even climbing the ladder is unrealistic. "It can't work in an AIDS pandemic or an endemic malaria zone. I don't have a strategy for a significant number of countries, other than we ought to help them stay alive and control disease and have clean water. You can't do this purely on market forces. The prospects for the Central African Republic are not the same as for Shanghai, and it doesn't do any good to give pep talks."

China, Chile and other nations show that under the right conditions, globalization can lift the poor out of misery. Hundreds of millions of poor people will never be helped by globalization, but hundreds of millions more could be benefiting now, if the rules had not been rigged to help the rich and follow abstract orthodoxies. Globalization can begin to work for the vast majority of the world's population only if it ceases to be viewed as an end in itself, and instead is treated as a tool in service of development: a way to provide food, health, housing and education to the wretched of the earth.

The End of the Nation State

Kenichi Ohmae

A funny—and, to many observers, a very troubling—thing has happened on the way to former US President Bush's so-called "new world order": the old world has fallen apart. Most visibly, with the ending of the Cold War, the long-familiar pattern of alliances and oppositions among industrialized nations has fractured beyond repair. Less visibly, but arguably far more important, the modern nation state itself—that artifact of the eighteenth and nineteenth centuries—has begun to crumble. [. . .]

In economics as in politics, the older patterns of nation-to-nation linkage have begun to lose their dominance. What is emerging in their place, however, is not a set of new channels based on culture instead of nations. Nor is it a simple realignment of previous flows of nation-based trade or investment.

In my view, what is realty at stake is not really which party or policy agenda dominates the apparatus of a nation state's central government. Nor is it the number of new, independent units into which that old center, which has held through the upheavals of industrialization and the agonies of two world wars, is likely to decompose. Nor is it the cultural fault lines along which it is likely to fragment.

Instead, what we are witnessing is the cumulative effect of fundamental changes in the currents of economic activity around the globe. So powerful have these currents become that they have carved out entirely new channels for themselves—channels that owe nothing to the lines of demarcation on traditional political maps. Put simply, in terms of real flows of economic activity, nation states have *already* lost their role as meaningful units of participation in the global economy of today's borderless world.

In the first place, these long-established, politically defined units have much less to contribute—and much less freedom to make contributions. The painful irony is that, driven by a concern to boost overall economic well-being, their efforts to assert traditional forms of economic sovereignty over the peoples and regions lying within their borders are now having precisely the opposite effect. Reflexive twinges of sovereignty make the desired economic success impossible, because the global economy punishes twinging countries by diverting investment and information elsewhere.

The uncomfortable truth is that, in terms of the global economy, nation states have become little more than bit actors. They may originally have been, in their mercantilist phase, independent, powerfully efficient engines of wealth creation. More recently, however, as the downward-ratcheting logic of electoral politics has placed a death grip on their economies, they have become—first and foremost—remarkably inefficient engines of wealth distribution. Elected political leaders gain and keep power by giving voters what they want, and what they want rarely entails a substantial decrease in the benefits, services, or subsidies handed out by the state.

Moreover, as the workings of genuinely global capital markets dwarf their ability to control exchange rates or protect their currency, nation states have become inescapably vulnerable to the discipline imposed by economic choices made elsewhere by people and institutions over which they have no practical control. Witness, for example, the recent, Maastricht-related bout of speculation against the franc, the pound, and the kronor. Witness, also, the unsustainable but self-imposed burden of Europe's various social programs. Finally, witness the complete absence of any economic value creation, save for those around the world who stand to benefit from pork-barrel excesses, in such decisions as the Japanese Diet's commitment—copied from the New Deal policies of Franklin Roosevelt—to build unnecessary highways and bridges on the remote islands of Hokkaido and Okinawa.

Second, and more to the point, the nation state is increasingly a nostalgic fiction. It makes even less sense today, for example, than it did a few years ago to speak of Italy or Russia or China as a single economic unit. Each is a motley combination of territories with vastly different needs and vastly different abilities to contribute. For a private sector manager or a public sector official to treat them as if they represented a single economic entity is to operate on the basis of demonstrably false, implausible, and nonexistent averages. This may still ge a political necessity, but it is a bald-faced economic lie.

Third, when you look closely at the goods and services now produced and traded around the world, as well as at the companies responsible for them, it is no easy matter to attach to them an accurate national label. Is an automobile sold under an American marque really a US product when a large percentage of its components comes from abroad? Is the performance of IBM's foreign subsidiaries or the performance of its R&D operations in Europe and Japan realty a measure of US excellence in technology? For that matter, are the jobs created by Japanese plants and factories in the Mississippi Valley really a measure of the health of the Japanese, and not the US, economy? The barbershop on the corner may indisputably be a part of the domestic American economy. But it is just not possible to make the same claim, with the same degree of confidence, about the firms active on the global stage.

Finally, when economic activity aggressively wears a national label these days, that tag is usually present neither for the sake of accuracy nor out of concern for the economic well-being of individual consumers. It is there primarily as a mini-flag of cheap nationalism—that is, as a jingoistic celebration of nationhood that places far more value on emotion-grabbing symbols than on real, concrete improvements in quality of life. By contrast, we don't hear much about feverish waves of Hong Kong nationalism, but the people in Hong Kong seem to live rather well. With much fanfare, Ukraine and the Baltic states have now become independent, but do their people have more food to eat or more energy to keep them warm during the winter or more electricity for light to see by?

An arresting, if often overlooked, fact about today's borderless economy is that people often have better access to low-cost, high-quality products when they are not produced "at home." Singaporeans, for example, enjoy better and cheaper agricultural products than do the Japanese, although Singapore has no farmers—and no farms—of its own. Much the same is true of construction materials, which are much less expensive in Singapore, which produces none of them, than in Japan, which does.

Now, given this decline in the relevance of nation states as units of economic activity, as well as the recent burst of economic growth in Asia, the burgeoning political self-consciousness of Islam, and the fragmentation, real or threatened, of such "official" political entities as Italy, Spain, Somalia, Rwanda, Canada, South Africa, and the former Yugoslavia, Czechoslovakia, and Soviet Union—given all this, it is easy to see why observers like Huntington should look to cultural, religious, ethnic, even tribal affiliations as the only plausible stopping point of the Centrifugal forces unleashed by the end of the Cold War.

Once bipolar discipline begins to lose its force, once traditional nation states no longer "hold," or so the argument goes, visionless leaders will start to give in to the feat that older fault lines will again make themselves felt. And given the bloody violence with which many of these lines have already begun to reappear, these leaders will find it hard to see where this process of backsliding can come to rest short of traditional groupings based on some sort of cultural affinity. In other words, in the absence of vision and the presence of slowly rising panic, the only groupings that seem to matter are based oil civilizations, not nations.

But are cultures or civilizations meaningful aggregates in terms of which to understand economic activity? Think, for a moment, of the ASEAN countries. In what sense is it useful to talk about them as a single, culturally defined economic area? As they affect local patterns of work, trade, and industry, the internal differences among their Buddhist, Islamic, Catholic (in the Philippines and the Sabah state of Malaysia), and Confucian traditions are every hit as large as, if not larger than, the differences separating any one of these traditions from the dominant business cultures of New York or London or Paris.

But in ASEAN, at least, differences of this sort do not provoke the same kinds of conflicts that often arise elsewhere. Most Western observers know, for example, that Spanish and Portuguese speakers can converse with each other, if with some minor degree of difficulty. Many fewer, however, know that the same is true of Indonesians and Malaysians. Or that, in border regions between Thailand and Malaysia, such as Phuket, there are peaceful, economically linked villages, some of which have mainly Buddhist and some mainly Islamic populations. These on-the-ground realities have made it possible for ASEAN leaders to accept and to reinforce, with little fear of internal friction, the development of cross-border economic ties like those stretching across the Strait of Malacca which are represented by the Greater Growth Triangle of Phuket, Medan, and Penang.

Even more important than such cultural differences within a civilization, and what Huntington's line of thought leaves out, is the issue of historical context. The particular dissolution of bipolar, "great power" discipline that so greatly affects us today is not taking place in the 1790s or the 1890s, but the 1990s. And that means it is taking place in a world whose peoples, no matter how far-flung geographically or disparate culturally, are all linked to much the same sources of global information. The immediacy and completeness of their access may vary, of course, and governments may try to impose restrictions and control. Even if they do, however, the barriers will not last forever, and leakages will occur all along the way. Indeed, the basic fact of linkage to global flows of information is a—perhaps, *the*—central, distinguishing fact of out moment in history. Whatever the civilization to which a particular group of people belongs, they now get to hear about the way other groups of people live, the kinds of products they buy, the changing focus of their tastes and preferences as consumers, and the styles of life they aspire to lead.

But they also get something more. For more than a decade, some of us have been talking about the progressive globalization of markets for consumer goods like Levi's jeans, Nike athletic shoes, and Hermés scarves—a process, driven by global exposure to the same information, the same cultural icons, and the same advertisements, that I have elsewhere referred to as the "California-ization" of taste. Today, however, the process of convergence goes faster and deeper. It reaches well beyond taste to much more fundamental dimensions of worldview, mind-set, and even thought process. There are now, for example, tens of millions of teenagers around the world who, having been raised in a multimedia-rich environment, have a lot more in common with each other than they do with members of older generations in their own cultures. For these budding consumers, technology-driven convergence does not rake place at the sluggish rate dictated by yesterday's media. It is instantaneous—a nanosecond migration of ideas and innovations.

The speed and immediacy of such migrations take us over an invisible political threshold. In the post-Cold War world, the information flows underlying economic activity in virtually all corners of the globe simply cannot be maintained as the possession of private elites or public officials. They are shared, increasingly, by all citizens and consumers. This sharing does not, of course, imply any necessary similarity in how local economic choices finally get made. But it does imply that there is a powerful centripetal force at work, counteracting and counterbalancing all the centrifugal forces noted above.

The emotional nexus of culture, in other words, is not the only web of shared interest able to contain the processes of disintegration unleashed by the reappearance of older fault lines. Information-driven participation in the global economy can do so, too, ahead of the fervid but empty posturing of both cheap nationalism and cultural messianism. The well-informed citizens of a global marketplace will not wait passively until nation states or cultural prophets deliver tangible improvements in lifestyle. They no longer trust them to do so. Instead, they want to build their own future, now, for themselves and by themselves. They want their own means of direct access to what has become a genuinely global economy. [. . .]

A Swing of the Pendulum

In the broad sweep of history, nation states have been a transitional form of organization for managing economic affairs. Their right—their prerogative—to manage them grew, in part, out of the control of military strength, but such strength is now an uncomfortably great burden to maintain. (It has also largely been exposed as a means to preserve the positions of those in power, not to advance the quality-of-life interests of their people.) Their right grew out of the control of natural resources and colonies, but the first is relatively unimportant as a source of value in a knowledge-intensive economy, and the second is less a source of low-cost resources than a bottomless drain on the home government's treasury. It grew out of the control of land, but prosperous economics can spread their influence through neighboring territories without any need for adjustment in formal divisions of sovereignty. And it grew out of the control of political independence, but such independence is of diminishing importance in a global economy that has less and less respect for national borders.

Moreover, as it grew, the nation state's organizational right to manage economic affairs fell victim to an inescapable cycle of decay. This should occasion no surprise. It comes as close to being a natural law as the messy universe of political economy allows. Whatever the form of government in power and whatever the political ideology that shapes it, demands for the civil minimum, for the support of special interests, and for the subsidization and protection of those left behind inexorably rise. In different circumstances, under different regimes, and during different eras, the speed of escalation varies. Good policy can slow the pace, bad policy can accelerate it. But no policy can stop it altogether. Nation states are political organisms, and in their economic bloodstreams cholesterol steadily builds up. Over time, arteries harden and the organism's vitality decays.

History, of course, also records the kinds of catastrophic, equilibrium-busting events that can stop or even reverse this aging process. Wars can do it, as can natural disasters like plagues, earthquakes, and volcanic eruptions. They have certainly done so in the past. But even for the most cold-blooded practitioners of *realpolitik*, these are hardly credible as purposeful instruments of economic policy.

Thus, in today's borderless economy, with its rapid cross-border [flows], there is really only one strategic degree of freedom that central governments have to counteract this remorseless buildup of economic cholesterol, only one legitimate instrument of policy to restore sustainable and self-reinforcing vitality, only one practical as well as morally acceptable way to meet their people's near-term needs without mortgaging the long-term prospects of their children and grandchildren. And that is to cede meaningful operational autonomy to the wealth-generating region states that lie within or across their borders, to catalyze the efforts of those region states to seek out global solutions, and to harness their distinctive ability to put global logic first and to function as ports of entry to the global economy. The only hope is to reverse the postfeudal, centralizing tendencies of the modern era and allow—or better, encourage—the economic pendulum to swing away from nations and hack toward regions. [. . .]

The Middle East: Religions in Collision

Jeff Haynes

The Middle East[1] is one of the first regions that many would think of when the issue of religion in politics arises. This is partly because of the decades-long struggle between Jews and (mostly Muslim) Arabs, especially since the founding of the State of Israel. Given their history of mutual antipathy, it might be assumed that there is something fundamental dividing the two religions, driving them inexorably towards conflict and confrontation. Yet both religions actually come from the same roots and have many theological similarities. The main issue dividing the Jews and the Arabs is not religious, but is a question of who is permanently to control Palestine with its holy places. But religion has become the main *symbol* of the division between the two peoples, exemplified by the rise of religious radicals posing serious challenges to modernizing governments. Such regimes share a desire to privatize religion, to reduce significantly its political importance.[2] But tensions between rulers and ruled over the public role of religion in the region are by no means novel. As Vatikiotis (1987: 56) points out, 'rulers of Middle Eastern states have for over a century now relentlessly eroded the religious character of the State. The expansion of State functions has been purely at the expense of the role of certain religious leaders and institutions.'

This chapter focuses on four countries: Israel, Turkey, Egypt and Algeria; the first is predominantly Jewish, the remainder preponderantly Muslim. In each, religion has emerged—or re-emerged—as an important political actor since the 1970s. What all four countries have in common is that despite long periods of modernization—involving State attempts to privatize religion—religion has great political importance. There is continuing civil war in Algeria, during which an estimated 60,000 people have died since 1991, between the State and Islamists.

Something similar is occurring in Egypt where Islamists seek the Islamic State, often by violent means. In Turkey politics was dominated in 1997 by a stand-off between the Government and the military over the public role of Islam; evidently the military triumphed and Islamist-orientated regime fell. Finally, in Israel, the Prime Minister, Yitzhak Rabin, was assassinated by a religious Jew in November 1995, focusing attention on the growing polarization between non-religious and religious Jews, often called Jewish 'fundamentalists' (Silberstein 1993). The emergence of Jewish fundamentalism—represented by organizations such as *Gush Emunim*—is often explained by the impact of Israel's victory over the Arabs in their 1967 war. Jewish fundamentalism is considered by Lustick (1993) and Sprinzak (1993), among others, as a product of the victory. For many religious Jews this was a particular triumph: it led to the regaining of the holiest sites in Judaism from the Arabs: Jerusalem, the Temple Mount, the Western Wall and Hebron and was, they believed, a sign of divine deliverance, an indication of impending redemption. Even some secular Jews spoke of it in theological terms.

For Arabs, on the other hand, Israel's victory exemplified the social and political crises enveloping their countries. For Piscatori (1986), the emergence of Islamist movements can only be understood against the background of Arab military defeats, especially that of 1967. The political and cultural crises they engendered created a situation of political instability and religious turmoil. Loss of control of holy Muslim sites, such as Jerusalem, the Temple Mount, the Dome of the Rock and the El Aksa mosque, generated a religious crisis. This loss, Silberstein (1993: 15) suggests, coupled with 'the ensuing political vacuum, opened the way for the growth of [Islamic] fundamentalist movements . . . fueled by the ongoing sense of shame, frustration, and victimization fostered by the continued occupation by Israel of an Arab population of 1.5 million in Jerusalem, the West Bank, and Gaza'. As I will explain, however, this is only part of the *raison d'être* for Islamist groups. As their rise in once strongly secular, non-Arab Turkey shows, they are also reactive against secularization, enforced modernization and a corresponding decline in Islam's social importance. Like their counterparts in Egypt and Algeria, Turkey's Islamists have profited from a declining economic situation, growing unemployment and serious State-level corruption presided over by self-proclaimed modernizing governments.

A number of factors—history, culture, religion, colonial experiences, constraints of underdevelopment and the ideologies and self-interest of political elites—were important in modelling the characteristics of the region's post-colonial States. Governments relied on centralist and centralizing development strategies and modes of rule. However, while importing doctrines of nationalism with its structure of the nation-state, many failed to provide acceptable alternative bases for the legitimacy of the State and its patterns of authority. The point is that the narrow political issue of 'nation' and nationalism have particular complexities in the Middle East. In the post-colonial period the view of the 'nation' that was given primacy in efforts at 'nation-building' was the citizenry occupying the territory of the new states. Subsidiary identities—especially those pertaining to shared religious and cultural identities—were dismissed as atavistic by modernizing regimes. Because of the cultural importance of both Jewish and Muslim identities, however, there were other possible bases for identity; particularly for the latter, whether in locally focused Islamist world views or in transnational ideologies such as pan-Islam.

The pursuit of modernity resulted in sharp divergences from Islamic or Judaic sources of authority, without integration on an alternative consensual basis. The result was an impasse regarding society's future direction. Currently, throughout the region the main challenges to political stability came from religious activists intent on changing the status quo. In the next two sections, I want to examine the religious and political characteristics of Islam and Judaism in order to put the following case studies into their proper contexts.

Islam and Judaism in Political Perspective

Islam and Politics

From its inception in the seventh century CE from a parlicularist religio-political community in present-day Saudi Arabia, Islam has developed into a world religion, albeit with different and rival, Shia and Sunni interpretations.[3] Islam is the unique historical case of a religion founded simultaneously as both a religious charismatic community of salvation and as a political community. This was expressed in the dual religious and political charisma of its founder, Muhammad, who was both God's messenger and a political and military leader. It is even more literally expressed by the fact that the Islamic era begins not with the birth or death of a founder or with the date of revelation but, rather, with the *hijra*, or migration, which marks the foundation of the Islamic political community in Medina ('the City'). There Muhammad established a political community, the *umma*, the importance of whose founding is commemorated in the Islamic calendar which begins from its inception in 622 CE rather than 610 CE, the year of God's first revelation to the Prophet. Under his leadership, the Muslims established their dominance over much of the Arabian peninsular, resulting in the welding of the disparate Arab tribes into a single polity with common institutions and a common ideology, a unity which endured until Muhammad's death in 632 CE.

Muhammad's passing was the prelude to the establishment of the caliphate period (632–1258), during which Islamic ideology and institutions as they are understood by Muslims today were formed and developed. This period is of special importance in the context of the rule of the first caliph (*kalifa* or 'successor'), since it is the period to which contemporary Islamic radicals turn to for guidance in attempting to define the preferred character of their putative Islamic states.

The process of creating a Middle Eastern Islamic civilization took 600 years, from the beginning of the seventh to the thirteenth century CE. The consolidation of Muslim rule was followed by its spreading to other regions. By the end of the fifteenth century Islam had established itself as the dominant religion in North Africa, and was of growing importance in sub-Saharan Africa and in many parts of Asia. The spread of Muslim power and the mass conversions with which it was accompanied brought into the faith a wide range of beliefs, superstitions, religious practices and social customs. The result was that Islam was no longer a simple, rational anti-idolatrous faith, characteristics with which it had initially been marked. The several types of Islamic societies—in the Middle East, Africa and Asia—can therefore be analysed in terms of various patterns of institutional arrangements involving State, parochial and Muslim religious institutions. In each case the pattern of relations describes a variant form of Muslim society. Although inherited patterns would be a powerful force in the shaping of Muslim societies in the post-colonial era, as they entered the modern era they were to be drastically changed. This was the result of three main developments: internal reorganization, European imperialism and the growth of the global economy.

There are two important themes in Islam that traditionally impact upon politics. First, it is often suggested that religion and politics are inseparable in Islam. It is said that the *umma*, the Islamic community, has traditionally seen itself as simultaneously both religious *and* political community, that is, the community of believers and the nation of Islam. The result is that it is completely 'natural' for religious actors to seek to gain political goals. Such a suggestion does not, however, go unchallenged; others believe that it is quite inaccurate to argue that Islam has no differentiated religious and political spheres. Indeed, it is suggested, the history of Islam is best viewed as the history of the various institutionalizations of the dual religious and political charisma of Muhammad into bilateral and differentiated religious and political institutions.

Certainly Islam's holy book, the Quran, depicts the faith as a belief system encompassing both religion and politics. The Quran, divine revelation received by Muhammad, and the *hadith*, prescriptions laid down by him on the basis of his own reflections, are sacred texts for Muslims. *Sharia* law, at least theoretically and in many cases practically, also helps regulate Muslims' conduct. Partly as a result, it is widely assumed, especially by non-Muslims, that politics and religion cannot logically be separated in Islam. However, at the very least the all-encompassing nature of this assumption can be strongly challenged. As respected scholars like Ayubi (1991), Piscatori (1986) and Owen (1992) have convincingly argued, Islam has a history above all of pragmatism. And, as Asad (1986) points out, there has never been a Muslim society in which *sharia* law has governed more than a fragment of social life. In practice, there is, on the one hand, very often separation between the essence of the religious principles and institutions and those of the temporal ruler and State. On the other, there has frequently developed a pragmatic compatability between Islam's precepts and the very different imperatives of a world of secularizing states. The important point is that Islamic history contains innumerable examples of thought and action where *din* (religion) and *dawla* (State) have been sharply distinguished. What this amounts to is that the most spectacular recent example of Islam's political involvement—Iran's Islamic revolution of 1978–9—is not the norm: actually it is historically novel. Further, there would appear to be no insurmountable obstacle of principle to a fair degree of compatability between 'Islamic' precepts and pragmatically modernizing State practice as regards citizenship and the nature of socio-political organization.

The second main theme is that most *ulama* (learned clergy) have historically been close to those who wield political power. So close has this relationship been that in some countries such religious figures are known as the 'ulama of the establishment' (Gaffney 1994), denoting their close identification with the politico, religious status quo. Numerous ulama—normally proponents of establishment Islam adhering closely to the ideal as described in texts and interpreted by religious scholars—have connived with State authorities in the name of perpetuation of their interpretation of Islam. 'In return for material favours and recognition of their status' many ulama have sought to use their positions to underline the importance of obedience to authority, in the process closely identifying themselves with government (Bill and Springborg 1994: 59). In short, 'establishment' Islam is in many instances the State religion and as such is formally bound up in the legitimacy of government. The establishment ulama are often in conflict with two tendencies: (a) popular' Islam, that is, the Sufi *tariqas* (orders)[4] and (b) Islamists. Popular Islam comprises those religious beliefs and practices which prevail among the ordinary people. Due to a variety of factors, many Muslims—especially the poorly educated and those residing away from Islamic centres—may not have access to religious scholars and written texts. Because of this it is natural for them to adhere to their own unorthodox interpretations of Islam.

While the Sufi orders have often incurred the suspicion of both religious and secular authorities over time, a more recent development has been the emergence of the Islamists with their overt threat to the political and religious status quo. They are often regarded by governments and analysts alike as representing the very epitome of the religiously negative, because they are regarded as both defensive and backward-looking. Islamists are said to champion a 'set of strategies by which beleaguered believers attempt to preserve their distinctive identity as a people or group' in response to real or imagined attacks from those who wish to draw them into a 'syncretistic, areligious or irreligious cultural milieu' (Marty and Scott Appleby 1993: 3). Some portray them as appealing exclusively to poor, simple people, especially those disoriented by the stresses and strains of modernization. Such people are judged to be easy prey for the Islamists, allegedly cynical, manipulative champions of a vision of religious dogma which promises spectacular improvements in the lives of ordinary people once the Islamic State—where life is governed according to religious laws—is a reality. In fact, the character and impact of Islamist doctrines are located within a nexus of moral, social and political issues revolving around State–society interactions. Islamist groups pose a challenge to State power because of their sharp critiques of existing religious and political elites. Their ideas amount to a 'manifesto'—a programme of political action—for social change and reform of the status quo. Apart from the perceived attack on religion by their modernizing governments, the rise of the Islamists has also been in response to the military defeats of the Arabs by Israel and as a result of the stimulus provided by the Iranian revolution.

The point is that the Islamists are counter-elites who perceive establishment ulama, the unorthodox *tariqas* and the State collectively as the 'enemies of Islam'. The expansion and contraction of Western colonialism, the dissolution of the Ottoman Empire, and the emergence of Muslim nation-states after World War II all undermined the traditional forms of institutionalization of the *umma* as a dual religious and political community. It opened up the way for all kinds of religious-political experiments in the name of returning to the original *umma*. It is misleading, therefore, to view the emergence of the Islamists as primarily an anti-modern traditionalist reaction. It is more appropriate to view them in their various manifestations as experiments in Islamic 'reformation' and 'revolution'. Below I examine Islamist groups in Algeria, Egypt and Turkey. First, however, I examine Jewish fundamentalism, in some ways a parallel to its Islamist counterpart.

Judaism and Politics

Islam is, more perhaps than any other religion, a *blueprint* of a social order. It is in the *totality* in which Islam is a social movement which sets it apart from Judaism. However, like Islam, Jewish identity has been understood, traditionally, as an overlapping combination of religion and nation. Put another way, the people of Israel think of themselves as a nation inhabiting a *Jewish State* created by their covenant with God. The interpretation of the covenant and its implications gives rise to the characteristic beliefs and practices of the Jewish people. Vital to this covenant is the promise of the land of Israel. Following their historical dispersions under first the Babylonians and then the Romans, Jews had prayed for centuries for the end of their exile and a return to Israel. However, except for small numbers, Jews lived in exile, in separate communities, for centuries. During the diaspora while awaiting divine redemption to return them to their homeland, Jews' lives were defined by *halacha* (religious law), which largely maintained the national component of Jewish identity. The Jews' historical suffering during the diaspora was understood as a necessary continuation of the special dedication of the community to God.

While monotheistic, Judaism lacks the universalist and proselytizing tendencies of Islam and Christianity. As former Chief Rabbi Epstein put it: 'when paganism gave place to Christianity and later also to Islam, Judaism withdrew from the missionary field and was satisfied to leave the task of spreading the religion of humanity to daughter faiths' (quoted in Parrinder 1977: 67). Jews have a different view of revelation from Christians. For the latter, the proclaimed messiah—Jesus Christ—has already come; Jews, however, look forward to the arrival of their *Mashiach* at some future date.

There are two main strands of the Jewish faith, Orthodox and Reform Judaism. The division between them is ostensibly on the question of whether tradition can be changed in the face of new situations. In other words, is the Torah, the Jewish holy book (essentially the first five books of the Hebrew Bible), totally immutable in theory? Over time, the hegemony of Orthodoxy has declined. In medieval times Jewish ritual life had been highly elaborated as a result of the dominance of the rabbis, both spiritual counsellors and teachers of the traditions of the Torah. Various injunctions of the Torah controlled nearly all acts of everyday life in both the home and the synagogue, serving constantly to remind Jews that they were God's chosen people (Smart 1989: 265). Ethically, Jews were expected to keep to the high standard of the Ten Commandments and other injunctions promulgated by the rabbis, such as monogamy. Regarding doctrine, the insistence on strict monotheism has always been vital.

The traditional view of Judaism as a revealed religion governing every aspect of life began to face severe challenges at the end of the eighteenth century following the French and American Revolutions. Henceforward, many Jews began to participate fully in the life of Western society, increasingly to share in its values, 'in contradiction to traditional Jewish life and values' (Jacobs 1992: 31). A consequence was the emergence of the *Haskalah* (Enlightenment) movement, led by a German Jew, Moses Mendelssohn. The *Haskalah* aimed to influence

Jewish intellectuals towards a greater appreciation of the need to adapt to the new order. They did not seek to reject tradition, but to promote a new approach whereby it could live side by side with new learning and social forms. Essentially, the *Haskalah* was a Jewish Renaissance whereby the Jewish Middle Ages came to an end. It spread to Eastern Europe where it met with considerable hostility on the part of traditional rabbis but its impact was such that no Jew could be impervious to its claims (Jacobs 1992: 31).

During the second half of the nineteenth century, Zionism—the political endeavour to create a national home for Jews—emerged. Fundamental to Zionism is the recognition of the national identity of the Jews, the rejection of the exile and a belief in the impossibility of assimilation. While the Bible is central to secular Zionists as a 'historical' document, many seem to be unclear concerning the centrality of religious elements in Jewish cultural history and the rejection of orthodox practice. The 'political' Zionism of Theodor Herzl's[5] World Zionist Organization (WZO), founded 1897, was condemned as 'idolatry' by many of the orthodox, who felt it replaced reverence for God and the Torah (law) by secular nationalism and the 'worship' of the land. Some orthodox Jews, instrumental in founding the *Mizrahi* party (*Merkaz Ruhani* or Spiritual Centre) in 1902 and *Agudat Israel* (Association of Israel, founded 1912), did, however, support Zionist efforts to establish a Jewish State. By the 1930s there was growing support for the idea of Israel from many orthodox Jews, although the Holocaust in Nazi-controlled Germany—some six million Jews were killed—was pivotal in the founding of the State of Israel in 1948.

Endnotes

1. In this chapter the term 'Middle East' refers to the Arab countries plus Turkey and Iran. Despite its importance in the context of religion and politics in the region, I do not focus upon the latter. This is because there are many existing sources of information for those interested. See, for example, Owen (1992) Haynes (1993), Bill and Springborg (1994) and Keddie (1995).
2. This is a debatable contention in the case of Israel where, since the Likud victory of 1977, regimes of both right and left have been obliged to accept the presence of religious parties in government due to the vagaries of the electoral system.
3. There is inadequate space in the present work to examine the theological and other differences between the two rival at interpretations of Islam. Those interested are directed to Haynes (1993).

4. The *tariqas* are brotherhoods of Islamic mystics who search for divine knowledge through the emotions rather than timely through the intellect. The Sufi orders emerged from the ninth century as an antidote to the austere, scripturalist, rational nature of Islam. Sufism has always met with, at best, ambivalence, at worst, outright condemnation, from most ulama. Periodically, brotherhoods have been outlawed by the authorities.

5. Theodor Herzl (1860–1904) was a Hungarian journalist living in Vienna. He was persuaded by the Russian pogroms and the Dreyfus trial France to conclude in his pamphlet *Der Judenstaat* (1896) that the only way Jewish people could live was to have their own nation-state. In 1897, at the first WZO congress in Basle, Switzerland, the leading Jewish intellectual and organizer, Chaim Weizmann (1874–1952), called for a Jewish homeland to be created in Palestine.

Terror in the Mind of God

Mark Juergensmeyer

When plastic explosives attached to a Hamas suicide bomber ripped through the gentrified Ben Yehuda shopping mall in Jerusalem in September 1997, the blast damaged not only lives and property but also the confidence with which most people view the world. As images of the bloodied victims were projected from the scene, the double arches of a McDonald's restaurant were visible in the background, their cheerful familiarity appearing oddly out of place with the surrounding carnage. Many who viewed these pictures saw symbols of their own ordinary lives assaulted and vicariously felt the anxiety—the terror—of those who experienced it firsthand. After all, the wounded could have included anyone who has ever visited a McDonald's—which is to say virtually anyone in the developed world. In this sense, the blast was an attack not only on Israel but also on normal life as most people know it.

This loss of innocence was keenly felt by many Americans after news of ethnic shootings in California and Illinois in 1999; the attack on American embassies in Africa in 1998; abortion clinic bombings in Alabama and Georgia in 1997; the bomb blast at the Olympics in Atlanta and the destruction of a U.S. military housing complex in Dhahran, Saudi Arabia, in 1996; the tragic destruction of the federal building at Oklahoma City in 1995; and the explosion at the World Trade Center in New York City in 1993. These incidents and a host of violent episodes associated with American religious extremists—including the Christian militia, the Christian Identity movement, and Christian anti-abortion activists—have brought Americans into the same uneasy position occupied by many in the rest of the world. Increasingly, global society must confront religious violence on a routine basis.

The French, for example, have dealt with subway bombs planted by Algerian Islamic activists, the British with exploding trucks and buses ignited by Irish Catholic nationalists, and the Japanese with nerve gas placed in Tokyo subways by members of a Hindu-Buddhist sect. In India residents of Delhi have experienced car bombings by both Sikh and Kashmiri separatists, in Sri Lanka whole sections of the city of Colombo have been destroyed both by Tamils and by Sinhalese militants, Egyptians have been forced to live with militant Islamic attacks in coffeehouses and riverboats, Algerians have lost entire villages to savage attacks perpetrated allegedly by supporters of the Islamic Salvation Front, and Israelis and Palestinians have confronted the deadly deeds of both Jewish and Muslim extremists. For many Middle Easterners, terrorist attacks have become a way of life.

In addition to their contemporaneity, all these instances share two striking characteristics. First, they have been violent—even vicious—in a manner calculated to be terrifying. And, second, they have been motivated by religion.

The Meaning of Religious Terrorism

The ferocity of religious violence was brought home to me in 1998 when I received the news that a car bomb had exploded in a Belfast neighborhood I had visited the day before. The following day firebombs ripped through several pubs and stores, apparently in protest against the fragile peace agreement signed earlier in the year. It was an eerie repetition of what had happened several years before. A suicide bombing claimed by the militant wing of the Palestinian Muslim political movement, Hamas, tore apart a bus near Hebrew University in 1995 the day after I had visited the university on, I believe, the very same bus. The pictures of the mangled bodies on the Jerusalem street and the images of Belfast's bombed-out pub, therefore, had a direct and immediate impact on my view of the world.

What I realized then is the same thing that all of us perceive on some level when we view pictures of terrorist events: on a different day, at a different time, perhaps in a different bus, one of the bodies torn to shreds by any of these terrorist acts could have been ours. What came to mind as I heard the news of the Belfast and Jerusalem bombings, however, was not so much a feeling of relief for my safety as a sense of betrayal—that the personal security and order that is usually a basic assumption of public life cannot in fact be taken for granted in a world where terrorist acts exist.

That, I take it, is largely the point: terrorism is meant to terrify. The word comes from the Latin *terrere*, "to cause to tremble," and came into common usage in the political sense, as an assault on civil order, during the Reign of Terror in the French Revolution at the close of the eighteenth century. Hence the public response to the violence—the trembling that terrorism effects—is part of the meaning of the term. It is appropriate, then, that the definition of a terrorist act is provided by us, the witnesses—the ones terrified—and not by the party committing the act. It is we—or more often our public agents, the news media—who affix the label on acts of violence that makes them terrorism. These are public acts of destruction, committed without a clear military objective, that arouse a widespread sense of fear.

This fear often turns to anger when we discover the other characteristic that frequently attends these acts of public violence: their justification by religion. Most people feel that religion should provide tranquility and peace, not terror. Yet in many of these cases religion has supplied not only the ideology but also the motivation and the organizational structure for the perpetrators. It is true that some terrorist acts are committed by public officials invoking a sort of "state terrorism" in order to subjugate the populace. The pogroms of Stalin, the government-supported death squads in El Salvador, the genocidal killings of the Khmer Rouge in Cambodia, ethnic cleansing in Bosnia and Kosovo, and government-spurred violence of the Hutus and Tutsis in Central Africa all come to mind. The United States has rightfully been accused of terrorism in the atrocities committed during the Vietnam War, and there is some basis for considering the nuclear bombings of Hiroshima and Nagasaki as terrorist acts.

But the term "terrorism" has more frequently been associated with violence committed by disenfranchised groups desperately attempting to gain a shred of power or influence. Although these groups cannot kill on the scale that governments with all their military power can, their sheer numbers, their intense dedication, and their dangerous unpredictability have given them influence vastly out of proportion with their meager military resources. Some of these groups have been inspired by purely secular causes. They have been motivated by leftist ideologies, as in the cases of the Shining Path and the Tupac Amaru in Peru, and the Red Army in Japan; and they have been propelled by a desire for ethnic or regional separatism, as in the cases of Basque militants in Spain and the Kurdish nationalists in the Middle East.

But more often it has been religion—sometimes in combination with these other factors, sometimes as the primary motivation—that has incited terrorist acts. The common perception that there has been a rise in religious violence around the world in the last decades of the twentieth century has been borne out by those who keep records of such things. In 1980 the U.S. State Department roster of international terrorist groups listed scarcely a single religious organization. In 1998 U.S. Secretary of State Madeleine Albright listed thirty of the world's most dangerous groups; over half were religious.[1] They were Jewish, Muslim, and Buddhist. If one added to this list other violent religious groups around the world, including the many Christian militia and other paramilitary organizations found domestically in the United States, the number of religious terrorist groups would be considerable. According to the RAND–St. Andrews Chronology of International Terrorism, the proportion of religious groups increased from sixteen of forty-nine terrorist groups identified in 1994 to twenty-six of the fifty-six groups listed the following year.[2] For this reason former U.S. Secretary of State Warren Christopher said that terrorist acts in the name of religion and ethnic identity have become "one of the most important security challenges we face in the wake of the Cold War."[3]

Throughout this study we will be looking at this odd attraction of religion and violence. Although some observers try to explain away religion's recent ties to violence as an aberration, a result of political ideology, or the characteristic of a mutant form of religion—fundamentalism—these are not my views. Rather, I look for explanations in the current forces of geopolitics and in a strain of violence that may be found at the deepest levels of religious imagination.

Within the histories of religious traditions—from biblical wars to crusading ventures and great acts of martyrdom—violence has lurked as a shadowy presence. It has colored religion's darker, more mysterious symbols. Images of death have never been far from the heart of religion's power to stir the imagination. One of the haunting questions asked by some of the great scholars of religion—including Emile Durkheim, Marcel Mauss, and Sigmund Freud—is why this is the case. Why does religion seem to need violence, and violence religion, and why is a divine mandate for destruction accepted with such certainty by some believers?

These are questions that have taken on a sense of urgency in recent years, when religious violence has reappeared in a form often calculated to terrify on a massive scale. These contemporary acts of violence are often justified by the historical precedent of religion's violent past. Yet the forces that combine to produce religious violence are particular to each moment of history. For this reason, I will focus on case studies of religious violence both within their own cultural contexts and within the framework of global social and political changes that are distinctive to our time.

This is a book about religious terrorism. It is about public acts of violence at the turn of the century for which religion has provided the motivation, the justification, the organization, and the world view. In this book, I have tried to get inside the mindset of those who perpetrated and supported such acts. My goal is to understand why these acts were often associated with religious causes and why they have occurred with such frequency at this juncture in history. Although it is not my purpose to be sympathetic to people who have done terrible things, I do want to understand them and their world views well enough to know how they and their supporters can morally justify what they have done.

What puzzles me is not why bad things are done by bad people, but rather why bad things are done by people who otherwise appear to be good—in cases of religious terrorism, by pious people dedicated to a moral vision of the world. Considering the high-sounding rhetoric with which their purposes are often stated, it is perhaps all the more tragic that the acts of violence meant to achieve them have caused suffering and disruption in many lives—not only those who were injured by the acts, but also those who witnessed them, even from a distance.

Because I want to understand the cultural contexts that produce these acts of violence, my focus is on the ideas and the communities of support that lie behind the acts rather than on the "terrorists" who commit them. In fact, for the purposes of this study, the word "terrorist" is problematic. For one thing, the term makes no clear distinction between the organizers of an attack, those who carry it out, and the many who support it both directly and indirectly. Are they all terrorists, or just some of them—and if the latter, which ones? Another problem with the word is that it can be taken to single out a certain limited species of people called "terrorists" who are committed to violent acts. The implication is that such terrorists are hell-bent to commit terrorism for whatever reason—sometimes choosing religion, sometimes another ideology, to justify their mischief. This logic concludes that terrorism exists because terrorists exist, and if we just got rid of them, the world would be a more pleasant place.

Although such a solution is enticing, the fact is that the line is very thin between "terrorists" and their "non-terrorist" supporters. It is also not clear that there is such a thing as a "terrorist" before someone conspires to perpetrate a terrorist act. Although every society contains sociopaths and others who sadistically enjoy killing, it is seldom such persons who are involved in the deliberate public events that we associate with terrorism, and few studies of terrorism focus exclusively on personality. The studies of the psychology of terrorism deal largely with social psychology; that is, they are concerned with the way people respond to certain group situations that make violent public acts possible.[4] I know of no study that suggests that people are terrorist by nature. Although some activists involved in religious terrorism have been troubled by mental problems, others are people who appear to be normal and socially well adjusted, but who are caught up in extraordinary communities and share extreme world views.

Most of the people involved in acts of religious terrorism are not unlike Dr. Baruch Goldstein, who killed over thirty Muslims as they were praying at the Tomb of the Patriarchs in Hebron on February 25, 1994. Goldstein was a medical doctor who grew up in a middle-class community in Brooklyn and received his professional training at Albert Einstein College of Medicine in the Bronx. His commitment to an extreme form of Zionism brought him to Israel and the Kiryat Arba settlement, and although he was politically active for many years—he was Rabbi Meir Kahane's campaign manager when he ran for the Israeli parliament—Goldstein did not appear to be an irrational or vicious person. Prior to the attack at Hebron, his most publicized political act had been a letter to the editor of the *New York Times*.[5] If Goldstein had deep and perverse personality flaws that eventually surfaced and made him a terrorist, we do not know about them. The evidence about him is to the contrary: it idicates that, like his counterparts in Hamas, he was an otherwise decent man who became overwhelmed by a great sense of dedication to a religious vision shared by many in the community of which he was a part. He became convinced that this vision and community were profoundly assaulted, and this compelled him to a desperate and tragic act. He was certainly single-minded about his religious concerns—even obsessed over them—but to label Goldstein a terrorist prior to the horrible act he committed implies that he was a terrorist by nature and that his religiosity was simply a charade. The evidence does not indicate either to be the case.

For this reason I use the term "terrorist" sparingly. When I do use it, I employ it in the same sense as the word "murderer": it applies to specific persons only after they have been found guilty of committing such a crime, or planning to commit one. Even then I am somewhat cautious about using the term, since a violent act is "terrorism" technically only in the eyes of the courts, more publicly in the eyes of the media, and ultimately only in the eyes of the beholder. The old saying "One person's terrorist is another person's freedom-fighter" has some truth to it. The designation of terrorism is a subjective judgment about the legitimacy of certain violent acts as much as it is a descriptive statement about them.

When I interviewed militant religious activists and their supporters, I found that they seldom used the term "terrorist" to describe what their groups had done. Several told me that their groups should be labeled militant rather than terrorist. A Lutheran pastor who was convicted of bombing abortion clinics was not a terrorist, he told me, since he did not enjoy violence for its own sake. He employed violence only for a purpose, and for that reason he described these events as "defensive actions" on behalf of the "unborn."[6] Activists on both sides of the struggle in Belfast described themselves as "paramilitaries." A leader in India's Sikh separatist movement said that he preferred the term "militant" and told me that "'terrorist' had replaced the term 'witch'" as an excuse to persecute those whom one dislikes.[7] One of the men convicted of bombing the World Trade Center essentially agreed with the Sikh leader, telling me that the word "terrorist" was so "messy" it could not be used without a lot of qualifications.[8] The same point of view was expressed by the political leader of the Hamas movement with whom I talked in Gaza. He described his movement's suicide attacks as "operations."[9] Like many activists who used violence, he likened his group to an army that was planning defensive maneuvers and using violence strategically as necessary acts. Never did he use the word "terrorist" or "terrorism."

This is not just a semantic issue. Whether or not one uses "terrorist" to describe violent acts depends on whether one thinks that the acts are warranted. To a large extent the use of the term depends on one's world view: if the world is perceived as peaceful, violent acts appear as terrorism. If the world is thought to be at war, violent acts may be regarded as legitimate. They may be seen as preemptive strikes, as defensive tactics in an ongoing battle, or as symbols indicating to the world that it is indeed in a state of grave and ultimate conflict.

In most cases in this book, religious language is used to characterize this conflict. When it is, what difference does religion make? Do acts of violence conducted by Hamas have different characteristics from those conducted by secular movements, such as the Kurds? The question is whether religious terrorism is different from other kinds.

In this book it will become clear that, at least in some cases, religion does make a difference. Some of these differences are readily apparent—the transcendent moralism with which such acts are justified, for instance, and the ritual intensity with which they are committed. Other differences are more profound and go to the very heart of religion. The familiar religious images of struggle and transformation—concepts of cosmic war—have been employed in this-worldly social struggles. When these cosmic battles are conceived as occurring on the human plane, they result in real acts of violence.

This leads to yet another question: when religion justifies violence, is it simply being used for political purposes? This question is not as simple as it may first appear. It is complicated largely because of the renewed role that religion plays in various parts of the world as an ideology of public order—especially in movements of religious nationalism—in which religious and political ideologies are intertwined. As the cases in this book will show, religion is not innocent. But it does not ordinarily lead to violence. That happens only with the coalescence of a peculiar set of circumstances—political, social, and ideological—when religion becomes fused with violent expressions of social aspirations, personal pride, and movements for political change.

For these reasons, questions about why religious terrorism has occurred at this moment in history have to be raised in context. By "context" I mean the historical situations, social locations, and world views related to violent incidents. To understand these, we will explore not only the mindset of religious activists who have committed violence but also the groups that have supported them and the ideologies to which they subscribe.

Seeing Inside Cultures of Violence

Terrorism is seldom a lone act. When Dr. Baruch Goldstein entered the Tomb of the Patriarchs carrying an automatic weapon, he came with the tacit approval of many of his fellow Jewish settlers in the nearby community of Kiryat Arba. When Rev. Paul Hill stepped from a sidewalk in Pensacola, Florida, and shot Dr. John Britton and his security escort as they prepared to enter their clinic, he was cheered by a certain circle of militant Christian anti-abortion activists around the country. When the followers of Sheik Omar Abdul Rahman drove a rented truck to the underground garage of the World Trade Center, igniting it and its lethal cargo, they came as part of a well-orchestrated plan that involved dozens of coconspirators and thousands of sympathizers in the United States, Egypt, Palestine, and elsewhere throughout the world.

As these instances show, it takes a community of support and, in many cases, a large organizational network for an act of terrorism to succeed. It also requires an enormous amount of moral presumption for the perpetrators of these acts to justify the destruction of property on a massive scale or to condone a brutal attack on another life, especially the life of someone one scarcely knows and against whom one bears no personal enmity. And it requires a great deal of internal conviction, social acknowledgment, and the stamp of approval from a legitimizing ideology or authority one respects. Because of the moral, ideological, and organizational support necessary for such acts, most of them come as collective decisions—such as the conspiracy that led to the release of nerve gas in the Tokyo subways and the Hamas organization's carefully devised bombings.

Even those acts that appear to be solo ventures conducted by rogue activists often have networks of support and ideologies of validation behind them, whether or not these networks and ideologies are immediately apparent. Behind Yitzhak Rabin's assassin, Yigal Amir, for instance, was a large movement of Messianic Zionism in Israel and abroad. Behind convicted bomber Timothy McVeigh and Buford Furrow, the alleged attacker of a Jewish day-care center, was a subculture of militant Christian groups that extends throughout the United States. Behind Unabomber Theodore Kaczynski was the strident student activist culture of the late 1960s, in which one could easily become infected by the feeling that "terrible things" were going on.[10] Behind the two high school students who killed themselves and thirteen of their classmates in Littleton, Colorado, in 1999 was a quasi-religious "trenchcoat" culture of gothic symbolism. In all of these cases the activists thought that their acts were supported not only by other people but by a widely shared perception that the world was already violent: it was enmeshed in great struggles that gave their own violent actions moral meaning.

This is a significant feature of these cultures: the perception that their communities are already under attack—are being violated—and that their acts are therefore simply responses to the violence they have experienced. In some cases this perception is one to which sensitive people outside the movement can readily relate—the feeling of oppression held by Palestinian Muslims, for example, is one that many throughout the world consider to be an understandable though regrettable response to a situation of political control. In other instances, such as the imagined oppression of America's Christian militia or Japan's Aum Shinrikyo movement, the members' fears of black helicopters hovering over their homes at night or the allegations of collusion of international governments to deprive individuals of their freedoms are regarded by most people outside the movements as paranoid delusions. Still other cases—such as those involving Sikh militants in India, Jewish settlers on the West Bank, Muslim politicians in Algeria, Catholic and Protestant militants in Northern Ireland, and anti-abortion activists in the United States—are highly controversial. There are sober and sensitive people to argue each side.

Whether or not outsiders regard these perceptions of oppression as legitimate, they are certainly considered valid by those within the communities. It is these shared perceptions that constitute the cultures of violence that have flourished throughout the world—in neighborhoods of Jewish nationalists from Kiryat Arba to Brooklyn where the struggle to defend the Jewish nation is part of daily existence, in mountain towns in Idaho and Montana where religious and individual freedoms are thought to be imperiled by an enormous governmental conspiracy, and in pious Muslim communities around the world where Islam is felt to be at war with the surrounding secular forces of modern society. Although geographically dispersed, these cultures in some cases are fairly small: one should bear in mind that the culture of violence characterized by Hamas, for example, does not implicate all Palestinians, all Muslims, or even all Palestinian Muslims.

I could use the term "communities" or "ideologies" of terrorism rather than "cultures" of violence, but what I like about the term "culture" is that it entails both things—ideas and social groupings—that are related to terrorist acts. Needless to say, I am using the term "culture" beyond its narrow meaning as the aesthetic products of a society.[11] Rather, I employ it in a broad way to include the ethical and social values underlying the life of a particular social unit.

My way of thinking about culture is enriched by the ideas of several scholars. It encompasses the idea of "episteme" as described by Michel Foucault: a world view, or a paradigm of thinking that "defines the conditions . . . of all knowledge."[12] It also involves the notion of a nexus of socially embedded ideas about society. Pierre Bourdieu calls this a "habitus," which he describes as "a socially constituted system of cognitive and motivating structures."[13] It is the social basis for what Clifford Geertz described as the "cultural systems" of a people: the patterns of thought, the world views, and the meanings that are attached to the activities of a particular society. In Geertz's view, such cultural systems encompass both secular ideologies and religion.[14]

The cultural approach to the study of terrorism that I have adopted has advantages and disadvantages. Although it allows me to explore more fully the distinctive world view and moral justifications of each group, it means that I tend to study less closely the political calculations of movement leaders and the international networks of activists. For these aspects of terrorism I rely on other works: historical studies such as Bernard Lewis's classic *The Assassins;* comprehensive surveys such as Walter Laqueur's *Terrorism* (revised and republished as *The Age of Terrorism*) and Bruce Hoffman's *Inside Terrorism,* which covers both historical and contemporary incidents;[15] studies in the social psychology of terrorism by Walter Reich and Jerrold Post;[16] political analyses such as Martha Crenshaw's work on the structure of terrorist organizations in Algeria and Peter Merkl's analysis of left-wing terrorism in Germany;[17] the contributions of Paul Wilkinson and Brian Jenkins in analyzing terrorism as an instrument of political strategy.[18]

These works leave room for other scholars to develop a more cultural approach to analyzing terrorist movements—efforts at reconstructing the terrorists' world views from within. This research has led to a number of significant case studies, including analyses of the Christian militia by Jeffrey Kaplan, the Christian Identity movement by James Aho, Irish paramilitarists by Martin Dillon, Sikh militants by Cynthia Keppley Mahmood, Jewish activists by Ehud Sprinzak, and Hamas suicide bombers by Paul Steinberg and Anne Marie Oliver.[19] These and other works, along with my own case studies and some interesting reportage by international journalists, make possible an effort such as this one: a comparative cultural study of religious terrorism.

This book begins with case studies of religious activists who have used violence or who justify its use. The first half of the book contains chapters on Christians in America who supported abortion clinic bombings and militia actions such as the bombing of the Oklahoma City federal building, Catholics and Protestants who justified acts of terrorism in Northern Ireland, Muslims associated with the bombing of the World Trade Center in New York City and Hamas attacks in the Middle East, Jews who supported the assassination of Prime Minister Yitzhak Rabin and the attack in Hebron's Tomb of the Patriarchs, Sikhs identified with the killing of India's prime minister Indira Gandhi and Punjab's chief minister Beant Singh, and the Japanese Buddhists affiliated with the group accused of the nerve gas attack in Tokyo's subways.

Since these case studies are not only about those directly involved in terrorist acts but also about the world views of the cultures of violence that stand behind them, I have interviewed a number of people associated with these cultures. In the chapters that follow, however, I have chosen to focus on only a few. In some cases I have highlighted the established leaders of political organizations, such as Dr. Abdul Aziz Rantisi, Tom Hartley, and Simranjit Singh Mann. In other cases I have chosen outspoken activists who have been convicted of undertaking violent acts, such as Mahmud Abouhalima, Michael Bray, and Yoel Lerner. In yet other cases I have selected members from the lower echelons of activist movements, such as Takeshi Nakamura and Yochay Ron. The interviews that I have chosen to describe in detail are therefore diverse. But in each case—in my opinion—they best exemplify the world views of the cultures of violence of which the individuals are a part.

In the second half of the book I identify patterns—an overarching logic—found within the cultures of violence described in the first half. I try to explain why and how religion and violence are linked. In Chapter 7 I explain why acts of religious terrorism are undertaken not only to achieve a strategic target but also to accomplish a symbolic purpose. In Chapters 8 and 9, I describe how images of cosmic confrontation and warfare that are ordinarily found in the context of heaven or history are sometimes tied to this-worldly political battles, and I explain how the processes of satanization and symbolic empowerment develop in stages. In Chapter 10, I explore the way that religious violence has provided a sense of empowerment to alienated individuals, marginal groups, and visionary ideologues.

In the last chapter of this book I return to questions directly about religion: why anyone would believe that God could sanction terrorism and why the rediscovery of religion's power has appeared in recent years in such a bloody way—and what, if anything, can be done about it. I have applied what I have learned about religious terrorism to five scenarios in which violence comes to an end.

In order to respond to religious terrorism in a way that is effective and does not produce more terrorism in response, I believe it is necessary to understand why such acts occur. Behind this practical purpose in writing this book, however, is an attempt to understand the role that violence has always played in the religious imagination and how terror could be conceived in the mind of God.

These two purposes are connected. One of my conclusions is that this historical moment of global transformation has provided an occasion for religion—with all its images and ideas—to be reasserted as a public force. Lurking in the background of much of religion's unrest and the occasion for its political revival, I believe, is the devaluation of secular authority and the need for alternative ideologies of public order. It may be one of the ironies of history, graphically displayed in incidents of terrorism, that the answers to the questions of why the contemporary world still needs religion and of why it has suffered such public acts of violence, are surprisingly the same.

Endnotes

1. "Global Terror," *Los Angeles Times*, August 8, 1998, A16.
2. Bruce Hoffman, *Inside Terrorism* (New York: Columbia Press, 1998), 91.
3. Warren Christopher, "Fighting Terrorism: Challenges for Peacemakers," address to the Washington Institute for Near East Policy, May 21, 1996. Reprinted in Warren Christopher, *In the Stream of History: Shaping Foreign Policy for a New Era* (Stanford, CA: Stanford University Press, 1998), 446.
4. See, for example, the essays from a conference on the psychology of terrorism held at the Woodrow Wilson International Center for Scholars, in Walter Reich, ed., *Origins of Terrorism: Psychologies, Ideologies, Theologies, States of Mind.* (New York: Cambridge University Press, 1990).
5. Baruch Goldstein, letter to the editor, *New York Times*, June 30, 1981.
6. Interview with Rev. Michael Bray, Reformation Lutheran Church, Bowie, Maryland, April 25, 1996.
7. Interview with Sohan Singh, leader of the Sohan Singh Panthic Committee, Mohalli, Punjab, August 3, 1996.
8. Interview with Mahmud Abouhalima, convicted coconspirator in the World Trade Center bombing case, federal penitentiary Lompoc, California, September 30, 1997.
9. Interview with Abdul Aziz Rantisi, cofounder and political leader of Hamas, Khan Yunis, Gaza, March 1, 1998.
10. Lance W. Small, an assistant professor of mathematics at the University of California, Berkeley, at the time Kaczynski taught there, quoted in David Johnston and Janny Scott, "The Tortured Genius of Theodore Kaczynski," *New York Times*, May 26, 1996, A1. According to the authors, Kaczynski's brother David thought that Kaczynski was unaffected by any particular political movement at the time.
11. In using the phrase "cultures of violence," I realize that for some this will evoke the term "cultures of poverty," coined by Oscar Lewis and other anthropologists in the 1960s to describe the mindset of the barrios of Latin America and African American ghettos in the United States. Lewis was accused of presenting a static set of values, forged through desperate conditions, that on the one hand explained away many of the moral and intellectual shortcomings of the people who came from such cultures, and on the other hand seemed to imply that nothing could be done to help them. My term, "cultures of violence," does not carry these implications.
12. Michel Foucault, *The Order of Things: An Archaeology of Human Sciences* (New York: Vintage, 1973), 168.
13. Pierre Bourdieu, *Outline of a Theory of Practice* (Cambridge: Cambridge University Press, 1977), 76.

14. Clifford Geertz, "Ideology as a Cultural System," in David Apter, ed., *Ideology and Discontent* (New York: Free Press), 1964; and "Religion as a Cultural System," reprinted in William A. Lessa and Evon Z. Vogt, eds., *Reader in Comparative Religion: An Anthropological Approach*, 3rd ed. (New York: Harper & Row, 1972).

15. Bernard Lewis, *The Assassins: A Radical Sect in Islam* (London: Al Saqi Books, 1985); Walter Laqueur, *Terrorism* (Boston: Little, Brown, 1977), revised and republished as *The Age of Terrorism* (Boston: Little, Brown, 1987); Hoffman, *Inside Terrorism.*

16. Walter Reich, *Origins of Terrorism: Psychologies, Ideologies, Theologies, States of Mind* (New York: Cambridge University Press, 1990); Robert S. Robins and Jerrold Post, *Political Paranoia: The Psychopolitics of Hatred* (New Haven, CT: Yale University Press, 1997).

17. Martha Crenshaw, *Revolutionary Terrorism: The FLN in Algeria, 1954–1962* (Stanford, CA: Hoover Institution, 1978); Peter Merkl, "West German Left-Wing Terrorism," in Martha Crenshaw, ed., *Terrorism in Context* (University Park: Pennsylvania State University Press, 1995). See also Crenshaw's article on instrumental and organizational approaches to the study of terrorism, "Theories of Terrorism," in David C. Rapoport, ed., *Inside Terrorist Organizations* (New York: Columbia University Press, 1988).

18. Paul Wilkinson, *Political Terrorism* (London: Macmillan, 1974); Brian Jenkins, *International Terrorism: Trends and Potentialities* (Santa Monica, CA: RAND Corporation, 1978). See also Paul Wilkinson and A. M. Stewart, eds., *Contemporary Research on Terrorism* (Aberdeen: Aberdeen University Press, 1987); Bruce Hoffman, *An Agenda for Research on Terrorism and LIC [Low Intensity Conflict] in the 1990s* (Santa Monica, CA: RAND Corporation, 1991).

19. Jeffrey Kaplan, "The Context of American Millennarian Revolutionary Theology: The Case of the 'Identity Christian' Church of Israel," *Terrorism and Political Violence* 5:1, Spring 1993, 30–82, and "Right Wing Violence in North America," in Tore Bjørgo, ed., *Terror from the Extreme Right* (London: Frank Cass, 1995), 44–95; James Aho, *The Politics of Righteousness: Idaho Christian Patriotism* (Seattle: University of Washington Press, 1990); Martin Dillon, *God and the Gun: The Church and Irish Terrorism* (New York: Routledge, 1998); Cynthia Keppley Mahmood, *Fighting for Faith and Nation: Dialogues with Sikh Militants* (Philadelphia: University of Pennsylvania Press, 1997); Ehud Sprinzak, *The Ascendance of Israel's Radical Right* (New York: Oxford University Press, 1991); Paul Steinberg and Annamarie Oliver, *Rehearsals for a Happy Death: The Testimonies of Hamas Suicide Bombers* (New York: Oxford University Press, forthcoming).

Models of Religious Revolution: The Middle East

Mark Juergensmeyer

Although the rise of revolutionary movements that embrace a religious nation-state is new, the movements inherit a long tradition of religious protest and social change. Religion and polities have been intertwined throughout history and around the globe, and a number of rebellions against authority, from the Maccabean revolt in ancient Israel to the Taiping Rebellion in China, the Wahhabiya movement in Arabia, and Puritanism in England, have been religious in character. Some of them, like the movements to be discussed here, were rebellions against secular authorities. The Puritans, with their theocratic revolt against the increasing secularism of seventeenth-century English politics, may be regarded as precursors of modern antisecular radicals. [1]

The new movements are different from their historical predecessors in that they are reactions to, and are attempts to forge a synthesis with, a specific political form that originated in the modern West: the nation-state. In responding to it, religious nationalists evoke ethnic loyalties and religious commitments that are by definition specific. These movements are identified with particular geographic and linguistic regions. To understand the phenomenon, then, we have to see it in its diversity.

The Ingredients of a Religious Revolt

In this part of the book, we will look at confrontations involving movements of religious nationalism that have come to the fore in the Middle East, South Asia, and the formerly socialist areas of Central Asia and Europe. I have chosen these cases because they are well known and they show profound similarities. Taken together, they are not just a congeries of particular cases but a worldwide phenomenon.

In general, I have chosen movements that share these characteristics: they reject secular nationalism; they regard secular nationalism as Western and neo-colonial; their rejection is fundamental—often hostile arid violent; they wage their struggle with religious rhetoric, ideology, and leadership; and they offer a religious alternative to the secular nation-state.

All the movements discussed in the following chapters share these characteristics, although some fit the criteria better than do others. They are all revolutionary, in the sense that they challenge the legitimacy of the old order and call for changes that have far-reaching consequences. Calling them revolutionary, however, does not indicate the kind of politics the revolutionaries desire. In the descriptions that follow we will find great diversity: the religious nation-state they have in mind may be democratic, socialist, theocratic, or autocratic; and in many instances the leaders simply have not thought that far ahead.

Some social scientists have seen past revolutions as the eruption of change along fault lines in a social system where pressure has been building for years, and this model can be applied to the current cases as well.[2] Gary Sick has done so in describing the Iranian revolution as almost a "textbook case" of Crane Brinton's theory that revolutions occur when rising expectations are thwarted.[3] The model is not essential for understanding the cases that follow, however, and I prefer to burden the term *revolution* with a minimal amount of conceptual baggage: in my use of the term, a revolutionary movement is one that attempts to alter the social and political order at a basic level.

Saying that revolutionary movements attempt to change the system does not, of course, mean that they will succeed. Most of the movements described here have not resulted in new regimes. The major exceptions are Iran, Sudan, Afghanistan, and Tajikistan, and in each of these cases it is still not clear whether in the long run the most strident leaders of the regimes will remain in charge. Yet the revolutionary intent of the religious activists in these countries, and in many countries like them around the world, is serious indeed. Four heads of state have been assassinated by religious radicals—Anwar Sadat in Egypt, S.W.R.D. Bandaranaike in Sri Lanka, Indira Gandhi in India, and Mohammed Boudiaf in Algeria—and thousands of others, on both sides of the struggles, have lost their lives.

One could question whether the sights of these revolutionary movements are aimed solely at the national level. Like the ideological rhetoric of the old Cold War, the political rhetoric of many of the movements seems directed toward a supranational ideal. This is especially true of the Muslim movements. The longing for a global state of religious harmony is an old Islamic dream, and for years the great Islamic empires appeared to be on the verge of making that dream a reality. For this reason, many Muslim activists hesitate to speak of solely national interests and instead express pan-Islamic ideals. Many espouse Muslim nationalism in general; pictured on the wall of one of the Palestinian leaders in Gaza is a map of the world on which is superimposed the Qur'an drawn as if it had hands extending from Morocco to Indonesia.[4] Some Muslim writers go so far as to regard the very idea of nationalism as anti-Islamic. One has described nationalism as "the greatest evil that stalks the modern world," and although he acknowledges that many Muslim movements are indeed nationalist, he sees their nationalism as a short-term goal and looks forward to a Muslim unity "beyond the Muslim nation-states."[5]

Even though this yearning for a single Islamic nation runs deep in Muslim consciousness, most Muslim activists seem happy to settle for an Islamic nationalism that is limited to the particular countries in which they reside. In the modern period, as Ira Lapidus explains, "the capacity of Islam to symbolize social identity has been merged into national feeling."[6] The most obvious example is Iran; the Shi'ite form of Islam that predominates there is rarely found elsewhere. But even in Sunni areas, such as Egypt and Palestine—as the case studies in this chapter show—religious sentiments are fused with national concerns. The religious revolutionaries there fight for an Egyptian or a Palestinian identity as well as a Muslim one. Even the proponents of a worldwide Islamic nation concede the necessity for "a succession of Islamic Revolutions in all Muslim areas of the world."[7] They expect that these will eventually be united through "'open' or 'soft' frontiers" to replace the boundaries between Islamic states.[8] My guess, however, is that the borders will stay immutable and solid, for the pan-Islamic sentiments of Arabs and other Muslims have always been vexed by intra-Islamic rivalries, many of which were exacerbated in 1991 by the Gulf War.[9]

Even so, Islamic nationalism in one country can encourage the growth of Islamic nationalism in other countries. In the 1980s, the Islamic revolution in Iran served as a model for the emergence of modern Islamic nation-states elsewhere in the world. In the early 1900s, Islamic leaders in Sudan promoted Muslim activism throughout the region. After 1989, when Lieutenant General Omar Hassan Ahmed Bashir established an Islamic regime in Sudan, thousands of young Muslim revolutionaries came to study in Sudanese universities and to train in its military camps.[10] Hassan Abdullah Turabi, the Islamic leader described by an American reporter as the "behind-the-scenes power" in Khartoum, is also mentioned as "one of the key architects" of Islamic movements in Algeria, Tunisia, Egypt, Ethiopia, Nigeria, Chad, and Afghanistan.[11]

In each of these countries, however, the impetus toward an Islamic national-ism was distinctively tied to each country's history and culture, and it is doubtful that Sudanese or any other external agents made a decisive difference. In Algiers, for instance, when the Islamic Salvation Front in 1991 soundly defeated the party that had ruled Algeria since its independence from the French in 1956, the Islamic leaders were consciously attempting to emulate the earlier independence move-ment and promised to fulfill it by giving Algeria "a firm beginning for building an Islamic state."[12] It was a short-lived promise, however, for in January 1992, the army annulled the elections and established a secular military junta, accomplish-ing, as the leader of a local mosque put it, "a *coup d'état* against the [Algerian] Islamic state before it was created."[13] Leaders of the Islamic Salvation Front were jailed, and a ban was imposed on meetings at mosques, which had become ven-ues of protest and organization for the Islamic opposition. On March 5 the party was officially outlawed. Later in 1992, the standoff between the army and Muslim activists erupted into violence, and the Casbah in Algiers' Old City became an arena of guerrilla warfare reminiscent of Algeria's war of independence from the French.[14] Hundreds of supporters of the Islamic Salvation Front were killed, and on June 29 Boudiaf, the civilian head of the military-supported Council of State, was assassinated, allegedly by militant supporters of the Salvation Front.[15]

In other nations, Islamic political movements have also been directed toward local and national concerns. In neighboring Tunisia, the outlawed Islamic Renaissance Party and the Nahda movement have mounted a serious opposition to the government, and in Jordan, where Muslim activists' accession to power has been less violent than in Algeria, it has, in many ways, been as effective. In elec-tions held after the Gulf War in 1991, members of the Muslim Brotherhood became the largest single bloc in the Jordanian parliament. Since then, even more extreme Muslim groups have threatened to destabilize the Jordanian govern-ment.[16] In Lebanon, Shi'ite and Christian allegiances have defined the major fac-tions, both of them claiming to represent a true Lebanese nationalism. In Syria, Islamic activists opposed to the Ba'ath Party's socialist ideology and its attempts to pander to Christians and other minority groups have attempted to unseat the party.[17] They disdain the secular style of Hafez al-Asad, whom they accused of "gross corruption, brutal repression of dissent, collusion with Zionism and impe-rialism, and sectarianism."[18]

In Saudi Arabia, Kuwait, and the other Gulf Emirates, where a kind of state Islamic culture prevails and Islamic law is honored, strident and democratic-minded Muslim activists threaten the status quo. These kingdoms, the last of the old-style Muslim states, have been protected against both the Western secularism of the left and the radical Muslim popularism of the right. In Saudi Arabia, Muslim activists have railed against the royal family and its alliance with the United

States by means of fiery speeches recorded on illicit cassette tapes that have been distributed by the thousands.[19]

Outside the Arab sphere, Muslim activists have also taken up local political causes and in some cases have scored spectacular successes. The triumph of Islamic revolutionaries in Afghanistan and Tajikistan will be discussed later in this book. Islam is also linked with the rise of new ethnic politics in such disparate places as Croatia and Bosnia-Herzegovina in Yugoslavia; Kosovo province in Albania; the Aceh region of Indonesia; southern Philippines; Xinjiang, Ningxia, Gansu, and Yunnan in China; Azerbaijan, Uzbekistan, Turkmenistan, Kazakhstan, and Kyrgyzstan; and the Islamic regions of Russia.

Muslim political activism is on the rise throughout the world, but it is not orchestrated by a central command, nor are its goals antithetical to national interests. Many Muslim activists are indeed nationalists; some support subnational, local, and ethnic entities; and a few favor a pan-Islamic federation of states. Most, however, are united in their stand against the adoption of Western secular nationalism. Like religious activists everywhere, they criticize secular rule from a religious perspective; they employ religious language, leadership, and organization in their attempts to change it; and they hold up the promise of a new religious order as a shining ideal.

Iran: The Paradigmatic Religious Revolution

The event that set the standard for religious revolution throughout the Muslim world was the Islamic revolution in Iran. "An entire population has risen up against the Shah," the Ayatollah Khomeini proclaimed to a professor from the University of California who visited him in France during the last, declining days of the Pahlavi regime.[20] This "revolutionary movement," as the Ayatollah described it, was an "explosion" that occurred as a direct result of "American intervention" and the repression of Islam over the preceding fifty years. At the time of the interview, in 1978, the ayatollah felt that the situation had "intensified to an extraordinary degree."[21] A few days later the Ayatollah was bound for Iran and his headquarters in Qom, where he presided over the new revolutionary Islamic regime until his death on June 4, 1989.

Even though the revolution was marked by the unique personality of the ayatollah, the particular circumstances of Iranian politics, and the distinctive character of Shi'ite Islam, this regime and the remarkable transfer of power that inaugurated it are seen as the paradigmatic form of religious revolution. The demon of the revolution was a nationalism and a secular rule patterned on the West and ineptly promoted by the shah. The critique of the shah's Westernized regime was couched in religious terms, the rebellion was led by religious figures, and the new order was fashioned as a utopian religious state. It was not simply a revival of an earlier form of Muslim rule, but a new form of Islamic politics. In a curious way, it was the shah's vision of an Iranian nationalism come true.

The new politics of the Iranian revolution was fundamentally Muslim—and particularly Shi'ite. Politics of various kinds have always been part and parcel of Islam. The Prophet himself was a military as well as a spiritual leader, and there have been strong Muslim rulers virtually from the tradition's inception. "In classical Islam there was no distinction between Church and state," writes Bernard Lewis, who goes on to say that the concept of secularism did not exist in the Islamic mind until quite recently.[22] There was not even a word in Arabic to express it.[23] All aspects of social and personal behavior were subject to divine guidance, and all political authority ultimately derived from sacred authority. This continues to be a general principle in Islamic societies; what is novel about the new Islamic movements is their struggle to install—in a distinctively modern way—this religious authority in secular states.

Perhaps nowhere in Islam is struggle more a part of its tradition than in Shi'ite societies. The world of Islam is largely Sunni, and only a small minority are Shi'a (partisans). They are found in southern Lebanon, Iraq, Pakistan, and especially in Iran, where 90 percent are Shi'a of a particular form. This dominant, Ithna Ashari (Twelver) brand of Shi'ism is based on the belief that there will be twelve great leaders, or imams, in world history. Shi'ite Islam began with a political struggle, and over time the tradition developed its own separate theological emphases. In his interpretation of the tradition, Khomeini capitalized on traditional Shi'ite themes, sharpening them to fit the situation of revolutionary Iran. The most important of these themes are the Shi'a tradition of struggle against oppression, the investment of political power in the clergy and a pattern of messianic and utopian expectations.

Struggle against oppression. Shi'ism was born in conflict, in the struggle for power immediately after the death of the Prophet Muhammad. The dispute was between those who felt that the spiritual and temporal authority of Islam resided in the caliphs who followed him and who believed that it dwelled in the members of the Prophet's own family—specifically in the descendants of Ali, who was both the prophet's cousin and his son-in-law. The critical moment in this conflict came in 680 C.E., with the assassination of Ali's son, Husain, who led the Shi'ite community in Karbala (in present-day Iraq). The assassin, Yazid, was a caliph of the Sunni's Umayyad dynasty. To this day that event is recognized as the somber turning point in Shi'ite history—rather as the crucifixion is regarded in Christian history.

Once a year, the assassination of Husain is remembered in massive and mournful parades throughout the Shi'ite world. Men stripped to the waist march down the city streets, flagellating themselves with whips and barbed wire until their backs become raw and bloody. On these occasions—the Ashura celebrations held every year during the first ten days of the Islamic month of Muharram—the faithful remember the suffering of Husain and experience both sorrow for his wrongful death and their own vicarious guilt for not having stood by him in his time of trial. In Iran, from the early 1960s on, this occasion took a special turn. The Ayatollah Khomeini and his colleagues began to alter the emphasis from personal mourning to collective outrage against oppression. They had in mind especially the shah's oppression of Islam, and they likened the shah to Yazid, the man who had killed Husain. In his messages the ayatollah urged his followers to avenge the martyrdom of Husain by attacking the Yazids of the present age. "With the approach of Muharram," he told his flock, "we are about to begin the month of epic heroism and self sacrifice—the month in which blood triumphed over the sword, . . . the month in which the leader of the Muslims taught us how to struggle against all the tyrants of history."[24] In case the listener still did not get the point, Khomeini would soon mention by name the particular tyrant he had in mind.

Political power of the clergy. Islam is primarily a layperson's religion, and although political leaders are expected to be religious and to use the state's apparatus to administer Muslim law, the clergy in most parts of the Muslim world have little political influence. In such Sunni societies as Egypt and Syria, for instance, they have been relatively uninvolved in radical Islamic politics.[25] The Shi'a tradition is different, in part for theological reasons. The idea of an imam, a great leader who shapes world history, has conditioned Shi'ites to expect strong leadership in what we would regard as both worldly and religious spheres. During a period of history when an imam is not physically present—such as the contemporary period, when the imam is supposedly "hidden"—the power of the imam is to be found in the mullahs, the Shi'a clergy. Another source for the power of certain religious leaders is their ancestral ties to the family of Ali and hence to the Prophet himself. The Ayatollah Khomeini could claim such ties, and even the modern Iraqi leader, Saddam Hussein, has let it be known that he has such connections as well. The shah's Pahlavi family, however, lacked such spiritual links, and from the point of view of the Shi'a clergy, that made them unfit for leadership. The mullahs, however, have been quite ready to speak out on social and political matters when they felt the situation called for it.

Rebellions of one sort or another have been led by the Shi'a clergy in Iran for at least a century. In 1892 a revolt against the use of tobacco was led by the mullahs, and their influence on the Constitutional Revolution of 1905–9 ensured that laws would not be passed that the mullahs deemed injurious to Islam. During the 1950s, after the campaign of the shah to blunt the influence of the mullahs, some of them became involved in conspiratorial plots against secular Iranian leaders, several of whom were assassinated. The groups they organized included the Fedayeen-i-Islam (Supporters of Islam) and the Mujahadin-i-Islam (Fighters for Islam), led by Mullah Nawab Safavi and the Ayatollah Abul Qasim Kashani, respectively. By 1963, the radical opposition to the shah had crystalized around the leadership of the Ayatollah Khomeini, and the Iranian revolution began in earnest.

Messianic and utopian expectations. In the Shi'a view of history, the hidden imam will return again at the end of history in the form of the Mahdi, the Messiah who will overthrow all the evil forces and institute a realm of justice and freedom. It would have been heretical to suggest that the Ayatollah Khomeini was the Mahdi and the Iranian revolution was that realm, and no Shi'ite dared to do so. It is true that the title that most of Khomeini's followers in Iran preferred to give him was *imam* (rather than *ayatollah*, the label by which he is best known in the West), but the title is often applied to Shi'ite religious leaders with no implication that they are in the pantheon of the twelve great imams.[26] Even so, some of Khomeini's followers claimed that he was actually a "mystical emanation issuing directly from the Mahdi," serving as a harbinger of the Mahdi's return.[27] Even if this attitude was not widespread, the very notion of a Mahdi helps to create the cultural conditions in which the figure of a savior/leader is expected and widely accepted.

These three aspects of Shi'ite Islam—its history of struggle against oppression, the political power it has traditionally vested in the clergy, and its tradition of messianic and utopian expectations—made the Islamic movement in Iran a revolution waiting to happen. That it happened so easily was due in part to the vulnerability of its adversaries. Few characters in the Shi'ite drama of the forces of good struggling against the forces of evil have so effectively played the role of evil as the members of the Pahlavi dynasty—Riza Shah, who established a military dictatorship in 1921, and his son Muhammad Riza Shah, who succeeded him in 1941. The Pahlavi reign was interrupted from 1951 to 1953 by a democratically elected prime minister, Mohammed Mossadegh (Musaddiq), who attempted to nationalize the oil industry and, with the help of the American Central Intelligence Agency, was promptly overthrown.

When the shah returned lie attempted to mollify the mullahs by giving them a free reign in developing their organizations and publications, and helping them to finance Islamic schools. To some extent this policy was successful, and even Khomeini's predecessor, Ayatollah Hosain Burujirdi, supported the shah in the 1950s; at this time the clergy was accused of being a "pillar of the Pahlavi state."[28] This accommodation of the mullahs changed in the 1960s, however, when the shah attempted land reforms that threatened religious institutions and extended the right to vote to women. Impressed by Atatürk's experiment at secularization in Turkey, the shah attempted similar sweeping reforms, replacing most of Islamic law with a secular code adopted from the French. Although they tried publicly to appear to be good Muslims, the Pahlavis were seen as destroying traditional Muslim schools and seminaries, Westernizing the universities, and creating a modern bureaucracy to administer the state. Women were forbidden to wear the veil. In Teheran and other cities Western culture began to thrive, bringing in its wake not only Coca-Cola and Western movies but also discos, girlie magazines, and gay bars. It was not the Islamic utopia the mullahs had in mind. The mullahs described it, in fact, as "a satanic rule."[29]

The government's control of the media and the presence of the sinister SAVAK, the secret police, made opposition difficult. It was "impossible to breathe freely in Iran."[30] The group that was most difficult to contain and most able to organize was the clergy, who found a natural leader in Ruhullah al-Musavi al-Khomeini, who began his career as the protégé of one of Iran's leading theologians, Sheik 'Abd al-Karim Ha'iri of the pilgrimage city of Qom. Following the death of Ha'iri in 1937, the leadership fell to the Ayatollah Burujirdi; when he died in 1961, there was no immediate consensus over who the new leader at Qom should be. It is probably not a coincidence that Khomeini's increasingly outspoken public pronouncements against the shah at that time and the rise of his public popularity occurred simultaneously with the solidification of his power within his own religious community. In any event, the protest, and Khomeini's leadership of it, surfaced in a massive demonstration in Qom in the spring of 1963. This demonstration led to Khomeini's imprisonment, his release in 1964, and imprisonment again in that year followed by expulsion from the country. Khomeini was to remain abroad—first in Turkey, then in Iraq, and finally in France—until after the revolution was completed in 1979. Although he was out of the country during those critical years, he was certainly not silent, and perhaps he was able more effectively to articulate the grievances and lead the revolution from Neauphlele-Chateau than from Qom.

To the surprise of everyone, the end came quite suddenly. Perhaps most caught off guard were the Americans, who had great difficulty even conceiving the possibility that a band of bearded, black-robed rural mullahs could seriously confront the poised and urbane shah with all his worldly connections and military might.[31] Even more inconceivable was that the power of the shah should crumble so effortlessly. Only a few months before, Jimmy Carter had praised the shah for creating an "island of stability" in the region.

Although the new revolutionary regime has not lived up to its utopian promises, the changes it has wrought have made a dramatic difference. Islamic law is now the law of the land, and most marks of "Westoxification" have been systematically erased. These reforms have not always been brought about with subtlety—some 7,000 people were executed for crimes as varied as homosexuality and believing in the Baha'i faith—and the revolutionary spirit has not easily been bridled. For a time bands of young people in the Hizbollah (Party of God) roamed the streets, attacking anyone or anything that appeared anti-Islamic, and a group of rowdy youth, without government authorization (at least at the beginning), precipitated a foreign-policy crisis by taking hostages at the American Embassy in Teheran.[32] The course of the revolution and the attention needed for domestic problems were also deflected by a bloody, protracted war with Iraq.

In the thirteen years between 1979 and 1992 the revolutionary regime went through three stages. It began as a moderate, secular regime led first by Mehdi Bazargan and then by Abolhassan Bani-Sadr, until Khomeini used the hostage crisis as a way of continuing the revolution and forcing the moderates out.[33] After Bani-Sadr fled the country in 1981, a period of repression set in, during which thousands of persons were killed, moderate and leftist political forces were destroyed, and the power of the clergy was consolidated.[34] In 1985, the revolutionary regime began something of a Thermidorian return to a more pragmatic and moderate rule.

After the death of the Ayatollah Khomeini on June 4, 1989, his son, Ahmad Khomeini, remained as virtually the only radical clergy in the inner circles; the new president of Iran, Ali-Akbar Heshemi-Rafsanjani, continued to steer a pragmatic course. During the Gulf War, Rafsanjani refused to side with Iraq or to criticize the United States seriously, to the disappointment of the conservative clergy.[35] At the end of 1991, Iranian leaders arranged for the American hostages held in Lebanon for years to be released. In the first months of 1992, apparently to impress the conservative clergy that he had not fully capitulated to the Americans, Rafsanjani denounced the American-sponsored Arab-Israeli peace talks and referred to the United States as "an arrogant power."[36] Although the April 1992 election was a triumph for the moderates, it resulted largely in economic reforms. In 1993 Iran greatly increased its financial aid to Islamic political movements in Algeria, Bosnia, Lebanon, Pakistan, Tajikistan, and elsewhere in the world.[37]

Iran has become the grandfather of the current generation of revolutionary Islamic nationals. Perhaps the most enduring contributions of its revolution are the creation of the sense of Iranian nationalism that the shah tried but failed to achieve and the constitutional privilege granted to religion in Iran's public life.[38] There is now a fusion of Iranian nationalist goals with Shi'ite political ideology, access to power for the Muslim clergy, and provision for religious guidance at the top of the country's administration. This provision is particularly interesting, for the leaders of the revolution have taken the concept of the just ruler *(al-sultan al- 'adil)* in Shi'ite Islam and made it into a political position—an elder statesman who guides and advises the president and other governmental officials.[39] During Khomeini's lifetime he played that role, and after his death he was succeeded by the former president, Ayatollah Ali Khamenei. The position is intriguing, for, as Khomeini explained, "the religious leaders do not wish to be the government, but neither are they separate from the government."[40] Separate or not, the ayatollah warned that they would be prepared to "intervene" if the secular leaders of the government make "a false step."[41] Religious revolutionaries in other parts of the world would give almost anything to acquire this remarkable leverage of power.

Egypt's Incipient Religious Revolt

Can the religious revolution that Khomeini created in Iran be exported to other places in the Islamic world? Many observers think that it can, and the country that is often mentioned as a candidate for a Khomeini-style revolution is Egypt.[42] In fact, Iran is said to have given financial support to some of Egypt's most radical Muslim movements, including the group accused of bombing the World Trade Center in New York City and plotting to blow up the UN in 1993.

The al-Jamaa al-Islamiyya ("the Islamic group") began as a student movement in Egypt in the 1970s and became linked with the militant al-Jihad in the 1980s. Its spiritual authority, Sheik Omar Abdul-Rahman, a former professor of Islamic law, fled to America in 1990, soon becoming the leader of the storefront mosque in New Jersey with which many of the accused conspirators in the World Trade Center bombing were affiliated. He and his followers were committed to a vision of Islamic rule in Egypt that would rival Khomeini's Iran.

This concept of an Egyptian religious nationalism has been around long before Khomeini, but the demand for it increasingly has been expressed in violent acts. In 1981, President Sadat was assassinated by members of al-Jihad. In 1990, the speaker of the Egyptian Assembly, Rifaat al-Mahgoub, who at the time of his death was second in power only to President Hosni Mubarak, was brutally killed. Members of the al-Jamaa al-Islamiyya were charged with the crime, but were acquitted in 1993 through lack of evidence. At the time, Mahgoub's death was linked to Egypt's stand in the Gulf War, but another factor may have been his efforts to block the use of Islamic law in Egypt's courts.[43] In Egypt, as in many other Arab countries, trifling with the spread of Islam is a serious business.

However, Egypt is not necessarily going the way of Iran. The radical Islamic movements in Egypt are different in basic ways from their Iranian counterparts. Sunni Muslims have neither the theological nor the organizational connection to politics that Shi'ites do, nor has Egypt had the same pattern of suppression of Islam that Iran has had. The Egyptian movements are much less centralized. Despite the fear of many Westerners that the virus of Khomeinism would spread (and perhaps Khomeini's wish that it had), Muslim activists throughout the Sunni world seem surprisingly ignorant of and uninterested in the Iranian experiment.[44] They have their political problems," a member of the Muslim Brotherhood in Cairo told me, referring to the Iranians, "and we have ours."[45] Although there is sometimes a tremor of admiration in their voices when they speak of the power of the Iranian revolution, the Egyptians seldom offer that upheaval as a model for their own.[46]

Although some scholars see more of an Iranian influence in Egypt than meets the eye,[47] the more obvious interaction is the other way around: the influence of radical Egyptian Muslim movements on the Iranians. In the late 1940s and early 1950s, the Iranians' Fedayeen-i-Islam was created in imitation of the guerrilla Muslim Brotherhood (Jam'iyat al-Ikhwan al-Muslimin), which was spreading terror at the time throughout Egypt. Egypt's Muslim Brotherhood had been founded in 1928 by Hasan al-Banna, and another radical Muslim movement, the Young Egypt Society (which advocated a kind of Islamic socialism), was founded soon after, in 1933.[48]

The leaders of these early Egyptian movements of Islamic politics were reacting against the transnational modernism that remained as the legacy of the British Empire (and before it, the Ottoman). Western culture, political influence, and economic control were the elements of a modernity that some of the early nationalists wished to reject. For that reason, Egyptian nationalism from the outset grew in both religious and secular directions. The Muslim Brotherhood represented the Islamic form of Egyptian nationalism, and the Wafd Party represented its secular side. When King Faruk (Farooq) and the whole tradition of Egyptian monarchy were overthrown in 1952, it was largely the Wafd vision of a secular Egypt that emerged triumphant.

Yet even after Faruk, Islamic nationalism continued to be a potent force in Egyptian politics. The great leader of the revolution, Jamal 'Ahd al-Nasir (whom the Western world knows as Gamal Nasser), had at one time been allied with the Muslim Brotherhood, as had his successor, Sadat. Despite their willingness to defend the Islamic aspects of Egyptian nationalism, neither Nasser nor Sadat was sufficiently strident in his ideology nor obsequious enough in his response to the

Muslim leadership to remain in the favor of Islamic extremists. By the 1960s, the leaders of the Muslim Brotherhood and Nasser were locked in bitter opposition; some of the leaders attempted to overthrow Nasser's regime, and he promptly threw them in prison.

The love-hate relationship between Muslim leaders and secular politicians continued in the 1970s during Sadat's regime. On the one hand, Sadat released the leaders of the Muslim Brotherhood from prison, lifted a ban on the writings of Muslim radicals, and was instrumental in the drafting of the 1971 version of the Egyptian Constitution, which proclaimed, in Article Two, that the goal of the judicial system was eventually to make shari'a (Islamic law) the law of the land. On the other hand, he did little to carry out this goal or the other Islamic reforms he had earlier touted. Sadat's concessions to Coptic Christians were widely denounced, and his wife was portrayed as being promiscuous. Pictures of her dancing with Gerald Ford at a formal occasion at the White House were circulated as evidence of her infidelity. The accords with Israel arranged by Carter were considered further signs of Sadat's moral decay, and he eventually succeeded in "having everyone turn against him," as one Egyptian scholar explained, in part because "he tried too hard to please everyone."[49] His killers were members of al-Jihad.

Although al-Jihad has been at the fringes of the Muslim Brotherhood, and its various splinter organizations have made a deep political impact, its ideology is the antithesis of Sadat's moderate Muslim stand. But despite its violence, its leaders have not been lunatics. One of them, Abd Al-Salam Faraj, was the author of a remarkably cogent argument for waging war against the political enemies of Islam. His pamphlet, "Al-Faridah al-Gha'ibah" ("The Neglected Duty"), states more clearly than any other contemporary writing the religious justifications for radical Muslim acts. It was published and first circulated in Cairo in the early 1980s.[50] This document grounds the current activities of Islamic terrorists firmly in Islamic tradition, specifically in the sacred text of the Qur'an and the biographical accounts of the Prophet in the hadith.

Faraj argues that the Qur'an and the hadith are fundamentally about warfare. The concept of jihad, holy war, is meant to be taken literally, not allegorically. According to Faraj, the "duty" that has been profoundly "neglected" is jihad, and it calls for "fighting, which means confrontation and blood."[51] Moreover, Faraj regards anyone who deviates from the moral and social requirements of Islamic law to be fit targets for jihad; these targets include apostates within the Muslim community as well as the more expected enemies from without.[52] Perhaps the most chilling aspect of his thought is his conclusion that peaceful and legal means for fighting apostasy are inadequate. The true soldier for Islam is allowed to use virtually any means available to achieve a just goal.[53] Deceit, trickery, and violence are specifically mentioned as options available to the desperate soldier.[54] Faraj sets some moral limits to the tactics that may be used—for example, innocent bystanders and women are to be avoided, whenever possible, in assassination attempts—but emphasizes that the duty to engage in such actions when necessary is incumbent on all true Muslims. The reward for doing so is nothing less than an honored place in paradise. Such a place was presumably earned by Faraj himself in 1982 after he was tried and executed for his part in the assassination of Sadat.

This way of thinking, although extreme, is not idiosyncratic to Faraj. He stands in a tradition of radical Islamic political writers that reaches back to the beginning of this century and earlier. Among Sunni Muslims worldwide, the most important radical thinker has been Maulana Abu al-Ala Mawdudi, the founder and ideological spokesman for Pakistan's Jamaat-i-Islami (Islamic Association).[55] His ideas were echoed by Egypt's most influential writer in the radical Muslim political tradition, Sayyid Qutb. Qutb was born in 1906 and, like Faraj, was executed for his political activities.[56] Although he was not as explicit as Faraj in indicating the techniques of terror that were acceptable for the Islamic warrior, Qutb laid the groundwork for Faraj's understanding of jihad as an appropriate response to the advocates of those elements of modernity that seemed to be hostile to Islam. Specifically, Qutb railed against those who encouraged the cultural, political, and economic domination of the Egyptian government by the West. Qutb had spent several years in the United States studying educational administration, but this experience only confirmed his impression that American society was essentially racist and that American policy in the Middle East was dictated by Israel and what he regarded as the Jewish lobby in Washington, D.C.[57] Alarmed at the degree to which the new government in Egypt was modeled after Western political institutions and influenced by Western values, Qutb, in the early 1950s, advocated a radical return to Islamic values and Muslim law. In *This Religion of Islam*, Qutb argued that the most basic divisions within humanity are grounded in religion rather than race or nationality, and that religious war is the only form of killing that is morally sanctioned.[58] To Qutb's way of thinking, the ultimate war is between truth and falsehood, and satanic agents of falsehood were to be found well entrenched in the Egyptian government. It is no wonder that the government found such ideas dangerous. Qutb was put in prison for most of the rest of the 1950s and was silenced forever in 1966.

The radical ideas of Mawdudi, Qutb, and Faraj have circulated widely in Egypt through two significant networks: universities and the Muslim clergy. The two networks intersect in the Muslim educational system, especially in the schools and colleges directly supervised by the clergy. The most important of these are the ones connected with Cairo's Al-Azhar University. They enroll only a small percentage of Egyptian students—perhaps 5 percent or so—at all levels of the educational system.[59] It is a significant number, nonetheless, because of the impact of the Muslim teachers in relating the traditional truths of Islam to modern ideas. As the dean of the Faculty of Education at Al-Azhar University explained to me, the school's mission is to show how modern academic subjects arid fields of professional training—including business, medicine, law, and education—can be taught from an Islamic perspective.[60] Not surprisingly, the university is often viewed as a fountainhead of radical Islamic ideas, and a great number of militant Muslim activists receive their training there.

Despite its dreams, the radical Muslim movement has yet to be sufficiently united to threaten President Mubarak with anything like the revolution in Iran. Even though it showed its destructive power in the 1990 assassination of the speaker of the Assembly, it remains a small splinter organization. The larger parent movement, the Muslim Brotherhood, has become somewhat more moderate. Though not accepted as a legal party, it has been well represented in the legislature. Members of the Brotherhood, running as independent candidates in the 1987 elections, won 38 seats out of the 448 in the People's Assembly. The platform of the Brotherhood was clearly articulated by its leader, Abu al-Nasr, in an open letter to President Mubarak in February 1987. According to Nasr, the movement has four main positions: pride in its Egyptian identity and tradition, the conviction that the current problems of Egypt are largely spiritual and moral in nature, the expectation that Islamic values will be made the basis for all aspects of Egyptian society, and the desire for Islamic organizations to have the freedom to operate as they wish.[61]

These relatively reasonable positions make the Muslim Brotherhood look quite respectable—especially compared with the strident rhetoric of the extremists. In 1991, during the Persian Gulf War, divisions between moderate and radical factions widened.[62] In 1992 and 1993 the terrorist acts of al-Jamaa al-Islamiyya further alienated it from the Muslim mainstream. In addition to the World Trade Center explosion in New York, tourists were attacked near Luxor and in a cafe in Cairo, a luxury ship was fired on as it cruised down the Nile, and a bomb was placed in one of the pyramids. In contrast, the Muslim Brotherhood presented a more viable, if gradual, Islamic revolution. What worries its secular opponents is that the shifts of ideology and power in a gradual revolution are equally unsettling.

Religious Revolt in a Jewish State

Religious revolutionaries in Israel face a situation more like that in Egypt than in prerevolutionary Iran: rather than confronting a thoroughly secular shah, they oppose moderate leaders who are more than nominally committed to their nation's dominant religion. In fact, one might think of Israel as an example of religious nationalism achieved, and many Arab opponents of Israel regard it exactly that way. Muslim nationalism in the Middle East has been fueled in part by the fact that Jews have their own religious state, and some Egyptians feel the religious zeal in the Jewish nation—in contrast to the secular indifference in their own—contributed to Israel's victory and Egypt's defeat in the 1967 war.[63]

However, within Israel itself a sizable contingent of politically active Jews regard their homeland, at best, as the expression of an incomplete form of religious nationalism. Although Israelis hospitable to Jewish refugees, it is essentially a secular state, one that follows the rules and mores of European and American society, and that leaves many Jewish religious nationalists deeply dissatisfied.

One of the most vocal of these Jewish nationalists was the late Rabbi Meir Kahane, the strident spokesman for the radical Kach ('Thus!') Party. Not surprisingly, perhaps, he had a certain admiration for the Ayatollah Khomeini.[64] He told me that he felt closer to Khomeini and other militant Muslims than he did to such framers of secular political thought as John Locke or even to secular Jews.[65] The reason, he explained, was that Khomeini believed in the relevance of religion to everyday life and especially in the importance of religion in shaping the morality and communal identity of a nation. From Kahane's point of view, that belief was far more important than any politically expedient secular arrangement, even if, as in the case of Israel, it was one made primarily to favor Jews.

Kahane's views on Jewish nationalism are not entirely idiosyncratic in Israel. Tensions between the religious and secular dimensions of modern Israel have existed throughout the almost 100-year history of the movement for nationhood. When the first meeting of the World Zionist Organization (WZO) was held in 1897, the goal was to form a modern national community based on the common cultural and historical heritage of the Jewish people and explicitly not to re-create the biblical Israel. The founder of the WZO, Theodor Herzl, had dreamed of Jewish assimilation into European society and hoped to achieve that dream by providing the Jews with "a new, modern symbol system—a state, a social order of their own, above all a flag."[66]

For other Jews, however, a flag—especially the secular flag that Herzl designed, which featured symbols for the seven hours he proposed for the modern working day—was not enough. They formed another nationalist group, the Merkaz Ruhani, or Mizrahi, which called for the formation of a religious state, one that would follow the rules of the Torah. At the same time, another group of orthodox Jews, Agudat Israel, adopted a somewhat different attitude: its members were in favor of Jews settling in Palestine but were largely indifferent to whether it should become a Jewish state. From the Agudat Israel's point of view, until the Temple was rebuilt and a new David installed as king, there could be no true Israel.

These and other groups continued their assaults on secular Israel after the establishment of an independent state in 1948, even though significant compromises had been made. For one thing, Jewish religious courts created during the British Mandate from 1923 to 1947 became integrated into the new legal system. For another, the "status quo agreement" made between the religious parties and the prestate administration, the Jewish Agency, called for certain religious concessions. Among these were the government's observance of dietary laws and the state's maintenance of religious schools.

Yet many nationalist Jews in Israel regarded these concessions as insufficient. The most influential advocate of further religious reforms, the Mafdal party, was a direct descendant of the old Mizrahi party and its various offshoots. The Mafdal has consistently held a dozen or so seats in the Knesset and has been a coalition partner in virtually every government formed since Israel's independence. The Agudat Israel party, despite its ambivalence toward a Jewish state, maintains representation in the Knesset as well. The ties of these two parties to the Likud party during its long rule helped to pass laws against public obscenity, working on the sabbath, and the sale of pork.

A new force has been growing in Israel based on the idea that the present secular Jewish state is the precursor of an ideal religious Israel.[67] It is the revival of an old idea, one advocated by Rabbi Avraham Yitzhak ha-Kohen Kuk (Kook), the chief rabbi of pre-Israeli Palestine. According to Kuk (and, following him, his son and successor, Z. Y. Kuk) the secular state of Israel is the forerunner of the religious Israel to come; it contains a "hidden spark" of the sacred.[68] The implications of this way of thinking are that the coming of the Messiah is imminent and that the religious purification of the state of Israel could help make that arrival come about.

Kuk's ideas began to take on an electric charge after Israel's six-day war in 1967. The war had two results that were significant for the movements for Jewish nationalism. The very success of the military engagement led to a great sense of national euphoria, a feeling that Israel was suddenly moving in an expansive and triumphant direction. At the same time, the spoils of that success created huge problems, the most critical of which were the question of what to do with the conquered territory, and, even more important, the question of what to do with the conquered people, especially Palestinian Arabs on the West Bank and in the Gaza Strip.

Jewish nationalists who were impressed with the theology of Rabbi Kuk felt strongly that history was quickly leading to the moment of divine redemption and the re-creation of the biblical state of Israel. This meant that the Palestinians living in the West Bank were in the way: at best they were an annoyance to be controlled, at worst an enemy to be destroyed. The *intifada,* or 'rebellion,' that has been waged in the Arab areas of Gaza, Jerusalem, and the West Bank since December 1987, has not done anything to dampen the sentiments of the Kukists. If anything, it has sharpened their attacks. The influx of Soviet and Ethiopian Jews has increased the pressure on living space and visibly supported the claim that Jews throughout the world are looking toward Israel as a redemptive nation.

Perhaps the most vocal of the Jewish nationalists to diverge from the Kuk lineage was Rabbi Kahane. Kahane, an American who had a long history of Jewish political activism in Brooklyn, formed the Jewish Defense League (JDL) in the 1960s to counter acts of anti-semitism.[69] In 1971 he came to Israel and turned to a more messianic vision of Jewish politics; in 1974 he created the Kach party. The main position of the party was that Israel should be ruled strictly according to Jewish law; non-Jews—for that matter, even secular Jews—had no place in this sacred order. Unlike Kuk, Kahane saw nothing of religious significance in the establishment of a secular Jewish state: the true religious creation of Israel was yet to come. Unlike other Jewish conservatives with this point of view, however, he felt that it was going to happen fairly soon and that he and his partisans could help bring about that messianic act. Kahane was elected to the Knesset in 1984, but after he served a term, his party was banned in 1988 because of its "racist" and "undemocratic positions."[70]

Kahane adopted a "get-tough" stance toward Judaism's detractors that had worked well in the liberal political atmosphere of the United States. There the Jews were in the minority, and Kahane's JDL was portrayed in the mass media as a Jewish version of the Black Panthers, defending the rights of the oppressed. In Israel, however, where the Jews controlled the status quo, the same belligerence struck secular nationalists as a perverted form of racist bigotry—some called it a kind of Jewish Nazism. His statements about Arabs were compared word for word with those of Hitler's about Jews and were found to be surprisingly similar.[71] In the same vein, a biography of the rabbi appearing in the mid-1980s was sardonically titled *Heil Kahane.*[72]

The main inspiration for Kahane was not Hitler's thought, however, but the messianic ideas of Judaism. In Kahane's view, the coming of the Messiah was imminent, and the Arabs were simply in the wrong place at the wrong time. Kahane told me that he did not hate the Arabs; he "respected them" and felt that they "should not live in disgrace in an occupied land."[73] For that reason they should leave. The problem, for Kahane, was not that they were Arabs but that they were non-Jews living in a place designated by God for Jewish people since biblical times.[74] From a biblical point of view, Kahane argued, the true Israel is the

West Bank of the Jordan River and the hilly area around Jerusalem—not the plains where modern Tel Aviv is located.[75] The desire to reclaim the West Bank was therefore not just a matter of irredentism: it was a part of a sacred plan of redemption. Kahane felt that modern Jews could hasten the coming of the Messiah by beginning to reclaim the sacred land. "Miracles don't just happen," Kahane said, referring to the messianic return, "they are made." And, he added, his own efforts and those of his followers would help to "change the course of history."[76]

Although most Jewish settlers do not agree with Kahane's catastrophic messianism and subscribe, instead, to Kuk's incremental theory of messianic history, they view their occupation of the West Bank not only as a social experiment but as a religious act. Rabbi Moshe Levinger, a leader of the Gush Emunim—an organization that encourages the new settlements and claims Rabbi Kuk as its founder—told me that the settlers' "return to the land is the first aspect of the return of the Messiah."[77] The religious settlers are by no means the majority of those who have established residential colonies on the West Bank—they are only a small percentage—but their presence colors the whole movement. Many of them regard the Palestinian Arabs around them with a certain contempt. Hostility from the Arabs—and, for that matter, from many secular Jews—has hardened many of the members of the Gush Emunim and turned what began as a romantic venture into a militant cult.[78]

Much the same can be said about those who long for the rebuilding of the Temple in Jerusalem. According to Kuk's theology, the final event that will trigger the return of the Messiah and the start of the messianic age is the reconstruction of the Temple on Temple Mount.[79] Again, like the Jewish conquest of biblical lands, it is an act of God that invites human participation: Jewish activists can join this act of redemption by helping to rebuild the Temple. The main constraint against doing so is the fact that the most holy place in Judaism is simultaneously one of Islam's most sacred sites. The Dome of the Rock (Qubbat al-Sakhra) occupies precisely the Temple site, which is known by Arabs as Haram al-Sharif, the location from which the Prophet Muhammad is said to have ascended into heaven. No other location is acceptable for rebuilding the Temple, however, and for that reason many messianic Jews are convinced that sooner or later the Dome has to go.

This conviction has led to several attempts to destroy the existing Muslim shrine, some of them involving elaborate tunnels bored from a site near the Western Wall, the only portion of the original Temple still standing. According to a former colleague of Kahane who was once imprisoned for his involvement in a plot to blow up the Dome of the Rock, the three conditions necessary for messianic redemption are the restoration of the biblical lands, the revival of traditional

Jewish law, and the rebuilding of the Temple on Temple Mount.[80] He told me that Israel is well on its way to fulfilling the first two conditions; only the absence of the Temple persists as an obstacle to the realization of this messianic vision.

Another Jewish nationalist who laments the absence of the temple is Gershon Salomon; he heads a small group known as the Faithful of Temple Mount—one of several groups committed to rebuilding the Temple. Salomon explained to me that the construction of the Temple will precipitate an "awakening" of the Jewish people and the advent of the messianic age.[81] Each year, on the seventh day of the festival of Sukkot, Salomon and his small band of followers have marched on Temple Mount and attempted to pray, and, according to some, also lay the cornerstone for rebuilding the Temple.[82] Each year, the Waqf organization of Muslim clergy, which polices the area, has nervously turned Salomon away.

During the celebration of Sukkot in October 1990, the charged atmosphere of the *intifada* and the presence of American troops in nearby Saudi Arabia made the situation more tense than usual. As Salomon and his group slowly moved toward Temple Mount, the Waqf leaders were joined by a large number of young people associated with the Islamic Palestinian resistance movement, Hamas, and by a contingent of Israeli police who were, as it turned out, insufficient in number to control what became the ugliest incident between Muslims and Israelis in recent years. Salomon and his group were barred from the Temple Mount area, but the damage had been done: in the confusion rocks were thrown, bullets were fired, and ultimately seventeen Palestinians were killed by the Israeli police in the melee.[83] The Security Council of the United Nations censured Israel for its heavy-handedness and called for an outside investigation, which Israel refused to allow.

Less than a month after the Temple Mount incident, the messianic wing of Jewish nationalism received another shock with the killing of Kahane in New York City, where he had come to give a speech. The suspected assassin, El Sayyid A. Nosair, was a recent immigrant from Egypt associated with the al-Salam Mosque in Jersey City. Other members of the mosque had been arrested for attempting to send ammunition to the Palestine Liberation Organization (PLO), and leaders of the mosque echoed the theology of Muslim nationalists such as Qutb and Faraj. They explained that the killing of Kahane did not violate the Qur'an because Kahane was an enemy of Islam.[84] Within a day of Kahane's death, two elderly Palestinian farmers were shot dead along the roadside near the West Bank city of Nablus, apparently in retaliation for Kahane's killing. Thus the spiral of violence that Kahane encouraged continued even after his death. An editorial writer for the *New York Times*, who described Kahane's life as "a passionate tangle of anger and unreason," referred to his death as the product of a "legacy of hate."[85]

In September, 1993, when many Israelis were celebrating the mutual recognition of Israel and the PLO, leaders of Kahane's Kach party denounced the historic accord, claiming it a fraud. They joined members of opposition parties, the Gush Emunim, and West Bank settlers in launching a campaign of civil disobedience against it, and vowed to fight by "any means." The passion of their protest— reminiscent of the style of Rabbi Kahane, whom they consider a martyr—comes from the conviction that an Israeli retreat from the biblical lands of the West Bank is not only bad politics but bad religion. In their view, a religious state ruled by Jewish law and located on the site of biblical Israel is essential for the redemption of the entire cosmos. For this reason the followers of Salomon, Kuk, Kahane, and other messianic religious nationalists will continue to wage their political fights with sacred passion. Though few in number, they will be a potent force in the political life of Israel for some years to come.

The Islamic *Intifada:* A Revolt within the Palestinian Revolution

The day that Israel's Yitzhak Rabin and PLO's Yasser Arafat boarded airplanes to fly to Washington D.C. to witness the historic signing of an Israeli–PLO accord in September 1993, protests erupted in Israel, the West Bank, Gaza, and much of the adjacent Arab world, and eight were killed in Gaza alone. The demonstrations were waged not only by Jewish nationalists but also by their Muslim counterparts. Both Israeli Jewish and Palestinian Muslim activists have been conducting a double struggle: one against each other and the other against their own secular leaders. The anti-secular attacks are often more vicious. Some say that the secular leaders, Rabin and Arafat, were propelled into the September 1993 alliance in part because they feared the rising strength of the religious nationalists in their camps. In Israel, the most ardent opposition to the secular government was Kahane's Kach party and the Gush Emunim; in Palestine, it was Hamas.

Hamas is an underground movement—actually a coalition of several movements with no single leader. Prominent among those identified with the movement are several religious figures: Sheik 'Abd al-Aziz 'Odeh (Uda); Sheik As'ad Bayud al-Tamimi, a resident of Hebron who was a preacher at the al-Aksa Mosque in Jerusalem; and Sheik Ahmed Yassin from Gaza.[86] Yassin, who is described as "a charismatic and influential leader," commands the Islamic Assembly, which has ties to virtually all the mosques in Gaza and is able to gain 65 to 75 percent of the votes of both students and faculty in Gaza's Islamic University.[87] Yassin claims that he and his Muslim colleagues initiated the *intifada*, the popular uprising against the Israeli occupation of Gaza and the West Bank.[88]

Although Yassin is virtually incapacitated by a degenerative nerve condition and has to be carried from place to place, when I visited him in 1989 his small house at the outskirts of Gaza City was crowded with admirers and associates who came for his advice. They sat on the carpeted floor of a plain meeting room adjacent to his bedroom and listened patiently to the sheik's rambling discourse. His monologue on the evils of Israeli occupation and the virtues of Muslim society was interrupted only by an occasional question and by daily prayers. These Yassin managed with great difficulty, tottering back and forth as he uttered the words of the Qur'an. His mind was sharp, however, and his opinions on current political matters were crystal clear.

Yassin described his Islamic resistance movement as the heart of the Palestinian opposition. He said that the idea of a secular liberation movement for Palestine is profoundly misguided because there "is no such thing as a secular state in Islam."[89] At that time, prior to the September 1993 accords, he nominally supported the PLO. He referred to Arafat as "President Arafat" and claimed that after the liberation of Palestine, "the people will decide" whether there should be an Islamic state.[90] Clearly, Yassin was confident that the people would decide in favor of Islam.

Leaders of the PLO, however, are not as convinced as Yassin about the outcome of the vote, if it should ever come to that.[91] They are clearly nervous about the Hamas challenge to their legitimacy, and before I was allowed to interview Yassin, representatives of the PLO in Gaza stopped my car and insisted that the driver take me to a pro-PLO refugee camp where I could hear the other Palestinian point of view. On another occasion, Yasir Arafat's brother, Fathi, assured me that only "a small percentage of Palestinians are in favor of an Islamic state."[92] He felt that religion should be a personal matter. He would not want his daughter to wear the Islamic veil, he said, but he would respect the right of others to do so if they wished. Yet he affirmed that his movement is democratic: should the Palestinian people vote in favor of an Islamic state, he would support it.[93]

Most Palestinians are caught between these two competing visions of an independent Palestine. Some observers feel that it would be a tight race if Islamic nationalism became the issue. In Gaza, supporters of Hamas are said to be in the majority, and there is considerable support for Islamic nationalism on the West Bank as well.[94] Yet this sort of support is difficult to gauge because many Palestinians are as impressed with Arafat as they are with Yassin. "The distinction between the PLO and Hamas is artificial," said a Palestinian student leader who is now studying Islamic theology in Cairo. "We should now be united against a common enemy; tomorrow, when we are free, we can discuss our differences."[95]

Still, the differences are considerable. Arafat expects Palestine to be a modern nation-state, one that is patterned largely on the Western secular model, while Yassin thinks that "shari'a should be the sole basis for Islamic politics."[96] Although Yassin admires Khomeini's revolution in Iran and appreciates the conservative Islamic rule in Saudi Arabia, he has been critical of both the Iranians and the Saudis. Yassin has been influenced most by Islamic nationalist leaders in nearby Egypt; he is said to have read the writings of both Qutb and Faraj.

Even though militant Islamic organizations such as Hamas are fairly new in the PLO, the idea of an Islamic Palestine has been around for some years. In the 1970s, when the PLO was consolidating its power among the various movements of the Palestinian resistance, an Islamic alternative to the PLO was proposed: a united movement that based its ideological and political strategy on traditional Islamic values.[97] One of the constituent groups of the short-lived movement was a Palestinian version of the Muslim Brotherhood. This group, in which Sheik Yassin has been active, was kin to its namesake in Egypt. For many years, however, it did not play a significant role in Palestinian politics.

In the 1980s, many Palestinian Islamic activists associated with the Muslim Brotherhood became impatient with its quiescent stance and split off to form several new associations. Sheik Yassin became president of the al-Mujamma' al-Islami (the Muslim Gathering). It had ties to another confederation of groups known as the Islamic Jihad, over which Sheik 'Odeh presided.[98] In 1983 the Jihad was implicated in the killing of a young Israeli settler in the occupied territories. In October 1984 Sheik Yassin and his colleagues were arrested and put in jail for stockpiling weapons to be used for "the destruction of Israel and the creation of an Islamic state."[99] In 1986, after Yassin and other prisoners were freed through a prisoner exchange, the Islamic Jihad launched a cluster of new military actions aimed at Israeli military officers; in Gaza, especially, a number of Israeli soldiers were killed, as were members of the Jihad. Sheik 'Odeh was arrested and expelled from the country.[100] At the same time the Islamic resistance began to organize Palestinians outside the Israeli-occupied areas. Communiqués were circulated in Paris and London, and a magazine, *al-Islam wa Filastin (Islam and Palestine)*, began publication in Cyprus, with circulation throughout Europe and the United States. The magazine lists a mailing address in Tampa, Florida, in addition to the main Cyprus office. [101]

The last month of 1987 saw the beginning of the *intifada*—a popular uprising that relied not on sophisticated weapons used by a few well-trained cadres, but on rocks, barricades, and any other materials that ordinary Palestinians could marshal in their resistance to Israeli occupation. It was a dramatic turn in the liberation struggle, not only because the simplicity of the weaponry enabled virtually any Palestinian to be involved but also because its populist style gave the cause an image of a moral crusade rather than a terrorist plot. It also changed the nature of the Islamic resistance. As a popular and moral crusade, the *intifada* was easily identified with the religion—and the religious leaders—of the people. The Islamic resistance movement Hamas emerged at roughly the same time that the *intifada* did, and although there is no question that there is a connection between the two, there is some debate over Yassin's boast that he and other Muslim activists created the *intifada*. It is equally possible that the *intifada*, in a sense, created Hamas. Without the *intifada*, a broad-based Muslim activist movement outside the PLO would have been unrealizable.

The word *hamas* means zeal or enthusiasm, but it is also an acronym for the formal name of the movement: Harakat al-Muqawama al-Islamiyya (Islamic Resistance Movement). The name *Hamas* first appeared publicly in a communiqué circulated in mid-February 1988. The communiqué was one in a series that appeared about the time that the *intifada* began in December 1987, but it was not clear whether the Muslim Brotherhood, the Jihad organizations, or some other group was behind these early communiqués. Jean-François Legrain suggests that Yassin and the Muslim Brotherhood were not involved in sending the early communiqués or with the *intifada* but joined the *intifada* bandwagon only in February 1988.[102] The February communiqué that mentions the name *Hamas* describes the movement as "the powerful arm of the Association of Muslim Brothers."[103] It is possible, therefore, that Hamas marked a new phase in the Islamic resistance movement, one in which militant Palestinian Muslim activists were united under an old Muslim Brotherhood leadership based in Gaza for the purpose of capturing the leadership of the *intifada*.

Hamas places the ideology of Islam and the organization of the mosque at the service of *intifada*. The struggle between the Palestinians and the Israelis is described in eschatological terms as "the combat between Good and Evil."[104] Committees are set up in mosques to provide alternative education when schools are closed because of the *intifada*, and other mosque committees collect *zakat* (donations) to give to victims of the uprising. Most of the leaders of Hamas have religious titles. The movement's communiqués justify its positions on the basis of Islamic beliefs and tradition, and cast even the most specific issues of policy in a theological light. The communiqués include criticisms of the Arab states' compromises with Israeli and U.S. positions and call for general strikes to protest the sponsorship of peace envoys by the Americans. In August 1988 Hamas published a forty-page covenant, which presented its vision of an Islamic Palestine, and implied that the only true course was to reject the secular ideology and compromising strategy of the PLO and wage a direct jihad against Israel.[105]

The PLO did not take kindly to the Hamas declaration of independence from it, and for a month or so the PLO and Hamas seemed to be competing for public support. They announced general strikes at different times, and although the Hamas strikes were usually smaller, the movement was especially successful in garnering support in Gaza and increasingly in such West Bank cities as Nablus, Ramallah, Bethlehem, and Hebron. By late September 1988 Hamas and the PLO had at least temporarily patched up their differences; for some months after that, most of the general strikes were called by both groups at the same time.

The mutual suspicion that trials relations between Hamas and the PLO may be goaded, in part, by the Israeli government. In the last months of 1988, while members of the PLO were being put in prison, Sheik Yassin was interviewed on Israeli television. There were rumors that he and Hamas were being tolerated by the Israeli government because they were putting an Islamic obstacle in the path of the PLO.[106] By the middle of 1989, however, the leaders of Hamas were regarded as too troublesome to be ignored. The Israeli government rounded up many of them, including Sheik Yassin, who was put under house arrest.

Despite the suppression of its leaders, Hamas did not disappear. Its message was spread through underground circulars and journals, such as *Al-Sabil (The Way)*, which is printed in Oslo, Norway, and smuggled into Israel. For several reasons, the Islamic resistance movement in Palestine continued to grow. For one thing, the longer the *intifada* continued, the more restless the Palestinian populace became with the official PLO leadership. Moreover, the educated PLO elite was often aloof from the masses—and, in the case of those who were in exile, physically distant—whereas the Islamic leaders were a part of the local communities and close at hand. In addition, the masses of American troops assigned to Saudi Arabia in 1990 following Husein's invasion of Kuwait were seen by many Palestinians as a direct threat to them. The *intifada* became rejuvenated and, with it, the growing feeling that the conciliatory attitude of the PLO was not working and that further direct action was necessary.

This feeling was heightened by a second event in 1990, the October confrontation on Temple Mount. Temple Mount had become an increasingly important symbol in the Hamas resistance struggle. Unlike the PLO, which had only the utopian vision of a Palestinian capital to defend, Hamas had a real one: the Dome of the Rock and the al-Aksa Mosque. Defending the sacred shrine and cleansing it of "foreign" (Israeli) influence became a major theme in Hamas publications. The sacred hill also became an important site for the recruitment of young Palestinian men from Jerusalem—many of them former members of street gangs—to the cause. Many of them were initiated into the Hamas movement in a dramatic nighttime ritual at the Dome of the Rock.[107] When the Israeli activist Gershon Salomon and his followers in the Faithful of Temple Mount let it be known that they were going to march on the site and lay the cornerstone for a new temple, Hamas leaders excitedly spread the word among their youthful followers that the time had come to defend the faith against the Israeli intruders. What happened then, as I recounted in the previous section of this chapter, was one of the bloodiest incidents of the *intifada*.

Hamas made the most of the incident. The Temple Mount confrontation had the immediate effect of consolidating Hamas power in Arab Jerusalem and the West Bank. It also dramatically illustrated that the Palestinian struggle was not only about land and political rights but also about religion. "The massacre at al-Aksa," leaders explained in one of their communiqués, "showed that our fight with Zionism is a fight between Islam and Judaism."[108] Moreover, it demonstrated that members of the religious resistance would lay down their lives in defense of the faith at a time when their more secular compatriots were quiescent.

Several violent incidents involving Hamas in November and December 1990 indicated either that the movement was now becoming bolder and more aggressive or that bolder and more aggressive persons were now joining the movement and championing its cause as their own. In either event it was a significant change from the earlier position of Hamas. During those two months at least eight Israelis were killed by attackers associated with Hamas. Following the knife slaying of three Israeli workers in Jaffa in mid-December, nearly a thousand Palestinians associated with Hamas were said to have been arrested.[109] The number included 600 in Gaza and another 200 on the West Bank. Included among them was Abdul Aziz al-Rantisi, a colleague of Sheik Yassin, who was described by the *New York Times* as "the co-founder of Hamas."[110]

By 1991 the Islamic resistance movement had become a significant contender for Palestinian leadership, in large part because of the weakening of Arafat's power following the defeat of the PLO's ally, Iraq, in the Gulf War. Unlike Arafat, whose disastrous support of Hussein had decimated the PLO's coffers and undermined its political support, the leaders of Hamas took a restrained approach—perhaps stimulated by the fact that the government of Kuwait had been by far a greater financial supporter of Hamas than of the PLO.[111] After the Gulf War, Hamas began to demand greater representation on Palestinian councils, and for the first time in recent years Arafat's authority began to be challenged by local leaders. By the middle of 1991 internal feuds between religious and secular Palestinian leaders had turned violent.[112] Supporters of Hamas were beginning to will elections on the West Bank as well as in Gaza.[113] In October 1991, Sheik Yassin was imprisoned.

In 1992, the peace talks between Israeli and Palestinian leaders commanded the attention of most Palestinians, and the *intifada* degenerated from a popular uprising of largely peaceful protestors into armed struggle conducted by small groups of youthful cadres. Among these were groups associated with the Fateh and Marxist branches of the PLO as well as groups associated with Hamas.[114]

Many of the older leaders of Hamas adopted a wait-and-see attitude toward the peace talks, while the younger members fought, at times violently, against the members of the PLO who favored them.[115] Supporters of Hamas questioned the degree to which Islamic law and leadership would be factors in the settlement eventually negotiated with the Israelis.

As it turned out, Islamic principles were not even mentioned in the September 1993 accord sponsored by Israel's Rabin and the PLO's Arafat. From the Hamas point of view, the circumstances surrounding the accord could not have been worse: It was a thoroughly secular document, negotiated in secret with Israeli leaders, and signed in Washington with the blessings of what is often seen as Islam's global enemy, the government of the United States.

The day the document was signed, Hamas supporters in Gaza City used wooden clubs to disperse a rally sponsored by a new pro-agreement political party. Arafat supporters opened fire with submachine guns over the heads of those attending a rally organized by Hamas in the Gaza town of Rafah. And in Damascus, a coalition of ten anti-PLO groups—including Hamas and another radical Islamic group, the Islamic Jihad—pledged to demolish the accord, identifying Arafat as a traitor. The continuing tensions and attempts on his life prove the seriousness of these accusations. Many outside the Middle East wondered why Palestinians could be so adamantly opposed to what seems to be a major Israeli concession arid a giant step towards their own independence.

On one level, it is a matter of who leads the movement: the Hamas leadership comes from the poorest areas of the villages and towns. Like the Islamic revolution in Iran, this struggle has the potential for bringing into power an uneducated local leadership. On another level, Hamas asks what sort of Palestinian movement there should be and what sort of new Palestinian state should come into being. Sheik 'Odeh saw the increased Islamicization of the *intifada* as "a sign from God to the people that they need Islam as a center."[116] This attitude seriously challenges the PLO's monopoly of power. For although Sheik Yassin admits that a secular Palestinian government could go far in helping to protect Islamic values in Palestine, it could never go far enough. It ultimately would be an illegitimate form of government because, according to Yassin and many of his followers in Hamas, "the only true Palestinian state is an Islamic state," and that means strict adherence to shari'a and its moral rules.[117]

The establishment of a secular Palestinian government transformed the Palestinian Islamic movement. Rather than being a revolt within the Palestinian revolution, it became the vanguard of a new revolutionary movement: the enemy of the secular Palestinian state. In this sense, then, it became like its counterparts in Iran, Egypt, Israel, and elsewhere in the Middle East.

Each of these movements oppose not only secular nationalism but also the efforts of secular leaders to offer halfhearted compromises with religion. Each offers its own model of religious protest: the Shi'ite movement in Iran achieved a total revolution; the Sunni Muslim movement in Egypt combines violent extremism with nonviolent measures; the Israeli religious right attempts to move its nominally religious nation further in the direction of religious commitment; and the Muslim wing of the Palestinian liberation movement attempts to change the course of what had been a solely secular movement. Although the particular course that each movement has taken is distinctly its own, the pattern of religious reform that each illustrates has been replicated in movements for religious nationalism elsewhere in the world.

Endnotes

1. See Michael Walzer, *The Revolution of the Saints: A Study in the Origins of Radical Politics* (New York: Atheneum, 1974).
2. A stasis-disequilibrium model of society is presumed in the models of revolution developed by social scientists in the 1950s and 1960s. See, for examples, Crane Brinton, *The Anatomy of Revolution*, rev. ed. (New York: Random House, Vintage Books, 1957), 16–17; and Chalmers Johnson, *Revolutionary Change* (Boston: Little, Brown, 1966), *passim.* Arendt maintains a different view of revolutions, arguing that they must always be "something new," aiming at "freedom." Hannah Arendt, *On Revolution* (New York: Viking Press, 1963), 36. She concludes that revolutions are always, therefore, secular.
3. Gary Sick, *All Fall Down: America's Tragic Encounter with Iran*, rev. ed. (New York: Penguin, 1986), 187.
4. I saw this poster in the home of Sheik Ahmed Yassin in Gaza, January 14, 1989.
5. Kalim Siddiqui, "Nation-States as Obstacles to the Total Transformation of the *Ummah*," in M. Ghayasuddin, ed., *The Impact of Nationalism on the Muslim World* (London: Open Press, Al-Hoda, 1986), 1.
6. Ira M. Lapidus, *A History of Islamic Societies* (Cambridge: Cambridge University Press, 1988), 887.
7. Siddiqui, "Nation-States as Obstacles," 11.
8. Ibid., 6.
9. Some observers say that the Gulf War was the final nail in the coffin of the pan-Arab movement. See Auda, "An Uncertain Response," 122.
10. Kim Murphy, "Islamic Militants Build Power Base in Sudan," *Los Angeles Times*, April 6, 1992, p. A1.
11. Ibid., p. A9.

12. Abdelkadir Hachani, quoted in Kim Murphy, "Algerian Election to Test Strength of Radical Islam," *Los Angeles Times*, December 26, 1991, p. A18. After the Front won 55 percent of the vote in local elections in 1990, the army attempted to arrest and intimidate its members, and 4,000 of them lost their jobs as a result of going on strike against the government in the summer of 1991. The first stage of the national elections, on December 27, 1991, gave the Front 40 percent of the parliamentary seats, and a total of more than 60 percent were expected to be gleaned after the runoff elections on January 16, 1992. The Islamic movement has been a thorn in the side of Algerian nationalists since independence. See John P. Entelis, *Algeria: The Revolution Institutionalized* (Boulder, Colo,: Westview Press, 1986); and Hugh Roberts, "Radical Islamism and the Dilemma of Algerian Nationalism: The Embattled Arians of Algiers," *Third World Quarterly* 10, no. 2 (April 1988): 556–89.
13. Quoted in Robin Wright, "Muslims under the Gun," *Los Angeles Times*, January 28, 1992, p. B1.
14. Kim Murphy, "Revolution Again Echoes through the Casbah," *Los Angeles Times*, March 15, 1992, p. A15. The leader of the Islamic Salvation Front, Abdelkadir Hachani, urged his followers to respond nonviolently to the military and to confine their protests to attendance at mosques, which swelled significantly after Hachani was jailed on January 22, 1992. Robin Wright, "Muslims under the Gun," *Los Angeles Times*, January 28, 1992.
15. Jonathan C. Randall, "Algeria Leader Assassinated during Speech," *Los Angeles Times*, June 30, 1991, p. A1. Boudiaf, a hero of Algeria's war of independence, had openly supported the separation of religion and politics in Algeria and had defended the ban on the Islamic Salvation Front. He was killed in a complicated attack involving bombs and automatic-weapons fire as he was giving a speech in the Mediterranean port city of Annaba. On July 2, he was succeeded by Ali Kafi, another civilian member of the Council of State.
16. The Jordanian government uncovered a cache of weapons allegedly being held for that purpose. See Nick B. Williams, Jr., "Chasm Widening between Amman, Fundamentalists," *Los Angeles Times*, August 8, 1991, p. A4.
17. Raymond A. Hinnebusch, "The Islamic Movement in Syria: Sectarian Conflict and Urban Rebellion in an Authoritarian-Populist Regime," in Ali E. Hillal Dessouki, ed., *Islamic Resurgence in the Arab World* (New York: Praeger, 1982), 138–69.
18. Quoted in R. Stephen Humphreys, "The Contemporary Resurgence in the Context of Modem Islam," in Ali E. Hillal Dessouki, ed., *Islamic Resurgence in the Arab World* (New York: Praeger, 1982), 80.
19. Youssef M. Ibrahim, "Saudi Rulers Are Confronting Challenge by Islamic Radicals," *New York Times*, March 9, 1992, p. A1.
20. Interview with the Ayatollah Khomeini by Prof. Hamid Algar on December 29, 1978, at Neauphle-le-Chateau, France, in Khomeini, *Islam and Revolution*, 323.
21. Ibid., 322.
22. Lewis, *Political Language of Islam*, 2.

23. Ibid., 3.

24. Ayatollah Ruhullah Khomeini, "Muharram: The Triumph of Blood over the Sword," in Khomeini, *Islam and Revolution*, 242. For a general assessment of the ayatollah's politicization of Ashura, see Emmanuel Sivan, "Sunni Radicalism in the Middle East and the Iranian Revolution," *International Journal for Middle East Studies* 21 (1989): 16–17.

25. Sivan, "Sunni Radicalism," 8–11 and note 11 on p. 29.

26. Hamid Algar, "Foreword" to Khomeini, *Islam and Revolution*, 10.

27. Quoted in Sivan, "Sunni Radicalism," 12.

28. A. Ali-Babai, "An Open Letter to Khomeini, *Iranshahr*, June 15–July 16, 1982, quoted in Ervand Abrahamian, *Radical Islam: The Iranian Mojahedin* (London: I. B. Tauris, 1989), 19.

29. Khomeini, *Islam and Revolution*, 334.

30. Ibid., 335.

31. For the U.S. State Department's perspective on the crisis, see the revealing study by Sick, *All Fall Down.*

32. Ibid., 229–30.

33. The early years of the revolution and the mullahs' ascension to power are chronicled in Shaul Bakhash, *The Reign of the Ayatollahs: Iran and the Islamic Revolution* (New York: Basic Books, 1984).

34. Supporters of the moderate Islamic revolutionary movement, the Mojahedin, were especially targeted for repression because of the considerable power and popularity they had gained after the revolution. See Abrahamian, *Radical Islam.*

35. Said Amir Aijomand, "A Victory for the Pragmatists: The Islamic Fundamentalist Reaction in Inn," in James P. Piscatori, ed., *Islamic Fundamentalisms and the Gulf Crisis* (Chicago: Fundamentalism Project, American Academy of Arts and Sciences, 1991), 52.

36. Nick B. Williams, Jr., "Iran's Rafsanjani, Guarding His Political Flanks, Steers a More Militant Course," *Los Angeles Times*, January 13, 1992, p. A3.

37. Robin Wright, "Iran Extends Reach of Its Aid to Islamic Groups," *Los Angeles Times*, April 6, 1993, p. A4.

38. For interesting accounts of life in postrevolutionary Iran, see Robin Wright, *In the Name of God: The Khomeini Decade* (New York: Simon & Schuster, 1989); John Simpson, *Inside Iran: Life under Khomeini's Regime* (New York: St. Martin's Press, 1988); and Roy P. Mottahedeh, *The Mantle of the Prophet* (New York: Pantheon, 1986).

39. For the theological history of the concept, see Abdulaziz Abdulhussein Sachedina, *The Just Ruler (al-sultan al-'adil) in Shi'ite Islam: The Comprehensive Authority of the Jurist in Imamite Jurisprudence* (New York: Oxford University Press, 1988).

40. Khomeini, *Islam and Revolution*, 342.

41. Ibid., 343.

42. From my informal conversation with a group of journalists in Jerusalem, May 24, 1990.

43. Nejla Sammakia, "Egypt's No. 2 Man Slain by Assassins," *San Francisco Examiner*, October 13, 1990, national edition, p. A16.

44. According to one scholar, "Egypt has been influenced by Arab and Indian subcontinent themes far more than by Iranian ones." Shahrough Akhavi, "The Impact of the Iranian Revolution on Egypt," in John L. Esposito, ed., *The Iranian Revolution: Its Global Impact* (Miami: Florida International University Press, 1990), 138. For a comprehensive analysis of the separation between Sunni and Shi'a radical groups, see Sivan, "Sunni Radicalism."

45. Interview with el-Arian.

46. They do, however, occasionally refer to the Iranian revolution in discussing the worldwide development of Islamic political consciousness. See, for instance, the articles from *Al-Hilal*, July 1987, translated into French and summarized in *Revue de la presse égyptienne*, no. 27 (1987).

47. Bakhash, for example, implies that the Iranian revolution provides a model for Muslim radicals in Egypt and elsewhere. Bakhash, *Reign of the Ayatollahs*, 4.

48. For the rise of the Muslim Brotherhood in Egypt, see Charles Wendell, trans., *Five Tracts of Hasan al-Banna (1906–1949)* (Berkeley and Los Angeles: University of California Press, 1978), 40–68, 133–62; Bernard Lewis, "The Return of Islam," in Michael Curtis, ed., *Religion and Politics in the Middle East* (Boulder, Colo.: Westview Press, 1981), 14–16, 55–67, 77–128; Richard P. Mitchell, *The Society of the Muslim Brothers* (London: Oxford University Press, 1969); and Emmanuel Sivan, *Radical Islam: Medieval Theology and Modern Politics* (New Haven, Conn.: Yale University Press, 1985).

49. Interview with Ibrahim.

50. It was published in *Al-Ahrar*, an Egyptian newspaper, on December 14, 1981. An English translation, accompanied by an extensive essay about the document, is to be found in Johannes J. G. Jansen, *The Neglected Duty: The Creed of Sadat's Assassins and Islamic Resurgence in the Middle East* (New York: Macmillan, 1986). I have also found helpful the analysis of this document by David Rapoport in "Sacred Terror: A Case from Islam" (Paper delivered at the annual meeting of the American Political Science Association, Washington, D.C., September 1–4, 1988). Its political implications are discussed in Mohammed Heikal, *Autumn of Fury: The Assassination of Sadat* (London: Andre Deutsch, 1983).

51. Faraj, par. 84, in Jansen, *Neglected Duty*, 199.

52. In the description of jihad often given by Sunni theologians it applies only to the defense of Islam when it is under direct assault. See Rudolph Peters, *Islam and Colonialism: The Doctrine of Jihad in Modern History* (The Hague: Mouton, 1979), 121–35.

53. Faraj, pars. 102 and 109, in Jansen, *Neglected Duty*, 210–11.

54. Faraj, par. 113, in Jansen, *Neglected Duty*, 212–13; see also par. 109 on p. 211.

55. According to an Egyptian scholar who interviewed in prison members of the group responsible for Sadat's assassination, the writings of Mawdudi were "important in shaping the group's ideas." Saad Eddin Ibrahim, "Islamic Militancy as a Social Movement: The Case of Two Groups in Egypt," in Ali E. Hillal Dessouki, ed., *Islamic Resurgence in the Arab World* (New York: Praeger, 1982), 125.

56. For a discussion of the significance of Sayyid Quito's life and work, see Richard C. Martin, "Religious Violence in Islam: Towards an Understanding of the Discourse on *Jihad* in Modern Egypt," in Paul Wilkinson and A. M. Stewart, eds., *Contemporary Research on Terrorism* (Aberdeen: University Press, 1987), 54–71; Gilles Kepel, *Muslim Extremism in Egypt: The Prophet and Pharaoh* (Berkeley and Los Angeles: University of California Press, 1986), 36–69; Yvonne V. Haddad, "Sayyid Qutb: Ideologue of Islamic Revival," in John L. Esposito, ed., *Voices of Resurgent Islam* (New York: Oxford University Press, 1983); and Ronald L. Nettler, *Past Trials and Present Tribulations: A Muslim Fundamentalist's View of the Jews* (New York: Pergamon Press, 1987).

57. Qutb studied in Washington, D.C., and California from 1949 to 1951. Haddad, "Sayyid Qutb," 69.

58. Sayyid Qutb, *This Religion of Islam (Hadha 'd-Din)*, translated by Islamdust (Palo Alto, Calif.: Al-Manar Press, 1967), 87.

59. Interview with Prof. A. K. Ashur, dean of the Faculty of Education, Al-Azhar University, in Cairo, May 27, 1990.

60. Interview with Ashur.

61. These points are summarized in Marius Deeb, "Egypt," in Stuart Mews, ed., *Religion in Politics: A World Guide* (London: Longman, 1989), 64.

62. Initially the Muslim Brotherhood condemned Iraq for invading Kuwait, but when the United States became involved, it shifted its condemnation to the United States. This confusion "induced deep ideological and behavioral uncertainty in its ranks." Auda, "An Uncertain Response," 110.

63. Akhavi, "Impact of the Iranian Revolution," 144.

64. Interview with Kahane.

65. Interview with Kahane; see also an interview with Kahane published in Raphael Mergui and Philippe Simonnot, *Israel's Ayatollahs: Meir Kahane and the Far Right in Israel* (London: Saqi Books, 1987), 40–41.

66. Carl E. Schorske, *Fin-de-Siècle Vienna: Politics and Culture* (New York: Knopf, 1980), 165.

67. The best analysis of the new religious politics in Israel may be found in Ehud Sprinzak, *The Ascendance of Israel's Radical Right* (New York: Oxford University Press, 1991). See also Ian S. Lustick, *For the Land and the Lord: Jewish Fundamentalism in Israel* (New York: Council on Foreign Relations, 1989).

68. Alter B. Z. Metzger, *Rabbi Kook's Philosophy of Repentance: A Translation of "Orot Ha-Teshuvah,"* Studies in Torah Judaism 11 (New York: Yeshiva University Press, 1968), 111. See also Jacob B. Agus, *Banner of Jerusalem: The Life, Times, and Thought of Rabbi Abraham Isaac Kuk* (New York: Bloch, 1946).

69. There have been several biographies of Kahane. The most recent is Robert Friedman, *The False Prophet: Rabbi Meir Kahan—From FBI Informant to Knesset Member* (London: Faber and Faber, 1990). For a comprehensive study of the religious right in Israel that puts Kahane's movement in context, see Sprinzak, *The Ascendance of Israel's Radical Right.*

70. Quoted in John Kifner's obituary of Kahane, "A Militant Leader, Fiery Politician and Founder of Anti-Arab Crusade," *New York Times,* November 7, 1990, p. B12.

71. H. K. Michael Eitan's speech to the Knesset Rules Committee in 1984, quoted in Gerald Cromer, *The Debate about Kahanism in Israeli Society, 1984–1988,* Occasional Papers 3 (New York: Henry Frank Guggenheim Foundation, 1988), 37–38.

72. Yair Kotler, *Heil Kahane* (New York Adama Books, 1986).

73. Interview with Kahane.

74. According to Sprinzak, Kahane did not make the usual nationalist argument that the Jews deserved the land because it was their ancient birthplace; rather, the Jews *"expropriated* it in the name of God and his sovereign will." Sprinzak, *The Ascendance of Israel's Radical Right,* 225; italics in the original.

75. Kahane made this point during a function proclaiming a new state of Judea—one that would be established on the West Bank if and when the Israeli army retreated from those areas (from my notes taken at the function in Jerusalem, January 18, 1989).

76. Interview with Kahane. See also similar comments made by Kahane in the interview published in Mergui and Simonnot, *Israel's Ayatollahs,* 43, 44, 68, 76–77, 150.

77. Interview with Levinger.

78. See Ehud Sprinzak, "Fundamentalism, Terrorism, and Democracy: The Case of Gush Emunim Underground" (Colloquium paper given at the Woodrow Wilson International Center for Scholars, Washington, D.C., September 16, 1986); revised and expanded version published as "From Messianic Pioneering to Vigilante Terrorism: The Case of Gush Emunim Underground," *Journal of Strategic Studies* 10, no. 4 (December 1987): 194–216 (a special issue entitled "Inside Terrorist Organizations," edited by David C. Rapoport); reissued as a book: David C. Rapoport, ed., *Inside Terrorist Organizations* (New York: Columbia University Press, 1988).

79. The idea that the rebuilding of the Temple will be a part of the messianic age is a common theme in Jewish speculation. See, for example, George W. Buchanan, *Revelation and Redemption: Jewish Documents of Deliverance from the Fall of Jerusalem to the Death of Nahmanides* (Dillsboro, N.C.: Western North Carolina Press, 1978); and Jonathan Frankel, ed., *Jews and Messianism in the Modern Era: Metaphor and Meaning,* vol. 7 of *Studies in Contemporary Jewry* (New York: Oxford University Press, and Jerusalem: Institute of Contemporary Jewry, Hebrew University of Jerusalem, 1991), 197–213 and 34–67. I am grateful to Prof. Richard Hecht of the University of California, Santa Barbara, for bringing to my attention these and other references on Jewish nationalism.

80. Interview with Lerner.
81. Interview with Gershom Salomon, head, Faithful of Temple Mount, in Jerusalem, May 25, 1990.
82. I am grateful to Prof. Hecht for pointing out that the calendar has long been a critical element in clashes between Jews and Muslims at Temple Mount and that conflicts between two different groups of religious nationalists often involve a skirmish over sacred space. See also Bernard Wasserstein, "Patterns of Communal Conflict in Palestine," in Ada Rapoport and Steven J. Zipperstein, eds., *Jewish History: Essays in Honour of Chimen Abramsky* (London: Peter Halban, 1988), 611–28.
83. Although the American television news reports routinely described the incident as unprovoked rock throwing by Palestinians aimed at Jewish worshipers gathered at the Western Wall (directly below the scene of the clash in the Temple Mount area), a fairly full and accurate report of the incident, including the provocation by Salomon and his group, may be found in the October 9, 1990, editions of the *New York Times*, the *Los Angeles Times*, and the *Washington Post*. One of the most complete accounts is Jackson Diehl, "The Battle at Temple Mount: Neither Palestinian nor Israeli Version Tells Full Story," *Washington Post*, October 14, 1990, pp. A1, A23; and "Special File: The Haram al-Sharif (Temple Mount) Killings," *Journal of Palestine Studies* 20, no. 2 (Winter 1991), 134–59.
84. John Kifner, "Suspect in Kahane Case Is Muslim Born in Egypt," *New York Times*, November 7, 1990, p. B13.
85. "The Legacy of Hate," *New York Times*, November 7, 1990, p. A30.
86. See the essay by Elie Rekhess, "The Iranian Impact on the Islamic Jihad Movement in the Gaza Strip," in David Menashri, ed., *The Iranian Revolution and the Muslim World* (Boulder, Cob.: Westview Press, 1990). An excerpt from this article, under the title "The Growth of Khomeinism in Gaza," was published in the *Jerusalem Post Magazine*, January 26, 1991, p. 12.
87. Legrain, "Defining Moment," 72.
88. Interview with Yassin.
89. Interview with Yassin.
90. Interview with Yassin.
91. Many leaders of the PLO coalition have been eager to avoid a confrontation between religious and secular elements, and to use the ideology of Islam to their own advantage. See, for instance, Matti Steinberg, "The PLO and Palestinian Islamic Fundamentalism," *Jewish Quarterly* 52 (Fall 1989): 37–54.
92. Interview with Dr. Fathi Arafat, president, Palestine Red Crescent Society, in Cairo, May 30, 1990.
93. Interview with Arafat.

94. One poll conducted in 1991 claimed that Hamas was supported by 18 percent of the residents in Gaza, while the support for another militant Muslim group, the Islamic Jihad, garnered another 5 to 10 percent: a total of 25 percent. A Hamas leader described the poll as "nonsense" and claimed 60 percent support in Gaza and 50 percent on the West Bank. "Surveys Show Support for Moslem Hardliners Weaker Than Believed," *Mideast Mirror*, May 7, 1991, p. 3.

95. Interview with Saleh Zamlot, student leader, Fateh, Palestine Liberation Organization, in Al-Azhar University, Cairo, May 27, 1990.

96. Interview with Yassin.

97. See Jean-François Legrain, "Islamistes et lutte nationale pal estinienne dans les territoires occupés par Israel," *Revue Française de science politique* 36, no. 2 (April 1986): 227–47; and Ifrah Zilberman, "Hamas: Apocalypse Now," *Jerusalem Post Weekly*, January 12, 1991, p. 11.

98. Jean-François Legrain, "The Islamic Movement and the *Intifada*," in Jamal R. Nassar and Roger Heacock, eds., *Intifada: Palestine at the Crossroads* (New York: Praeger, 1990), 177, and "Defining Moment," 72–73. Legrain identifies Fathi Shqaqi, a pharmacist from Rafah, as the military commander of the Islamic Jihad, 'Odeh as the spiritual leader.

99. Legrain, "Islamic Movement," 177.

100. Ibid.

101. Ibid., 176. I am grateful to Dr. Ifrah Zilberman of Jerusalem for showing me a number of copies of *Islam and Palestine*, which he has in his possession.

102. Legrain, "Islamic Movement," 182.

103. Quoted in ibid.

104. Ibid., 183.

105. Reuven Paz, *Ha-'imna ha-islamit umichma'utah 'iyyon rechoni utargum (The Covenant of the Islamicists and Its Significance—Analysis and Translation)* (Tel Aviv: Dayan Center, Tel Aviv University, 1988).

106. These rumors were reported to me by Zilberman in my interview with him. See also Legrain, "Islamic Movement," 185. During the first months of 1989 Yassin was allowed to talk to journalists and foreigners such as myself.

107. This ritual, in which the young men were required to sleep beside the Dome of the Rock all night, was described in the newspaper *Al-Sabil*, April 1989.

108. Communiqué #66, October 31, 1990, quoted in Legrain, "Defining Moment," 83.

109. "Israelis Round Up Palestinians in Hunt for Killers," *New York Times*, December 16, 1990, international edition, p. A5. This article reported that an Israeli army spokesman said that the numbers of those arrested, provided by Palestinian sources, were "terribly exaggerated."

110. Ibid.

111. In the year before the Gulf War, Kuwait gave $60 million to Hamas and only $27 million to the PLO. Legrain, "Defining Moment," 79.

112. See "Three Hurt in Muslim-PLO Clash as Internal Feud Turns Violent," *Los Angeles Times*, June 3, 1991, p. A10. Clashes between Hamas and Fateh occurred in the Jabalya refugee camp in Gaza and in Nablus on the West Bank. Also, Hamas began to require women in Gaza to wear the Muslim head scarf *(hijab)*.

113. Joel Brinkley, "A West Bank Business Chamber Votes for Islamic Fundamentalists," *New York Times*, June 20, 1991, international edition, p. A10.

114. Daniel Williams, "Arab Revolt: From Rocks to Revenge," *Los Angeles Times*, May 5, 1992, p. H4.

115. Daniel Williams, "The Quiet Palestinian," *Los Angeles Times Magazine*, June 7, 1992, p. 53.

116. Interview with 'Odeh printed in *Islam and Palestine*, Leaflet 5 (Limasol, Cyprus, June 1988).

117. Interview with Yassin.

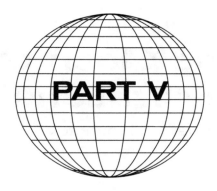

Looking Toward the Future

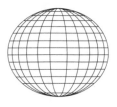

The Clash of Civilizations?

Samuel P. Huntington

The Next Pattern of Conflict

World politics is entering a new phase, and intellectuals have not hesitated to proliferate visions of what it will be—the end of history, the return of traditional
rivalries between nation states, and the decline of the nation state from the conflicting pulls of tribalism and globalism, among others. Each of these visions
catches aspects of the emerging reality. Yet they all miss a crucial, indeed a central, aspect of what global politics is likely to be in the coming years.

It is my hypothesis that the fundamental source of conflict in this new world
will not be primarily ideological or primarily economic. The great divisions
among humankind and the dominating source of conflict will be cultural. Nation
states will remain the most powerful actors in world affairs, but the principal conflicts of global politics will occur between nations and groups of different civilizations. The clash of civilizations will dominate global politics. The fault lines
between civilizations will be the battle lines of the future.

Conflict between civilizations will be the latest phase in the evolution of conflict in the modern world. For a century and a half after the emergence of the modern international system with the Peace of Westphalia, the conflicts of the Western
world were largely among princes—emperors, absolute monarchs and constitutional monarchs attempting too expand their bureaucracies, their armies, their
mercantilist economic strength and, most important, the territory they ruled. In
the process they created nation states, and beginning with the French Revolution
the principal lines of conflict were between nations rather than princes. In 1793,
as R. R. Palmer put it, "The wars of kings were over; the wars of peoples had
begun." This nineteenth-century pattern lasted until the end of World War I. Then,

---

as a result of the Russian Revolution and the reaction against it, the conflict of nations yielded to the conflict of ideologies, first among communism, fascism-Nazism and liberal democracy, and then between communism and liberal democracy. During the Cold War, this latter conflict became embodied in the struggle between the two superpowers, neither of which was a nation state in the classical European sense and each of which defined its identity in terms of its ideology.

These conflicts between princes, nation states and ideologies were primarily conflicts within Western civilization, "Western civil wars," as William Lind has labeled them. This was as true of the Cold War as it was of the world wars and the earlier wars of the seventeenth, eighteenth and nineteenth centuries. With the end of the Cold War, international politics moves out of its Western phase, and its centerpiece becomes the interaction between the West and non-Western civilizations and among non-Western civilizations. In the politics of civilizations, the peoples and governments of non-Western civilizations no longer remain the objects of history as targets of Western colonialism but join the West as movers and shapers of history. [. . .]

Why Civilizations Will Clash

Civilization identity will be increasingly important in the future, and the world will be shaped in large measure by the interactions among seven or eight major civilizations. These include Western, Confucian, Japanese, Islamic, Hindu, Slavic-Orthodox, Latin American and possibly African civilization. The most important conflicts of the future will occur along the cultural fault lines separating these civilizations from one another.

Why will this be the case?

First, differences among civilizations are not only real; they are basic. Civilizations are differentiated from each other by history, language, culture, tradition and, most important, religion. The people of different civilizations have different views on the relations between God and man, the individual and the group, the citizen and the state, parents and children, husband and wife, as well as differing views of the relative importance of rights and responsibilities, liberty and authority, equality and hierarchy. These differences are the product of centuries. They will not soon disappear. They are far more fundamental than differences among political ideologies and political regimes. Differences do not necessarily mean conflict, and conflict does not necessarily mean violence. Over the centuries, however, differences among civilizations have generated the most prolonged and the most violent conflicts.

Second, the world is becoming a smaller place. The interactions between peoples of different civilizations are increasing; these increasing interactions intensify civilization consciousness and awareness of differences between civilizations and Commonalities within civilizations. North African immigration to France generates hostility among Frenchmen and at the same time increased receptivity to immigration by "good" European Catholic Poles. Americans react far more negatively to Japanese investment than to larger investments from Canada and European countries. Similarly, as Donald Horowitz has pointed out, "An Ibo may be . . . an Owerri Ibo or an Onitsha Ibo in what was the Eastern region of Nigeria. In Lagos, he is simply an Ibo. In London, he is a Nigerian. In New York, he is an African." The interactions among peoples of different civilizations enhance the civilization consciousness of people that, in turn, invigorates differences and animosities stretching or thought to stretch back deep into history.

Third, the processes of economic modernization and social change throughout the world are separating people from longstanding local identities. They also weaken the nation state as a source of identity. In much of the world religion has moved in to fill this gap, often in the form of movements that are labeled "fundamentalist." Such movements are found in Western Christianity, Judaism, Buddhism and Hinduism, as well as in Islam. In most countries and most religions the people active in fundamentalist movements are young, college-educated, middle-class technicians, professionals and business persons. The "unsecularization of the world," George Weigel has remarked, "is one of the dominant social facts of life in the late twentieth century." The revival of religion, "la revanche de Dieu," as Gilles Kepel labeled it, provides a basis for identity and commitment that transcends national boundaries and unites civilizations.

Fourth, the growth of civilization-consciousness is enhanced by the dual role of the West. On the one hand, the West is at a peak of power. At the same time, however, and perhaps as a result, a return to the roots phenomenon is occurring among non-Western civilizations. Increasingly one hears references to trends toward a turning inward and "Asianization" in Japan, the end of the Nehru legacy and the "Hinduization" of India, the failure of Western ideas of socialism and nationalism and hence "re-Islamization" of the Middle East, and now a debate over Westernization versus Russianization in Boris Yeltsin's country. A West at the peak of its power confronts non-Wests that increasingly have the desire, the will and the resources to shape the world in non-Western ways.

In the past, the elites of non-Western societies were usually the people who were most involved with the West, had been educated at Oxford, the Sorbonne or Sandhurst, and had absorbed Western attitudes and values. At the same time, the populace in non-Western countries often remained deeply imbued with the indigenous culture. Now, however, these relationships are being reversed. A de-Westernization and indigenization of elites is occurring in many non-Western countries at the same time that Western, usually American, cultures, styles and habits become more popular among the mass of the people.

Fifth, cultural characteristics and differences are less mutable and hence less easily compromised and resolved than political and economic ones. In the former Soviet Union, communists can become democrats, the rich can become poor and the poor rich, but Russians cannot become Estonians and Azeris cannot become Armenians. In class and ideological conflicts, the key question was "Which side are you on?" and people could and did choose sides and change sides. In conflicts between civilizations, the question is "What are you?" That is a given that cannot be changed. And as we know, from Bosnia to the Caucasus to the Sudan, the wrong answer to that question can mean a bullet in the head. Even more than ethnicity, religion discriminates sharply and exclusively among people. A person can be half-French and half-Arab and simultaneously even a citizen of two countries. It is more difficult to be half-Catholic and half -Muslim.

Finally, economic regionalism is increasing. The proportions of total trade that were intraregional rose between 1980 and 1989 from 51 percent to 59 percent in Europe, 33 percent to 37 percent in East Asia, and 32 percent to 36 percent in North America. The importance of regional economic blocs is likely to continue to increase in the future. On the one hand, successful economic regionalism will reinforce civilization-consciousness. On the other hand, economic regionalism may succeed only when it is rooted in a common civilization. The European Community rests on the shared foundation of European culture and Western Christianity. The success of the North American Free Trade Area depends on the convergence now underway of Mexican, Canadian and American cultures. Japan, in contrast, faces difficulties in creating a comparable economic entity in East Asia because Japan is a society and civilization unique to itself. However strong the trade and investment links Japan may develop with other East Asian countries, its cultural differences with those countries inhibit and perhaps preclude its promoting regional economic integration like that in Europe and North America.

Common culture, in contrast, is clearly facilitating the rapid expansion of the economic relations between the People's Republic of China and Hong Kong, Taiwan, Singapore and the overseas Chinese communities in other Asian Countries. With the Cold War over, cultural commonalities increasingly overcome ideological differences, and mainland China and Taiwan move closer together. If cultural commonality is a prerequisite for economic integration, the principal East Asian economic bloc of the future is likely to be centered on China. This bloc is, in fact, already coming into existence. As Murray Weidenbaum has observed,

> Despite the current Japanese dominance of the region, the Chinese-based economy of Asia is rapidly emerging as a new epicenter for industry, commerce and finance. This strategic area contains substantial amounts of technology and manufacturing capability (Taiwan), outstanding entrepreneurial, marketing and services acumen (Hong Kong), a fine communications network (Singapore), a tremendous pool of financial capita (all three), and very large endowments of land, resources and labor (mainland China) . . . From Guangzhou to Singapore, from Kuala Lumpur to Manila, this influential network—often based on extensions of the traditional clans—has been described as the backbone of the East Asian economy.

Culture and religion also form the basis of the Economic Cooperation Organization, which brings together ten non-Arab Muslim countries: Iran, Pakistan, Turkey, Azerbaijan, Kazakhstan, Kyrgyzstan, Turkmenistan, Tadjikistan, Uzbekistan and Afghanistan. One impetus to the revival and expansion of this organization, founded originally in the 1960s by Turkey, Pakistan and Iran, is the realization by the leaders of several of these countries that they had no chance of admission to the European Community. Similarly, Caricom, the Central American Common Market and Mercosur rest on common cultural foundations. Efforts to build a broader Caribbean-Central American economic entity bridging the Anglo-Latin divide, however, have to date failed.

As people define their identity in ethnic and religious terms, they are likely to see an "us" versus "them" relation existing between themselves and people of different ethnicity or religion. The end of ideologically defined states in Eastern Europe and the former Soviet Union permits traditional ethnic identities and animosities to come to the fore. Differences in culture and religion create differences over policy issues, ranging from human rights to immigration to trade and commerce to the environment. Geographical propinquity gives rise to conflicting territorial claims from Bosnia to Mindanao. Most important, the efforts of the West to promote its values of democracy and liberalism as universal values, to maintain its military predominance and to advance its economic interests engender countering responses from other civilizations. Decreasingly able to mobilize support and form coalitions on the basis of ideology, governments and groups will increasingly attempt to mobilize support by appealing to common religion and civilization identity.

The clash of civilizations thus occurs at two levels. At the micro-level, adjacent groups along the fault lines between civilizations struggle, often violently, over the control of territory and each other. At the macro-level, states from different civilizations compete for relative military and economic power, struggle over the control of international institutions and third parties, and competitively promote their particular political and religious values.

The Fault Lines between Civilizations

The fault lines between civilizations are replacing the political and ideological boundaries of the Cold War as the flash points for crisis and bloodshed. The Cold War began when the Iron Curtain divided Europe politically and ideologically. The Cold War ended with the end of the Iron Curtain. As the ideological division of Europe has disappeared, the cultural division of Europe between Western Christianity, on the one hand, and Orthodox Christianity and Islam, on the other, has reemerged The most significant dividing line in Europe, as William Wallace has suggested, may well be the eastern boundary of Western Christianity in the year 1500. This line runs along what are now the boundaries between Finland and Russia and between the Baltic states and Russia, cuts through Belarus and Ukraine separating the more Catholic western Ukraine from Orthodox eastern Ukraine, swings westward separating Transylvania from the rest of Romania, and then goes through Yugoslavia almost exactly along the line now separating Croatia and Slovenia from the rest of Yugoslavia. In the Balkans this line, of course, coincides with the historic boundary between the Hapsburg and Ottoman empires. The peoples to the north and west of this line are Protestant or Catholic; they shared the common experiences of European history—feudalism, the Renaissance, the Reformation, the Enlightenment, the French Revolution, the Industrial Revolution; they are generally economically better off than the peoples to the east; and they may now look forward to increasing involvement in a common European economy and to the consolidation of democratic political systems. The peoples to the east and south of this line are Orthodox or Muslim; they historically belonged to the Ottoman or Tsarist empires and were only lightly touched by the shaping events in the rest of Europe; they are generally less advanced economically; they seem much less likely to develop stable democratic political systems. The Velvet Curtain of culture has replaced the Iron Curtain of ideology as the most significant dividing line in Europe. As the events in Yugoslavia show, it is not only a line of difference; it is also at times a line of bloody conflict.

Conflict along the fault line between Western and Islamic civilizations has been going on for 1,300 years. After the founding of Islam, the Arab and Moorish surge west and north only ended at Tours in 732. From the eleventh to the thirteenth century the Crusaders attempted with temporary success to bring Christianity and Christian rule to the Holy Land. From the fourteenth to the seventeenth century, the Ottoman Turks reversed the balance, extended their sway over the Middle East and the Balkans, captured Constantinople, and twice laid siege to Vienna. In the nineteenth and early twentieth centuries as Ottoman power declined Britain, France, and Italy established Western control over most of North Africa and the Middle East.

After World War II, the West, in turn, began to retreat; the colonial empires disappeared; first Arab nationalism and then Islamic fundamentalism manifested themselves; the West became heavily dependent on the Persian Gulf countries for its energy; the oil-rich Muslim countries became money-rich and, when they wished to, weapons-rich. Several wars occurred between Arabs and Israel (created by the West). France fought a bloody and ruthless war in Algeria for most of the 1950s; British and French forces invaded Egypt in 1956; American forces went into Lebanon in 1958; subsequently American forces returned to Lebanon, attacked Libya, and engaged in various military encounters with Iran; Arab and Islamic terrorists, supported by an least three Middle Eastern governments, employed the weapon of the weak and bombed Western planes and installations and seized Western hostages. This warfare between Arabs and the West culminated in 1990, when the United States sent a massive army to the Persian Gulf to defend some Arab countries against aggression by another. In its aftermath NATO planning is increasingly directed to potential threats and instability along its "southern tier."

This centuries-old military interaction between the West and Islam is unlikely to decline. It could become more virulent. The Gulf War left some Arabs feeling proud that Saddam Hussein had attacked Israel and stood up to the West. It also left many feeling humiliated and resentful of the West's military presence in the Persian Gulf, the West's overwhelming military dominance, and their own apparent inability to shape their destiny. Many Arab countries, in addition to the oil exporters, are reaching levels of economic and social development where autocratic forms of government become inappropriate and efforts to introduce democracy become stronger. Some openings in Arab political systems have already occurred. The principal beneficiaries of these openings have been Islamist movements. In the Arab world, in short, Western democracy strengthens anti-Western political forces. This may be a passing phenomenon, but it surely complicates relations between Islamic countries and the West. [. . .]

The West versus the Rest

The west is now at an extraordinary peak of power in relation to other civilizations. Its superpower opponent has disappeared from the map. Military conflict among Western states is unthinkable, and Western military power is unrivaled. Apart from Japan, the West faces no economic challenge. It dominates international political and security institutions and with Japan international economic institutions. Global political and security issues are effectively settled by a directorate of the United States, Britain and France, world economic issues by a directorate of the United States, Germany and Japan, all of which maintain extraordinarily close relations with each other to the exclusion of lesser and largely non-Western countries. Decisions made at the UN Security Council or in the International Monetary Fund that reflect the interests of the West are presented to the world as reflecting the desires of the world community. The very phrase "the world community" has become the euphemistic collective noun (replacing "the Free World") to give global legitimacy to actions reflecting the interests of the United States and other Western powers. Through the IMF and other international economic institutions, the West promotes its economic interests and imposes on other nations the economic policies it thinks appropriate. In any poll of non-Western peoples, the IMF undoubtedly would win the support of finance ministers and a few others, but get an overwhelmingly unfavorable rating from just about everyone else, who would agree with Georgy Arbatov's characterization of IMF officials as "neo-Bolsheviks who love expropriating other people's money, imposing undemocratic and alien rules of economic and political conduct and stifling economic freedom."

Western domination of the UN Security Council and its decisions, tempered only by occasional abstention by China, produced UN legitimation of the West's use of force to drive Iraq out of Kuwait and its elimination of Iraq's sophisticated weapons and capacity to produce such weapons. It also produced the quite unprecedented action by the United States, Britain and France in getting the Security Council to demand that Libya hand over the Pan Am 103 bombing suspects and then to impose sanctions when Libya refused. After defeating the largest Arab army, the West did not hesitate to throw its weight around in the Arab world. The West in effect is using international institutions, military power and economic resources to run the world in ways that will maintain Western predominance, protect Western interests and promote Western political and economic values.

That at least is the way in which non-Westerners see the new world, and there is a significant element of truth in their view. Differences in power and struggles for military, economic and institutional power are thus one source of conflict between the West and other civilizations. Differences in culture, that is basic values and beliefs, are a second source of conflict. V. S. Naipaul has argued that Western civilization is the "universal civilization" that "fits all men." At a superficial level much of Western culture has indeed permeated the rest of the world. At a more basic level, however, Western concepts differ fundamentally from those prevalent in other civilizations. Western ideas of individualism, liberalism, constitutionalism, human rights, equality, liberty, the rule of law, democracy, free markets, the separation of church and state, often have little resonance in Islamic, Confucian, Japanese, Hindu, Buddhist or Orthodox cultures. Western efforts to propagate such ideas produce instead a reaction against "human rights imperialism" and a reaffirmation of indigenous values, as can be seen in the support for religious fundamentalism by the younger generation in non-Western cultures. The very notion that there could be a "universal civilization" is a Western idea, directly at odds with the paricularism of most Asian societies and their emphasis on what distinguishes one people from another. Indeed, the author of a review of 100 comparative studies of values in different societies concluded that "the values that are most important in the West are least important worldwide." In the political realm, of course, these differences are most manifest in the efforts of the United States and other Western powers to induce other peoples to adopt Western ideas concerning democracy and human rights. Modern democratic government originated in the West. When it has developed in non-Western societies it has usually been the product of Western colonialism or imposition.

The central axis of world politics in the future is likely to be, in Kishore Mahbubani's phrase, the conflict between "the West and the Rest" and the responses of non-Western civilizations to Western power and values. Those responses generally take one or a combination of three forms. At one extreme, non-Western states can, like Burma and North Korea, attempt to pursue a course of isolation, to insulate their societies from penetration or "corruption" by the West, and, in effect, to opt out of participation in the Western-dominated global community. The costs of this course, however, are high, and few states have pursued it exclusively. A second alternative, the equivalent of "band-wagoning" in international relations theory, is to attempt to join the West and accept its values and institutions. The third alternative is to attempt to "balance" the West by developing economic and military power and cooperating with other non-Western societies against the West, while preserving indigenous values and institutions; in short, to modernize but not to Westernize. [. . .]

Western civilization is both Western and modern. Non-Western civilizations have attempted to become modern without becoming Western. To date only Japan has fully succeeded in this quest. Non-Western civilizations will continue to attempt to acquire the wealth, technology, skills, machines and weapons that are part of being modern. They will also attempt to reconcile this modernity with their traditional culture and values. Their economic and military strength relative to the West will increase. Hence the West will increasingly have to accommodate these non-Western modern civilizations whose power approaches that of the West but whose values and interests differ significantly from those of the West. This will require the West to maintain the economic and military power necessary to protect its interests in relation to these civilizations. It will also, however, require the West to develop a more profound understanding of the basic religious and philosophical assumptions underlying other civilizations and the ways in which people in those civilizations see their interests. It will require an effort to identify elements of commonality between Western and other civilizations. For the relevant future, there will be no universal civilization, but instead a world of different civilizations, each of which will have to learn to coexist with the others.

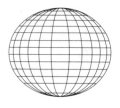

Draft of a Global Program

Jeremy Brecher
Tim Costello
Brendan Smith

We wrote in Chapter 1 that participants in the movement for globalization from below have varied goals, but the movement's unifying goal is "to bring about sufficient democratic control over states, markets, and corporations to permit people and the planet to survive and begin to shape a viable future." In this chapter we present the draft of a program to impose such democratic control. It proposes institutions and practices designed to turn global norms into enforceable rules.

This draft program is offered as a contribution to the ongoing process of constructing a program for globalization from below. It is not derived from an underlying political philosophy, but rather is synthesized from the solutions that diverse constituencies have proposed on their itineraries to globalization from below. It represents a work in progress, based on elements that have been percolating through the movement. Similar approaches have been formulated in previous programs presented by transnational groupings of various kinds.[1] Many of these elements have been included in the Global Sustainable Development Resolution cosponsored by a group of progressive members of the US Congress.[2]

This synthesis is guided by Chapter 1's analysis of the conflict between globalization from above and globalization from below; Chapter 2's concept of social movements imposing norms; Chapter 3's emphasis on addressing the different levels from the local to the global; Chapter 4's approach to integrating the needs of people and nature and of North and South; and Chapter 5's delineation of the origins and functions of a program.

This program is not the design for a utopia or a plan to fix all the world's ills. Its purpose is to provide a win-win framework for the many constituencies converging into globalization from below. It seeks ways that their needs, concerns, and interests can be complementary rather than contradictory.[3] Rather than treating trade, finance, development, labor, environment, agriculture, and other aspects of globalization as separate, unrelated compartments, this draft program addresses the global economy holistically. While each element also requires detailed elaboration, all are presented here as parts of an integrated project.

While this program aims to change the global economy, it is designed to be fought for and implemented as much in local arenas as in Washington or Geneva. For example, local struggles over the right to organize unions and control over corporate waste disposal can help level labor and environmental conditions upward, especially if they receive solidarity support from a broad coalition around the world. Reducing the volatility of the global economy involves local economic development protected from the gyrations of the global casino. While this program ultimately envisions new rules and institutions for the global economy, many of its objectives can implemented piecemeal through pressure on particular corporations, governments, and institutions.

The goals of globalization from below are often expressed in broad language advocating just and sustainable development. One formulation describes the movement's goal as "a new economy based on fairness and justice, on a sound ecology and a health environment, one that protects human rights and serves freedom."[4] Another calls for a "sustainable, socially just and democratically accountable" system.[5] Our sketch of a program for globalization from below is organized around seven basic principles:

1. Level labor, environmental, social, and human rights conditions upward.
2. Democratize institutions at every level from local to global.
3. Make decisions as close as possible to those they affect.
4. Equalize global wealth and power.
5. Convert the global economy to environmental sustainability.
6. Create prosperity by meeting human and environmental needs.
7. Protect against global boom and bust.

1. Level Labor, Environmental, Social, and Human Rights Conditions Upward

Globalization from above is creating a race to the bottom, an economic war of all against all in which each workforce, community, and country is forced to compete by offering lower labor, social, environmental, and human rights conditions.

The result is impoverishment, inequality, volatility, degradation of democracy, and environmental destruction. Halting the race to the bottom requires raising labor, environmental, social, and human rights conditions for those at the bottom. Such upward leveling can start with specific struggles to raise conditions for those who are being driven downward. Ultimately, minimum environmental, labor, social, and human rights standards must be incorporated in national and international law. Such standards protect communities and countries from the pressure to compete by sacrificing their rights and environment. Rising conditions for those at the bottom can also expand employment and markets and generate a virtuous circle of economic growth.

Raise labor, environmental, social, and human rights conditions locally: The fight to reverse the race to the bottom can begin at home. For example, living wage campaigns in local communities can be part of the process of upward leveling for wages. Organizing unions, ensuring the right to organize, establishing rights for workers in contingent jobs, and creating an adequate social safety net all establish rights and raise standards for those threatened by the downward pressures of the global economy. Campaigns for environmental justice and the protection of local environments similarly resist the environmental race to the bottom.[6]

Force standards on corporations: Workers and other citizens, acting in civil society, should pressure global corporation to negotiate minimum global standards for labor and environment.[7] National governments should be pressured to incorporate such standards in national trade laws and international financial and trade organizations.

Incorporate global standards in national law: Internationally recognized labor rights are regularly violated not only in the third world but also in the US. Every country's law should enforce those rights at home and require their corporations to meet international labor standards throughout the world.

Put floors, not ceilings, in international trade agreements: NAFTA, the WTO, and other trade agreements often forbid labor, environmental, health, and other regulations that exceed the agreement's own standards. Such ceilings should be eliminated to allow communities and countries to set their own minimum standards.

Negotiate agreements to protect minimum standards for labor, environment, and human rights: Such agreements can be implemented by established institutions such as international trade organizations or the UN, or by new ones established for the purpose.[8]

2. Democratize Institutions at Every Level from Local to Global

Globalization from above has restricted the power of self-government for people all over the world. At the heart of globalization from below lies democratization—making institutions accountable to those they affect.

Open the dialogue on the future of the global economy to all: The movement has already initiated a participatory global dialogue on democratizing the global economy. That dialogue should be expanded in every local community, in every country, and worldwide. A model here is the movement in Canada, which organized community forums across the country to discuss a people's alternative to the MAI [Multilateral Agreement on Investment].[9]

Establish a Global Economy Truth Commission: Globalization has been conducted behind the back of the world's people. A truth commission can provide citizens of the world with the information they need to monitor the results, impacts, and failures of economic institutions and policy at every level. The Truth Commission's inquest should be given the powers to investigate, publicize, and refer abuses in the use of international funds and the powers of international financial institutions to other authorities.

Democratize international trade and financial institutions: It is unacceptable that a few rich countries monopolize decision making regarding the global economy's future through their control of the IMP, World Bank, and WTO and through the control of major policy decisions by the G-7. Voting in international financial and trade institutions must move toward the standard of equal representation for the world's people.[10] International economic policy making must move from the rich men's club of the G-7 to forums where poor countries are fairly represented. International economic institutions must be made transparent in all their operations.

Let those affected by international economic policies participate in making them: Instead of closed negotiations with top government and corporate officials, decisions about international economic agreements and loans should require participation by labor unions, environmental groups, women's organizations, development organizations, and other major sectors of civil society in each country.

Establish an enforceable code of conduct for global corporations: Corporations that operate in more than one country should be subject to a global code of conduct with minimum requirements for disclosure of activities and compliance with labor and environmental standards. The UN Center on Transnational Corporations was in the process of developing such a code, but it was stopped by US opposition.[11]

Make corporations legally accountable: Corporations should be held legally liable for harms caused abroad and be subject to actions for relief in home-country courts. They should be required to disclose their use, emission, and accidental discharge of toxic substances and the names and addresses of their fully or partially owned facilities, contractors, and subcontractors.

End the domination of politics by big money: Ending "crony capitalism" means reducing the domination of political systems and media by economic oligarchs and increasing the capacity of people to organize themselves at the grassroots. This is as necessary in the United States as in Indonesia, Mexico, or Russia.[12]

3. Make Decisions as Close as Possible to Those They Affect

The movement for globalization from below should aim to construct a multilevel global economy. In accordance with the subsidiarity principle, power and initiative should be concentrated at as low a level as possible, with higher-level regulation established where and only where necessary. This approach envisions relatively self-reliant, self-governing communities, states, provinces, countries, and regions, with global regulation only sufficient to protect the environment, redistribute resources, block the race to the bottom, and perform other essential functions.

Build a community-controlled economic sector: A key strategy for protecting local communities from the vagaries of the global economy is to create an economic sector that is partially insulated from global markets. This sector needs to be rooted in and controlled by local people and based on meeting local needs. Creating such a sector involves initiating local projects, such as worker and community-owned businesses, cooperatives, development banks, and loan funds. It also involves supportive public policies, such as government procurement and funding policies that support sustainable local development.

Make corporations locally accountable: Local labor unions, community groups, and governments should pressure corporations to negotiate with them regarding acceptable norms of behavior.

Establish local control of local environments: In accord with the principle of subsidiarity, any activity with potential impact on the local environment should require the informed consent of the people in that community.[13]

Protect local and national economic development capacity: Current trade agreements often interfere with the right of countries and communities to pursue local economic development objectives, such as job creation and targeting development for needy groups. International agreements should instead protect that right.

Establish regional "no raiding" pacts: States and provinces should agree not to compete to provide subsidies to lure companies to relocate. No-raiding rules exist in the EU, and corporations have been heavily fined for taking state and provincial subsidies to relocate. Unions in the northeastern US have proposed a multistate agreement that would block the regional race to the bottom by punishing companies that relocate to areas with lower standards.[14]

4. Equalize Global Wealth and Power

The current gap between the global rich and poor is unacceptable; it is unconscionable to act as if it can be a permanent feature of the global economy. It is equally unacceptable to assume that the rich countries of the world can call all the shots regarding the global economy's future. Policy at every level should prioritize economic advancement of the most oppressed and exploited people, including women, immigrants, racial and ethnic minorities, and indigenous peoples. It should increase power, capability, resources, and income for those at the bottom.

Shop and invest ethically: Individual consumers, institutions, and governments should use their buying power to purchase goods, services, and investments that support acceptable labor, environmental, and social conditions. Consumer power is already being used in such areas as the boycott of companies that invest in Burma and of World Bank bonds. Consumer purchasing power is also being harnessed to support fair trade—for example, through the Rugmark consumer seal for rugs produced without child labor; the creation of organizations to certify that garments and other products are not produced under sweatshop conditions; and the marketing of crafts and coffee from fairly paid workers and employee-owned cooperatives.

Revive the North-South Dialogue: In the 1970s, the rich and poor countries of the world initiated the North-South Dialogue, a series of ongoing UN discussions designed to establish a New International Economic Order that would support third world development. This dialogue, terminated by Ronald Reagan, should be revived as a step toward providing poor countries with a greater voice in global policies.

End global debt slavery: Today poor countries are forced to run their economies to pay debts promoted by foreign investors and taken on by corrupt governments that did not represent their people. The wealthy countries and the international financial institutions should immediately cancel the debts of the poorest countries. Repayment requirements should be limited for all underdeveloped countries.[15] No poor country should be required to use more than a small proportion of its income for debt repayment.

Make global markets work for developing economies: Rather than promoting indiscriminate free trade, trade policy should specifically encourage development of poor countries by providing them with preferential access to first world markets. (This is already done in a modest way with the Generalized System of Preferences, which reduces tariffs for developing countries.) To reverse the fall in commodity prices that has devastated third world producers and to prevent a global race to the bottom in commodities, commodity agreements to promote stability in price and production levels should be encouraged.

Provide developing countries access to technical knowledge: International trade agreements have enormously expanded the so-called intellectual property rights of corporations. This blocks poor countries from the knowledge they need to develop and become more self-reliant. Often this causes terrible hardship, such as the murderous drug company policy of using their "intellectual property rights" to price lifesaving drugs out of reach of the world's ordinary citizens. Global policy should encourage rapid and inexpensive access to all forms of technical knowledge to aid sustainable development. Those with access to such knowledge should, when necessary, commit "intellectual civil disobedience" by helping make it available to those who need it.

Invest in sustainable development: Global investment should be redirected from private financial speculation to one or more public international investment funds. The primary purpose of these funds should be to meet human and environmental needs by channeling money into locally controlled, environmentally sustainable, long-term investment. Sources for funding could include a Tobin Tax on international currency transactions; a global tax on carbon use designed to reduce greenhouse gas emissions; reductions in military spending; and public and private investment.[16] Such funds could also counter global economic cycles by appropriate expansion and contraction of their activities.

5. Convert the Global Economy to Environmental Sustainability

The world is in the midst of a global environmental catastrophe. Ill-conceived economic activity is disrupting the basic balances of climate and ecology on which human life depends. Globalization is rapidly accelerating that ongoing catastrophe. The sources of environmental destruction lie primarily in the wrongly developed countries of the North and in the activities of global corporations in the South. The only way to reverse this catastrophe is to halt the present dynamic of globalization and meet human needs by technologies and social practices that progressively reduce the negative impact of the economy on the environment.

Transform the production and consumption patterns of wrongly developed countries: The so-called developed or industrialized countries of the North produce the lion's share of the world's pollution and climate-changing carbon emissions. The technological and social means to change their destructive patterns exist but are not being utilized. Public policy, including taxation, regulation, planning, and investment, must be directed to completely rebuilding these wrongly developed economies on an environmentally sustainable basis.

Make international environmental agreements enforceable: International agreements have been developed to combat global warming, protect endangered species, and restrict foreign dumping of toxic waste. But these agreements have little provision for enforcement. For example, many countries have ignored the agreements they signed at the Rio conference on environment and development. Such agreements should now be made enforceable by incorporating sanctions like those for protection of international property rights in the WTO.[17]

Incorporate environmental protections in trade agreements: The WTO, NAFTA, and other trade agreements should discourage environmentally destructive practices. Countries should be free to ban import of goods produced under conditions that violate environmental principles.

End the despoiling of natural resources for export: Countries should not be required by the IMF, World Bank, or global investors to chop down their forests, overfarm their lands, and overfish their waters to service their debts or increase investor profit.

Encourage sustainable development: Establish sustainable development plans at local and national levels. Pursue "conservation-based development" that combines good jobs and income with environmental enhancement. Focus international aid on helping to implement sustainable development plans.

6. Create Prosperity by Meeting Human and Environmental Needs

Today, an estimated I billion people are unemployed. Millions are forced to leave rural areas and migrate to cities or around the world seeking work. Meanwhile, the world's vast need for goods and services to alleviate poverty and to reconstruct society on an environmentally sustainable basis goes unmet. A goal of economic policy at every level must be to create a new kind of full employment based on meeting those needs.

Encourage development, not austerity: Neoliberalism, the IMF, and the World Bank have imposed austerity policies on much of the world, leading to massive unemployment and the destruction of small businesses and farms. Instead, local, national, and global policies should aim to ensure livable wages. They should make credit available for small and medium-sized locally owned businesses and farms. They should pursue a progressive tax policy that reduces the burden on the poor. This will help reverse the destructive competition that is promoted by globalization from above.

Promote local food production for local needs: Today's global economy subsidizes corporate food exports while forcing countries to open up to foreign food imports, thereby driving millions of small-scale farmers off the land. Instead, global policy should promote small-scale, environmentally sound farming for local markets. It should end agricultural export dumping. It should encourage countries to provide basic food security for their people.[18]

Utilize development planning techniques: Governments should revive the development planning techniques that have been forbidden by neoliberalism and its institutions. Such tools include reserving some economic sectors for public, state, or national ownership. They also include performance requirements designed to achieve local, regional, or national economic objectives, such as requirements for local inputs and local hiring preferences.

Promote long-term investment: Short-term foreign investment that just skims off speculative profits does little or nothing for economic development. Only long-term investment that builds economic capacity and protects the environment is likely to benefit poorer countries. Public policy should encourage investment that leads to genuine sustainable development, not exploitation of people and resources for short-term gain.

Reestablish national full employment policies: Neoliberal economic policies have used mass unemployment to keep wages low, allegedly to fight inflation. National governments should instead use tax, budget, and monetary policies to ensure full employment.

7. Protect against Global Boom and Bust

The era of globalization has been an era of volatility. Its repeated crises have destroyed local and national economies overnight and driven hundreds of millions of people into poverty. An unregulated global economy has led to huge flows of speculative funds that can swamp national economies. No one country can control these forces on its own. Yet neoliberal economics and the major economic powers have resisted any changes that might restrict the freedom of capital. Economic security for ordinary people requires just such restrictions.

Utilize capital controls: Under the articles of the IMF, countries have the power to impose controls on the movement of capital across their borders. This power, which was used regularly by most countries for many decades, helps protect against wild rushes of money into and out of a country. But the current policies of the IMF and other institutions and the pressures of globalization have largely undermined the capacity of individual countries to use such controls effectively. Countries and international institutions should cooperate to restore their effectiveness.

Establish a "hot money" tax: A global tax on short-term hot money transactions—known as a Tobin Tax—will reduce global speculation, as well as provide resources for world development and environmental protection.

Coordinate demand in the major economies: The maintenance of prosperity worldwide requires cooperation of the major economic powers working parallel to ensure demand adequate to help all economies grow.[19]

Assure global liquidity: Financial crises have been a regular part of globalization. When such crises occur, short-term lack of liquidity can cause long-term economic devastation. Provisions should be made in advance to reduce the effects of such liquidity crises, especially on poorer countries. In the 1970s, for example, a system of Special Drawing Rights was established to protect the global economy from liquidity squeezes. The expansion of this or an equivalent system is required today.

Stabilize exchange rates: An effective system to prevent wild fluctuations in currency exchange rates existed for decades under the original design of the Bretton Woods agreement, but it was abandoned in the early 1970s. Such a system should be revived through international cooperation. It should aim to help countries adjust to changing conditions without drastic devaluations and massive increases in exports.[20]

Make speculators pay for their losses: International bailouts have insulated large banks and investors from the consequences of their high-risk speculations. This leads to what economists call moral hazard—encouraging more such speculative ventures. The result is even more international volatility. Assistance provided for economies in trouble must go to benefit the people, not to line the pockets of the international investors who lured them into trouble in the first place.

Establish a permanent insolvency mechanism for indebted countries: Such a mechanism can draw on the experience of other bankruptcy procedures for governments, such as the municipal insolvency provisions of Chapter 9 of US bankruptcy law. Arbitration panels should represent both debtors and creditors, and should establish the debtor country's capacity to pay, taking into account necessary expenditures for social safety nets to protect a minimum of human dignity of the poor and the debtor's economic future.[21]

Develop international monetary regulation: Over the course of centuries, nations developed central banks to regulate private banks, control the supply of money, and counter booms and busts. But globalization has undermined their capacity to do so, creating a global monetary system that is wildly out of control. That makes it necessary to develop international institutions to perform or assist with functions of monetary regulation currently performed inadequately by national central banks. Regulating global banks, for example, requires international cooperation. Equally important, the non-bank financial services companies that have grown explosively in the past decades need to be brought under national and international regulation. And, since money has become global, an international equivalent to the national regulation of interest rates and money supply is needed.[22] Such regulation must support basic objectives of just and sustainable development.

* * *

The movement for globalization from below is indeed developing an alternative vision for the global economy. It is not just a nostalgic desire to return to the past, nor a fearful rejection of a wider world, nor a laundry list of wishes and hopes. It is a program for the transformation of the global economy. Its elements are concrete enough to implement. They fit together well enough to be synergistic. They address the needs of the overwhelming majority of the world's people.

People can begin to implement these elements wherever and whenever they have the power to do so. As some elements are implemented, that can help strengthen the capacity to implement others.

That doesn't mean that the program presented here is adequate or final. On the contrary, it represents only an early attempt to put the proposals of different parts of the movement together into a common whole. The next step is to review this and other such syntheses in the light of the problems and concerns of different constituencies and to revise the whole in the light of the various needs to which it must respond. That is a work for many hands.

Endnotes

1. For such a common program for the Americans, see "Alternatives for the Americas: Building a People's Hemispheric Agreement," which is available on-line at http://www.web.net/comfort/alts4americas/eng/eng.html; summary in Anderson et al., *Field Guide to the Global Economy*, pp. 130ff. For a synthesis from the Asian-Pacific network PP21, see Muto Ichiyo, "For an Alliance of Hope," in Brecher et al., *Global Visions*, pp. 147ff. For trade issues, see "WTO—Shrink or Sink: The Turn Around Agenda" (http://www.tradewatch.org). For financial issues, see "From Speculation to the Real Economy: An Emerging North-South Labor-Citizens Agenda on Global Finance," the summary of recommendations from the 1998 conference, "Toward a Progressive International Economy," sponsored by Friends of the Earth, the International Forum on Globalization, and the Third World Network, in Anderson et al., *Field Guide to the Global Economy*, pp. 128ff. Similar ideas are spelled out more fully in Sarah Anderson and John Cavanagh, *Bearing the Burden: The Impact of Global Financial Crisis on Workers and Alternative Agendas for the IMF and Other Institutions* (Washington: Institute for Policy Studies, April 2000). Many similar proposals are presented in UNDP, *Human Development Report 1999*, and in its previous annual editions. Many significant labor proposals regarding reform of the global economy are available on-line at the AFL-CIO web site: http://www.aflcio.org. Several valuable recent articles on alternatives for the global economy are collected in "Section Four: Ways to Restructure the Global Economy" in Danaher and Burbach, *Globalize This!* See also the wide-ranging synthesis of proposals for reform of the global economy presented by William Greider in a series of articles in *The Nation:* "Global Agenda" (January 31, 2000), "Shopping Till We Drop" (April 10, 2000), and "Time to Rein in Global Finance" (April 24, 2000). For ongoing coverage of third world proposals relating to international negotiations, see the magazine *Third World Resurgence.*

2. H. Res., 479, text available on-line through the US House of Representatives web site: http://thomas.loc.gov/. For additional information visit Representative Bernie Sanders' (I-VT) web site: http://bernie.house.gov/imf/global.asp. See also "Whose Globalization?" *The Nation*, March 22, 1999, and Ellen Frank, "Bye Bye IMF?: A New Blueprint for the Global Economy," in *Dollars and Sense* 224 (July–August 1999).

3. It is often assumed that these interests are inherently contradictory. For example, it is assumed that rising living standards in the South necessitate lowered living standards in the North or that protection and restoration of the environment simply worse living standards for some or all of the world's people. While neither poverty nor environmental destruction can be reversed without major change worldwide, such change does not require the impoverishment of ordinary citizens of the North. Ending wasteful and destructive use of the world's resources and putting its unused and poorly used resources, particularly its one billion unemployed, to work could

largely eliminate poverty and environmental degradation without reducing the real quality of life in the North. Change in consumption patterns will be necessary—for example, reduced dependence on fossil fuels—and the lifestyles of the rich will not doubt need to take a hit, but this does not imply a reduction in overall quality of life for the majority in the North.

4. Starhawk, "How We Really Shut Down the WTO," in Danaber and Burbach, *Globalize This!* pp. 39–40.
5. "WTO—Shrink or Sink!" (http://www.tradewatch.org).
6. See Jeremy Brecher, Tim Costello, and Brendan Smith, *Fight When You Stand! Why Globalization Matters in Your Community and Workplace and How to Address It at the Grassroots* (Boston: Campaign on Contingent Work/Commonwork, 2000).
7. Professor Andy Banks of the George Meany Center has proposed that international law mandate that companies recognize and bargain with global union structures composed of unions representing all their workers worldwide. The law would mandate a minimum standard agreement which those structures would have the power to enforce through legally protected local monitoring committees. Personal communication, May 18, 2000. See also Andy Banks, "Monitoring: A Trade Union Perspective" (unpublished paper).
8. There has been considerable debate regarding the appropriate venues for such standards. The international trade union movement, for example, has strongly advocated that such standards be included in the WTO, while third world governments and many NGOs have opposed that proposal and have argued that such issues belong instead in the ILO. In fact, this question is currently moot, since the opposition to incorporating such standards in any international agreement is overwhelming. For the time being, labor rights will have to be imposed on corporations primarily by direct pressure in civil society. As other means for imposing them, such as national policy or international agreement open up, those opportunities should be seized without regard to preconceptions about appropriate venues.

   As we argued in Chapter 4, the emerging structures regulating the global economy tend to be multiple and overlapping. And, as Waldon Bello has argued, such pluralism is desirable: "Trade, development, and environmental issued must be formulated and interpreted by a wider body of global organizations [than the WTO], including UNCTAD, the International Labor Organization (ILO), the implementing bodies of multilateral environmental agreements, and regional economic blocs" ("UNCTAD: Time to Lead, Time to Challenge the WTO," in Danaher and Burbach, *Glabalize This!* p. 172). Steven Shrybman similarly argues that environmental regulations should be embodies both within trade organizations like the WTO and in international environmental agreements ("Trade Now, Pay Later," in Danaher and Burbach, *Glabalize This!* p. 162). Ultimately, such standards should be incorporated in a wide range of rule-making structures. For an extended discussion of issues regarding implementation of labor rights requirements, see Pharis J. Harvey and Terry Collingsworth, "Developing Effective Mechanisms for Implementing Labor

Rights in the Global Economy" (Discussion Draft, International Labor Rights Fund, March 9, 1998).

9. "Economic Forum: MAI Foes to Hold Inquiry to View Alternatives," *Vancouver Sun*, September 11, 1998. A discussion paper about this process and its results, "Towards a Citizens' MAI: An alternative Approach to Developing a Global Investment Treaty Based on Citizens' Rights and Democratic Control" (1998), was prepared by the Polaris Instituted in Canada with input from scholars and activists around the world.

10. Proposals include restoring the original Bretton Woods conception that the UN Economic and Social Council (ECOSOC) oversee and coordinate the work of international trade and financial institutions; changing the weighted voting in international financial institutions to correspond to population rather than just investments; adding additional countries to international institution governing boards; establishing elected regional boards of directors; and creating a directly elected Global People's Assembly within the UN system.

11. For the UN Center on Transnational Corporations corporate code of conduct efforts, see Walter A. Chudson, "An Impressionistic Tour of International Investment Codes, 1948–1994," in Orin Kirshoer ed, *The Bretton Woods—GATT System* (Armonk, New York: M.E. Sharpe, 1996), p. 177.

12. For detailed suggestions for reclaiming popular control of national governments, see "Democratic Governance," a working paper prepared by Tony Clarke of the Polaris Institute in Canada for the International Forum on Globalization.

13. See Vandana Soiva, "The Greening of the Global Reach," in Breecher et al., *Global Visions*, p. 59.

14. Regional efforts can themselves be transnational. The Great Lakes Regional Compact brings together US states and Canadian provinces for economic development and environmental protection. PP21 has established regional networks of grassroots organizations across national boundaries in several major Asian river valleys.

15. See, for example, Rev. Dr. Robert W. Edgar, "Jubilee 2000: Paying Our Debts," *The Nation*, April 24, 2000, pp. 20–21.

16. For a detailed proposal for such and international investment fund, see Jane D'Arista, "Financial Regulation in a Liberalized Global Environment," paper prepared for the Conference on International Capital Markets and the Future of Economic Policy, Queens' College, University of Cambridge, April 16–17, 1998. For D'Arista's proposals and related work, see the Financial Markets Center web site at http://www.fmcenter.org. As discussed below, the purpose of the Tobin Tax is not simply to raise revenue, but also to put "speed bumps" in the flow of speculative capital. For information on the Tobin Tax and on the campaign promoting it, visit the web site of the Tobin Tax Initiative USA at http://www.tobintax.org. The United Nations Conference on Trade and Development (UNCTAD) predicts that a .25 percent transaction tax would reduce global foreign-exchange transactions by

up to 30 percent, while generating around $300 billion in tax revenues. ("Financial Globalization vs. Free Trade: The Case for the Tobin Tax," *UNCTAD Bulletin*, January–March 1996.) For a discussion of issues around global taxation, also see Howard M. Wachtel, "The Mosaic of Global Taxes," in Pieterse ed., *Global Futures*, pp. 83ff. The Association for the Taxation of Financial Transactions for the Aid of Citizens [ATTAC], an international effort initiated in France, has drawn tens of thousands of people into discussion of the Tobin Tax and related issues. Visit the association's web site on-line at http://www.atac.org.

Peter Dorman has suggested that such funds could provide a transition to a generally more democratic global economy in which securities

> would pass progressively into the ownership of a class of financial intermediaries chartered on condition of extensive public input. Competition between these institutions and transparency in their operations would preserve incentives for efficient investment, but governments or other agents of the public would increasingly find it in their power to loosely guide or set limits to portfolio choice. This leverage would mitigate pressures toward financial instability and the excessive power of financial markets over democratic institutions . . . [and] the intermediaries themselves would acquire global scope, providing a venue for democratic processes across national borders.

Peter Dorman, "Actually Existing Globalization," in Preet Aulakh and Michael Schechter ed., *Rethinking Globalization(s): From Corporate Transnationalism to Local Interventions* (New York: St. Martin's Press, 2000).

17. See Steven Shrybman, "Trade Now, Pay Later," in Danaher and Burbach, *Globalize This!*
18. For background on global agricultural issues, see Mark Ritchie, "Rural-Urban Cooperation: Out Populist History and Future," in Breacher and Costello, *Building Bridges*. See also Peter Rosser, "A New Food Movement Comes of Age in Seattle," in Danaher and Burbach, *Globalize This!*
19. See, for example, Oskar Lafontaine, "The Future of German Social Democracy," extract of the text of a speech to the SPD Conference, Hanover, December 2–4, 1997, in *New Left Review* 227 (January–February 1998): 72ff. Lafontaine tried to develop cooperative international policies along these lines during his brief tenure as Germany's finance minister.
20. See the various proposals in Jo Marie Griesgraber and Bernhard G. Gunter eds., *The World's Monetary System: Toward Stability and Sustainability in the Twenty-First Century* (London: Pluto Press, 1996).
21. Proposals for so insolvency mechanism have been developed by Prof. Kunibert Raffer. See Kunibert Raffer, "Applying Chapter 9 Insolvency to International Debts: An Economically Efficient Solution with a Human Face," *World Development* 18: 2 (February 1990): 301ff.

22. Jane D'Arista has proposed one valuable model for such regulation. It involves the regulation of banks and all other financial institutions by national and international regulatory authorities; internationally coordinated minimum reserve requirements on the consolidated global balance sheets of all financial firms; and utilization of reserve requirements to counter cyclical variations in global growth rates. See D'Arista, "Financial Regulation in a Liberalized Global Environment." For D'Arista's proposals and related work, see the Financial Markets Center web site at http://www.fmcenter.org. For more establishment-oriented advocacy of expanded global financial regulation, see John Earwell and Lance Taylor, "International Capital markets and the Future of Economic Policy," Center for Economic Policy Analysis, August 1998, and Jeffrey E. Garten, "Needed: A Fed for the World," *New York Times*, September 23, 1998.

Workers of the World at Century's End

Giovanni Arrighi

In an article written in 1990, I noted how "over the last fifteen to twenty years, labor unions, working-class parties and states ruled by socialist governments, particularly of the Communist variety, have all been under considerable pressure to restructure themselves and change their orientation or face decline. . . . Some may be able to stave off the decline, even prosper, through a simple change in strategy. Others can attain the same result but only through a process of thorough self-restructuring. And others again can only decline, no matter what they do" (Arrighi, 1990: 179).

I traced this tendency to the fact that all existing working-class organizations had formed under the circumstances of world-market disintegration typical of the first half of the twentieth century. Under those circumstances, organized labor in high income ("core") countries—the United States included—had acquired considerable social power and political influence, while Communist revolution had made great advances in middle income ("semiperipheral") and low income ("peripheral") countries—first and foremost, in Russia and China. But the revitalization of world market forces that occurred under U.S. hegemony progressively undermined the conditions of national economic seclusion on which the social power of organized labor in core countries and the advances of Communist revolution in semiperipheral and peripheral countries were based. Under the emerging circumstances, all working-class organizations—no matter how effective they had been in meeting the challenges and seizing the opportunities of the bygone age–would find it difficult, or impossible, to meet the challenges and seize the opportunities created by the reintegration of national economies into a single world market. Since this was written, Communist parties have become nearly extinct throughout Europe; Social Democratic and Labor parties have transformed themselves out of recognition; and once powerful labor unions have been struggling to stave off decline in membership and political influence. If my diagnosis of the joint crisis of organized labor and Communist regimes underestimated anything, it was the speed at which the crisis was unfolding and the extent to which it would result in the extinction rather than the transformation of existing working-class organizations. But the very pace and destructiveness of the crisis confirm with a vengeance the validity of my contention that the working-class organizations that had been "made" in the early twentieth century were in the process of being "unmade" at the end of the century.

This does not mean that the world labor movement has no future. What it does mean is that, in order to be at all effective, the world labor movement in the twenty-first century will have to develop strategies and structures as different from those of the twentieth century as the latter were from those of the nineteenth. World capitalism evolves continually, and so do the conditions under which the working classes of the world make their own history.

In order to grasp how these conditions are evolving, we must first of all dispel two misconceptions concerning the present crisis of world labor. First, that the crisis is due primarily either to a decline in the disposition of workers to struggle to protect or improve their working and living conditions, or to the effects of the relocation of industrial activities from high income to lower income countries. Secondly, that the crisis demonstrates the failure of the world labor movement as instituted in the first half of the twentieth century to attain its objectives, as well as the capacity of world capitalism to overcome indefinitely its limits and contradictions.

The first misconception is based on a narrow focus on the labor movement in core countries, and a lack of attention to the wider and longer-term effects of the relocation of industrial activities. Capital, U.S. capital in particular, has been relocating its activities to lower income countries throughout the twentieth century. U.S. corporations became transnational almost as soon as they had completed their continent-wide domestic integration at the turn of the century; and by 1914 U.S. direct investment abroad amounted to 7% of U.S. Gross National Product (GNP), the same percentage as in the late 1960's and a slightly higher percentage than today (Hymer, 1972: 121; Wilkins, 1970: 201–02; Kapstein, 1991/92: 57). These relocations contained, and at times rolled back, the bargaining power and disposition to struggle of the U.S. working class. But these domestic effects were more than counterbalanced on a world scale by the strengthening of the bargaining power and disposition to struggle of the working classes of the countries to which industrial activities were relocated (Arrighi & Silver, 1984).

More generally, new worldwide data on labor unrest based on reports in *The New York Times* and in the *Times* (London), has revealed that labor unrest since the end of the Second World War shows a declining trend only in core countries. In semiperipheral countries throughout the same period, and in peripheral countries since 1970, in contrast, there has been a rising trend in labor unrest (Silver, 1995: 177–79). As Beverly Silver explains,

> Corporations were initially attracted to particular semiperipheral sites because they appeared to offer cheap and docile workers (e.g., Spain, Brazil, South Africa, South Korea). The subsequent inflow of (direct and indirect) foreign investment contributed to a series of semiperipheral "economic miracles" in the 1970's and 1980's. But the expansion of capital-intensive mass production industries that accompanied these "economic miracles" also created new and militant working classes with significant disruptive power. Workers exercised this power in waves of struggle that spread throughout the semiperipheral miracles of the 1970's and 1980's—from Brazil . . . and South Africa . . . in the 1970's to South Korea in the 1980's (Silver, 1995: 182).

Had spatial relocation been the main thrust of the ongoing restructuring of world capitalism, the chances are that in the 1980's and early 1990's we would have witnessed massive labor unrest worldwide; and today, it would not even occur to us to speak of a crisis of world labor. If we are speaking of such a crisis, it is because the spatial relocation of industrial activities to lower income countries—even the faster relocation made possible by the latest technological developments—is not the most fundamental aspect of the capitalist restructuring of the last 25 years.

As argued at length elsewhere (Arrighi, 1994), the primary aspect of this restructuring is a change of phase of processes of capital accumulation on a world scale from material to financial expansion. This change is not at all an aberration but a normal development of the capitalist accumulation of capital. From its earliest beginnings 600 years ago down to the present, the capitalist world-economy has always expanded through two alternating phases: a phase of material expansion—where a growing mass of money capital was channeled into trade and production—and a phase of financial expansion, where a growing mass of capital reverted to its money form and went into lending, borrowing, and speculation. As Fernand Braudel remarked in pointing out the recurrence of this pattern in the sixteenth, eighteenth, and nineteenth centuries, "every capitalist development of this order seems, by reaching the stage of financial expansion, to have in some sense announced its maturity: it was a sign of autumn" (Braudel, 1984: 246).

As Braudel was writing, the great expansion of world trade and production of the 1950's and 1960's—the so-called "golden age of capitalism"—began announcing its own maturity by turning into the financial expansion of the 1970's and 1980's. In the 1970's, the expansion of financial activities was associated with, and in many ways contributed to, an expansion of capital flows from high to lower income countries. In the 1980's, cross-border borrowing and lending continued to grow exponentially—the stock of international bank lending rising from 4% of the total Gross Domestic Product (GDP) of all Organization for Economic Cooperation and Development (OECD) countries in 1980 to 44% in 1991. But capital flows from high to lower income countries, after contracting sharply in the early 1980's, began to recover only towards the end of the decade (*The Economist*, "World Economy Survey," Sept. 19, 1992: 6–9; 14–17). The ultimate and privileged destination of the capital withdrawn from trade and production in core locations, in other words, has not been lower income countries but the "hidden abodes" of financial speculation that connect high income countries to one another. It was this withdrawal, rather than relocation, that in the 1980's precipitated the crisis of world labor.

As previously mentioned, this crisis should not be misconstrued as evidence that the world labor movement in the first half of the twentieth century failed to attain its objectives, or that world capitalism can indefinitely overcome its limits and contradictions. Powerful working-class organizations of the Trade Unionist, Social Democratic, and Communist varieties established themselves in the first half of the twentieth century as key institutions of world society under conditions of almost uninterrupted warfare or preparation for war among capitalist states. The establishment of Communist revolution as a force in world politics, first in Russia and then in China, was of course a direct result of the ravages of the two World Wars. But even in core capitalist countries, the greatest waves of class struggle occurred towards the end and immediately after the two World Wars (Silver, 1995: 158–73, 177).

The U.S. Cold War world order, and the great expansion of world trade and production that occurred under the auspices of that order, were thoroughly shaped by this joint advance of organized labor in core countries and of Communist revolution in semiperipheral arid peripheral countries. By the end of the Second World War this joint advance was widely perceived as constituting a fundamental threat for the very survival of world capitalism. If the advance was not contained and eventually reversed, the only question that seemed to remain open was not whether world capitalism would survive but by what combination of reforms and revolutions it would die. The U.S. "invention" of the Cold War was primarily a response to this situation of emergency for world capitalism.

Under the Cold War world order the advances of the world labor movement of the first half of the twentieth century were indeed contained and, eventually, reversed but only through a partial accommodation of its objectives. Core capitalist states were encouraged to appropriate the working-class objectives of job security ("full employment") and high mass consumption. Colonial states were granted juridical sovereignty. Along with other peripheral and semiperipheral states, they were also encouraged to pursue modernization and "development," so as to be able, in a more or less distant future, to provide their own working classes with the job security and high mass consumption that for the time being only workers in core states would enjoy.

To be sure, the pursuit of welfare for core workers and "development" for noncore workers became objectives of governmental action primarily as means of an anti-Communist crusade and, as such, it came to be embedded in a U.S.-centered system of military alliances and in an armament race between the U.S. and the U.S.S.R. that had no historical peacetime precedent. But the Cold War between the two superpowers did remain "cold" and, moreover, it became the basis of a fundamental reorganization of world capitalism designed to ensure a lasting peace among its various national components.

The importance of this reorganization cannot be emphasized too strongly. Ever since President Wilson had responded to Lenin's summons to world revolution with his Fourteen Points (Barraclough, 1967: 127), the more enlightened factions of the U.S. ruling classes had implicitly concurred with Lenin that the greatest threat to world capitalism came from its internecine struggles over colonies and territory. It is not surprising, therefore, that once the Second World War had validated Lenin's hopes and Wilson's fears, the U.S. government skillfully exploited the fear of Communist revolution to induce the governments of western Europe to renounce colonialism, to enter into long-term military cooperation with the United States, and to integrate their national economies into a single common market of continental dimension. By so doing, the United States created in western Europe and in the former colonial world new arenas of profitable expansion for U.S. corporate capital. But it also created durable structures of political and economic cooperation among western European states that undermined their disposition and capability to engage in mutual war.

The achievements of the U.S. reformation of world capitalism went beyond the rosiest expectations of its promoters. The 1950's and 1960's, in Thomas McCormick's words, were "the most sustained and profitable period of economic growth in the history of world capitalism" (McCormick, 1989: 99). Communist revolution continued to advance—in Cuba, in Indochina, and in Africa—but in ever more peripheral locations. What's more, the two original centers of Communist revolution developed mutual antagonisms that made it easier for the United States and its allies to play one center against the other. And while Communist revolution was peripheralized or tamed, industrial conflict in core countries was progressively routinized; and after a brief revival in the late 1960's, it started to decline precipitously.

By no stretch of the imagination, however, can this miraculous recovery of world capitalism be construed as a failure of the world labor movement, and even less as a lasting resolution of the contradictions of capitalism. On the contrary, the recovery of world capitalism was based primarily, not on the negation, but on the partial realization by world capitalism itself of the objectives of the world labor movement of the preceding half century. This accommodation demonstrates the extraordinary adaptability of world capitalism as an historical social system. But the onset of a new financial expansion around 1970 shows that this adaptability has limits, and that the approaching of these limits brings back to the fore the crisis tendencies of capitalism in old and new forms.

* * *

Financial expansions are moments of crisis and fundamental reorganization of the capitalist world-economy. As in all the financial expansions of previous centuries, the driving force behind the present diversion of capital from the purchase and sale of commodities (including wage labor, plant, and equipment) to borrowing, lending, and speculation has been a major intensification of inter-capitalist competition, itself a consequence of the preceding expansion of world trade and production. This is discussed at length and documented (Arrighi, 1994). As old and new enterprises invested a growing mass of capital in the purchase and sale of commodities, they brought down profit margins in their respective lines of business. And as an increasing number of enterprises sought to counter diminishing returns by diversifying their activities across locations and lines of business, they invaded one another's market niches and thereby further intensified competitive pressures and uncertainty in all branches of trade and production.

Under these circumstances, it is only natural that a growing mass of capital should be withdrawn from trade and production arid held liquid to avoid the risks and troubles of investment in an increasingly competitive and uncertain business environment. This large and growing mass of surplus capital—capital, that is, that cannot be reinvested profitably in the purchase arid sale of commodities—in itself creates all kinds of profitable opportunities for financial intermediaries to borrow, lend, and speculate. Historically, however, the full flourishing of financial expansions has always been associated with an intensification of interstate competition for the capital that was being withdrawn from trade and production. As competition in commodity markets escalated, governments tended to step into the struggle and to compete with one another for the capital needed to overpower rivals, mostly, though not exclusively, through an escalation in the armament race. This competition, in turn, multiplied opportunities to profit from the mobilization of surplus capital in borrowing, lending, and speculation.

This pattern can be clearly recognized in present and in past financial expansions. Throughout the 1970's, surplus capital was channeled in directions—lending to semiperipheral and peripheral countries and speculation in currency markets—that further increased competitive pressures and uncertainty in world trade and production without increasing returns in financial markets. Abundant and cheap credit encouraged semiperipheral and peripheral countries to step up their industrialization and modernization efforts and, therefore, to compete over markets and resources (most notably, oil) that had previously been the privileged preserve of core countries. Speculation in currency markets, for its part, first undermined, and then destroyed the system of fixed exchange rates that had contributed to the stability of world economic conditions in the 1950's and 1960's. This further increase in competitive pressures and uncertainty strengthened the overall tendency of capital to withdraw from trade and production; it widened the disequilibrium between a rapidly expanding supply and a stagnant demand for surplus capital; and it depressed returns in financial markets.[1]

It was only after 1979 that the U.S. government, first under President Carter, and then with much greater determination under President Reagan, took steps that created highly favorable demand conditions for the ongoing financial expansion. These steps were taken in the context of a major escalation of the ideological struggle and armament race with the U.S.S.R.—what Fred Halliday has called the Second Cold War. Responding to the serious deterioration of U.S. power and prestige that ensued from military defeat in Indochina and diplomatic defeat in Iran, the U.S. government came to the rescue of a battered dollar by aggressively bidding up real interest rates in world financial markets. It then used the seemingly unlimited credit that it gained through these measures to escalate the armament race well beyond what the U.S.S.R. could afford and, simultaneously, to cut taxes to win electoral support for the new anti-Communist crusade. The result was an increase of historic proportions in the U.S. national debt, which provided domestic and foreign surplus capital with a far more secure and remunerative outlet than it had been able to find since the outset of the financial expansion.[2]

An escalation in the interstate power struggle thus played as critical a role in sustaining the current financial expansion as it did in the past. As we shall see, in this as in other respects the dynamic of the present financial expansion diverges significantly from past experience. But before we turn to these differences, we must deal with two more analogies that bear directly on our attempt to understand the main thrust of the present restructuring of world capitalism.

Both analogies relate to the fact that all past financial expansions have not just been the "closing season" of a major material expansion of the capitalist world-economy. The intensification of intercapitalist competition that underlay the financial expansions also brought about epochal changes in the spatial configuration and in the organizational structure of processes of capital accumulation on a world scale—changes which prepared the ground for, and in due course translated into, a new phase of expansion of world trade and production. Epochal changes of this kind have always taken long periods of time to complete—as a rule, more than half a century from the beginning of the financial expansions. Initially, the previously dominant center always had the means to turn to its advantage the intensification of intercapitalist competition. As Halford MacKinder put it in 1899, commenting on Britain's relative decline in industrial competitiveness, "we [the British] are essentially the people with capital, and those who have capital always share in the activity of brains and muscles of other countries" (quoted in Hugill, 1993: 305).

Over time, however, even "the greatest ownership of capital" did not help the previously dominant centers in meeting the costs and in compensating for the disruptions of the escalating competitive struggle, the benefits of which accrued disproportionately to newly emerging centers. Thus, Britain's heavy borrowing from the United States during the First World War initiated that change of guard between the two countries at the commanding heights of the capitalist world-economy that was completed by more borrowing during the Second World War. Although the parallel should not be pushed too far, something similar seems to have happened in the 1980's. For all its spectacular results in reflating the U.S. economy and in bankrupting the U.S.S.R., the historic inflation of the U.S. national debt during the Second Cold War may well have sent the United States down a path of decline analogous to Britain's. As Kevin Phillips notes, "Formerly the world's leading creditor, the United States had borrowed enough money overseas—shades of 1914–45 Britain's—to become the world's leading debtor" (Phillips, 1993: 220).

Equally important, the decline of U.S. financial supremacy has been accompanied by the spectacular rise of the East Asian region, not just as the main "container of world liquidity," but as the "workshop of the world" as well. Britain's victory in both World Wars, far from slowing down, accelerated the ongoing shift of the geopolitical center of world-scale processes of capital accumulation from northwestern Europe to North America. So, we should not be surprised if, in retrospect, the U.S. victory in the Second Cold War turned out to have sealed a similar shift from North America to East Asia.

That this might indeed be the case is suggested by another analogy between the present and past financial expansions. As theorists of "informalization" and "flexible specialization" have underscored, the relative decline of U.S. economic power since 1970 has been associated with a major reversal in the organizational thrust of capitalism over the preceding century. In the words of Manuel Castells and Alejandro Portes,

> The large corporation, with its national vertical structure and the separation of its functions between staff and line, does not appear any more as the last stage of a necessary evolution toward rationalized industrial management. Networks of economic activities, networks of firms, and coordinated clusters of workers appear to comprise an emergent model of successful production and distribution (1989: 29–30).

In a similar vein, Michael Piore and Charles Sable have argued that

> the technologies and operating procedures of most modern corporations; the forms of labor-market control defended by many labor movements; the instruments of macroeconomic control developed by bureaucrats and economists in the welfare states; and the rules of the international monetary and trading systems established immediately after World War II—all must be modified even discarded, if the chronic economic diseases of our times are to be cured (1984: 4–5).

Reversals of the main organizational thrust of world capitalism are no novelty of the late twentieth century. Thus, some 80 years ago Henri Pirenne observed the great regularity with which phases of "economic freedom" and phases of "economic regulation" followed one another in the social history of European capitalism. Each swing of capitalist organization in one direction, he noted, called forth a movement in the opposite direction, which became dominant in the subsequent stage of capitalist development. Thus, the movement towards "economic freedom" of the sixteenth century led to the movement towards "economic regulation" of the seventeenth and eighteenth centuries. This, in turn, led to the movement towards "economic freedom" of the nineteenth century, which led to the movement towards "economic regulation" of the twentieth century (Pirenne, 1953: 515–16).

All these reversals in the main organizational thrust of capitalism have occurred in periods of financial expansion and have been closely associated with the changes in the spatial configuration of world-scale processes of capital accumulation discussed above. The alternation of "deregulatory" and "regulatory" thrusts underscored by Pirenne is but one aspect of this recurrent reversal. Other and equally relevant aspects are captured by such antinomies as "informalization versus formalization," "flexible versus rigid specialization," "extensive versus intensive accumulation," "market versus corporate capitalism" (Arrighi, 1994: 127–74, 239–300).

As theorists of informalization and of flexible specialization have underscored, there is plenty of evidence of an ongoing reversal of the trend of the past century towards formally organized and rigidly specialized governmental and business structures. But not all regions of time world-economy have equal chances in the struggle to benefit rather than lose from the emerging trend towards informality and flexible specialization. After 600 years in which "gifts" of history and geography made the West the primary seat of world capitalism, it now seems that the civilization(s) of East Asia are best positioned to take advantage of this latest reversal in the organizational thrust of world capitalism (cf. Hamilton, 1994; Arrighi, 1994: epilogue).

This is a first important difference between the present and past financial expansions. During past financial expansions the geopolitical center of world-scale processes of capital accumulation shifted from one region to another of the Western world. During the present financial expansion, in contrast, the center seems to be shifting to a region of the non-Western world.

Equally important, this latest shift of the geopolitical center of world-scale processes of capital accumulation is anomalous in another respect. In the past, shifts of this kind were associated with the formation at the commanding heights of the capitalist world-economy of a complex of governmental and business organizations that was more powerful both militarily and financially than the previously dominant complex: the U.S. complex relative to the British, the British relative to the Dutch, and the Dutch relative to the governmental and business organizations of Italian city-states. Past financial expansions and the competitive struggles that underlay them, in other words, resulted in an increasingly powerful *fusion* of world military and financial power within the organizational domains of the hegemonic center. The present financial expansion, in contrast, has thus far resulted in a *fission* of the two kinds of power. While financial power is increasingly concentrated in East Asian hands, military power is more than ever concentrated in U.S. hands.

This second anomaly of the present financial expansion is closely related to a third. Contrary to what happened in the course of all past financial expansions, the escalation in the interstate power struggle of the 1980's did not turn into open warfare. The United States "won" by financial means a *cold* war that it could not win by military and diplomatic means, but the Cold War remained "cold." To be sure, during and after the Second Cold War, "hot" wars have been proliferating in most peripheral and semiperiplieral regions of the world-economy—in Latin America and the Caribbeans, Africa, southeastern Europe, West, South, and Central Asia, often with the direct or indirect participation of core capitalist states. Nevertheless, even after the end of the Cold War, the mutual quarrels that invariably set capitalist states against one another have shown no tendency to deteriorate into open warfare, as they did in all previous financial expansions.

These anomalies of the present financial expansion can be interpreted as reflecting a fundamental limit of the long-term tendency of historical capitalism to expand through the formation of political organizations endowed with greater military power than their predecessors. Historically, the emergence of these increasingly powerful organizations has been the outcome of protracted and generalized wars among rising and declining capitalist states. Eventually, however, this process is bound to attain its limits by bringing into existence an organization that is so powerful as to be unchallengeable militarily by newly emerging capitalist states. World capitalism under U.S. hegemony may well have attained these limits by bringing about such a concentration of military power in the hands of the United States and its closest allies as to make interstate warfare an obsolete instrument of capitalist competition.

This does not mean, of course, that the United States is not vulnerable to the consequences of capitalist competition by means other than interstate warfare, or to the proliferation of local wars in peripheral and semiperipheral countries. On the contrary, the consolidation of the U.S. quasimonopoly of global—as opposed to merely local or regional—military power during the Second Cold War has left a legacy of fixed costs and frames of mind that hampers seriously the capacity of U.S. governmental and business agencies to compete effectively in a world trading system of unprecedented scale, scope, and density. This is particularly the case in relation to the governmental and business agencies of regions like East Asia that "gifts" of history and geography have endowed with low protection and reproduction costs. Ironically, therefore, the military power without historical precedent that has accumulated in U.S. hands cannot prevent, and may actually contribute to, the "migration" across the Pacific of the geopolitical center of world-scale processes of capital accumulation.

* * *

Let us now return to the issue of what changes in the conditions of working-class struggles can be expected to ensue from the ongoing restructuring and reorganization of the capitalist world-economy. The world labor movement of the twentieth century developed in response to the crisis of world capitalism as instituted under British hegemony. What are the chances that the "autumn" of world capitalism as instituted tinder U.S. hegemony will give rise to a world labor movement as effective as its predecessor? And what would such a labor movement look like?

A first answer to these questions is that it is still too early to tell. The first 25 years of the late-nineteenth century financial expansion were characterized by an extreme instability in working-class organization and by many more defeats than victories for the working classes of most countries. It took another 25 years before the ideological and organizational contours of the world labor movement began to crystallize and be discernible, and yet another 25 before that movement became powerful enough to impose some of its objectives on world capitalism (Arrighi, 1990: 24–47). There is no reason, of course, for supposing that the world labor movement of the twenty-first century will develop at the same pace and along the same trajectory as its predecessor. But whether it is actually emerging, what form it is going to take, and how effective it is going to be—these are issues that cannot be decided on the basis of the tendencies of the last, or even of the next, 10–20 years.

It is nonetheless not too early to tell that the conditions under which the workers of the world will make their own history in the twenty-first century will differ radically from the conditions of the past century. To be sure, the present financial expansion, like the preceding one, marks the beginning of a transition of world capitalism from one kind of spatial configuration and organizational structure to another. But each transition has peculiarities of its own, which make the conditions of working-class struggles different from what they had been during the preceding transition.

A first difference is that the changing spatial configuration of the capitalist world-economy can be expected to shift the epicenter of working-class struggles towards peripheral and semiperipheral countries in general and towards East Asia in particular. As previously noted, the notion that the world labor movement has been weakened by a massive relocation of industrial activities from high to low and middle income countries is a myth. Had such a massive relocation actually occurred, the chances are that the world labor movement would have already been revitalized. The main reason why it has not is that in the 1980's the primary destination of the flight of capital has not been low and middle income countries but extraterritorial financial markets.

The main exception to this general tendency has been East Asia, where the financial expansion has been accompanied by a rapid growth of trade and production. Should this tendency continue, there can be little doubt that this region, China included, will witness the formation of a vigorous labor movement. And to the extent that the material expansion of the East Asian regional economy will develop sufficient momentum to translate into a new material expansion of the entire world-economy, the chances are that this vigorous labor movement will become global in scope.

A second difference is that the reversal of the trend of the past century towards formally organized and rigidly specialized governmental and business structures can be expected to change the main thrust of the world labor movement as well. The increasing bureaucratization of capital in the century following 1870 created favorable conditions for the bureaucratization of labor movements as well. It is quite possible that the reversal of this tendency will create the conditions for the revival in entirely new forms of the more flexible and informal organizational structures typical of the labor movement of the nineteenth century.

If and when this revival will occur, we should expect also a major change in the ethnic/racial and gender composition of the world labor movement. The joint bureaucratization of capital and labor in the twentieth century benefited primarily the core white male component of the world labor force. As labor and commodity markets were "internalized" within the bureaucratic structures of core capital,[3] and the objectives of "full employment" and high mass consumption were taken over by the governments of core capitalist countries, white male workers succeeded in monopolizing the better paid and more secure jobs. But the intensification of intercapitalist competition since 1970 has induced capital to seek cheaper and more flexible sources of labor, not just in low and middle income countries, but also among women and nonwhite males in all countries. In the short run, the main impact of this tendency has been to heighten the "fear of falling" of white male workers in core countries. In the longer run, however, its main effect may well be the emergence of a world labor movement in which women and people of color have a far greater weight and influence than they have had in the past.

Finally, the obsolescence of interstate warfare as an instrument of capitalist competition can be expected to weaken the nationalist and statist orientation of the world labor movement. As previously noted, the world labor movement of the twentieth century developed under conditions of almost uninterrupted warfare or preparation for war among capitalist states. Under these circumstances, the military power of states could be presented by the ruling classes, and be perceived by the subordinate classes (workers included) as a key ingredient of national wealth and welfare. As a result, in the twentieth century nationalism became an integral component of labor movements almost everywhere, and the class struggle became inextricably interwoven with the interstate power struggle.

To the extent that the obsolescence of interstate warfare as an instrument of capitalist competition will be confirmed by future trends, the class struggle will be progressively disentangled from the interstate power struggle. There is of course no guarantee that this disentanglement will translate into a more internationalist rather than "tribalist" disposition among the workers of the world. The invention of new, or the consolidation of old, "imagined communities" along ethnic or religious lines is no doubt an easier response to the intensification of world market competition and state breakdowns than the formation of class solidarity across borders or cultural divides. As the experience of former Yugoslavia illustrates tragically, however, the easier response may well be a cure much worse than the disease.

The Croatian and Serb militias may well prefigure the predominant form of proletarian organization of the twenty-first century. But there is at least an equal chance that the predominant form will be prefigured by the kind of working-class cooperation that is being organized slowly and loosely from below across the U.S.-Mexican border. Whether the now weaker wind of internationalism will eventually prevail over the wind of "tribalism"—that's ultimately in the hands of the workers of the world themselves.

Endnotes

1. In the mid-1970's, real interest rates in the United States apparently plunged below zero. See World Bank (1985: 5).
2. Between 1981, when Reagan entered the White House, and 1991, the U. S. budget deficit increased from $74 billion to $300 billion a year and the U. S. national debt from $1 trillion to $4 trillion. As a result, net federal interest payments skyrocketed to $195 billion a year, more than ten times what they had been in the mid-1970's. (Phillips, 1993: 210, 220; Kennedy, 1993: 297).
3. On the "internalization" of markets see Doeringer & Piore, (1971) and Arrighi (1994: 239–42, 287–89).

References

Arrighi, Giovarnni (1990). "Marxist Century, American Century: The Making and Remaking of the World Labor Movement,' *New Left Review*, No. 179, Jan./Feb., 29–63.

Arrighi, Giovanni (1994). *The Long Twentieth Century: Money, Power, and the Origins of our Times*. London: Verso.

Arrighi, Giovanni & Silver, Beverly J. (1984). "Labor Movements and Capital Migration: The United States and Western Europe in World Historical Perspective." in C. Bergquist, ed., *Labor in the Capitalist World-Economy*. Beverly Hills: Sage, 183–216.

Barraclough, Geoffrey (1967). *An Introduction to Contemporary History*. Hammondsworth: Penguin Books.

Braudel, Fernand (1981). *The Perspective of the World*. New York: Harper and Row.

Castells, Manuel & Tortes, Alejandro (1989). "World Underneath: The Origins, Dynamics, and Effects of the Informal Economy," in A. Portes, M. Castells & L. A. Benton, eds., *The Informal Economy: Studies in Advanced and Less Developed Countries*. Baltimore: Johns Hopkins Univ. Press, 11–37.

Derringer, Peter B. & Piore, Michael J. (1971). *Internal Labor Markets and Manpower Analysis*. Lexington MA: D. C. Heath & Co.

Hamilton, Gary (1994), "Civilizations and the Organization of Economies," in N. Smelser & R. Swedberg, eds., *The Handbook of Economic Sociology*. Princeton: Princeton Univ. Press, 183–205.

Hugill, Peter J. (1993). *World Trade since 1431. Geography, Technology, and Capitalism*. Baltimore: Johns Hopkins Univ. Press.

Hymer, Stephen (1972). "The Multinational Corporation and the Law of Uneven Development," in J. N. Bhagwati, ed., *Economic and World Order*. New York: Macmillan, 113–60.

Kapstein, Ethan (1991/92). "We are Us: The Myth of the Multinational," *The National Interest*, No. 26, Win., 55–62.

Kennedy, Paul (1993). *Preparing for the Twenty First Century*. New York: Random House.

McCormick, Thomas J. (1989). *America's Half Century: United States Foreign Policy in the Cold War*. Baltimore: Johns Hopkins Univ. Press.

Phillips, Ken (1993). *Boiling Point: Republicans, Democrats and the Decline of Middle Class Prosperity*. New York: Random House.

Piore, Michael J. & Sable, Charles F. (1984). *The Second Industrial Divide: Possibilities for Prosperity*. New York: Basic Books.

Pirenne, Henri (1953). "Stages in the Social History of Capitalism," in R. Bendix & S. Lipset, eds., *Class, Status and Power: A Reader in Social Stratification*. Glencoe: The Free Press, 501–16.

Silver, Beverly J. (1995). "World-Scale Patterns of Labor-Capital Conflict: Labor Unrest, Long Waves and Cycles of Hegemony," *Review*, XVIII, 1, Win., 155–92.

Wilkins, Mira (1970). *The Emergence of Multinational Enterprise*. Cambridge: Cambridge Univ. Press.

World Bank (1985). *World Development Report*. New York: Oxford Univ. Press.